WONDER WOMAN
VOL.2 YEAR ONE

GREG RUCKA
writer

NICOLA SCOTT
artist

BILQUIS EVELY
artist ("Interlude")

ROMULO FAJARDO JR.
colorist

JODI WYNNE
letterer

NICOLA SCOTT & ROMULO FAJARDO JR.
collection cover artists

WONDER WOMAN created by WILLIAM MOULTON MARSTON

W9-CBD-268

MARK DOYLE Editor - Original Series ◆ **REBECCA TAYLOR** Associate Editor - Original Series
JEB WOODARD Group Editor - Collected Editions ◆ **ROBIN WILDMAN** Editor - Collected Edition
STEVE COOK Design Director - Books ◆ **MONIQUE GRUSPE** Publication Design

BOB HARRAS Senior VP - Editor-in-Chief, DC Comics

DIANE NELSON President ◆ **DAN DiDIO** Publisher ◆ **JIM LEE** Publisher ◆ **GEOFF JOHNS** President & Chief Creative Officer
AMIT DESAI Executive VP - Business & Marketing Strategy, Direct to Consumer & Global Franchise Management ◆ **SAM ADES** Senior VP - Direct to Consumer
BOBBIE CHASE VP - Talent Development ◆ **MARK CHIARELLO** Senior VP - Art, Design & Collected Editions
JOHN CUNNINGHAM Senior VP - Sales & Trade Marketing ◆ **ANNE DePIES** Senior VP - Business Strategy, Finance & Administration
DON FALLETTI VP - Manufacturing Operations ◆ **LAWRENCE GANEM** VP - Editorial Administration & Talent Relations
ALISON GILL Senior VP - Manufacturing & Operations ◆ **HANK KANALZ** Senior VP - Editorial Strategy & Administration
JAY KOGAN VP - Legal Affairs ◆ **THOMAS LOFTUS** VP - Business Affairs
JACK MAHAN VP - Business Affairs ◆ **NICK J. NAPOLITANO** VP - Manufacturing Administration
EDDIE SCANNELL VP - Consumer Marketing ◆ **COURTNEY SIMMONS** Senior VP - Publicity & Communications
JIM (SKI) SOKOLOWSKI VP - Comic Book Specialty Sales & Trade Marketing ◆ **NANCY SPEARS** VP - Mass, Book, Digital Sales & Trade Marketing

WONDER WOMAN VOLUME 2: YEAR ONE

Published by DC Comics. Compilation and all new material Copyright © 2017 DC Comics. All Rights Reserved.
Originally published in single magazine form in WONDER WOMAN 2, 4, 6, 8, 10, 12, 14. Copyright © 2016, 2017 DC Comics.
All Rights Reserved. All characters, their distinctive likenesses and related elements featured in this publication are trademarks of DC Comics.
The stories, characters and incidents featured in this publication are entirely fictional.
DC Comics does not read or accept unsolicited ideas, stories or artwork.

DC Comics, 2900 West Alameda Ave., Burbank, CA 91505. Printed by LSC Communications, Salem, VA, USA. 3/31/17.
First Printing. ISBN: 978-1-4012-6880-0

Library of Congress Cataloging-in-Publication Data is available.

PEFC Certified

Printed on paper from
sustainably managed
forests, controlled
sources

PEFC

PEFC/29-31-337   www.pefc.org

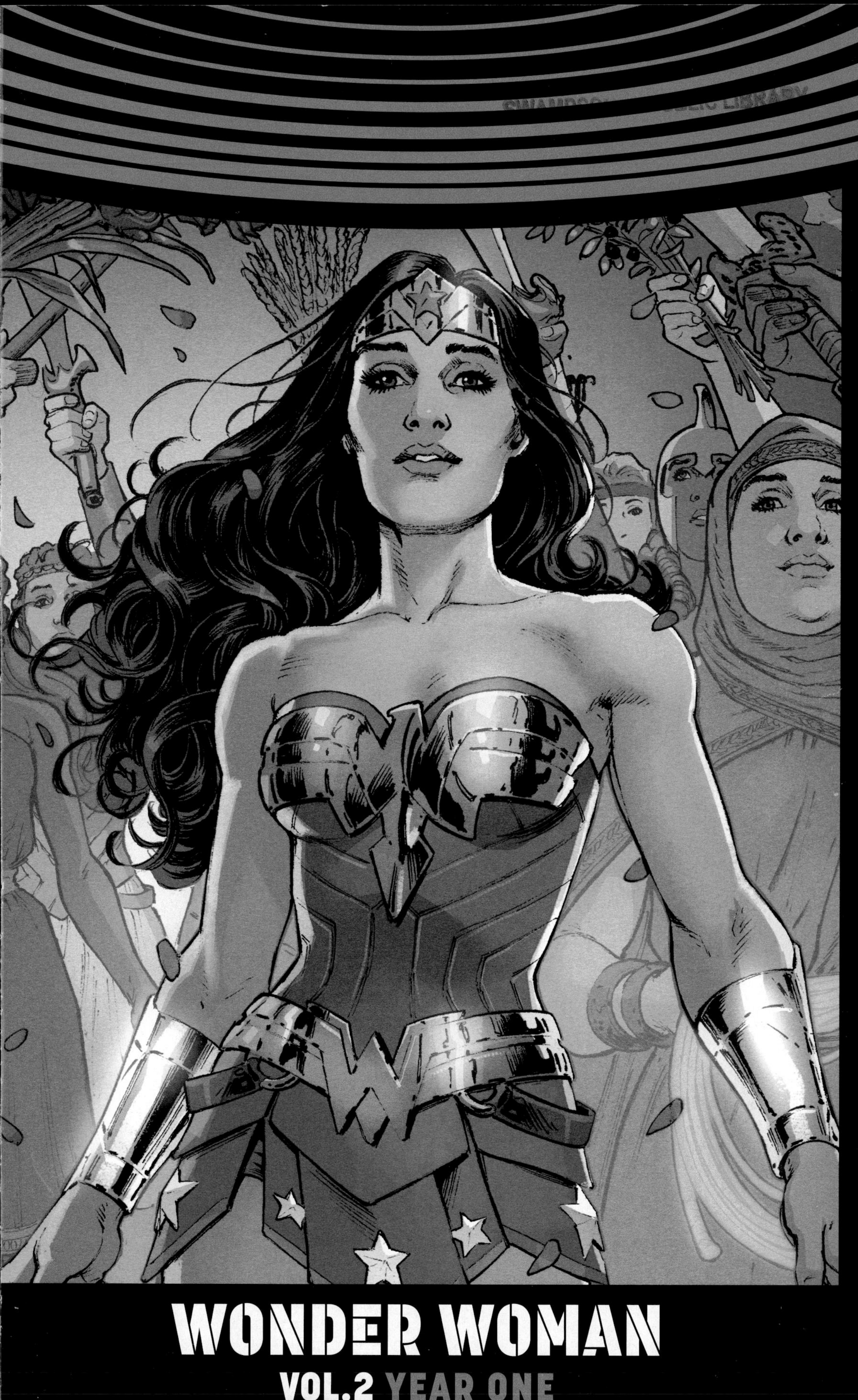

WONDER WOMAN

VOL.2 YEAR ONE

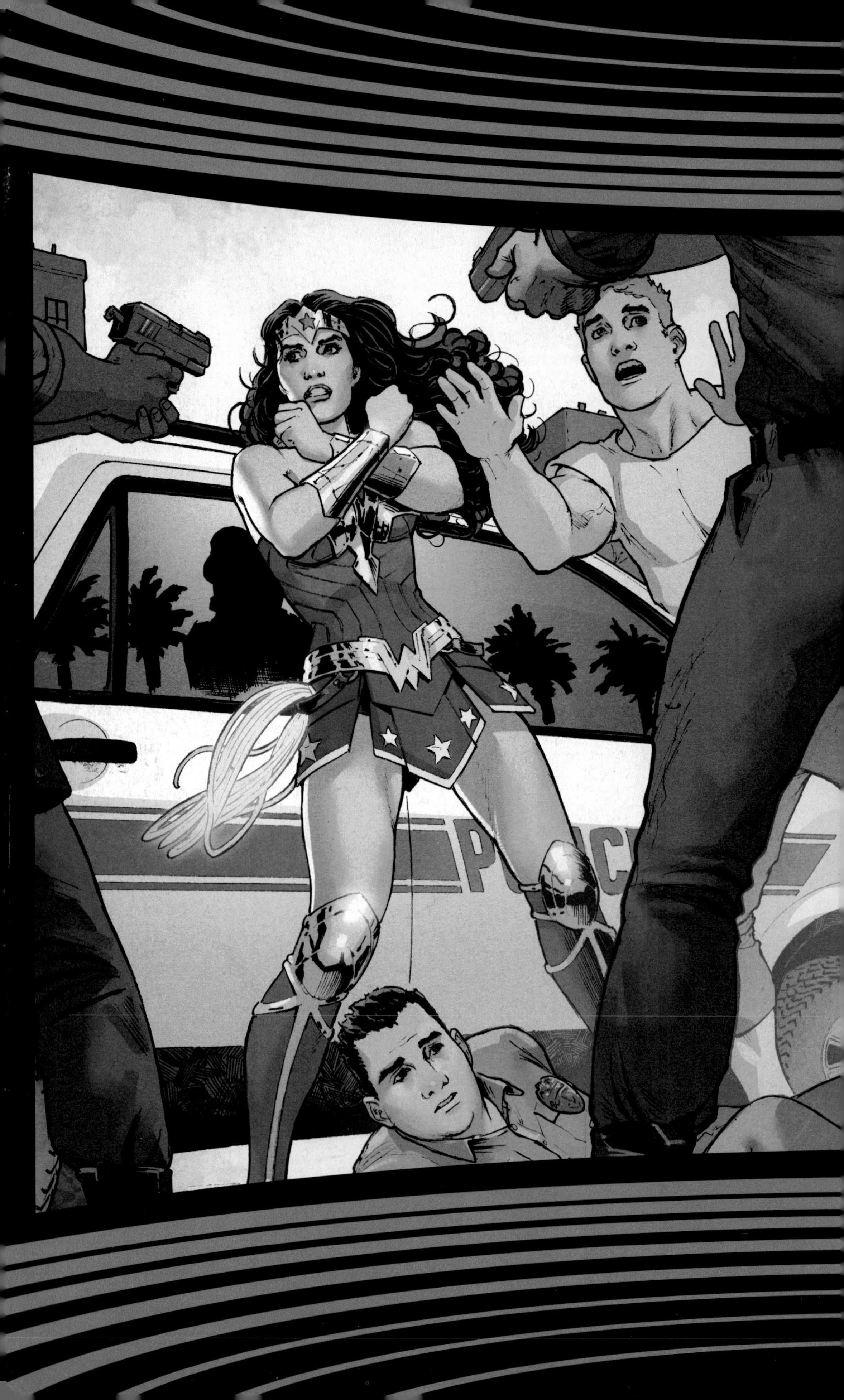

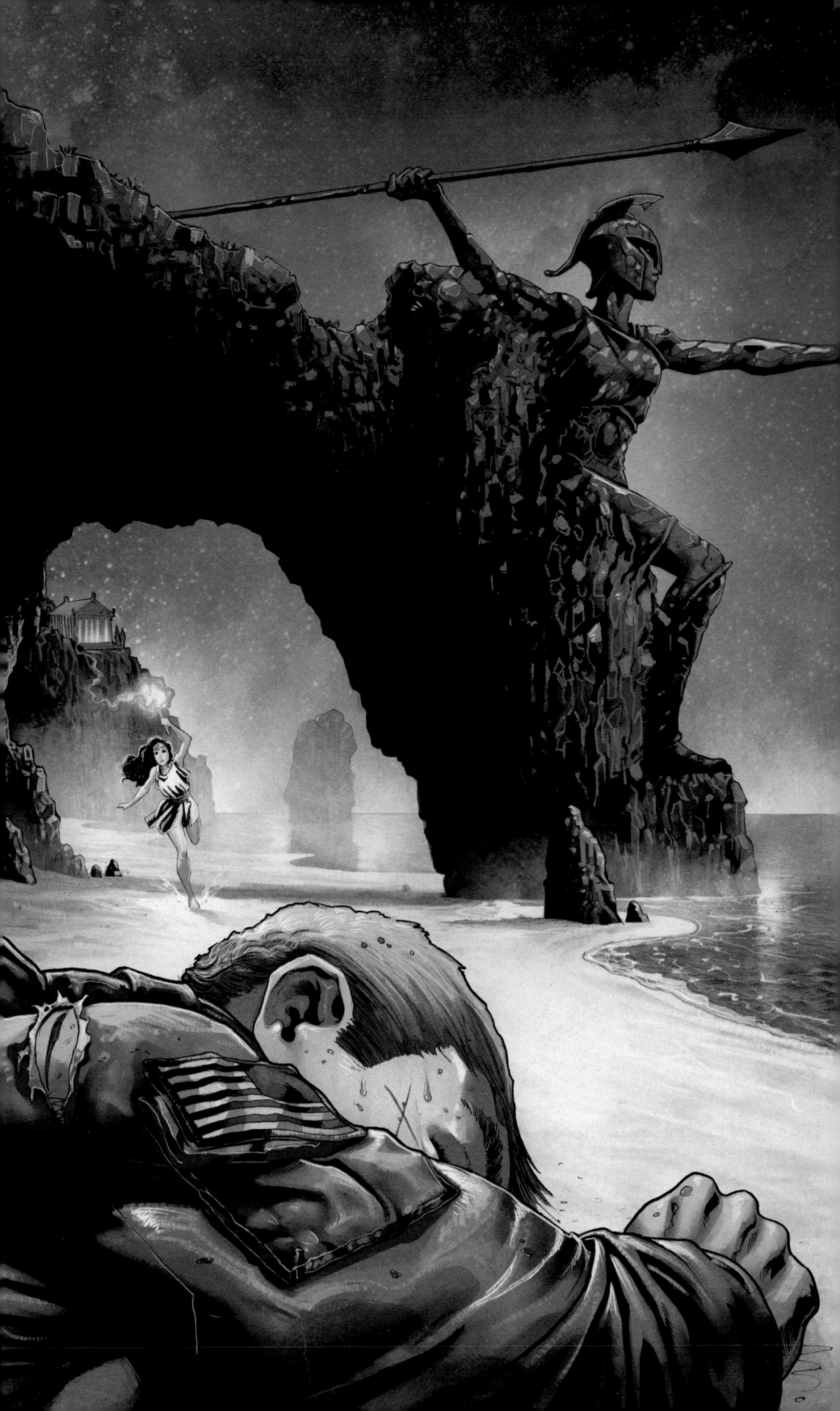

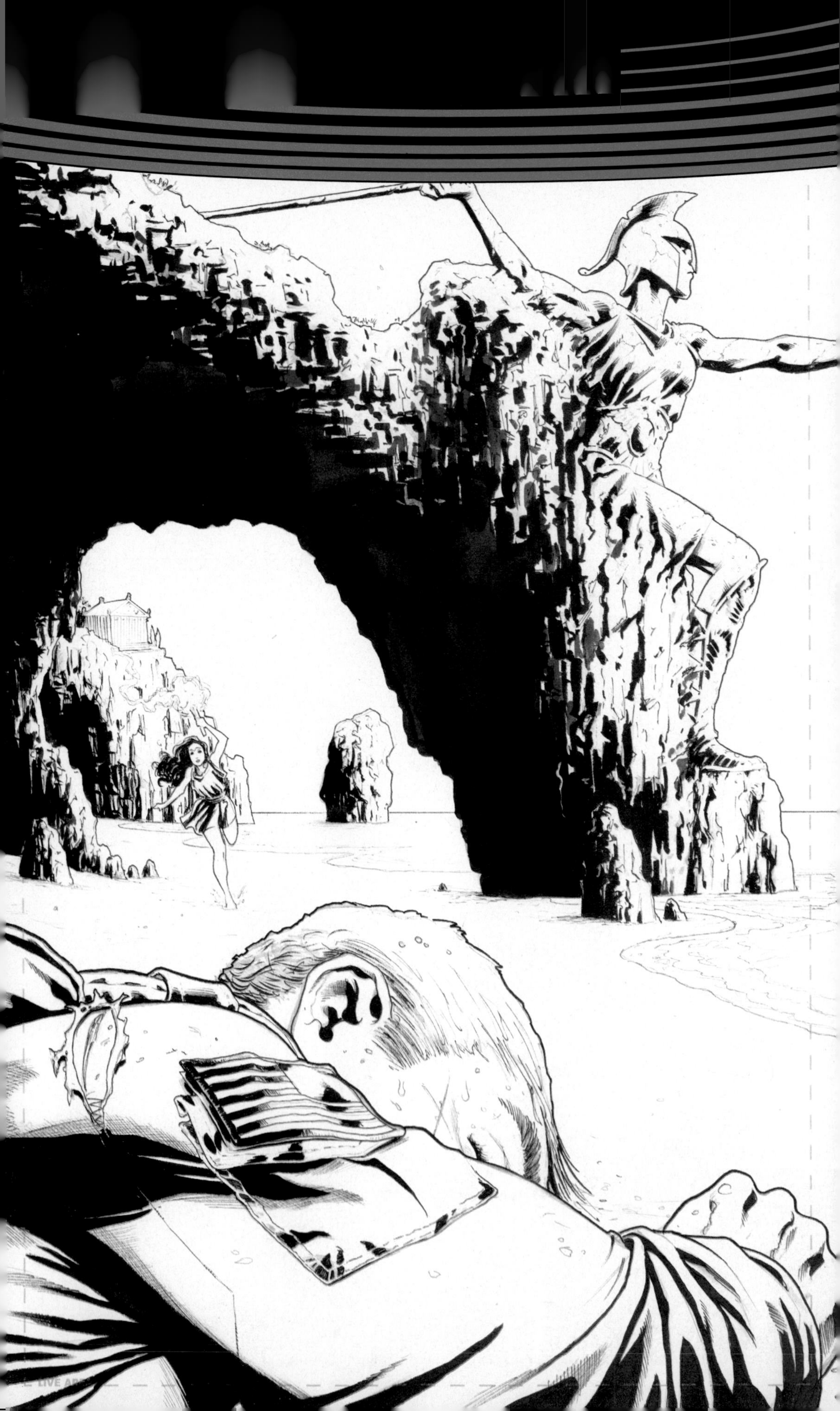

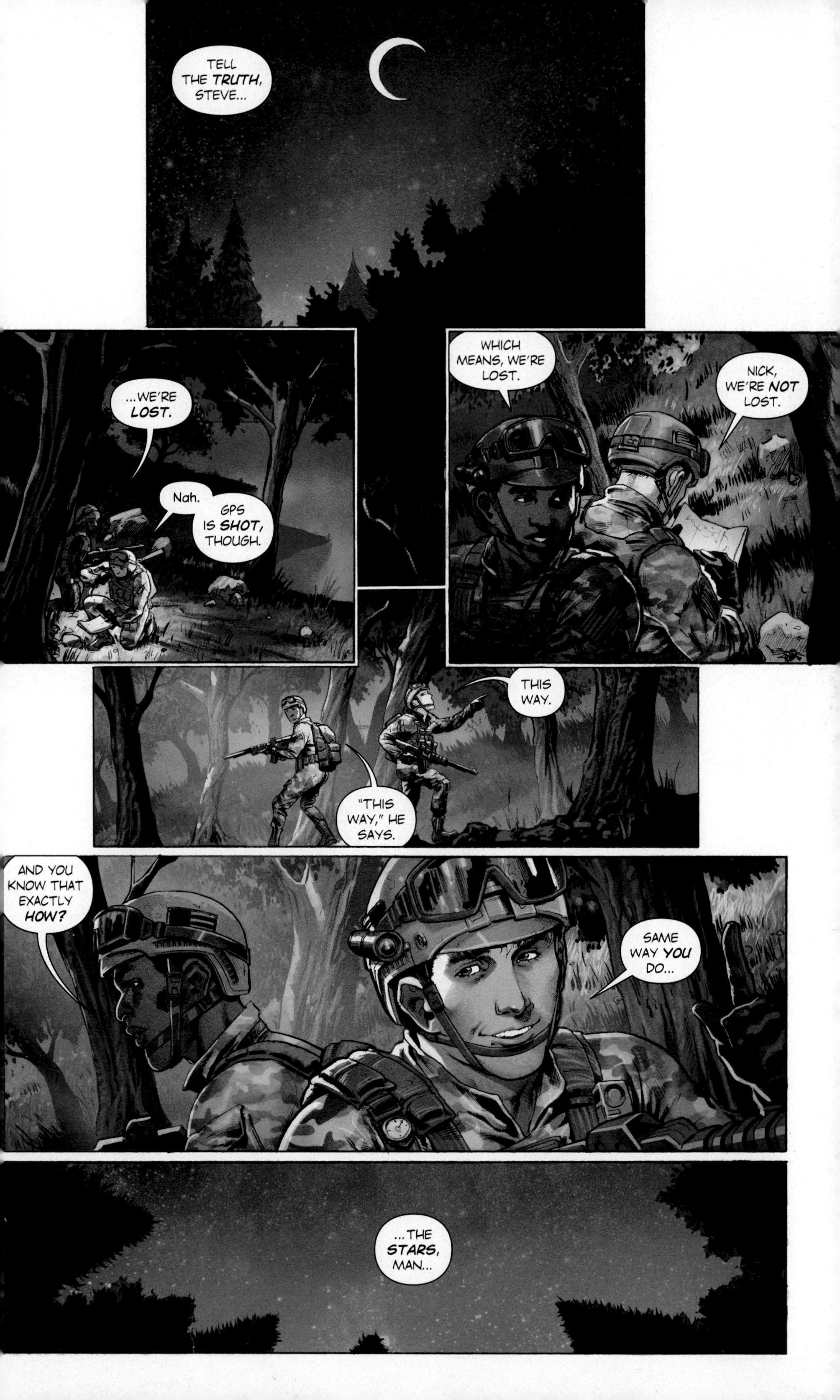
TELL THE TRUTH, STEVE...
...WE'RE LOST.
Nah.
GPS IS SHOT, THOUGH.
WHICH MEANS, WE'RE LOST.
NICK, WE'RE NOT LOST.
THIS WAY.
"THIS WAY," HE SAYS.
AND YOU KNOW THAT EXACTLY HOW?
SAME WAY YOU DO...
...THE STARS, MAN...

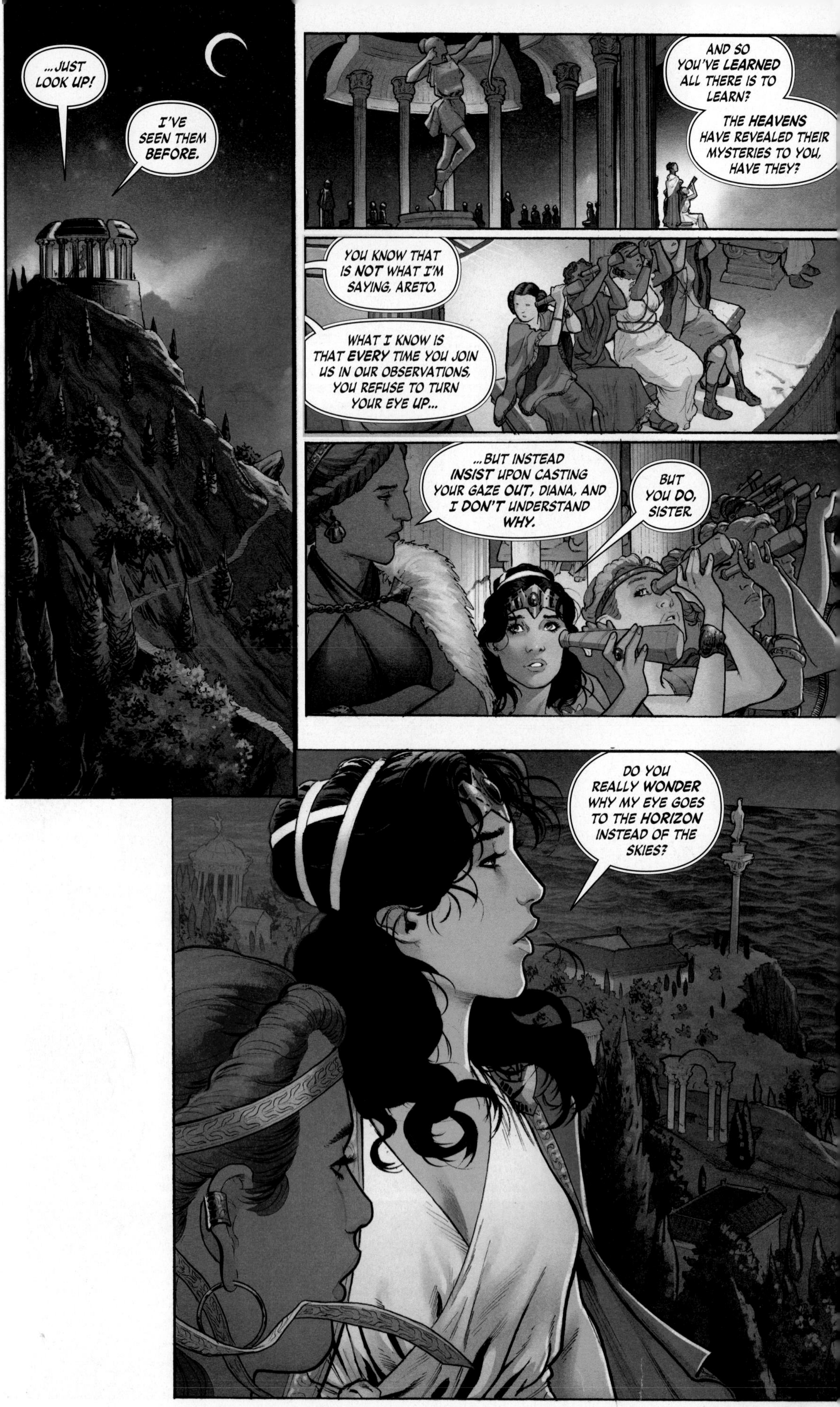
...JUST LOOK UP!
I'VE SEEN THEM BEFORE.
AND SO YOU'VE LEARNED ALL THERE IS TO LEARN?
THE HEAVENS HAVE REVEALED THEIR MYSTERIES TO YOU, HAVE THEY?
YOU KNOW THAT IS NOT WHAT I'M SAYING, ARETO.
WHAT I KNOW IS THAT EVERY TIME YOU JOIN US IN OUR OBSERVATIONS, YOU REFUSE TO TURN YOUR EYE UP...
...BUT INSTEAD INSIST UPON CASTING YOUR GAZE OUT, DIANA, AND I DON'T UNDERSTAND WHY.
BUT YOU DO, SISTER.
DO YOU REALLY WONDER WHY MY EYE GOES TO THE HORIZON INSTEAD OF THE SKIES?

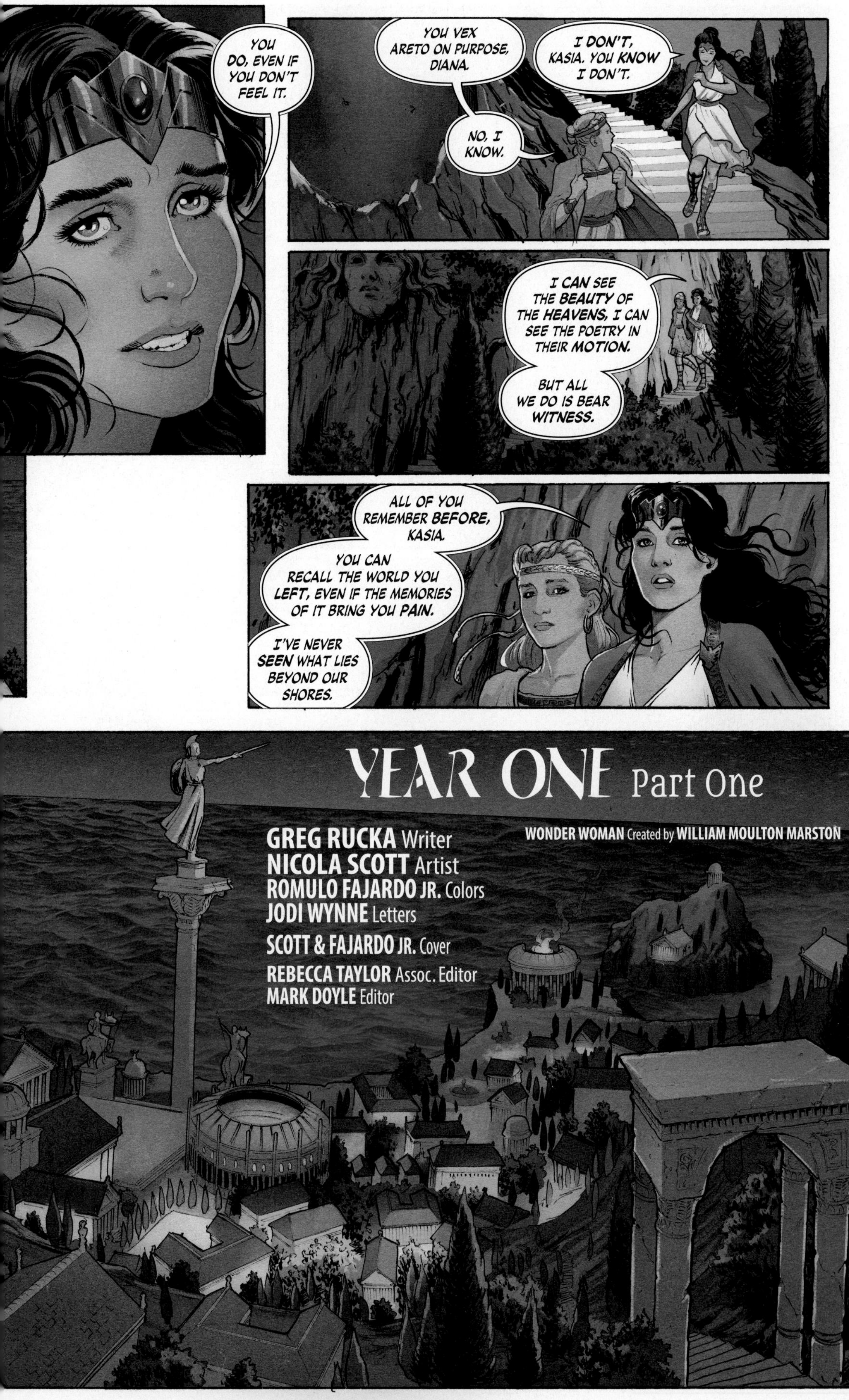

YOU VEX ARETO ON PURPOSE, DIANA.
I DON'T, KASIA. YOU KNOW I DON'T.
NO, I KNOW.
YOU DO, EVEN IF YOU DON'T FEEL IT.
I CAN SEE THE BEAUTY OF THE HEAVENS, I CAN SEE THE POETRY IN THEIR MOTION.
BUT ALL WE DO IS BEAR WITNESS.
ALL OF YOU REMEMBER BEFORE, KASIA.
YOU CAN RECALL THE WORLD YOU LEFT, EVEN IF THE MEMORIES OF IT BRING YOU PAIN.
I'VE NEVER SEEN WHAT LIES BEYOND OUR SHORES.
YEAR ONE Part One
GREG RUCKA Writer
NICOLA SCOTT Artist
ROMULO FAJARDO JR. Colors
JODI WYNNE Letters
SCOTT & FAJARDO JR. Cover
REBECCA TAYLOR Assoc. Editor
MARK DOYLE Editor
WONDER WOMAN Created by WILLIAM MOULTON MARSTON

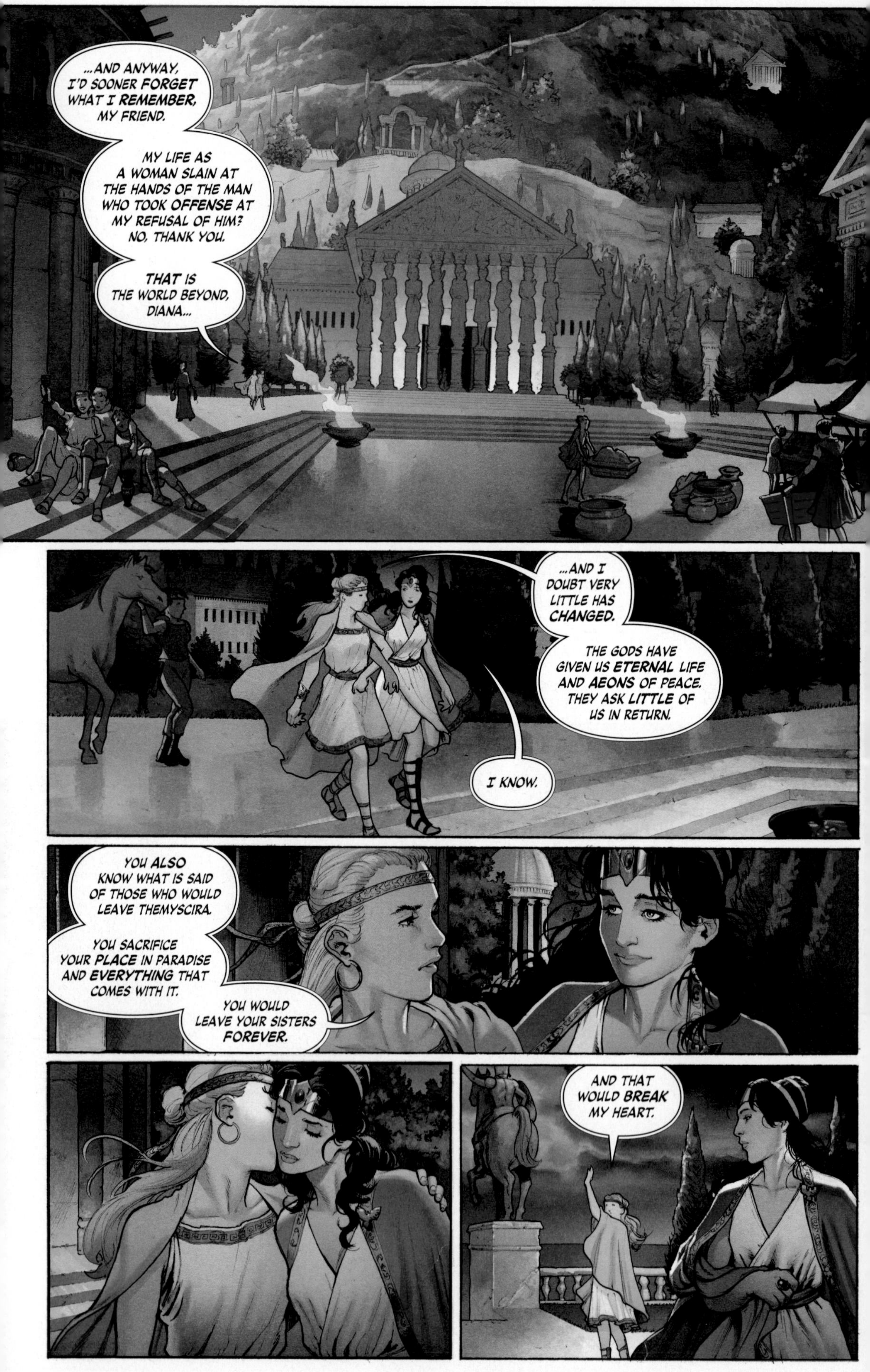
...AND ANYWAY, I'D SOONER FORGET WHAT I REMEMBER, MY FRIEND.
MY LIFE AS A WOMAN SLAIN AT THE HANDS OF THE MAN WHO TOOK OFFENSE AT MY REFUSAL OF HIM? NO, THANK YOU.
THAT IS THE WORLD BEYOND, DIANA...
...AND I DOUBT VERY LITTLE HAS CHANGED.
THE GODS HAVE GIVEN US ETERNAL LIFE AND AEONS OF PEACE. THEY ASK LITTLE OF US IN RETURN.
I KNOW.
YOU ALSO KNOW WHAT IS SAID OF THOSE WHO WOULD LEAVE THEMYSCIRA.
YOU SACRIFICE YOUR PLACE IN PARADISE AND EVERYTHING THAT COMES WITH IT.
YOU WOULD LEAVE YOUR SISTERS FOREVER.
AND THAT WOULD BREAK MY HEART.

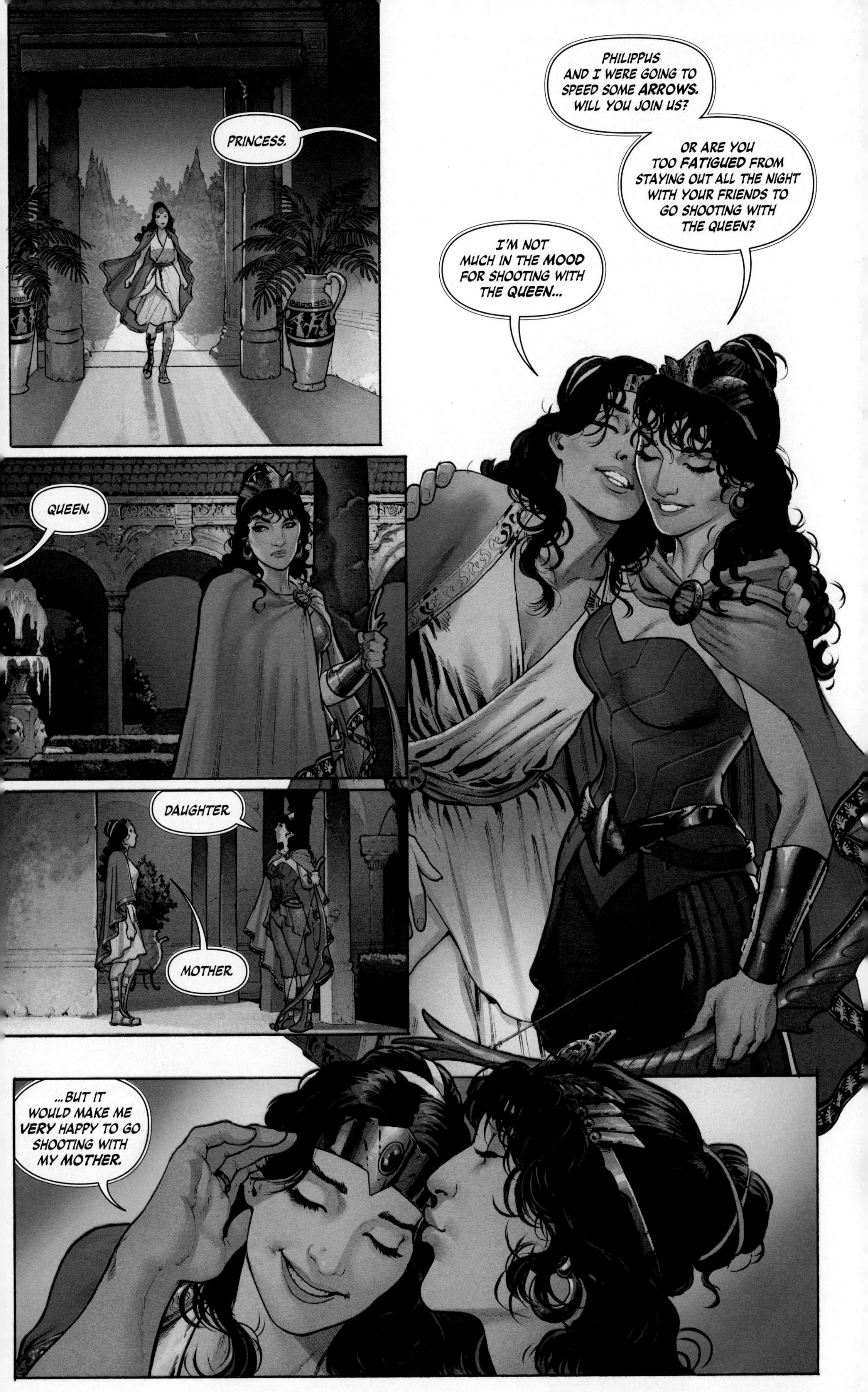
PRINCESS.
QUEEN.
DAUGHTER.
MOTHER.
PHILIPPUS AND I WERE GOING TO SPEED SOME ARROWS. WILL YOU JOIN US?
OR ARE YOU TOO FATIGUED FROM STAYING OUT ALL THE NIGHT WITH YOUR FRIENDS TO GO SHOOTING WITH THE QUEEN?
I'M NOT MUCH IN THE MOOD FOR SHOOTING WITH THE QUEEN...
...BUT IT WOULD MAKE ME VERY HAPPY TO GO SHOOTING WITH MY MOTHER.

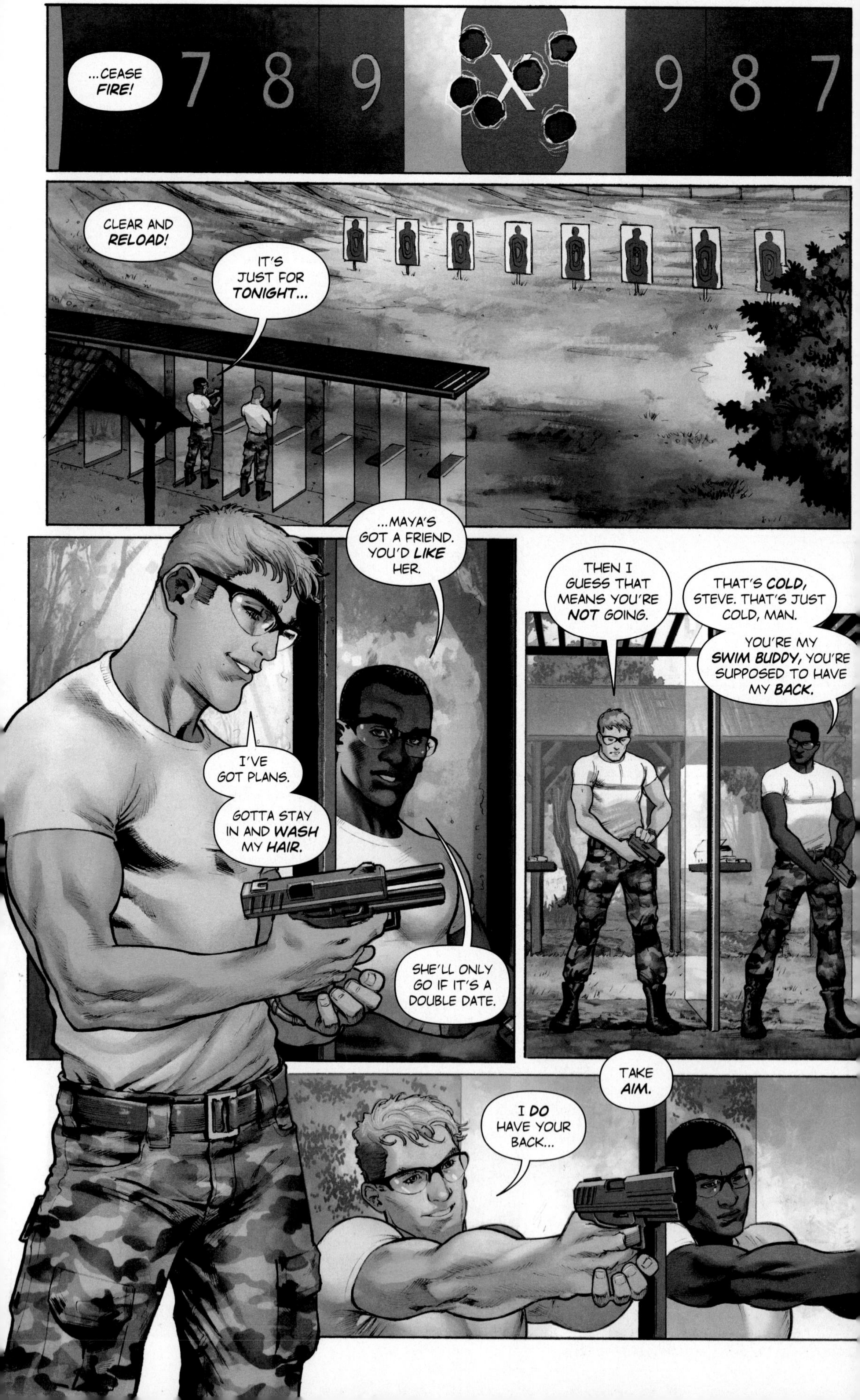

...CEASE FIRE!
7 8 9 X 9 8 7
CLEAR AND RELOAD!
IT'S JUST FOR TONIGHT...
...MAYA'S GOT A FRIEND. YOU'D LIKE HER.
I'VE GOT PLANS.
GOTTA STAY IN AND WASH MY HAIR.
SHE'LL ONLY GO IF IT'S A DOUBLE DATE.
THEN I GUESS THAT MEANS YOU'RE NOT GOING.
THAT'S COLD, STEVE. THAT'S JUST COLD, MAN.
YOU'RE MY SWIM BUDDY, YOU'RE SUPPOSED TO HAVE MY BACK.
TAKE AIM.
I DO HAVE YOUR BACK...

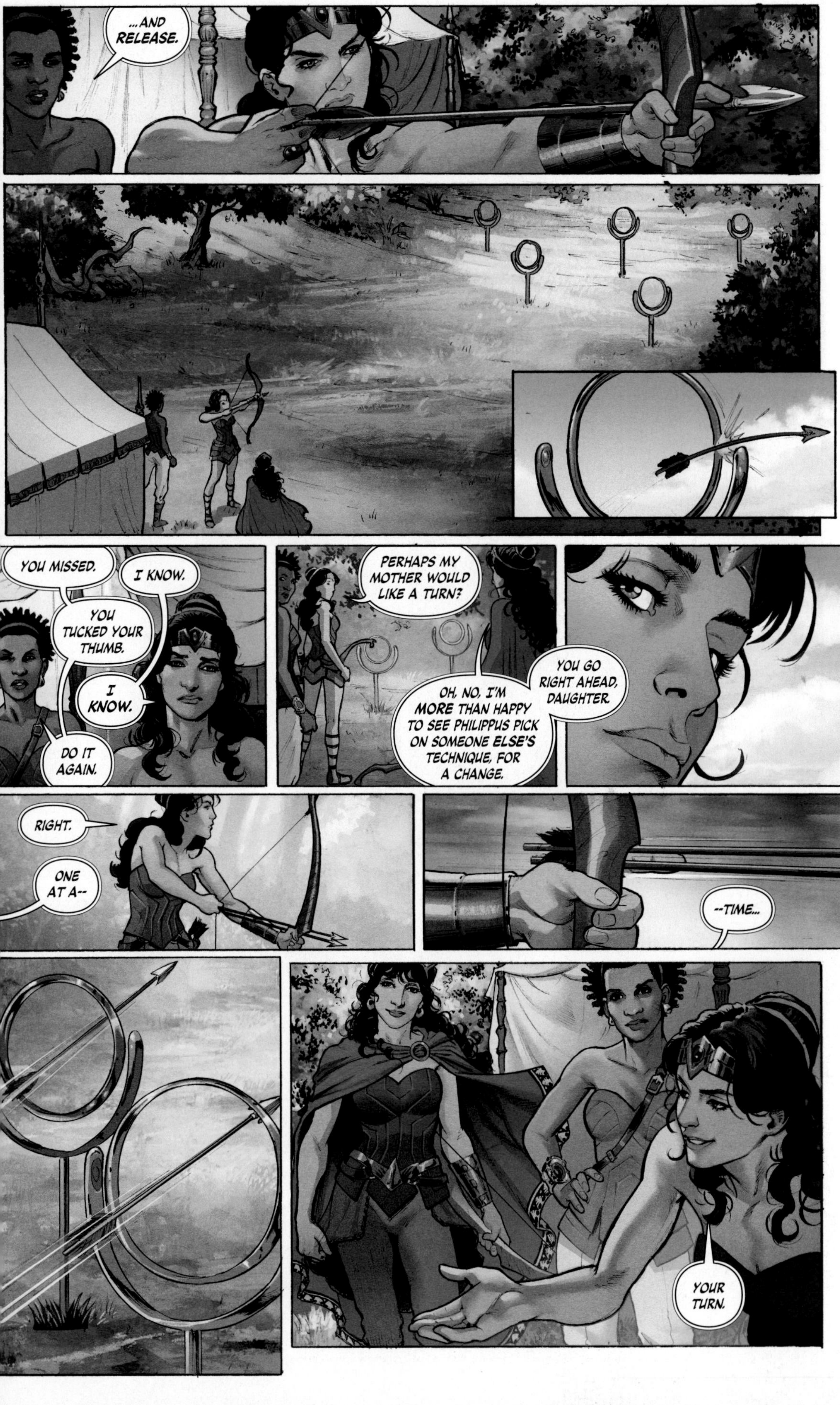
...AND RELEASE.
YOU MISSED.
I KNOW.
YOU TUCKED YOUR THUMB.
I KNOW.
DO IT AGAIN.
PERHAPS MY MOTHER WOULD LIKE A TURN?
OH, NO, I'M MORE THAN HAPPY TO SEE PHILIPPUS PICK ON SOMEONE ELSE'S TECHNIQUE, FOR A CHANGE.
YOU GO RIGHT AHEAD, DAUGHTER.
RIGHT.
ONE AT A--
--TIME...
YOUR TURN.

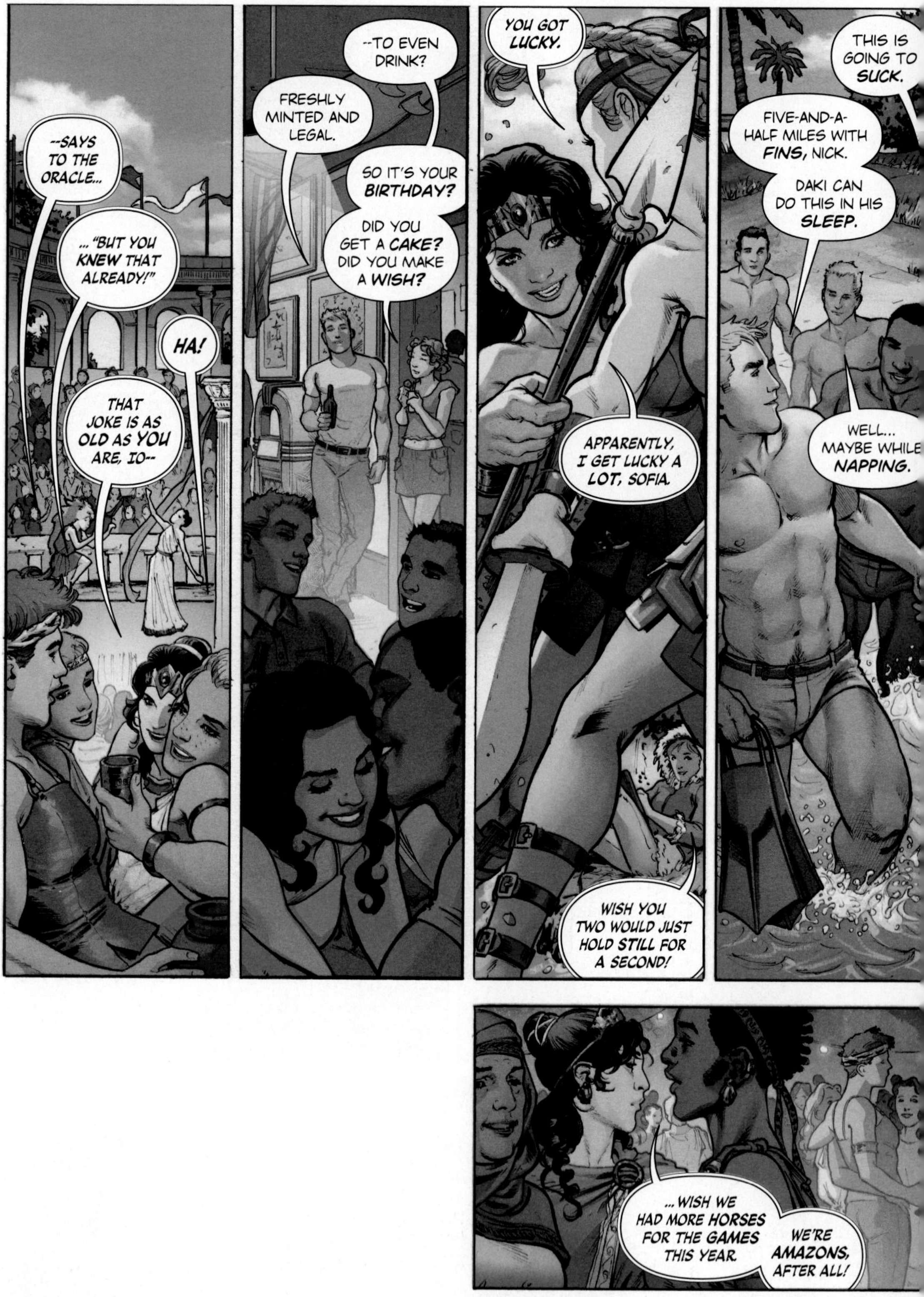
--SAYS TO THE ORACLE...
..."BUT YOU KNEW THAT ALREADY!"
HA!
THAT JOKE IS AS OLD AS YOU ARE, IO--
--TO EVEN DRINK?
FRESHLY MINTED AND LEGAL.
SO IT'S YOUR BIRTHDAY?
DID YOU GET A CAKE? DID YOU MAKE A WISH?
YOU GOT LUCKY.
APPARENTLY, I GET LUCKY A LOT, SOFIA.
WISH YOU TWO WOULD JUST HOLD STILL FOR A SECOND!
THIS IS GOING TO SUCK.
FIVE-AND-A-HALF MILES WITH FINS, NICK.
DAKI CAN DO THIS IN HIS SLEEP.
WELL... MAYBE WHILE NAPPING.
...WISH WE HAD MORE HORSES FOR THE GAMES THIS YEAR.
WE'RE AMAZONS, AFTER ALL!

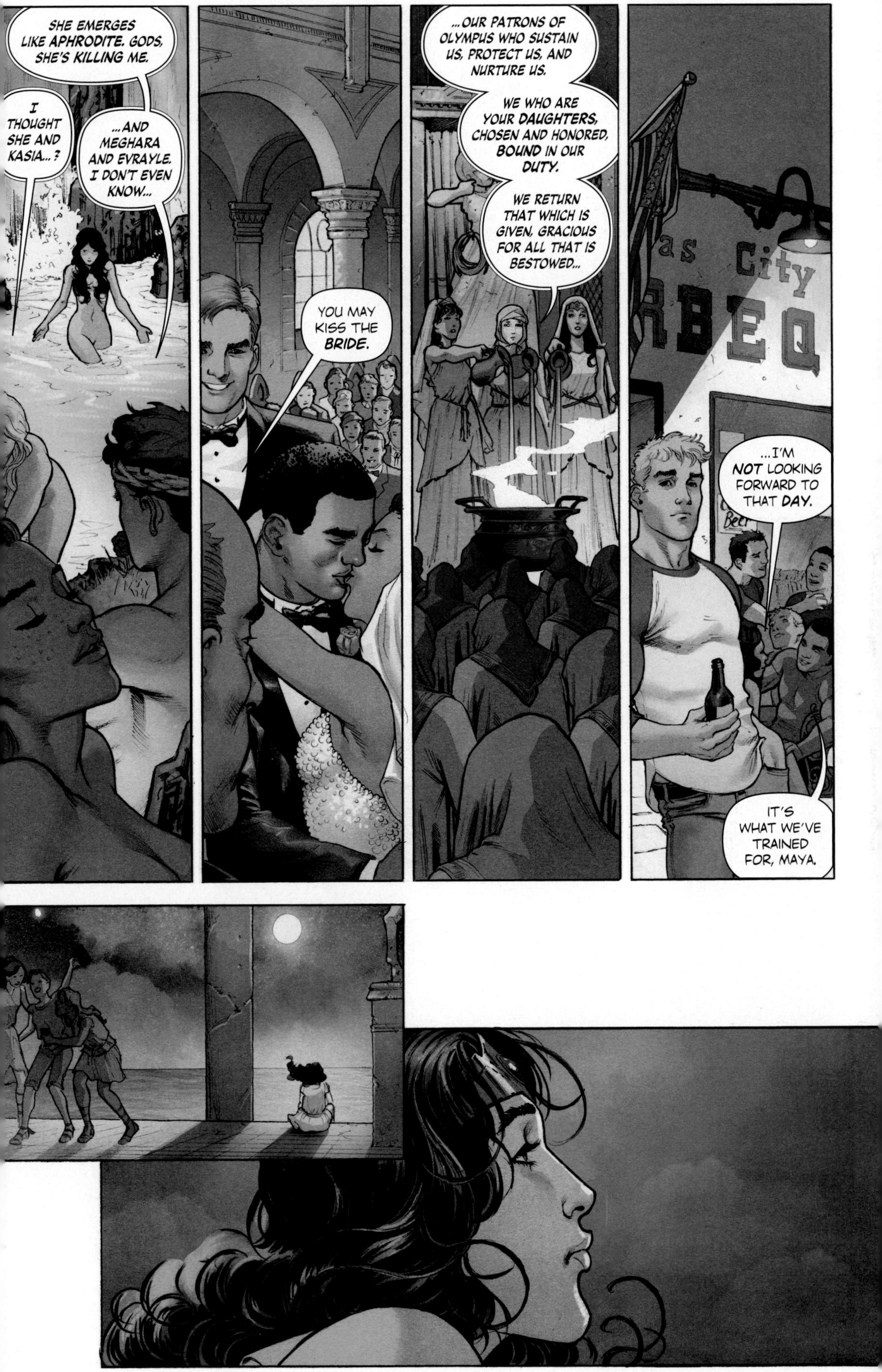
SHE EMERGES LIKE APHRODITE. GODS, SHE'S KILLING ME.
I THOUGHT SHE AND KASIA...?
...AND MEGHARA AND EVRAYLE. I DON'T EVEN KNOW...
YOU MAY KISS THE BRIDE.
...OUR PATRONS OF OLYMPUS WHO SUSTAIN US, PROTECT US, AND NURTURE US.
WE WHO ARE YOUR DAUGHTERS, CHOSEN AND HONORED, BOUND IN OUR DUTY.
WE RETURN THAT WHICH IS GIVEN, GRACIOUS FOR ALL THAT IS BESTOWED...
as City
RBEQ
Beer
...I'M NOT LOOKING FORWARD TO THAT DAY.
IT'S WHAT WE'VE TRAINED FOR, MAYA.

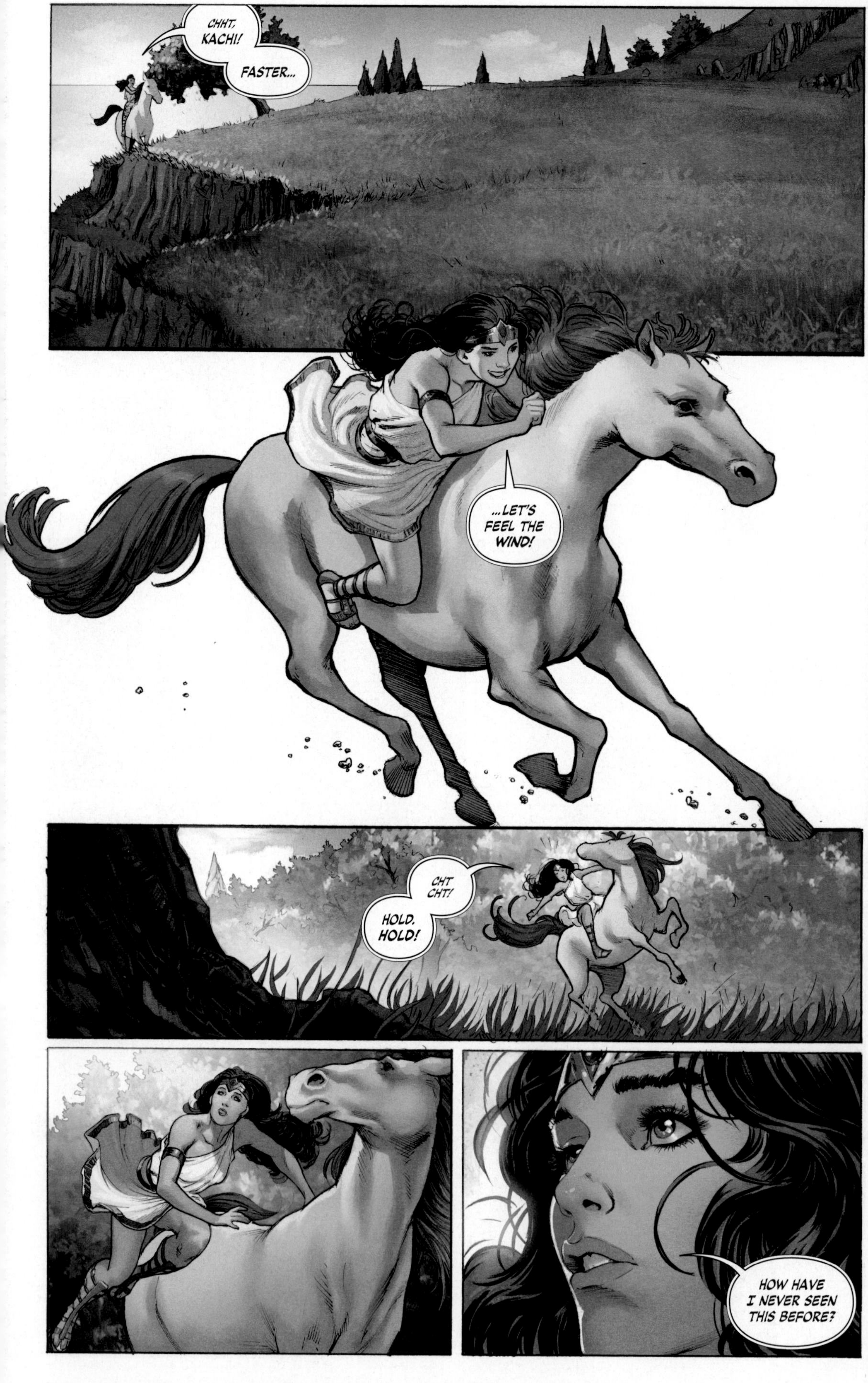
CHHT, KACHI!
FASTER...
...LET'S FEEL THE WIND!
CHT CHT!
HOLD, HOLD!
HOW HAVE I NEVER SEEN THIS BEFORE?

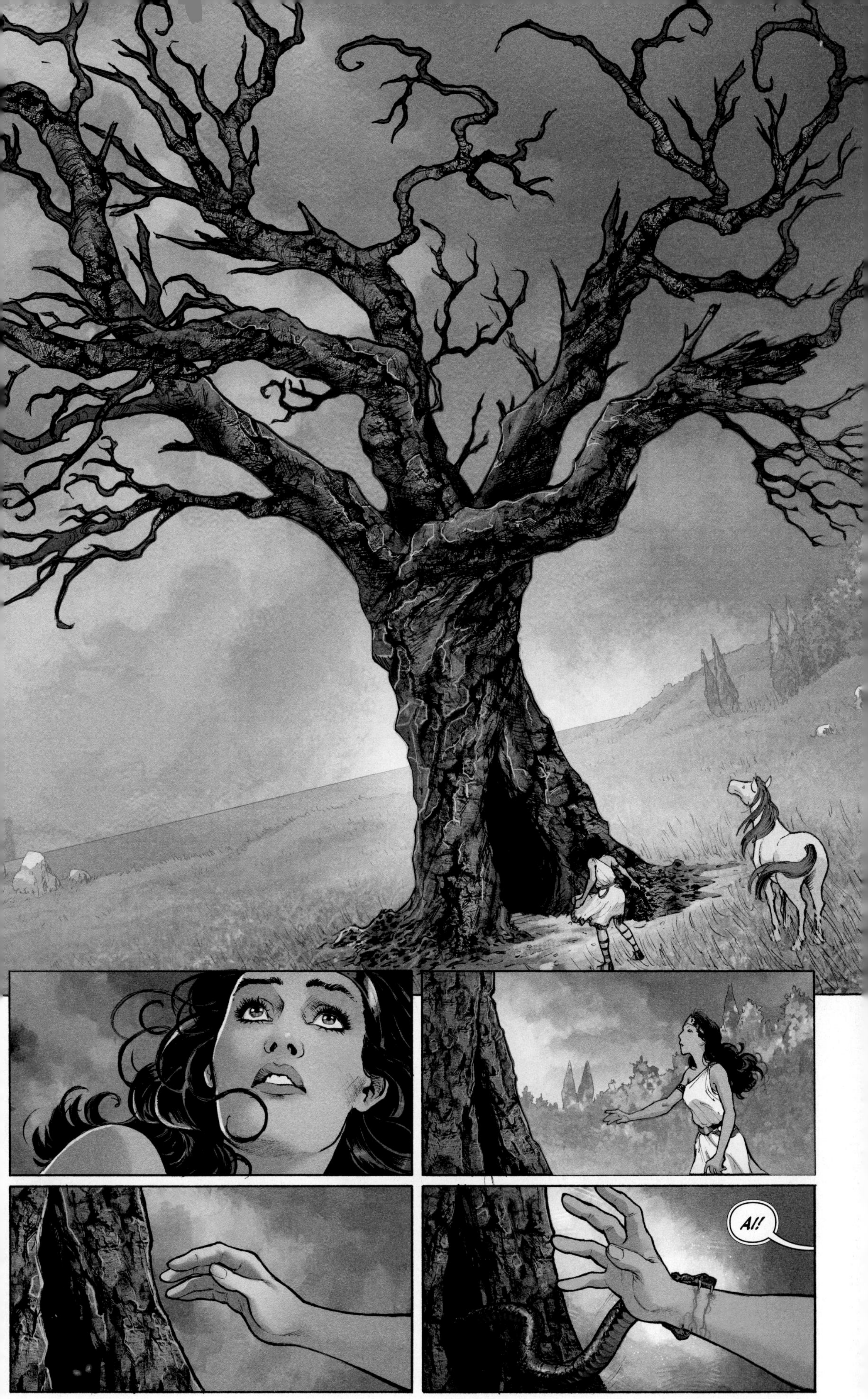
AI!

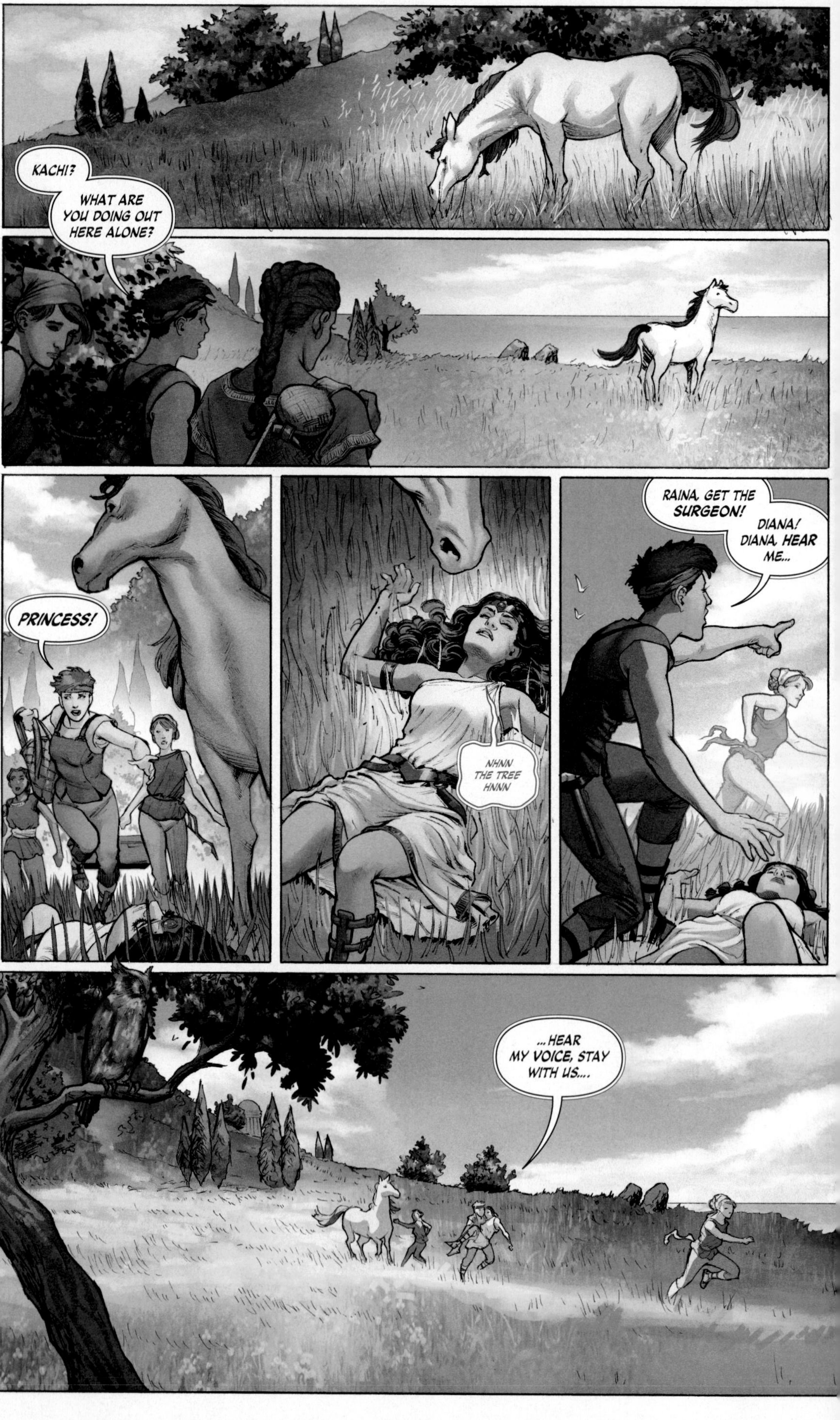
KACHI?
WHAT ARE YOU DOING OUT HERE ALONE?
PRINCESS!
NHNN THE TREE HNNN
RAINA, GET THE SURGEON!
DIANA! DIANA, HEAR ME...
...HEAR MY VOICE, STAY WITH US....

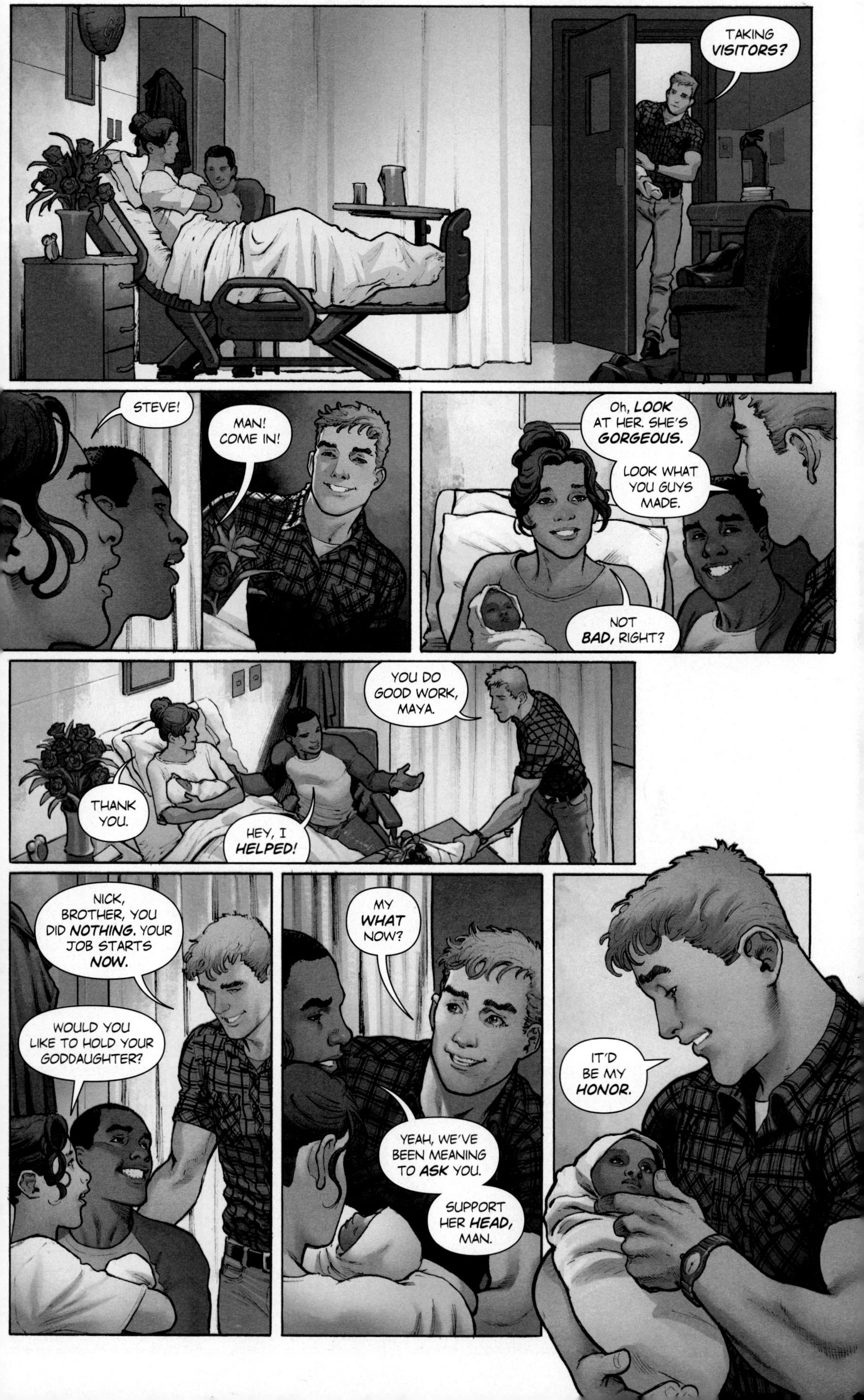
TAKING VISITORS?
STEVE!
MAN! COME IN!
Oh, LOOK AT HER. SHE'S GORGEOUS.
LOOK WHAT YOU GUYS MADE.
NOT BAD, RIGHT?
YOU DO GOOD WORK, MAYA.
THANK YOU.
HEY, I HELPED!
NICK, BROTHER, YOU DID NOTHING. YOUR JOB STARTS NOW.
WOULD YOU LIKE TO HOLD YOUR GODDAUGHTER?
MY WHAT NOW?
YEAH, WE'VE BEEN MEANING TO ASK YOU.
SUPPORT HER HEAD, MAN.
IT'D BE MY HONOR.

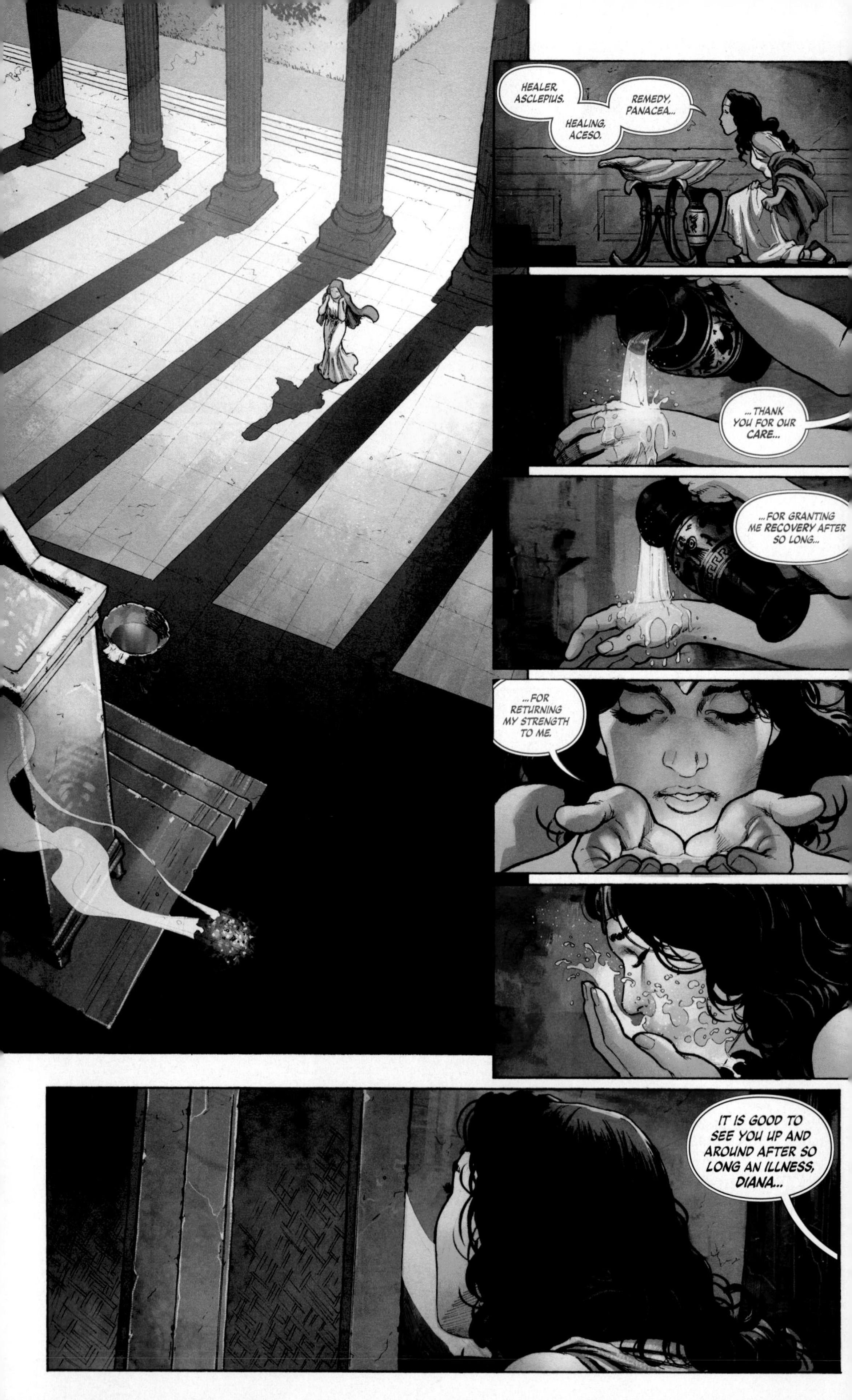
HEALER ASCLEPIUS.
HEALING, ACESO.
REMEDY, PANACEA...
...THANK YOU FOR OUR CARE...
...FOR GRANTING ME RECOVERY AFTER SO LONG...
...FOR RETURNING MY STRENGTH TO ME.
IT IS GOOD TO SEE YOU UP AND AROUND AFTER SO LONG AN ILLNESS, DIANA...

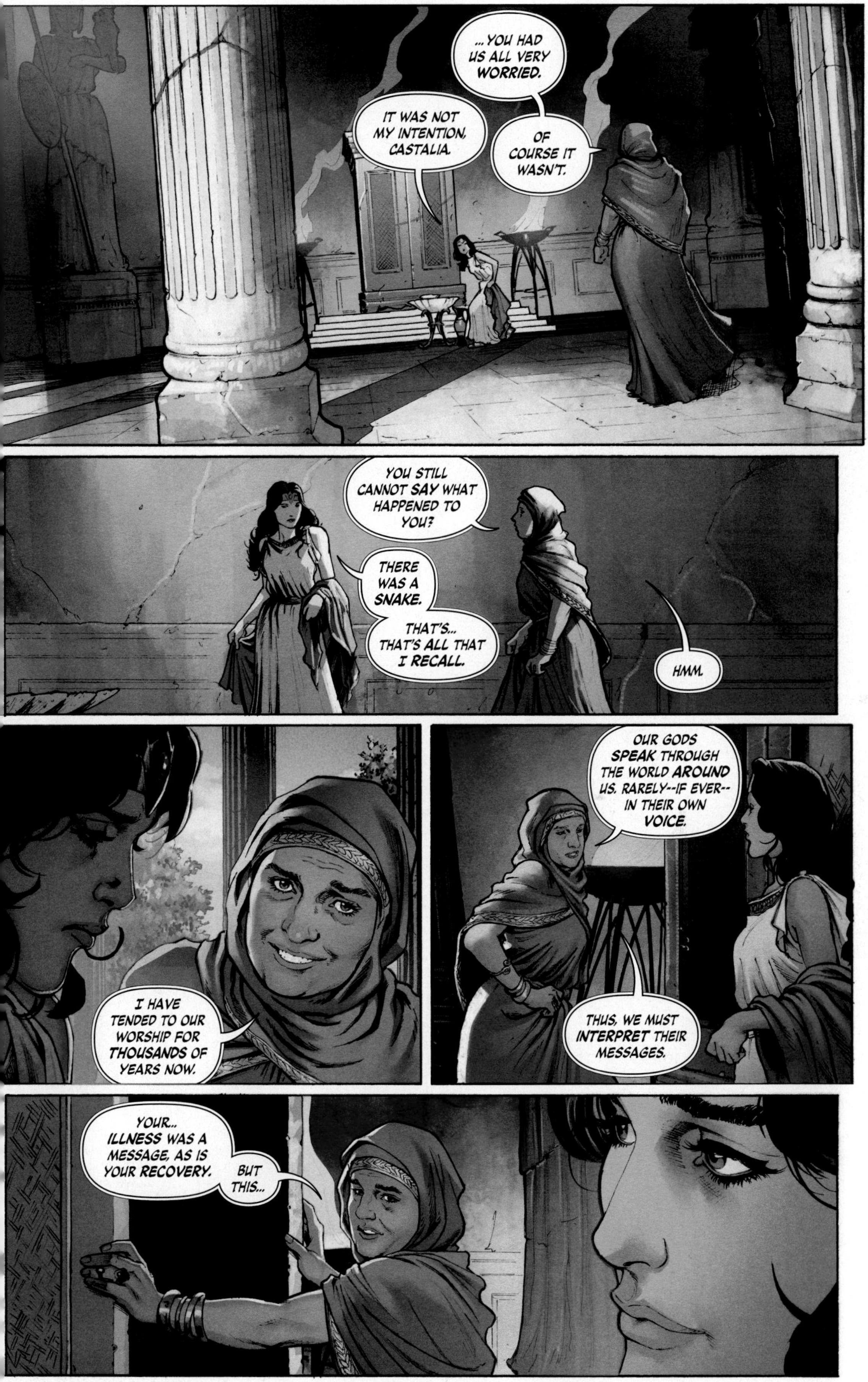

...YOU HAD US ALL VERY WORRIED.
IT WAS NOT MY INTENTION, CASTALIA.
OF COURSE IT WASN'T.
YOU STILL CANNOT SAY WHAT HAPPENED TO YOU?
THERE WAS A SNAKE.
THAT'S... THAT'S ALL THAT I RECALL.
HMM.
I HAVE TENDED TO OUR WORSHIP FOR THOUSANDS OF YEARS NOW.
OUR GODS SPEAK THROUGH THE WORLD AROUND US. RARELY--IF EVER--IN THEIR OWN VOICE.
THUS, WE MUST INTERPRET THEIR MESSAGES.
YOUR... ILLNESS WAS A MESSAGE, AS IS YOUR RECOVERY.
BUT THIS...

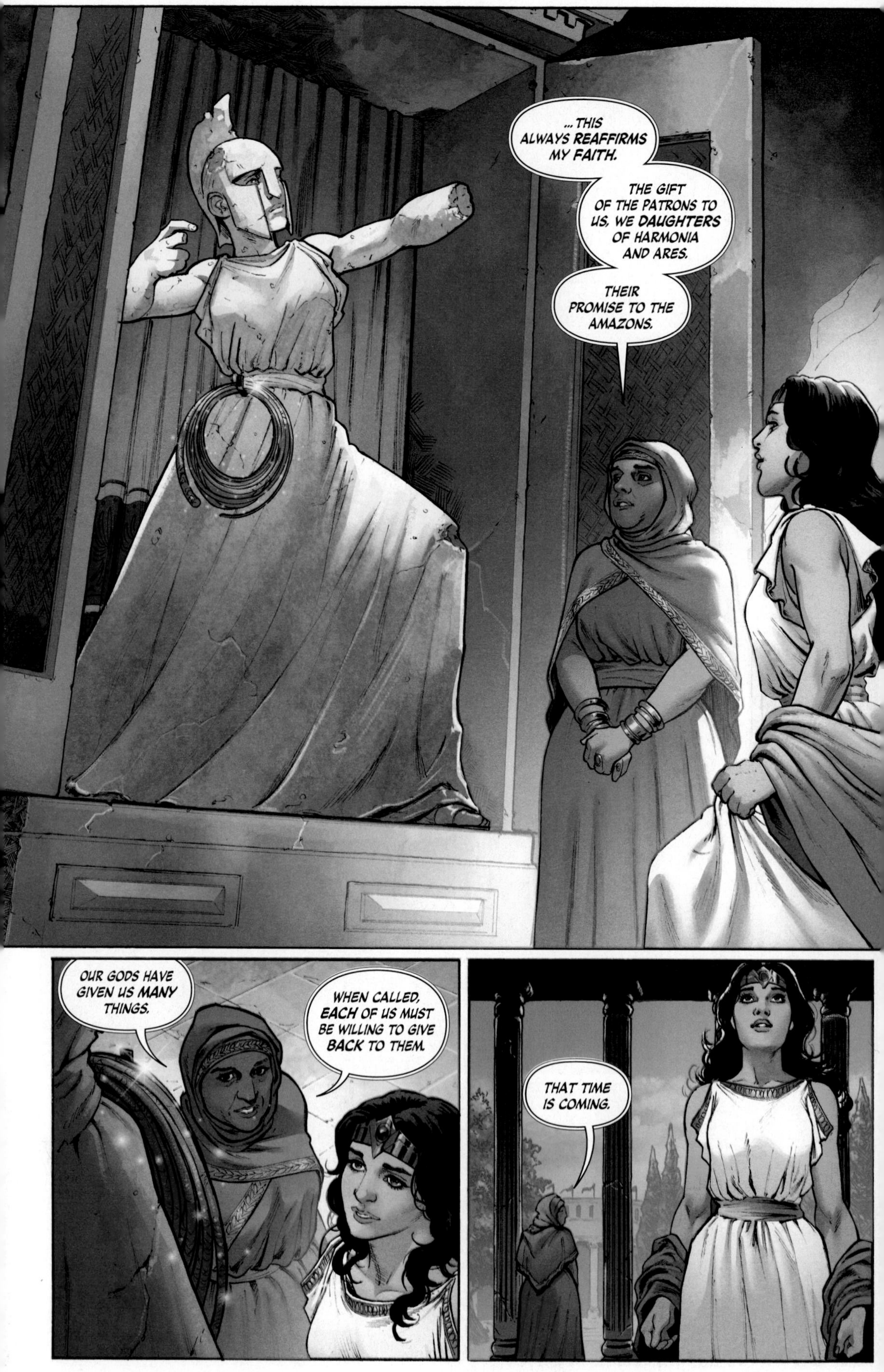
...THIS ALWAYS REAFFIRMS MY FAITH.
THE GIFT OF THE PATRONS TO US, WE DAUGHTERS OF HARMONIA AND ARES.
THEIR PROMISE TO THE AMAZONS.
OUR GODS HAVE GIVEN US MANY THINGS.
WHEN CALLED, EACH OF US MUST BE WILLING TO GIVE BACK TO THEM.
THAT TIME IS COMING.

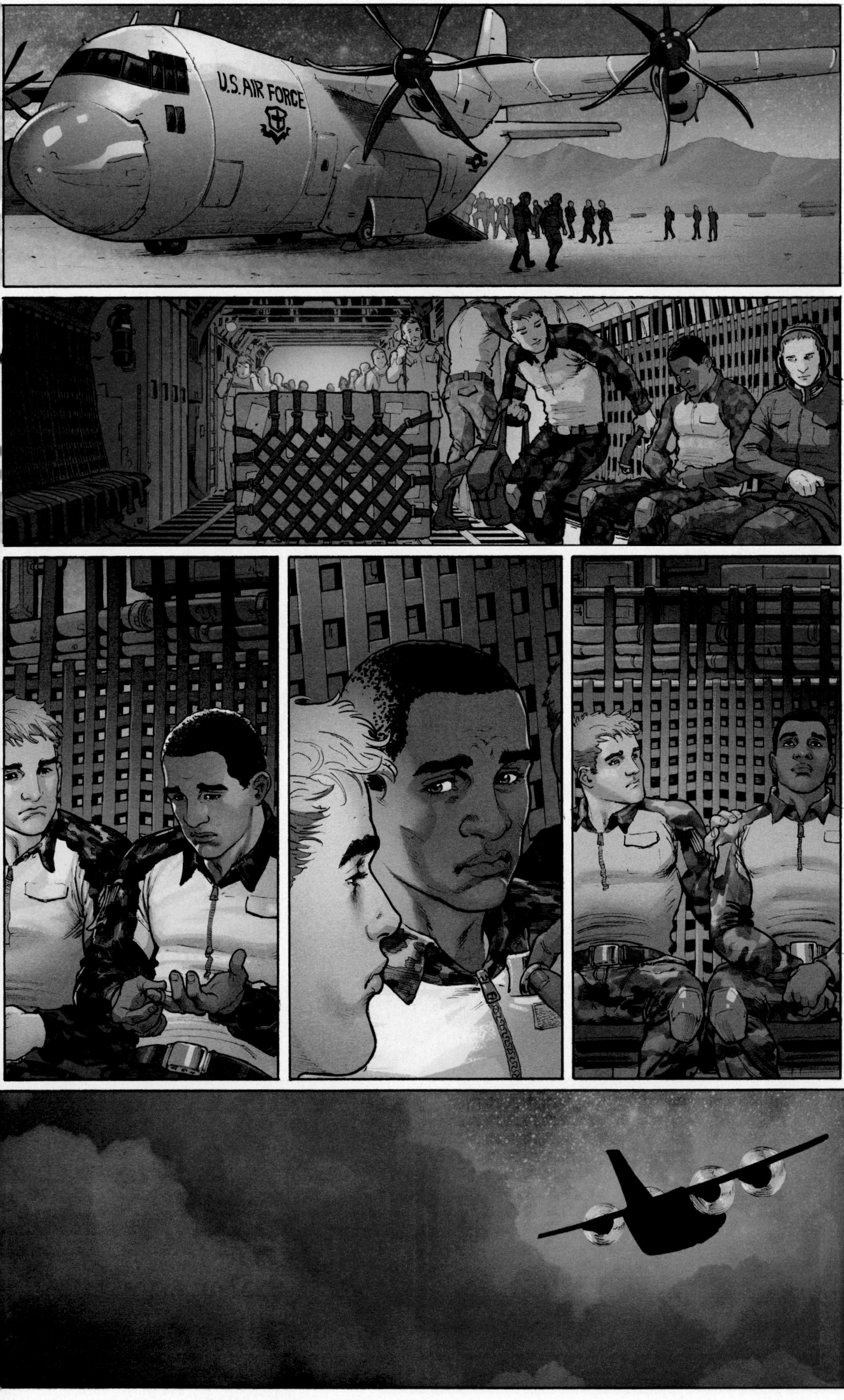
U.S. AIR FORCE

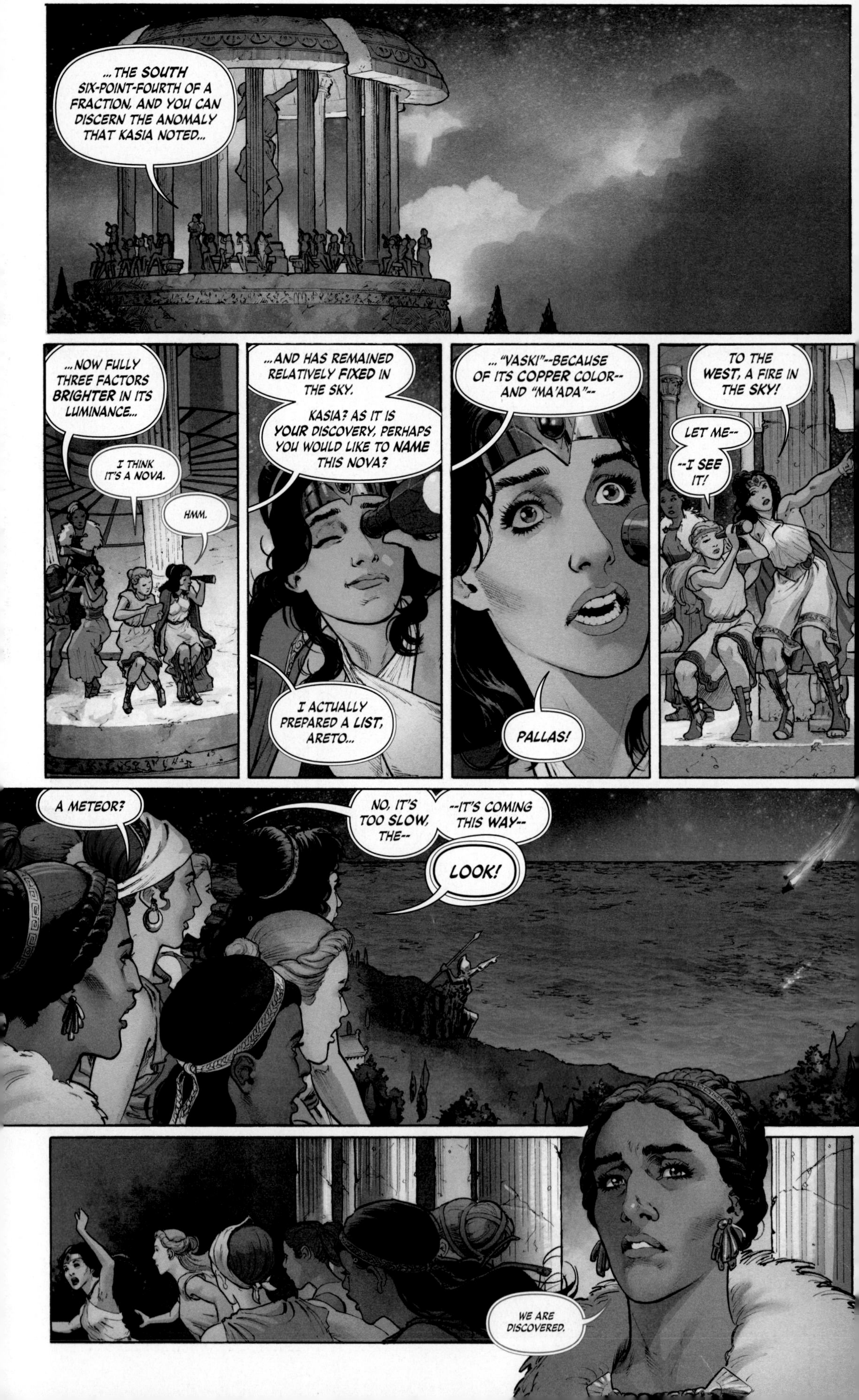
...THE SOUTH SIX-POINT-FOURTH OF A FRACTION, AND YOU CAN DISCERN THE ANOMALY THAT KASIA NOTED...
...NOW FULLY THREE FACTORS BRIGHTER IN ITS LUMINANCE...
I THINK IT'S A NOVA.
HMM.
...AND HAS REMAINED RELATIVELY FIXED IN THE SKY.
KASIA? AS IT IS YOUR DISCOVERY, PERHAPS YOU WOULD LIKE TO NAME THIS NOVA?
I ACTUALLY PREPARED A LIST, ARETO...
... "VASKI"--BECAUSE OF ITS COPPER COLOR-- AND "MA'ADA"--
PALLAS!
TO THE WEST, A FIRE IN THE SKY!
LET ME--
--I SEE IT!
A METEOR?
NO, IT'S TOO SLOW, THE--
--IT'S COMING THIS WAY--
LOOK!
WE ARE DISCOVERED.

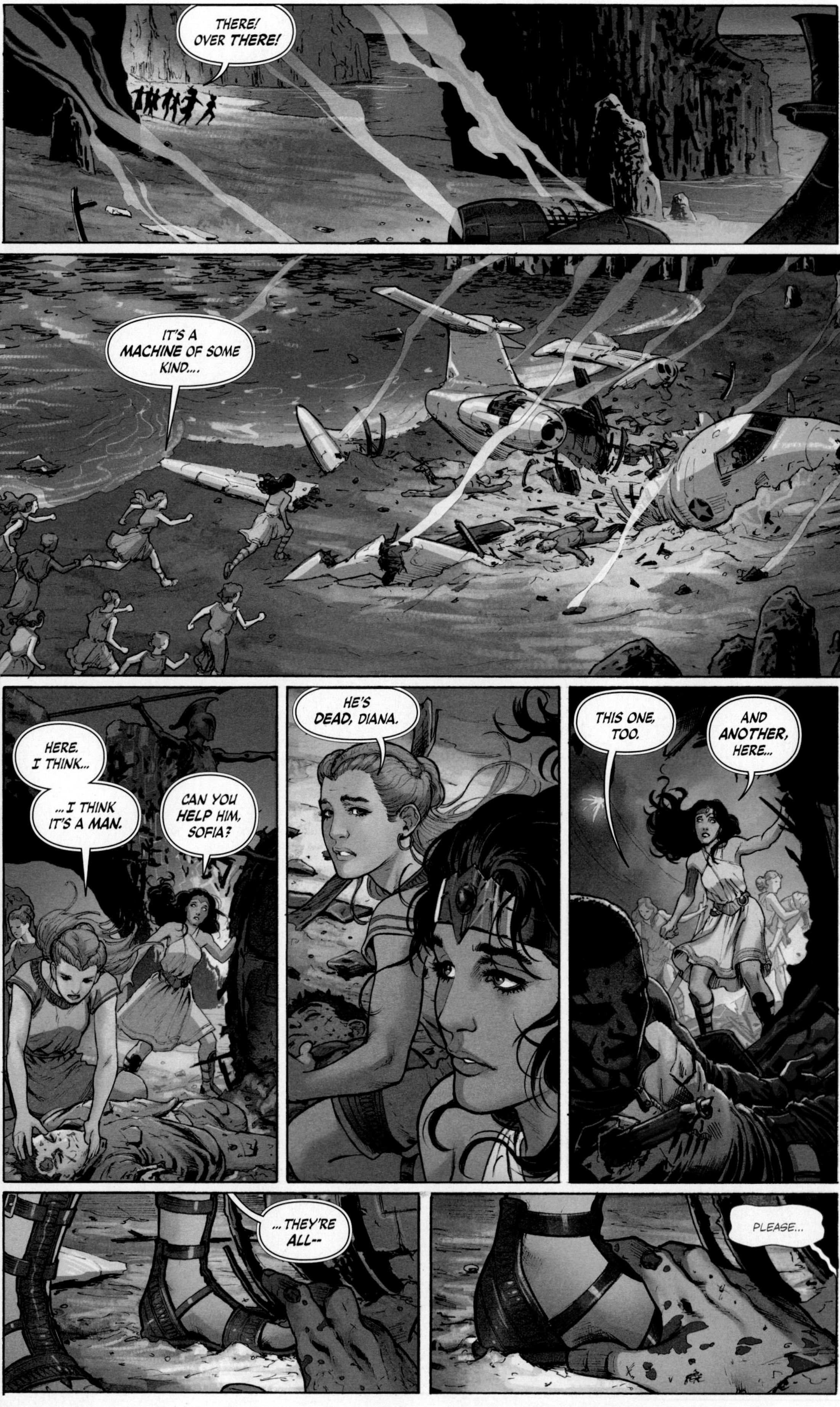
THERE! OVER THERE!
IT'S A MACHINE OF SOME KIND....
HERE. I THINK...
...I THINK IT'S A MAN.
CAN YOU HELP HIM, SOFIA?
HE'S DEAD, DIANA.
THIS ONE, TOO.
AND ANOTHER, HERE...
...THEY'RE ALL--
PLEASE...

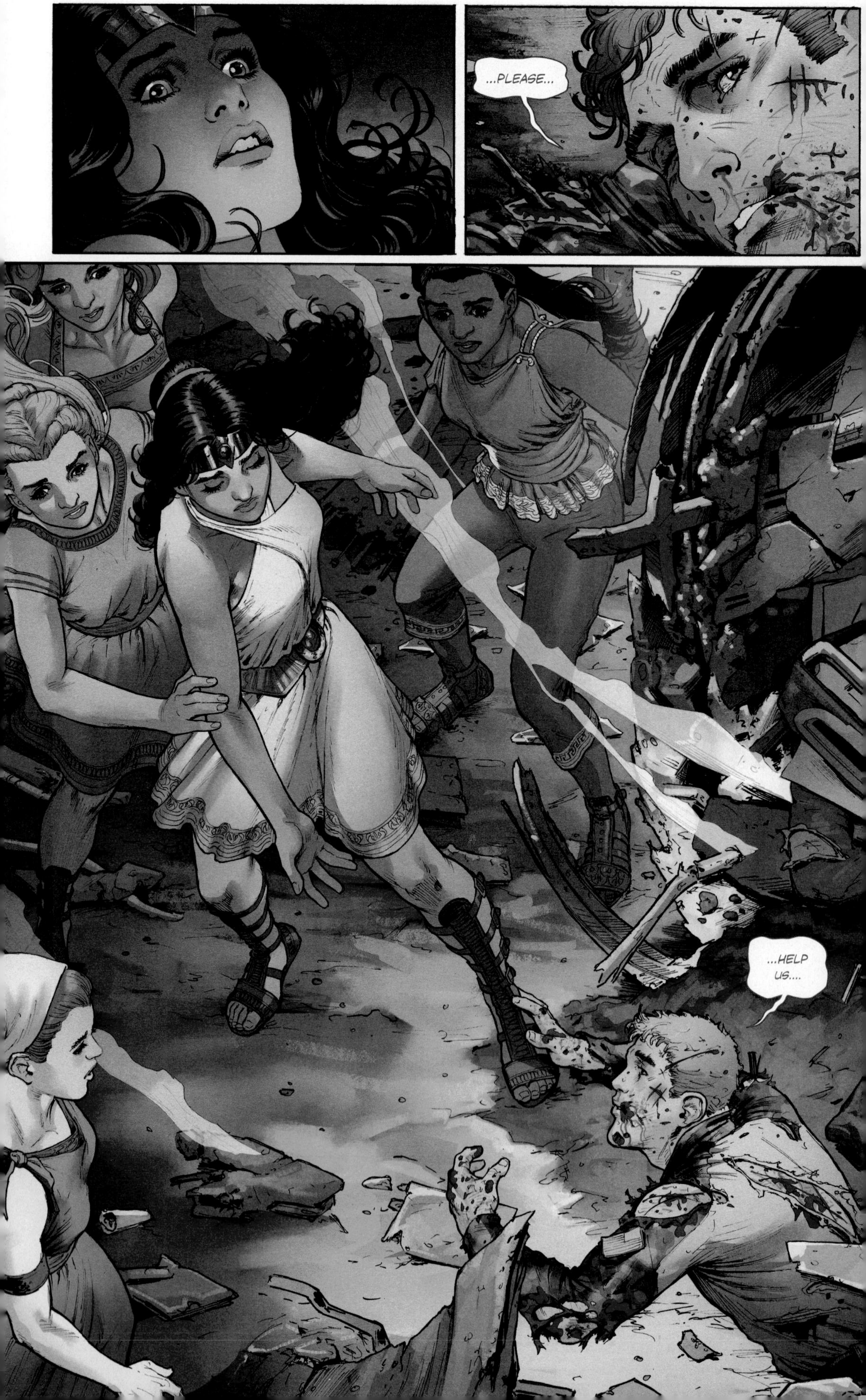
...PLEASE...
...HELP US....

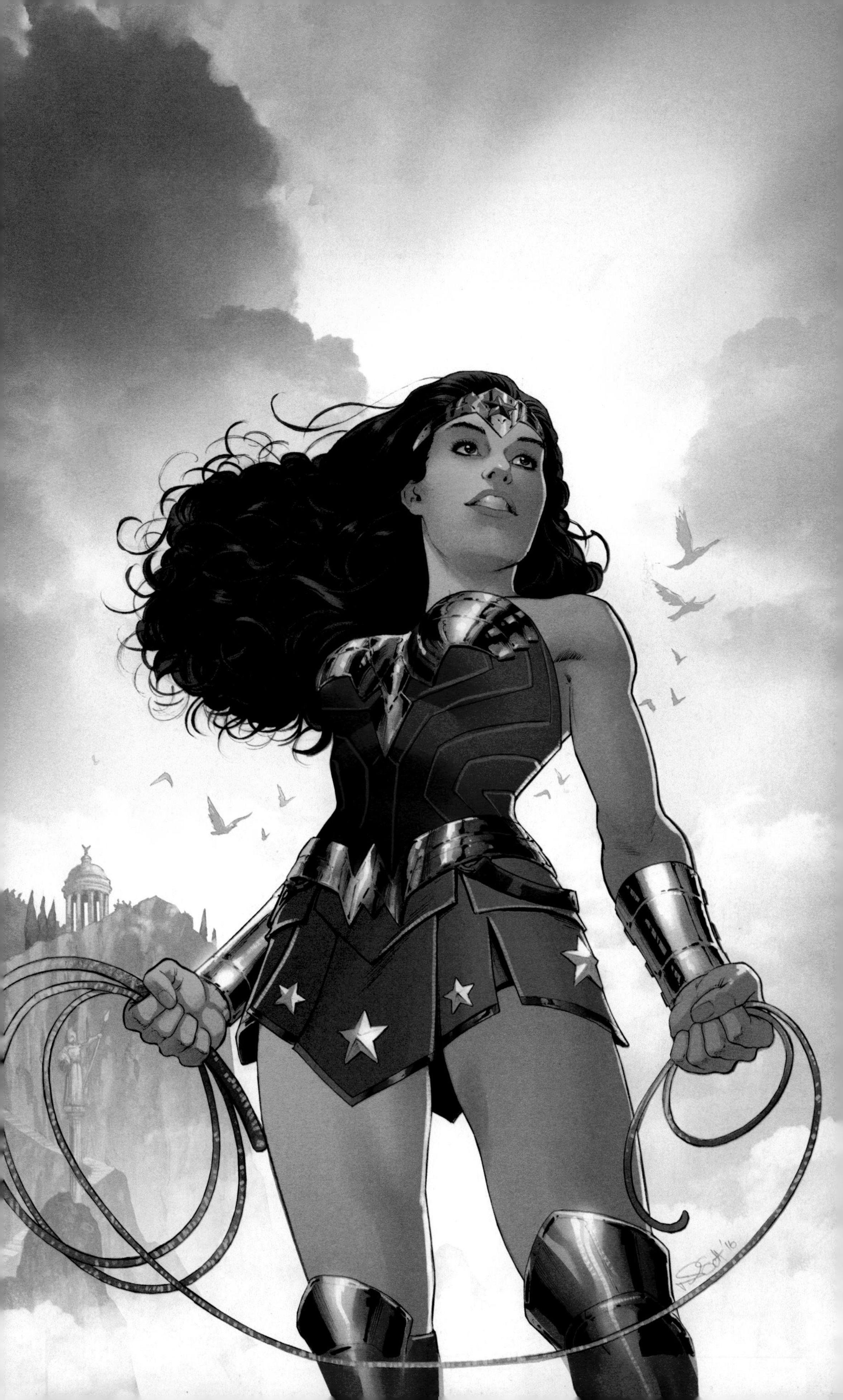

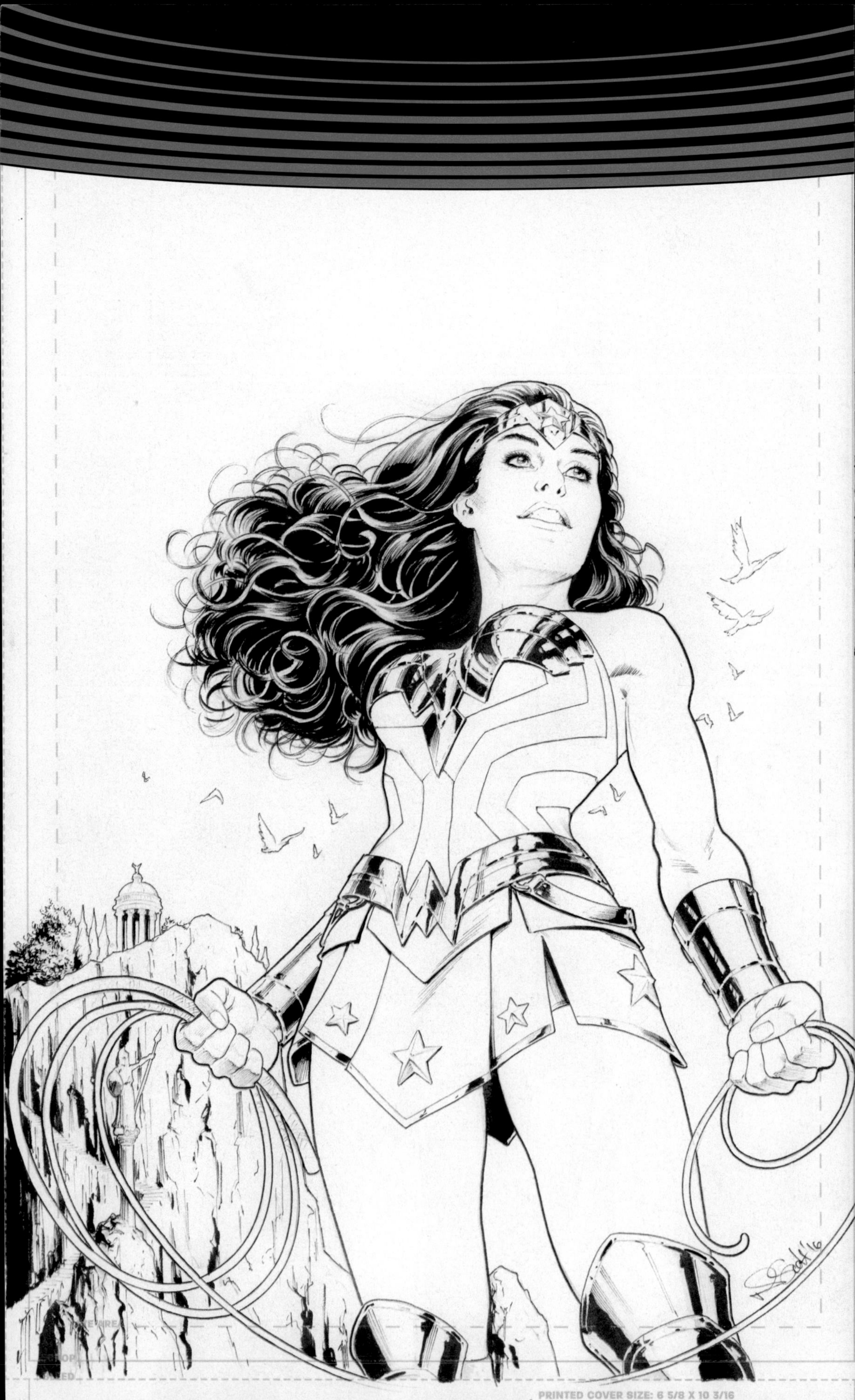

PRINTED COVER SIZE: 6 5/8 X 10 3/16

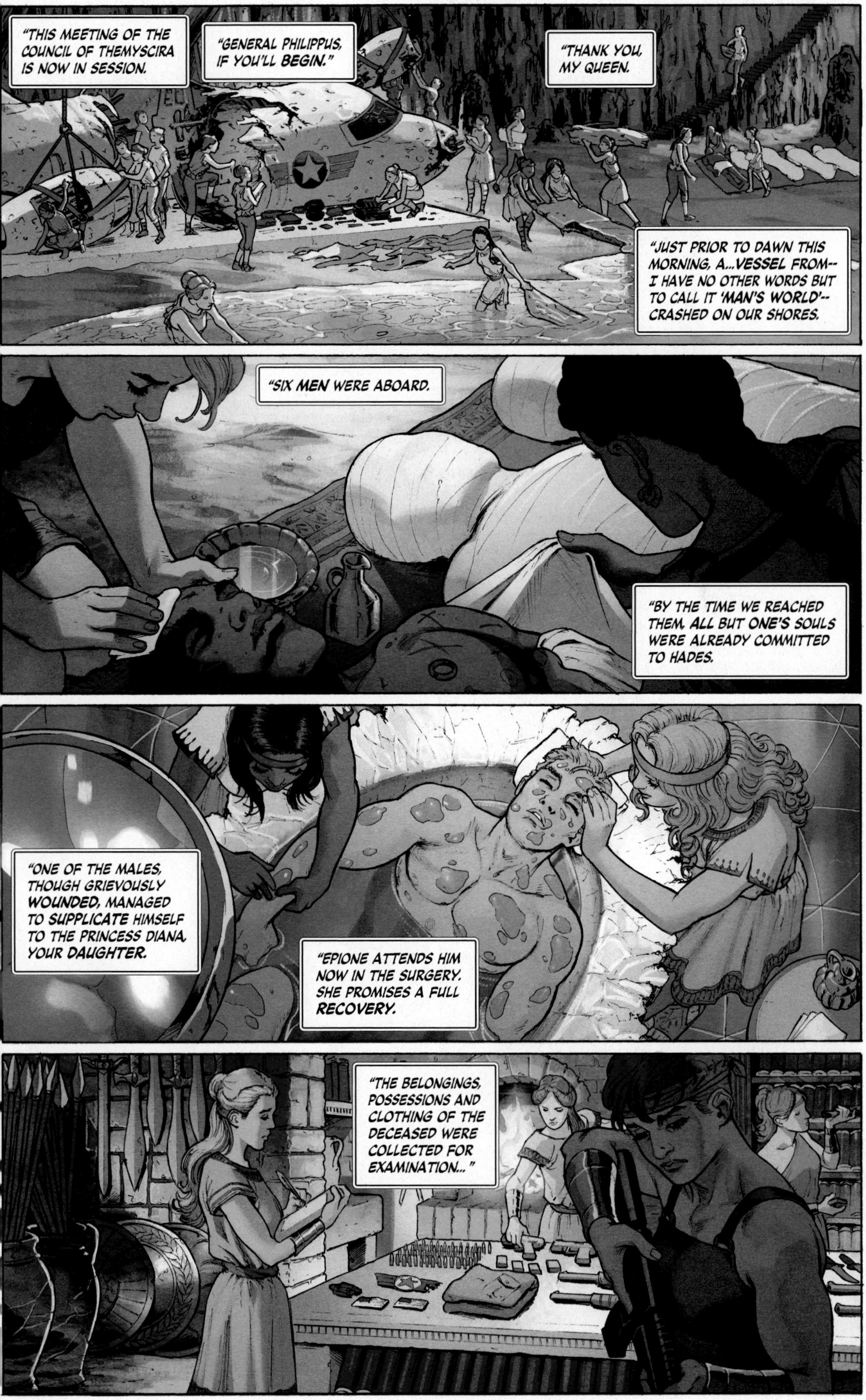
"THIS MEETING OF THE COUNCIL OF THEMYSCIRA IS NOW IN SESSION.
"GENERAL PHILIPPUS, IF YOU'LL BEGIN."
"THANK YOU, MY QUEEN.
"JUST PRIOR TO DAWN THIS MORNING, A...VESSEL FROM-- I HAVE NO OTHER WORDS BUT TO CALL IT 'MAN'S WORLD'-- CRASHED ON OUR SHORES.
"SIX MEN WERE ABOARD.
"BY THE TIME WE REACHED THEM, ALL BUT ONE'S SOULS WERE ALREADY COMMITTED TO HADES.
"ONE OF THE MALES, THOUGH GRIEVOUSLY WOUNDED, MANAGED TO SUPPLICATE HIMSELF TO THE PRINCESS DIANA, YOUR DAUGHTER.
"EPIONE ATTENDS HIM NOW IN THE SURGERY. SHE PROMISES A FULL RECOVERY.
"THE BELONGINGS, POSSESSIONS AND CLOTHING OF THE DECEASED WERE COLLECTED FOR EXAMINATION..."

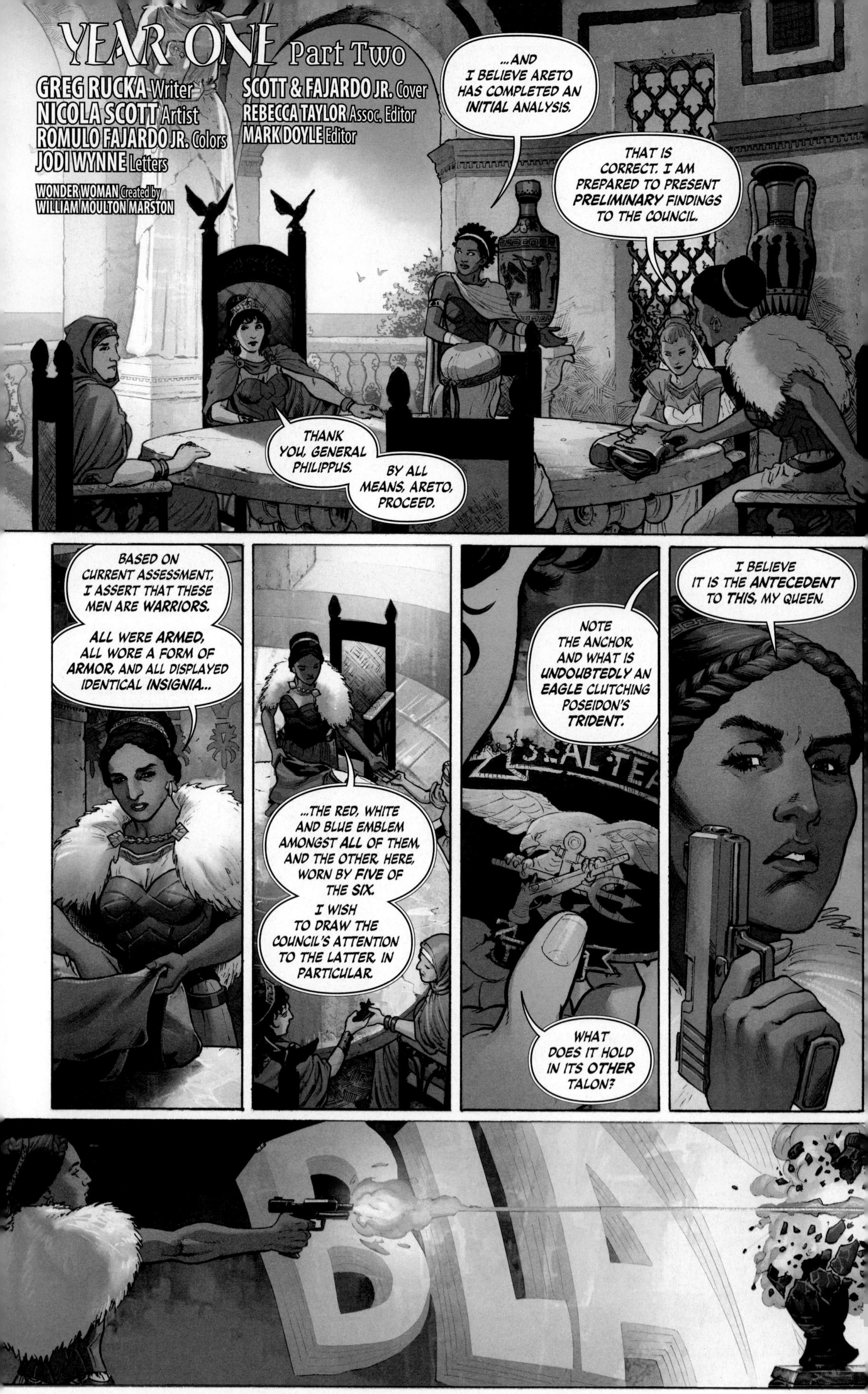

YEAR ONE Part Two
GREG RUCKA Writer
NICOLA SCOTT Artist
ROMULO FAJARDO JR. Colors
JODI WYNNE Letters
SCOTT & FAJARDO JR. Cover
REBECCA TAYLOR Assoc. Editor
MARK DOYLE Editor
WONDER WOMAN Created by WILLIAM MOULTON MARSTON
...AND I BELIEVE ARETO HAS COMPLETED AN INITIAL ANALYSIS.
THAT IS CORRECT. I AM PREPARED TO PRESENT PRELIMINARY FINDINGS TO THE COUNCIL.
THANK YOU, GENERAL PHILIPPUS.
BY ALL MEANS, ARETO, PROCEED.
BASED ON CURRENT ASSESSMENT, I ASSERT THAT THESE MEN ARE WARRIORS.
ALL WERE ARMED, ALL WORE A FORM OF ARMOR, AND ALL DISPLAYED IDENTICAL INSIGNIA...
...THE RED, WHITE AND BLUE EMBLEM AMONGST ALL OF THEM, AND THE OTHER HERE, WORN BY FIVE OF THE SIX.
I WISH TO DRAW THE COUNCIL'S ATTENTION TO THE LATTER, IN PARTICULAR.
NOTE THE ANCHOR AND WHAT IS UNDOUBTEDLY AN EAGLE CLUTCHING POSEIDON'S TRIDENT.
WHAT DOES IT HOLD IN ITS OTHER TALON?
I BELIEVE IT IS THE ANTECEDENT TO THIS, MY QUEEN.
BLA

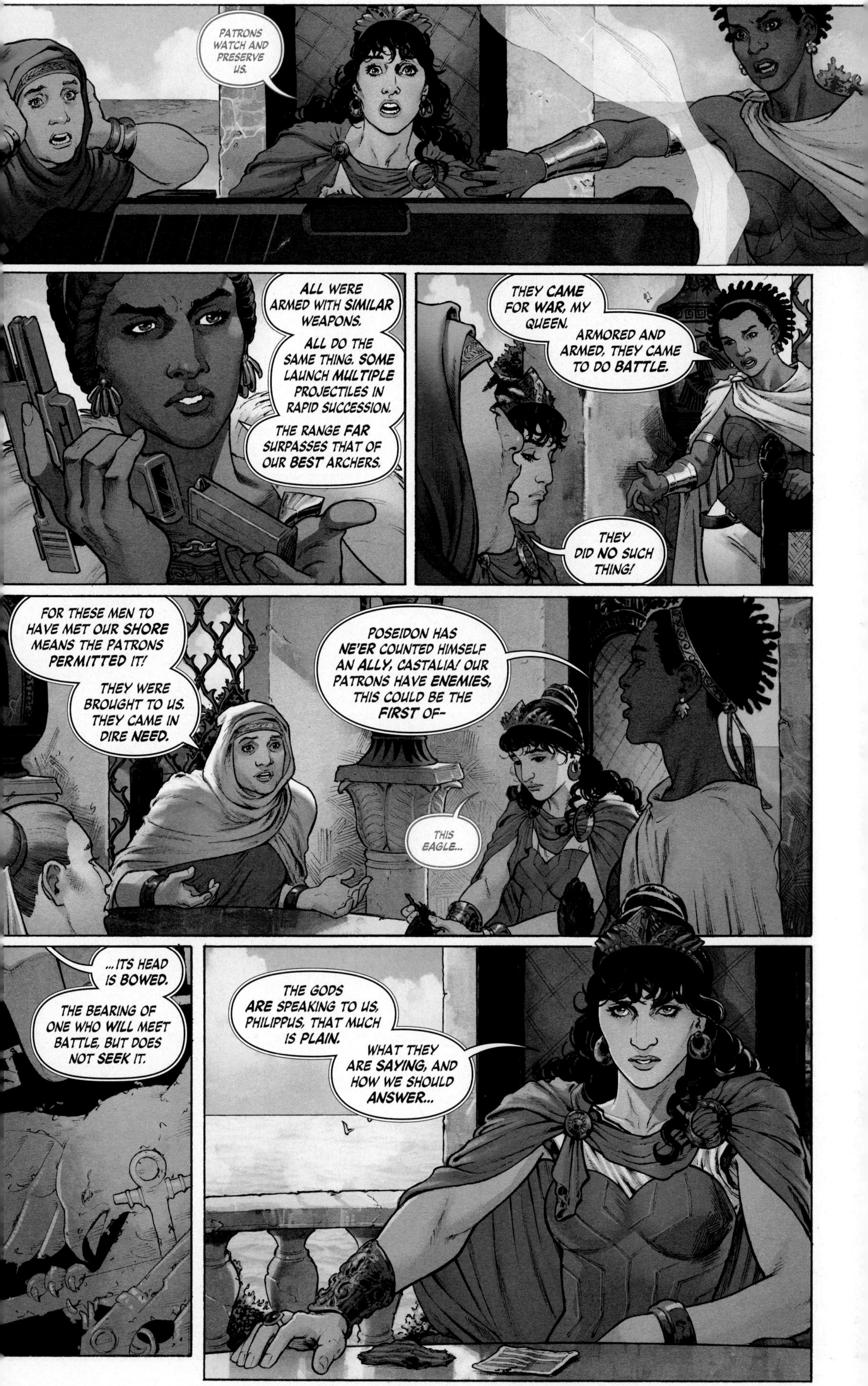

PATRONS WATCH AND PRESERVE US.
ALL WERE ARMED WITH SIMILAR WEAPONS.
ALL DO THE SAME THING. SOME LAUNCH MULTIPLE PROJECTILES IN RAPID SUCCESSION.
THE RANGE FAR SURPASSES THAT OF OUR BEST ARCHERS.
THEY CAME FOR WAR, MY QUEEN.
ARMORED AND ARMED, THEY CAME TO DO BATTLE.
THEY DID NO SUCH THING!
FOR THESE MEN TO HAVE MET OUR SHORE MEANS THE PATRONS PERMITTED IT!
THEY WERE BROUGHT TO US. THEY CAME IN DIRE NEED.
POSEIDON HAS NE'ER COUNTED HIMSELF AN ALLY, CASTALIA! OUR PATRONS HAVE ENEMIES, THIS COULD BE THE FIRST OF-
THIS EAGLE...
...ITS HEAD IS BOWED.
THE BEARING OF ONE WHO WILL MEET BATTLE, BUT DOES NOT SEEK IT.
THE GODS ARE SPEAKING TO US, PHILIPPUS, THAT MUCH IS PLAIN.
WHAT THEY ARE SAYING, AND HOW WE SHOULD ANSWER...

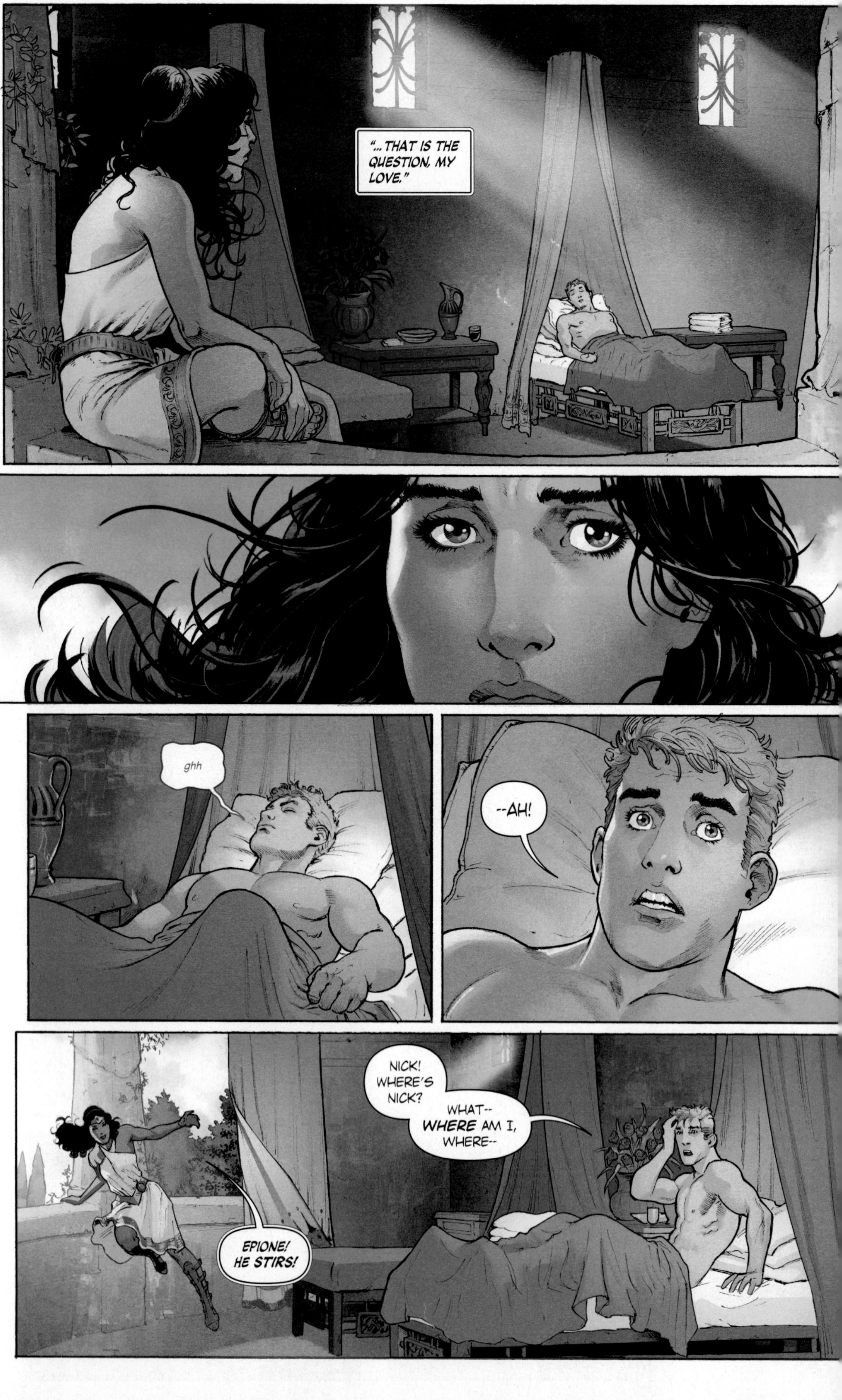
"...THAT IS THE QUESTION, MY LOVE."
ghh
--AH!
EPIONE! HE STIRS!
NICK! WHERE'S NICK?
WHAT-- WHERE AM I, WHERE--

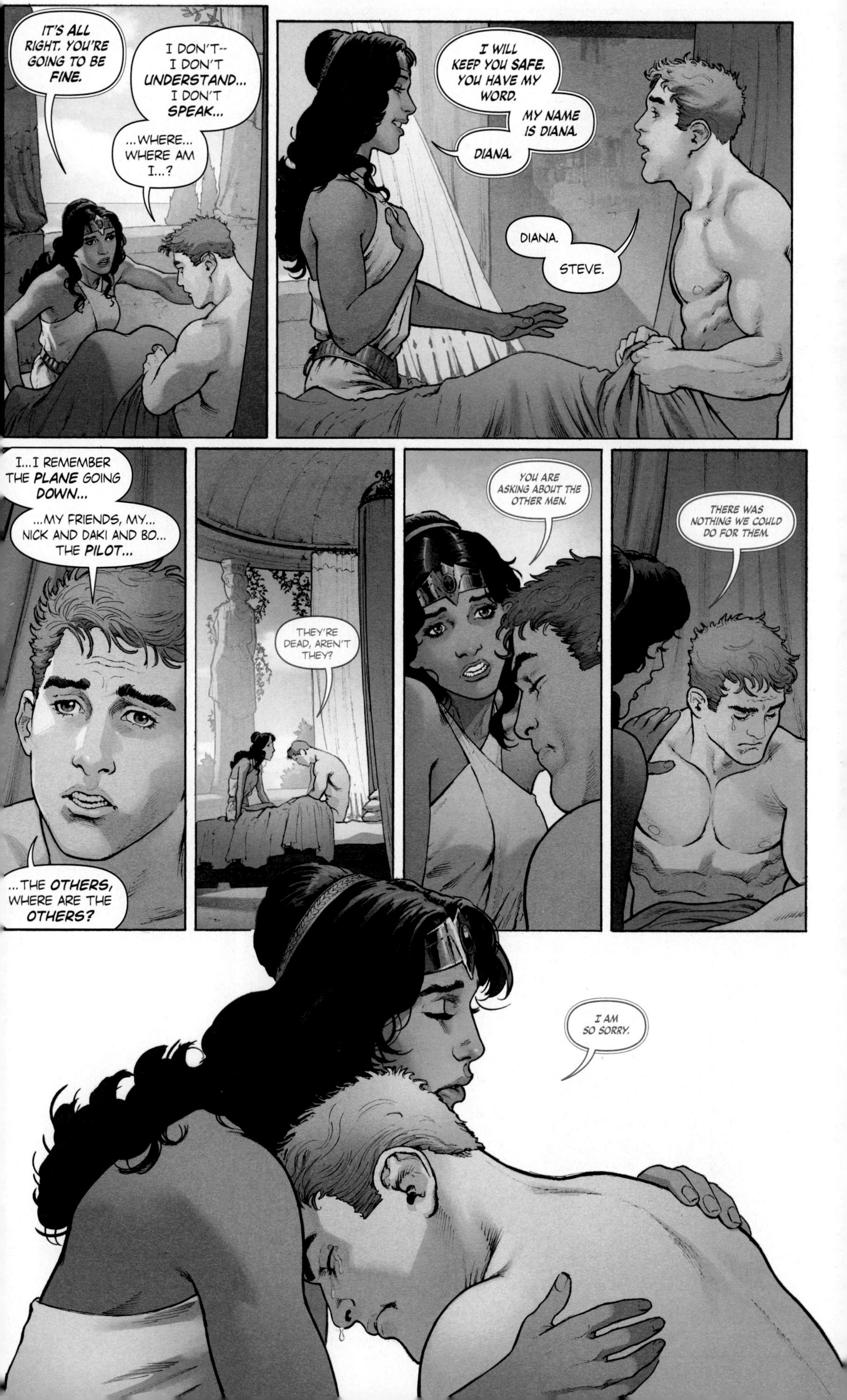
IT'S ALL RIGHT. YOU'RE GOING TO BE FINE.
I DON'T-- I DON'T UNDERSTAND... I DON'T SPEAK...
...WHERE... WHERE AM I...?
I WILL KEEP YOU SAFE. YOU HAVE MY WORD.
MY NAME IS DIANA.
DIANA.
DIANA.
STEVE.
I...I REMEMBER THE PLANE GOING DOWN...
...MY FRIENDS, MY... NICK AND DAKI AND BO... THE PILOT...
...THE OTHERS, WHERE ARE THE OTHERS?
THEY'RE DEAD, AREN'T THEY?
YOU ARE ASKING ABOUT THE OTHER MEN.
THERE WAS NOTHING WE COULD DO FOR THEM.
I AM SO SORRY.

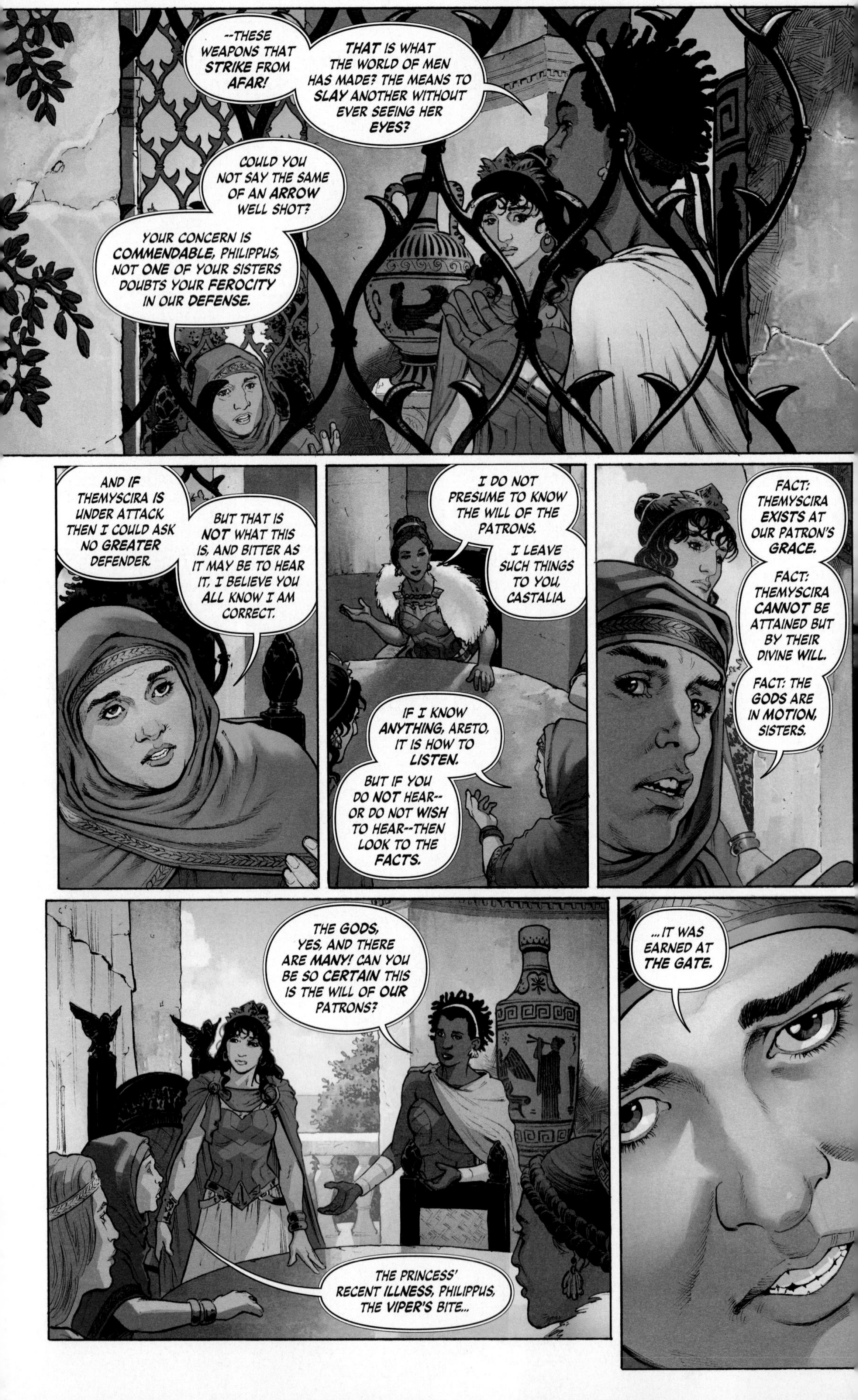
--THESE WEAPONS THAT STRIKE FROM AFAR!
THAT IS WHAT THE WORLD OF MEN HAS MADE? THE MEANS TO SLAY ANOTHER WITHOUT EVER SEEING HER EYES?
COULD YOU NOT SAY THE SAME OF AN ARROW WELL SHOT?
YOUR CONCERN IS COMMENDABLE, PHILIPPUS, NOT ONE OF YOUR SISTERS DOUBTS YOUR FEROCITY IN OUR DEFENSE.
AND IF THEMYSCIRA IS UNDER ATTACK, THEN I COULD ASK NO GREATER DEFENDER.
BUT THAT IS NOT WHAT THIS IS, AND BITTER AS IT MAY BE TO HEAR IT, I BELIEVE YOU ALL KNOW I AM CORRECT.
I DO NOT PRESUME TO KNOW THE WILL OF THE PATRONS.
I LEAVE SUCH THINGS TO YOU, CASTALIA.
IF I KNOW ANYTHING, ARETO, IT IS HOW TO LISTEN.
BUT IF YOU DO NOT HEAR-- OR DO NOT WISH TO HEAR--THEN LOOK TO THE FACTS.
FACT: THEMYSCIRA EXISTS AT OUR PATRON'S GRACE.
FACT: THEMYSCIRA CANNOT BE ATTAINED BUT BY THEIR DIVINE WILL.
FACT: THE GODS ARE IN MOTION, SISTERS.
THE GODS, YES, AND THERE ARE MANY! CAN YOU BE SO CERTAIN THIS IS THE WILL OF OUR PATRONS?
THE PRINCESS' RECENT ILLNESS, PHILIPPUS, THE VIPER'S BITE...
...IT WAS EARNED AT THE GATE.

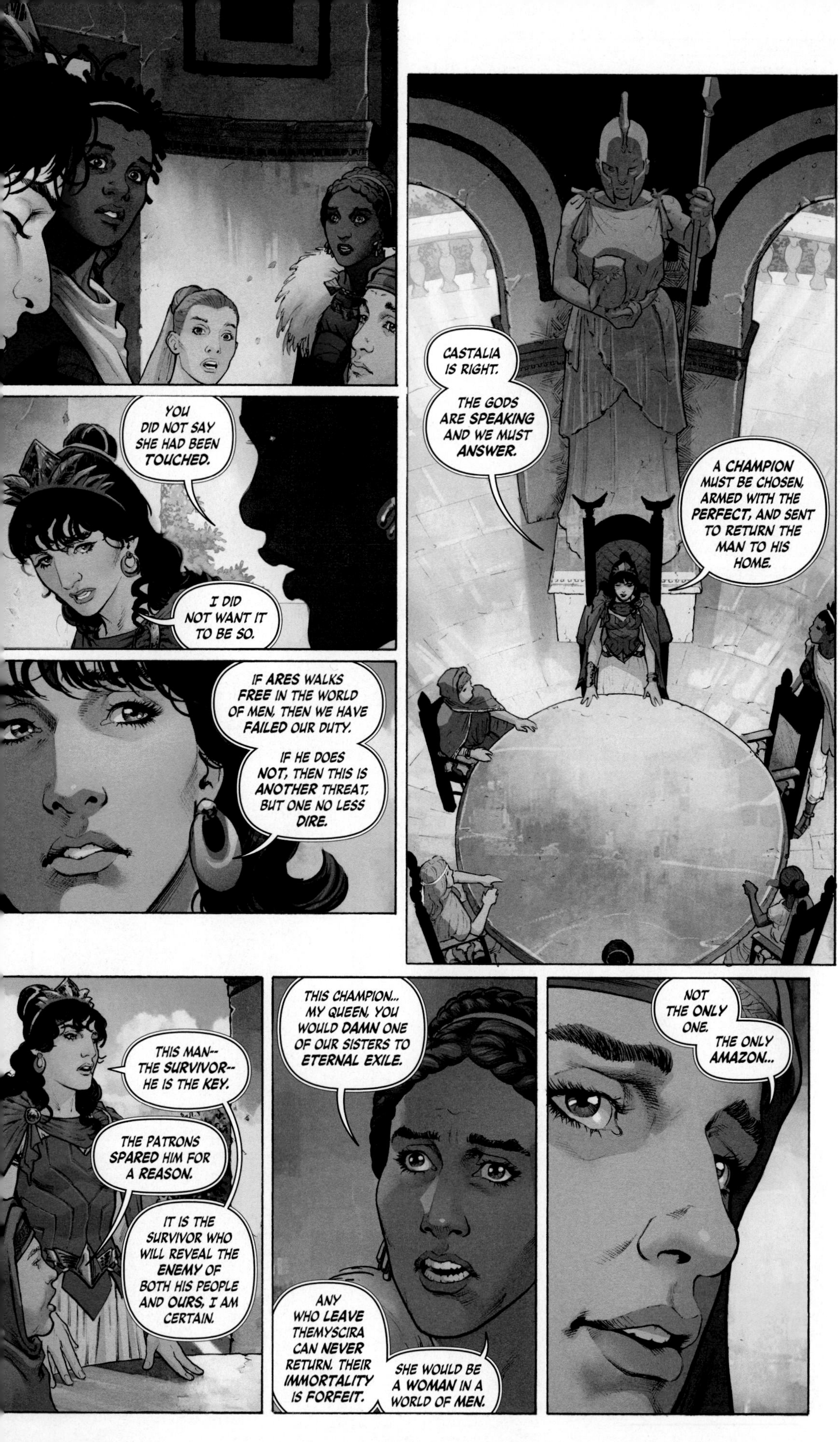
YOU DID NOT SAY SHE HAD BEEN TOUCHED.
I DID NOT WANT IT TO BE SO.
IF ARES WALKS FREE IN THE WORLD OF MEN, THEN WE HAVE FAILED OUR DUTY.
IF HE DOES NOT, THEN THIS IS ANOTHER THREAT, BUT ONE NO LESS DIRE.
CASTALIA IS RIGHT.
THE GODS ARE SPEAKING AND WE MUST ANSWER.
A CHAMPION MUST BE CHOSEN, ARMED WITH THE PERFECT, AND SENT TO RETURN THE MAN TO HIS HOME.
THIS MAN-- THE SURVIVOR-- HE IS THE KEY.
THE PATRONS SPARED HIM FOR A REASON.
IT IS THE SURVIVOR WHO WILL REVEAL THE ENEMY OF BOTH HIS PEOPLE AND OURS, I AM CERTAIN.
THIS CHAMPION... MY QUEEN, YOU WOULD DAMN ONE OF OUR SISTERS TO ETERNAL EXILE.
ANY WHO LEAVE THEMYSCIRA CAN NEVER RETURN. THEIR IMMORTALITY IS FORFEIT.
SHE WOULD BE A WOMAN IN A WORLD OF MEN.
NOT THE ONLY ONE.
THE ONLY AMAZON...

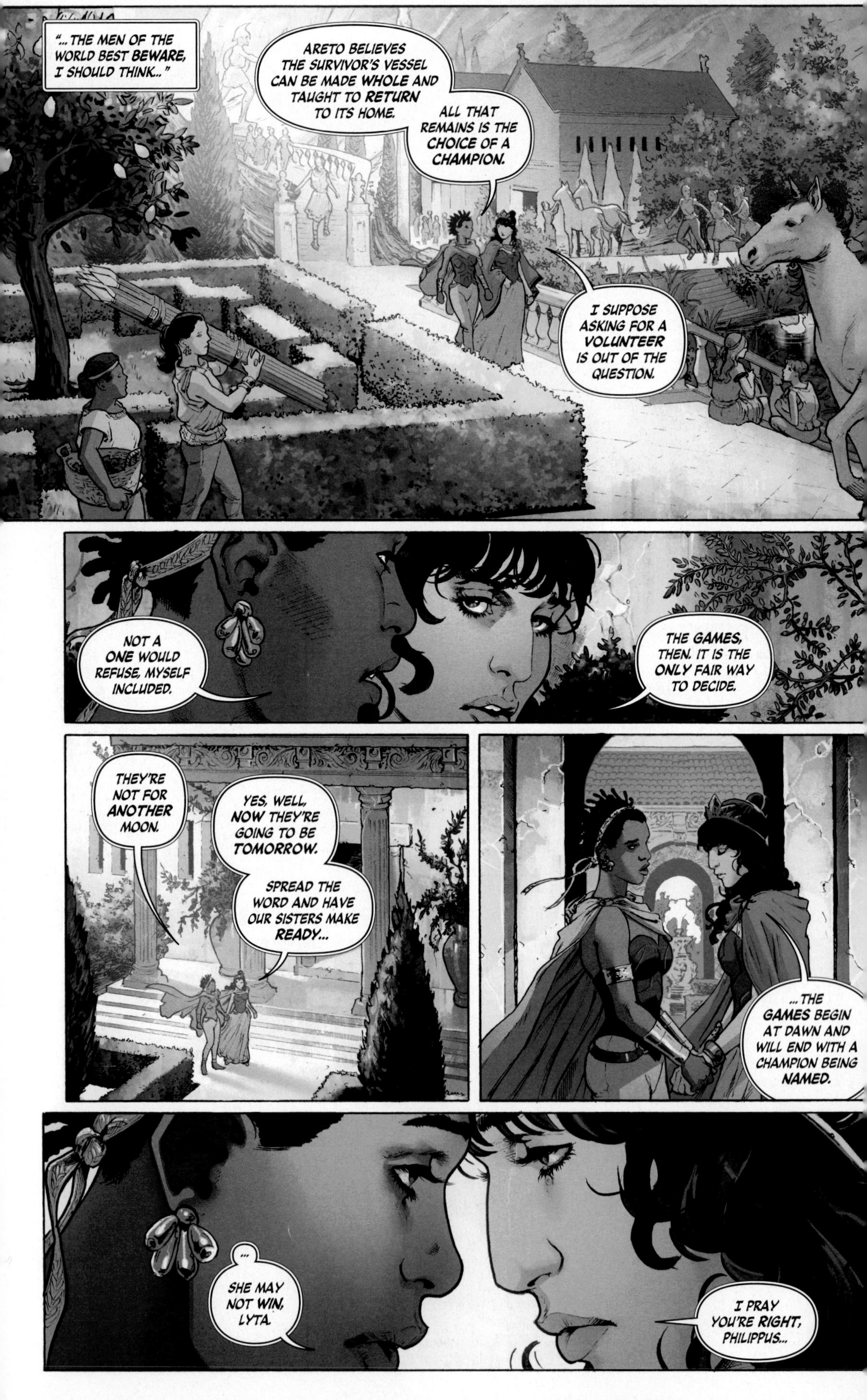
"... THE MEN OF THE WORLD BEST BEWARE, I SHOULD THINK..."
ARETO BELIEVES THE SURVIVOR'S VESSEL CAN BE MADE WHOLE AND TAUGHT TO RETURN TO ITS HOME.
ALL THAT REMAINS IS THE CHOICE OF A CHAMPION.
I SUPPOSE ASKING FOR A VOLUNTEER IS OUT OF THE QUESTION.
NOT A ONE WOULD REFUSE, MYSELF INCLUDED.
THE GAMES, THEN. IT IS THE ONLY FAIR WAY TO DECIDE.
THEY'RE NOT FOR ANOTHER MOON.
YES, WELL, NOW THEY'RE GOING TO BE TOMORROW.
SPREAD THE WORD AND HAVE OUR SISTERS MAKE READY...
... THE GAMES BEGIN AT DAWN AND WILL END WITH A CHAMPION BEING NAMED.
...
SHE MAY NOT WIN, LYTA.
I PRAY YOU'RE RIGHT, PHILIPPUS...

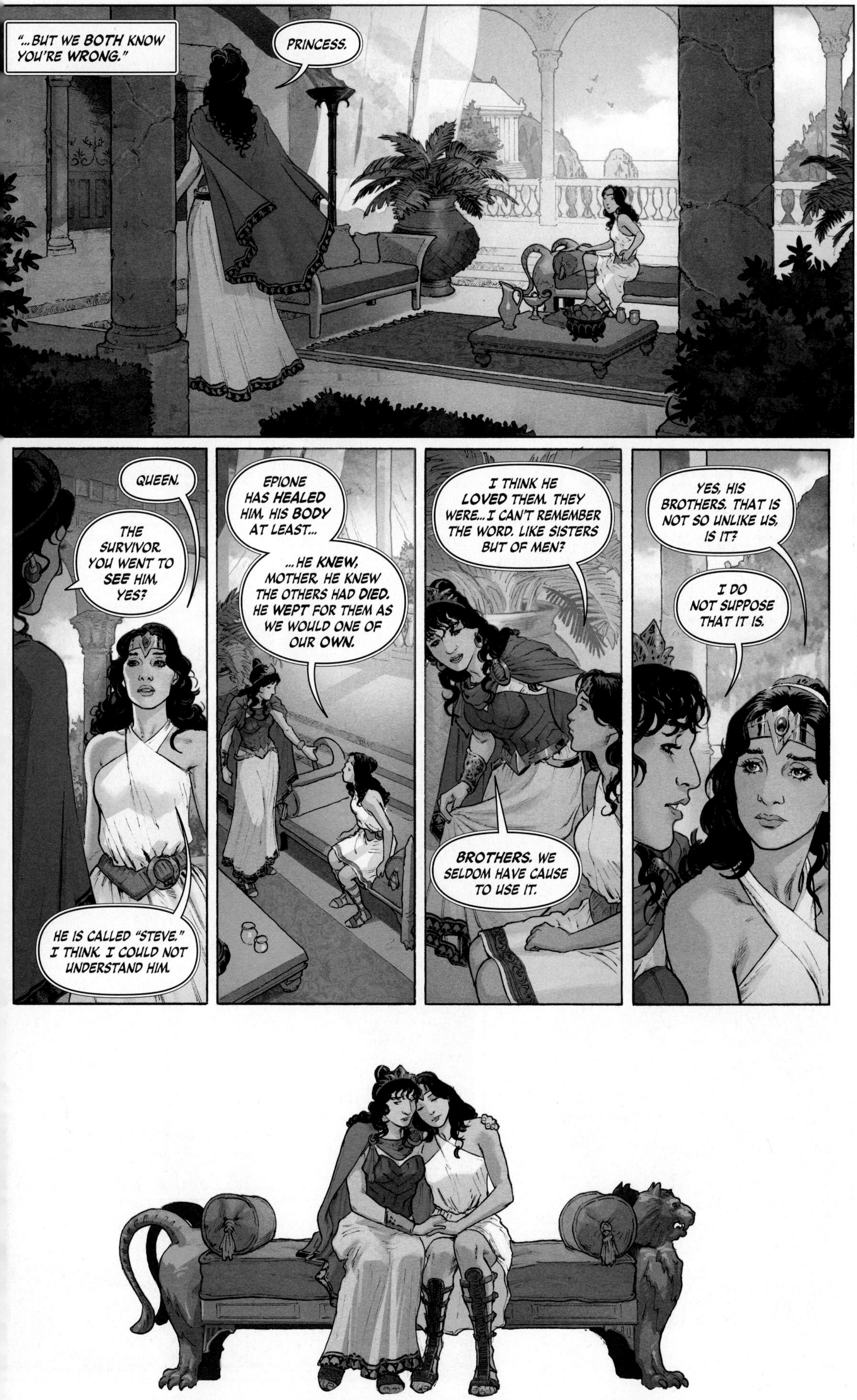
"...BUT WE BOTH KNOW YOU'RE WRONG."
PRINCESS.
QUEEN.
THE SURVIVOR. YOU WENT TO SEE HIM, YES?
HE IS CALLED "STEVE," I THINK. I COULD NOT UNDERSTAND HIM.
EPIONE HAS HEALED HIM. HIS BODY AT LEAST...
...HE KNEW, MOTHER. HE KNEW THE OTHERS HAD DIED. HE WEPT FOR THEM AS WE WOULD ONE OF OUR OWN.
I THINK HE LOVED THEM. THEY WERE... I CAN'T REMEMBER THE WORD. LIKE SISTERS BUT OF MEN?
BROTHERS. WE SELDOM HAVE CAUSE TO USE IT.
YES, HIS BROTHERS. THAT IS NOT SO UNLIKE US, IS IT?
I DO NOT SUPPOSE THAT IT IS.

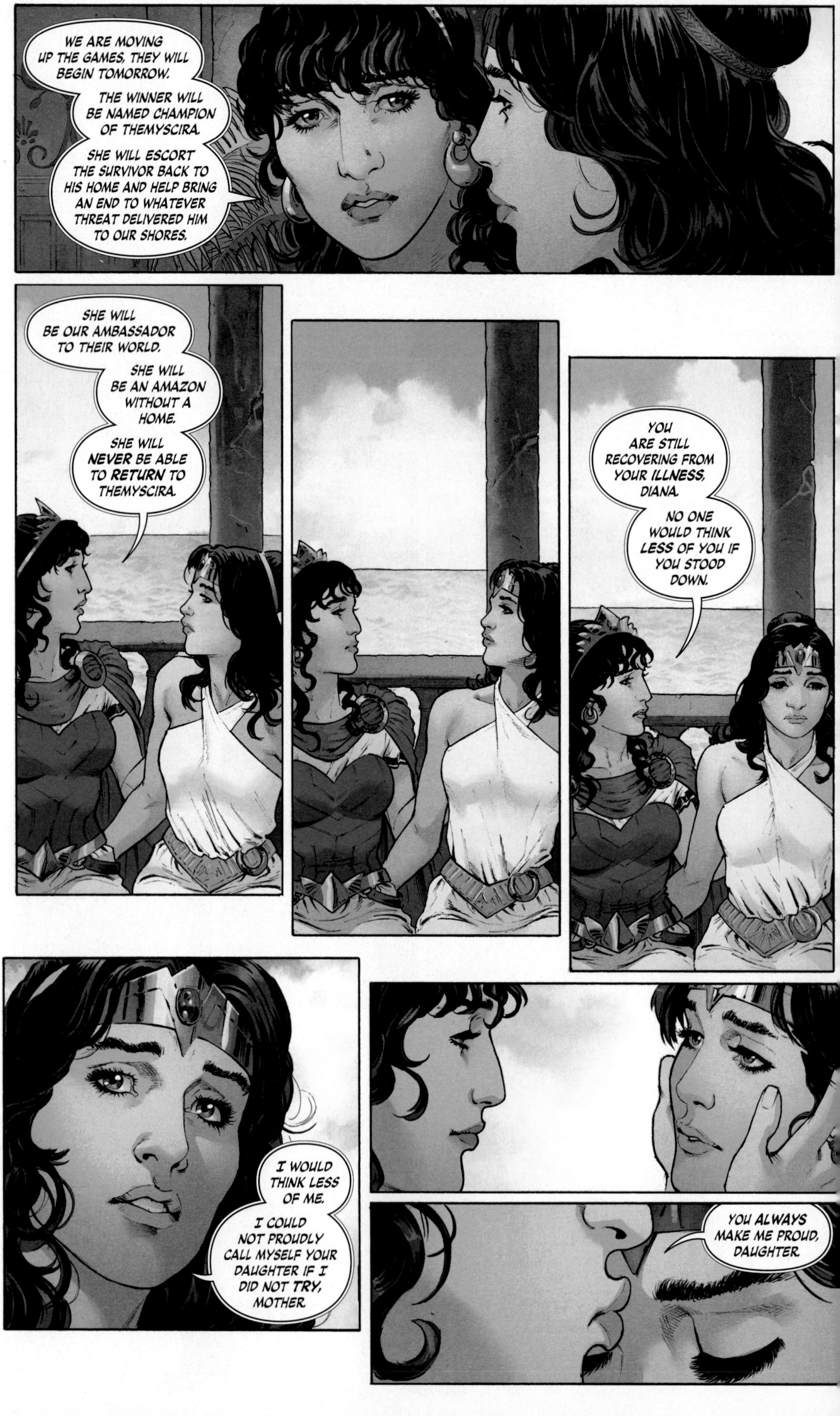
WE ARE MOVING UP THE GAMES, THEY WILL BEGIN TOMORROW.
THE WINNER WILL BE NAMED CHAMPION OF THEMYSCIRA.
SHE WILL ESCORT THE SURVIVOR BACK TO HIS HOME AND HELP BRING AN END TO WHATEVER THREAT DELIVERED HIM TO OUR SHORES.
SHE WILL BE OUR AMBASSADOR TO THEIR WORLD.
SHE WILL BE AN AMAZON WITHOUT A HOME.
SHE WILL NEVER BE ABLE TO RETURN TO THEMYSCIRA.
YOU ARE STILL RECOVERING FROM YOUR ILLNESS, DIANA.
NO ONE WOULD THINK LESS OF YOU IF YOU STOOD DOWN.
I WOULD THINK LESS OF ME.
I COULD NOT PROUDLY CALL MYSELF YOUR DAUGHTER IF I DID NOT TRY, MOTHER.
YOU ALWAYS MAKE ME PROUD, DAUGHTER.

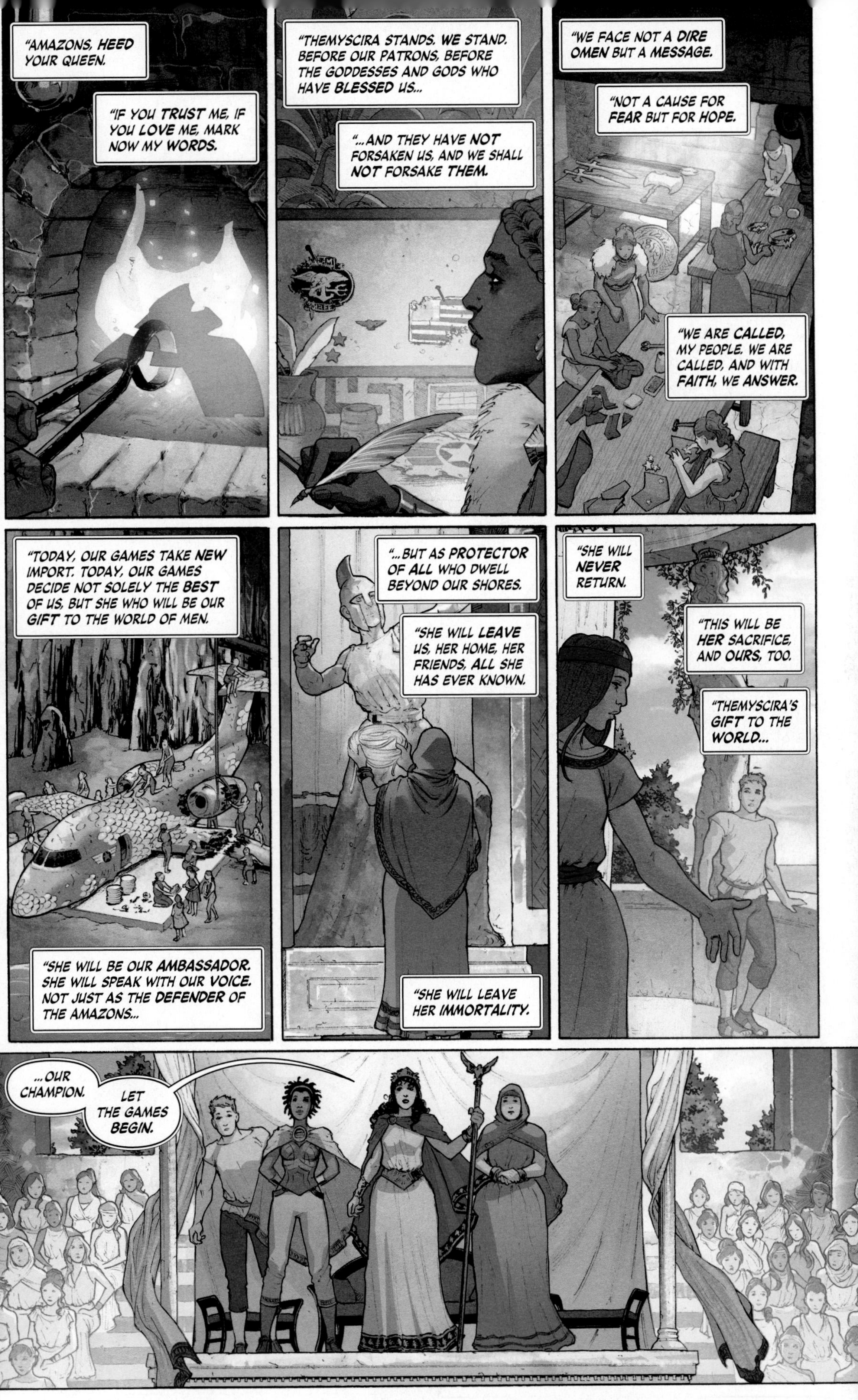
"AMAZONS, HEED YOUR QUEEN.
"IF YOU TRUST ME, IF YOU LOVE ME, MARK NOW MY WORDS.
"THEMYSCIRA STANDS. WE STAND. BEFORE OUR PATRONS, BEFORE THE GODDESSES AND GODS WHO HAVE BLESSED US...
"...AND THEY HAVE NOT FORSAKEN US, AND WE SHALL NOT FORSAKE THEM.
"WE FACE NOT A DIRE OMEN BUT A MESSAGE.
"NOT A CAUSE FOR FEAR BUT FOR HOPE.
"WE ARE CALLED, MY PEOPLE. WE ARE CALLED, AND WITH FAITH, WE ANSWER.
"TODAY, OUR GAMES TAKE NEW IMPORT. TODAY, OUR GAMES DECIDE NOT SOLELY THE BEST OF US, BUT SHE WHO WILL BE OUR GIFT TO THE WORLD OF MEN.
"SHE WILL BE OUR AMBASSADOR. SHE WILL SPEAK WITH OUR VOICE. NOT JUST AS THE DEFENDER OF THE AMAZONS...
"...BUT AS PROTECTOR OF ALL WHO DWELL BEYOND OUR SHORES.
"SHE WILL LEAVE US, HER HOME, HER FRIENDS, ALL SHE HAS EVER KNOWN.
"SHE WILL LEAVE HER IMMORTALITY.
"SHE WILL NEVER RETURN.
"THIS WILL BE HER SACRIFICE, AND OURS, TOO.
"THEMYSCIRA'S GIFT TO THE WORLD...
...OUR CHAMPION.
LET THE GAMES BEGIN.

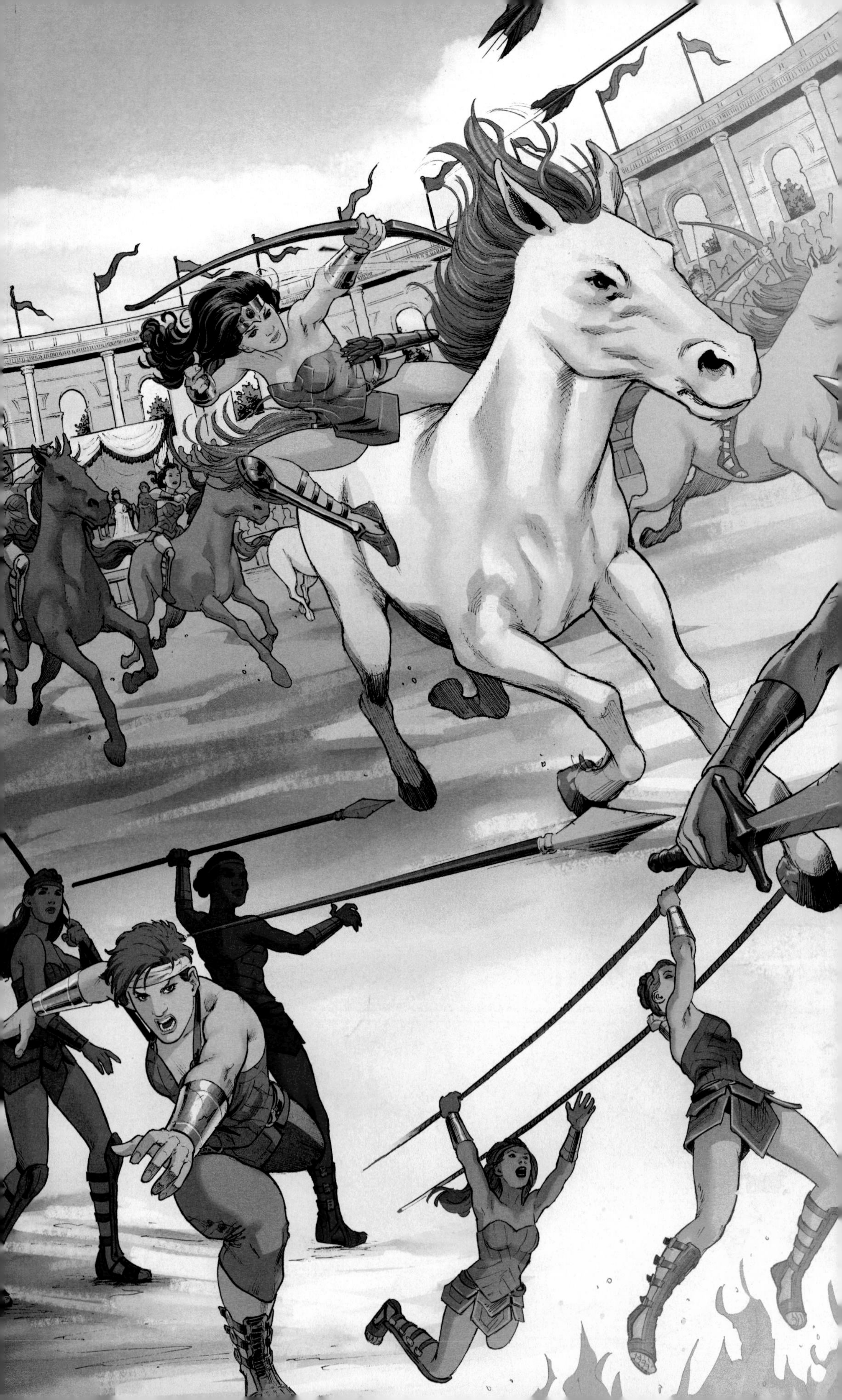

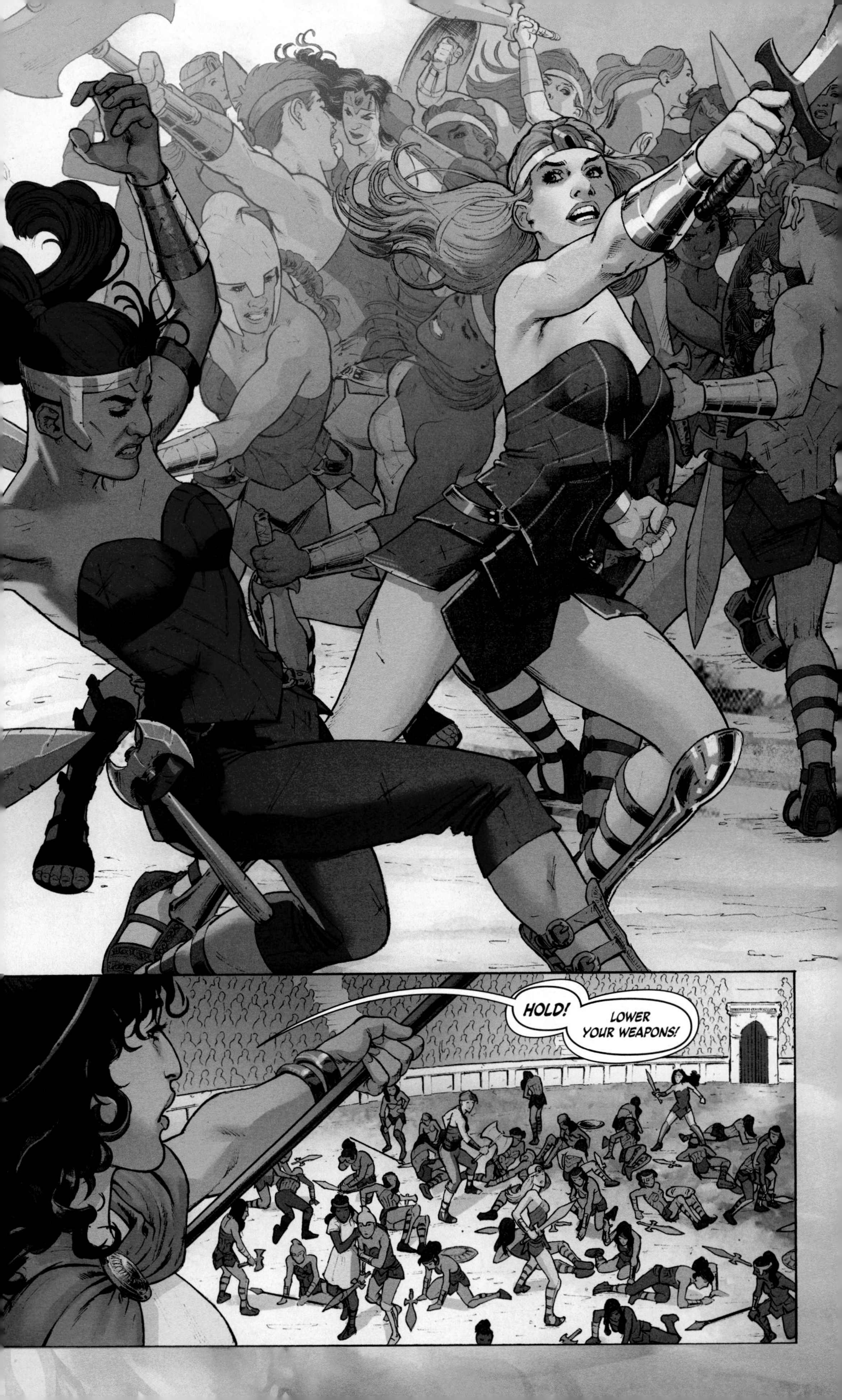
HOLD!
LOWER YOUR WEAPONS!

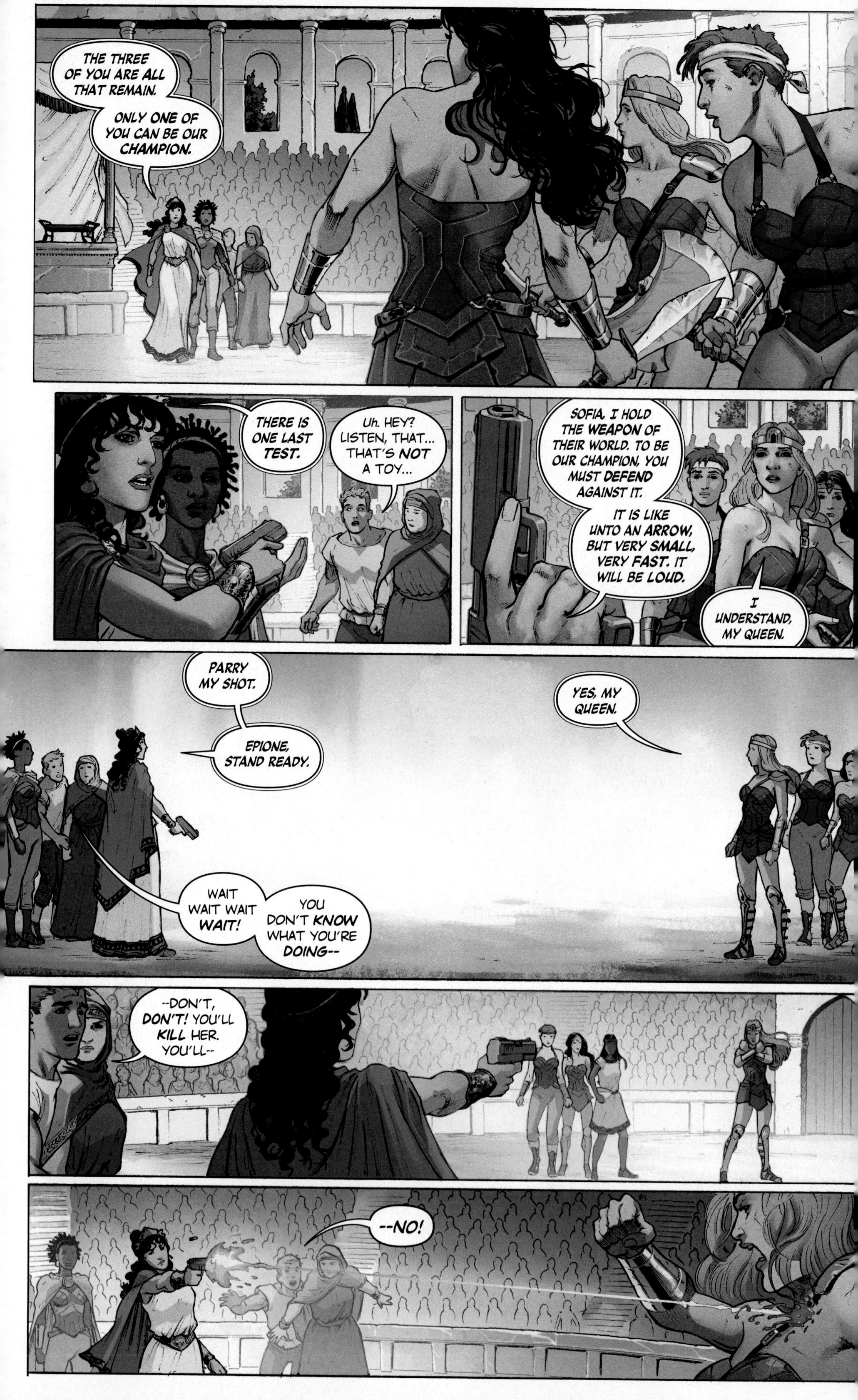
THE THREE OF YOU ARE ALL THAT REMAIN.
ONLY ONE OF YOU CAN BE OUR CHAMPION.
THERE IS ONE LAST TEST.
Uh. HEY? LISTEN, THAT... THAT'S NOT A TOY...
SOFIA, I HOLD THE WEAPON OF THEIR WORLD. TO BE OUR CHAMPION, YOU MUST DEFEND AGAINST IT.
IT IS LIKE UNTO AN ARROW, BUT VERY SMALL, VERY FAST. IT WILL BE LOUD.
I UNDERSTAND, MY QUEEN.
PARRY MY SHOT.
EPIONE, STAND READY.
YES, MY QUEEN.
WAIT WAIT WAIT WAIT!
YOU DON'T KNOW WHAT YOU'RE DOING--
--DON'T, DON'T! YOU'LL KILL HER. YOU'LL--
--NO!

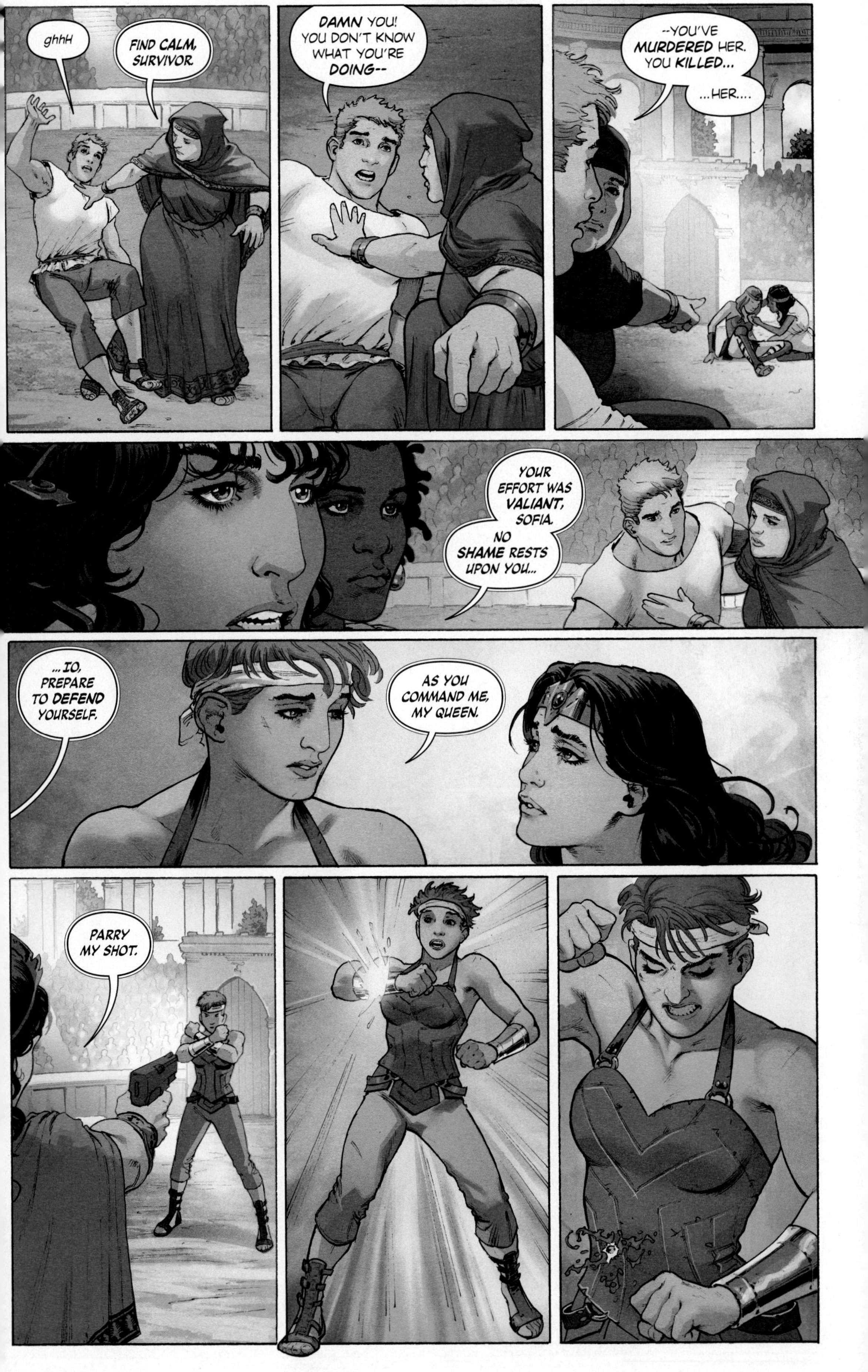

ghhH
FIND CALM, SURVIVOR.
DAMN YOU! YOU DON'T KNOW WHAT YOU'RE DOING--
--YOU'VE MURDERED HER. YOU KILLED...
...HER....
YOUR EFFORT WAS VALIANT, SOFIA.
NO SHAME RESTS UPON YOU...
...IO, PREPARE TO DEFEND YOURSELF.
AS YOU COMMAND ME, MY QUEEN.
PARRY MY SHOT.

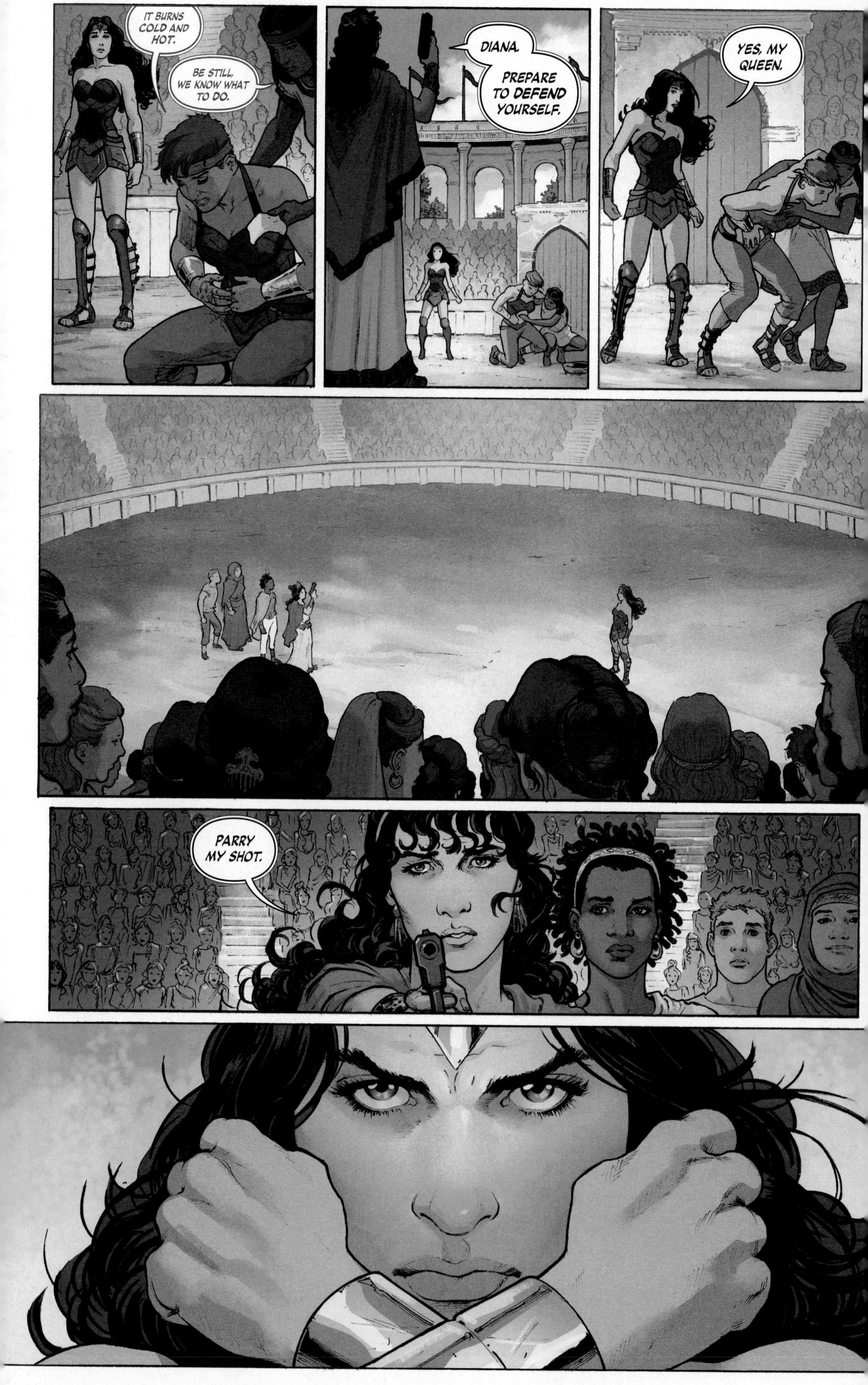
IT BURNS COLD AND HOT.
BE STILL, WE KNOW WHAT TO DO.
DIANA.
PREPARE TO DEFEND YOURSELF.
YES, MY QUEEN.
PARRY MY SHOT.

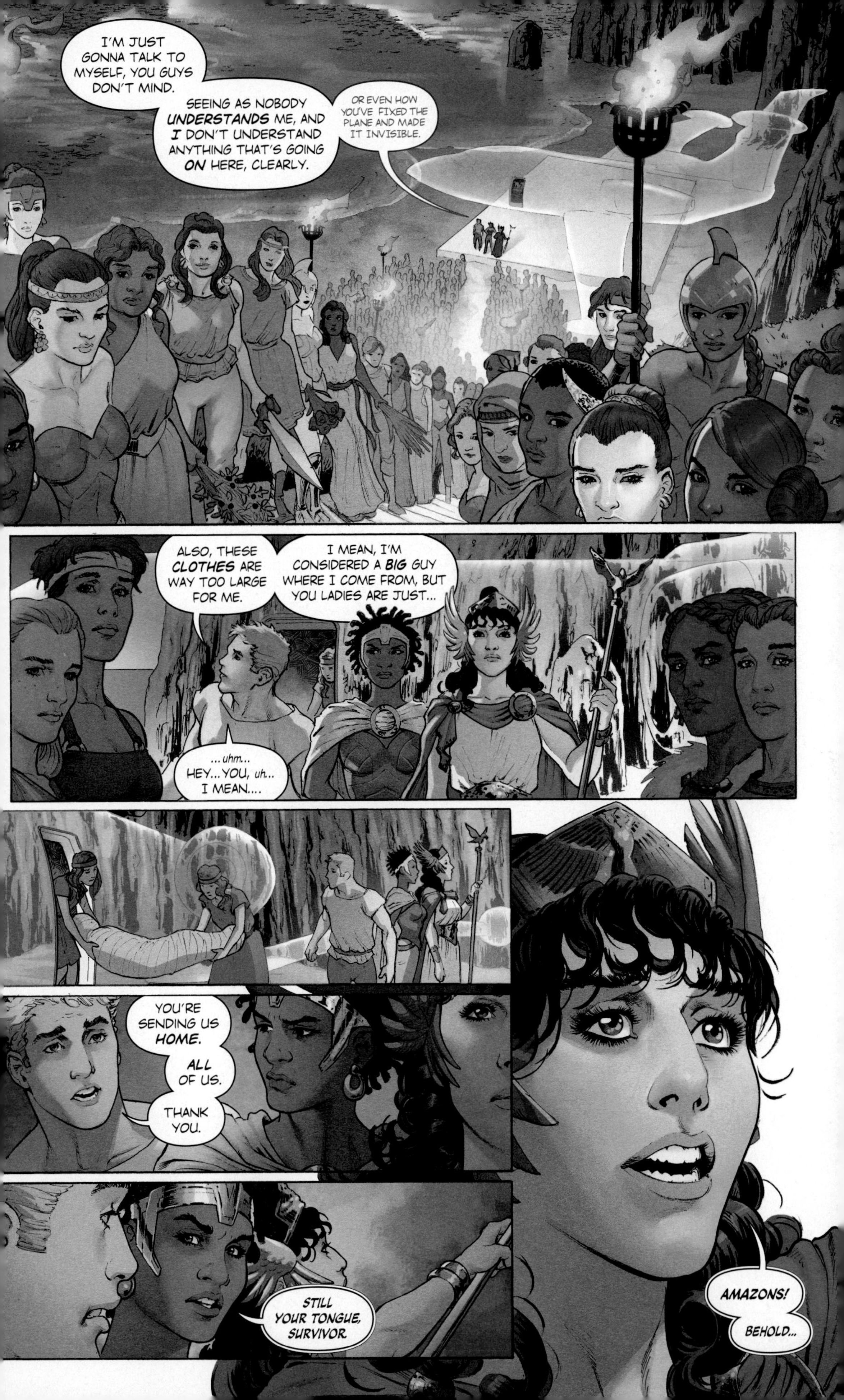
I'M JUST GONNA TALK TO MYSELF, YOU GUYS DON'T MIND.
SEEING AS NOBODY **UNDERSTANDS** ME, AND **I** DON'T UNDERSTAND ANYTHING THAT'S GOING **ON** HERE, CLEARLY.
OR EVEN HOW YOU'VE FIXED THE PLANE AND MADE IT INVISIBLE.
ALSO, THESE **CLOTHES** ARE WAY TOO LARGE FOR ME.
I MEAN, I'M CONSIDERED A **BIG** GUY WHERE I COME FROM, BUT YOU LADIES ARE JUST...
...*uhm*... HEY...YOU, *uh*... I MEAN....
YOU'RE SENDING US **HOME.**
ALL OF US.
THANK YOU.
STILL YOUR TONGUE, SURVIVOR.
AMAZONS!
BEHOLD...

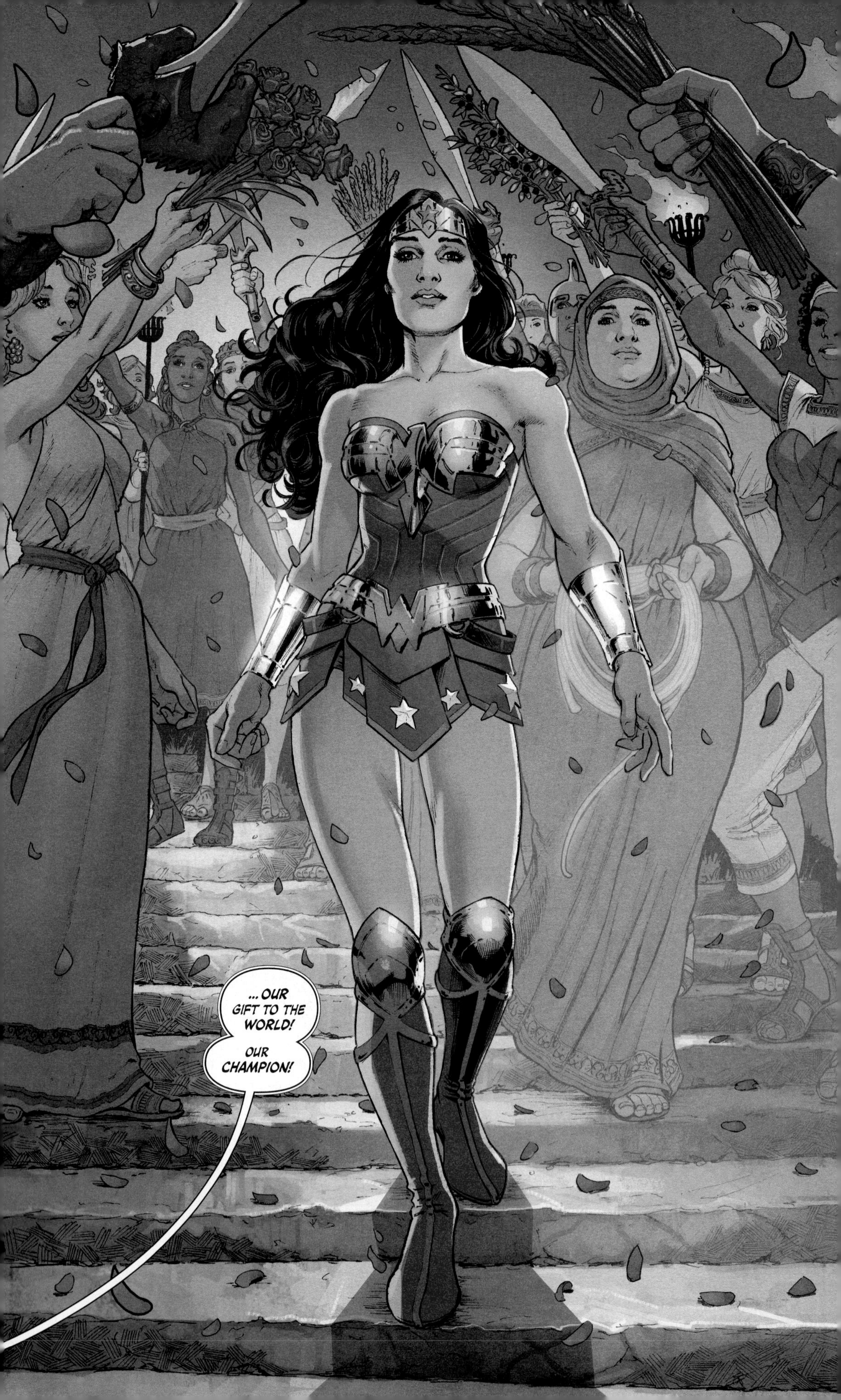
...OUR GIFT TO THE WORLD!
OUR CHAMPION!

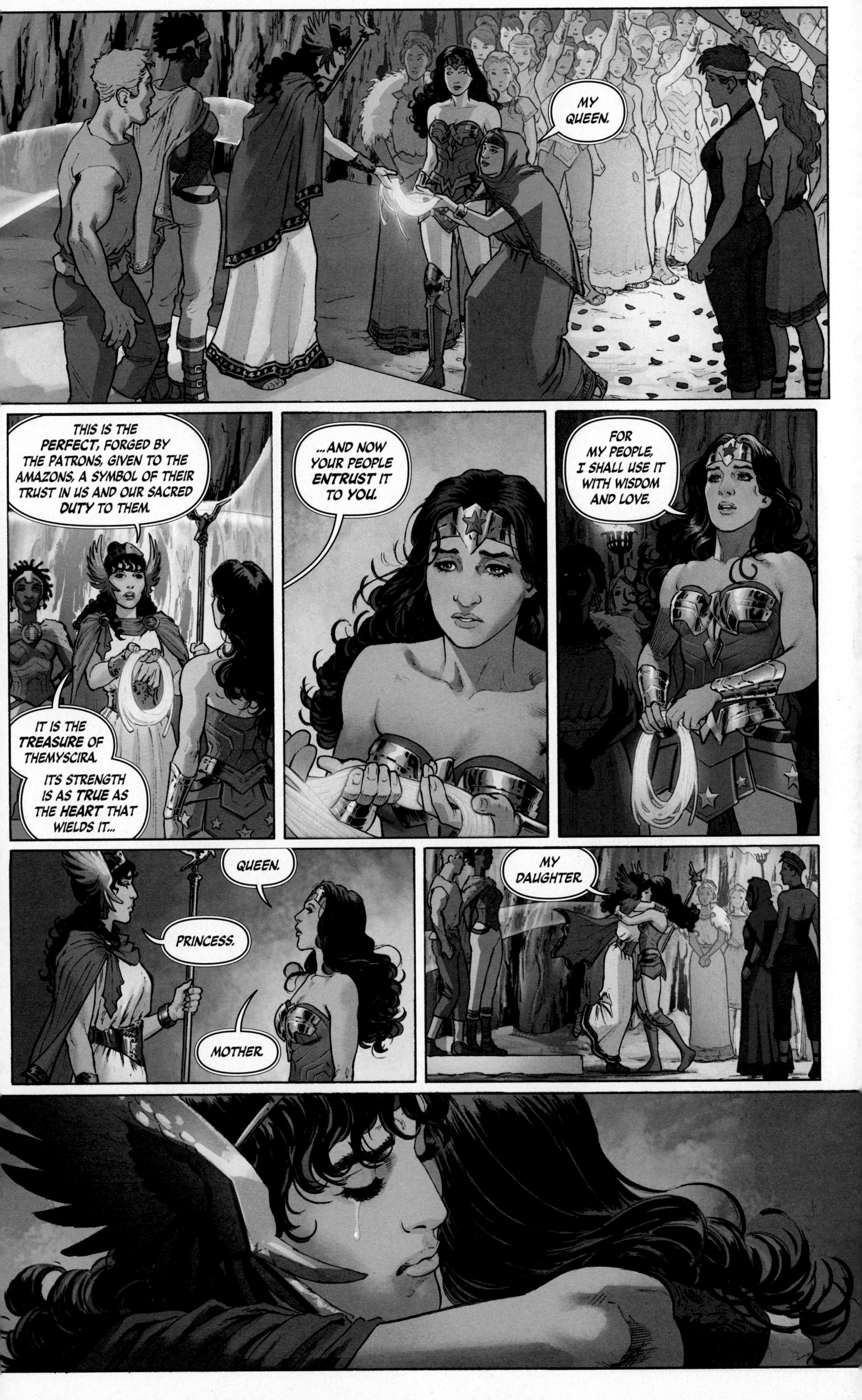

MY QUEEN.
THIS IS THE PERFECT, FORGED BY THE PATRONS, GIVEN TO THE AMAZONS, A SYMBOL OF THEIR TRUST IN US AND OUR SACRED DUTY TO THEM.
IT IS THE TREASURE OF THEMYSCIRA.
ITS STRENGTH IS AS TRUE AS THE HEART THAT WIELDS IT...
...AND NOW YOUR PEOPLE ENTRUST IT TO YOU.
FOR MY PEOPLE, I SHALL USE IT WITH WISDOM AND LOVE.
QUEEN.
PRINCESS.
MOTHER.
MY DAUGHTER.

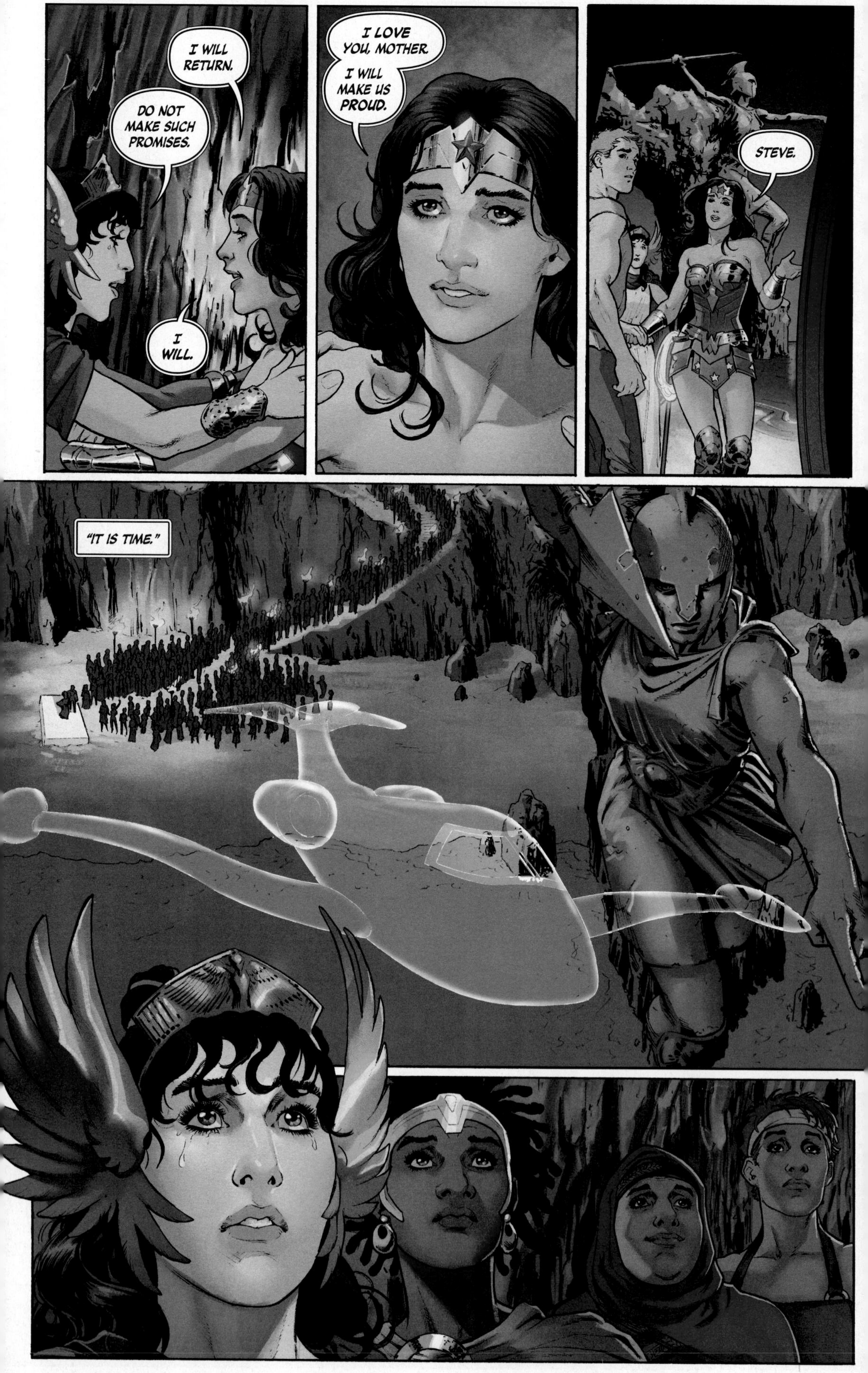
I WILL RETURN.
DO NOT MAKE SUCH PROMISES.
I WILL.
I LOVE YOU, MOTHER.
I WILL MAKE US PROUD.
STEVE.
"IT IS TIME."

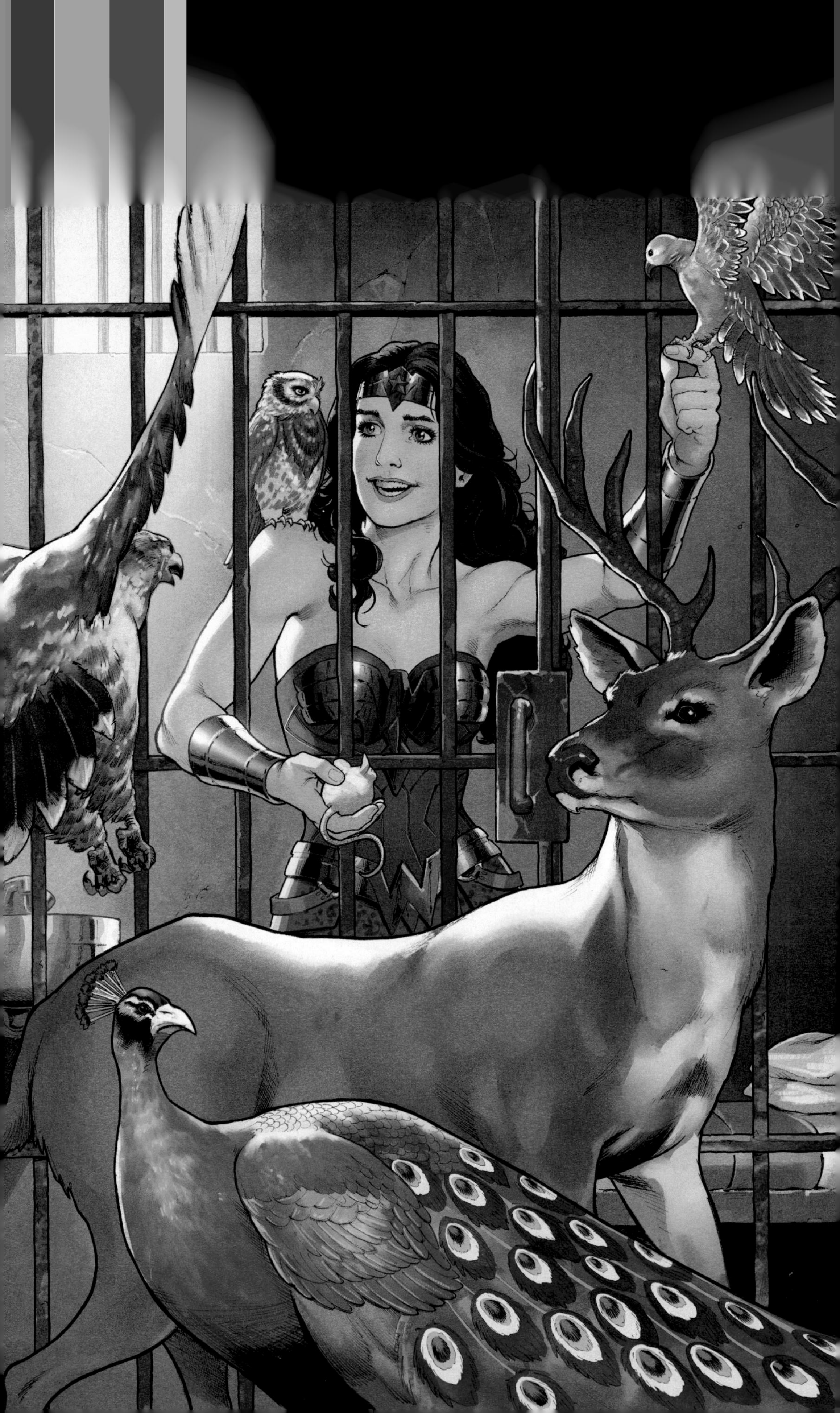

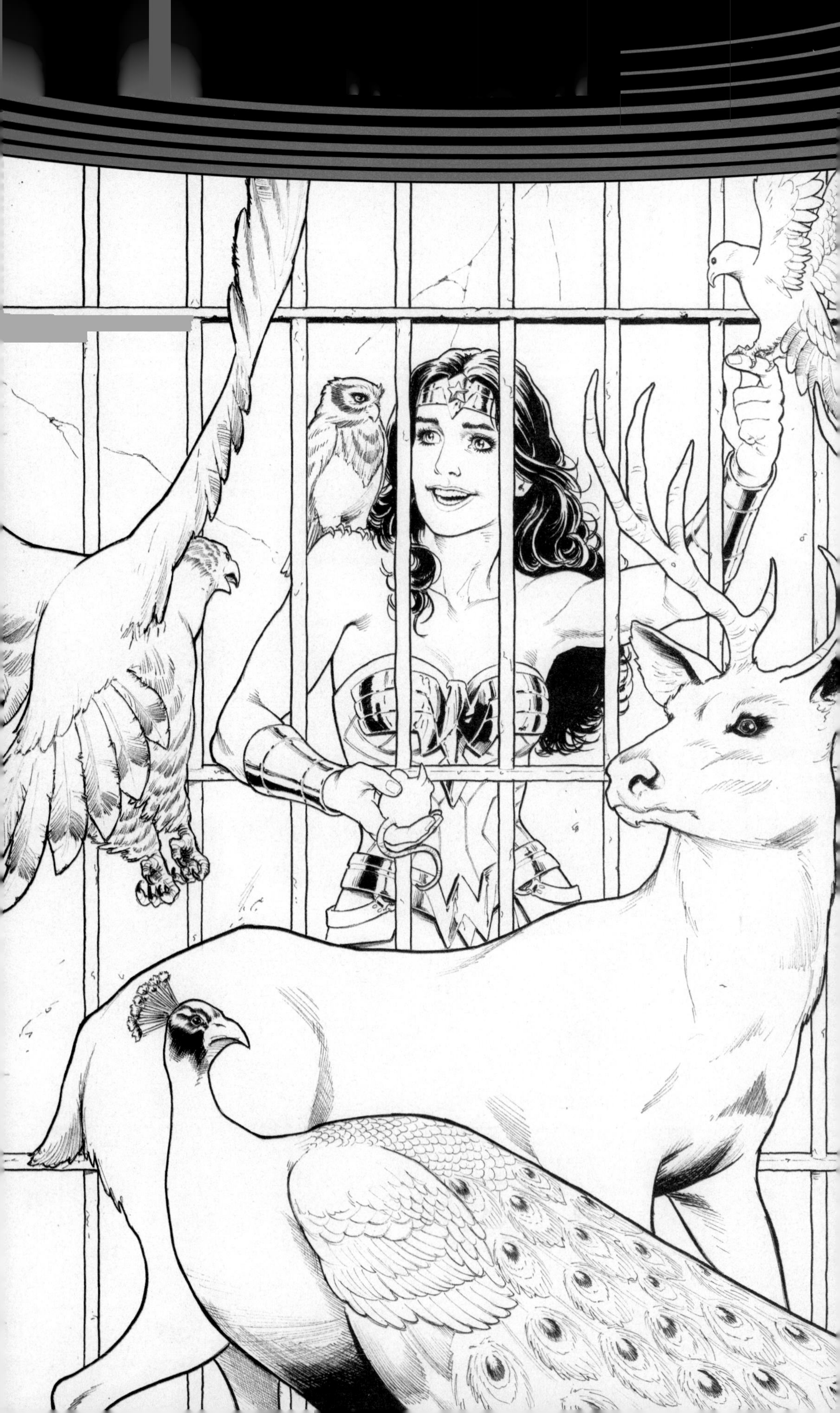

Uh. SO...

...YOU, uh... I MEAN, THIS *JET*, I...

...YOU'RE NOT REALLY *FLYING* IT, IT JUST...KINDA *KNOWS* WHERE IT'S SUPPOSED TO *GO* NOW, RIGHT?

YEAR ONE
Part Three

GREG RUCKA Writer
NICOLA SCOTT Artist
ROMULO FAJARDO JR. Colors
JODI WYNNE Letters

SCOTT & FAJARDO JR. Cover

REBECCA TAYLOR Assoc. Editor
MARK DOYLE Editor

WONDER WOMAN created by **WILLIAM MOULTON MARSTON**

I DO *NOT* UNDERSTAND A WORD YOU'RE *SAYING*.

YOU DON'T *UNDERSTAND* A WORD I'M *SAYING*.

STEVE.

DIANA.

I DO NOT UNDERSTAND A WORD YOU'RE SAYING.

YOU DON'T UNDERSTAND A *WORD* I'M SAYING, DO YOU?

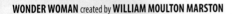

Whoa.

PLEASE TELL ME WE'RE *DESCENDING*...

...AND *NOT* CRASHING.

...HE SAID TO HIMSELF, HOPEFULLY....

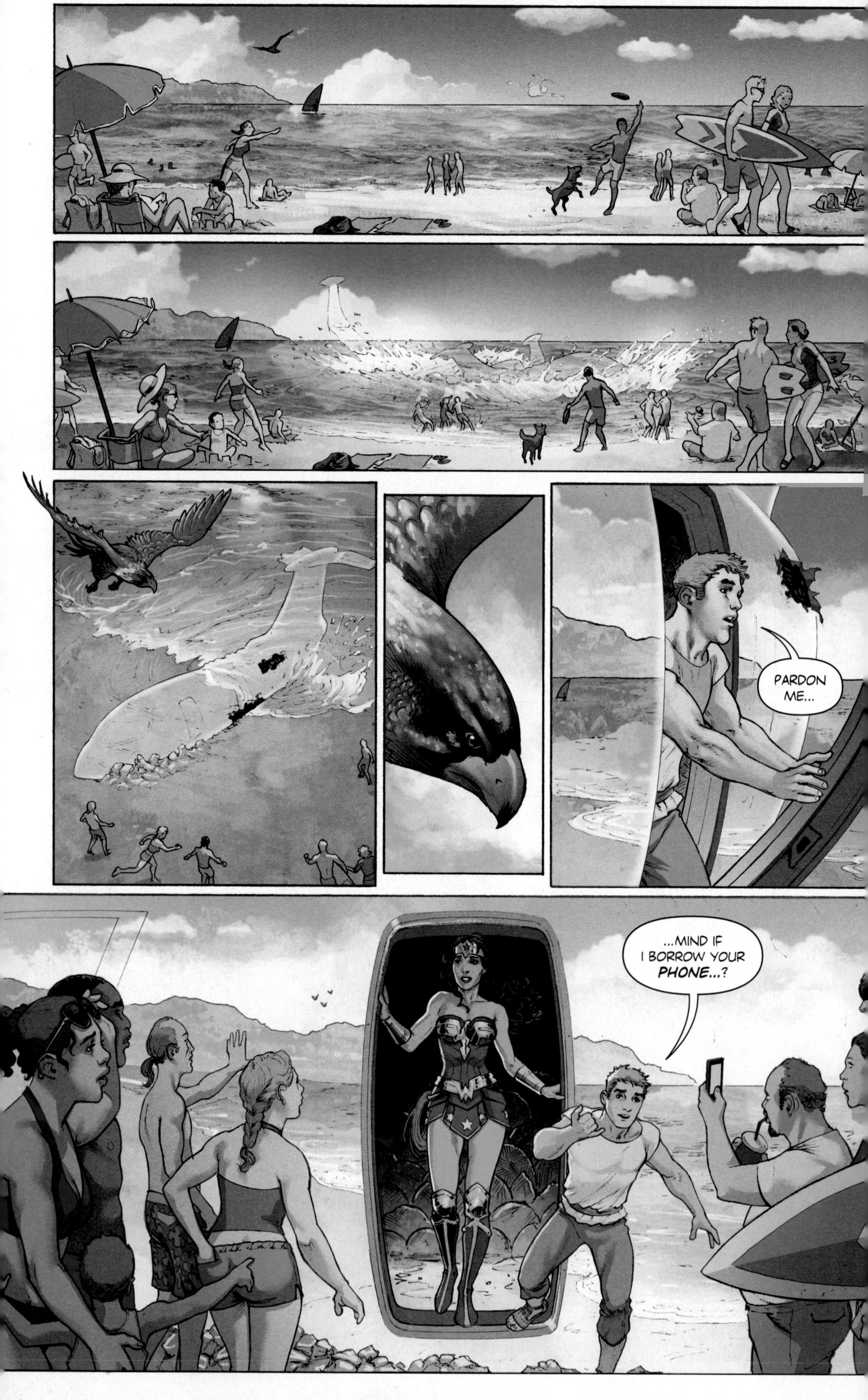
PARDON ME...
...MIND IF I BORROW YOUR PHONE...?

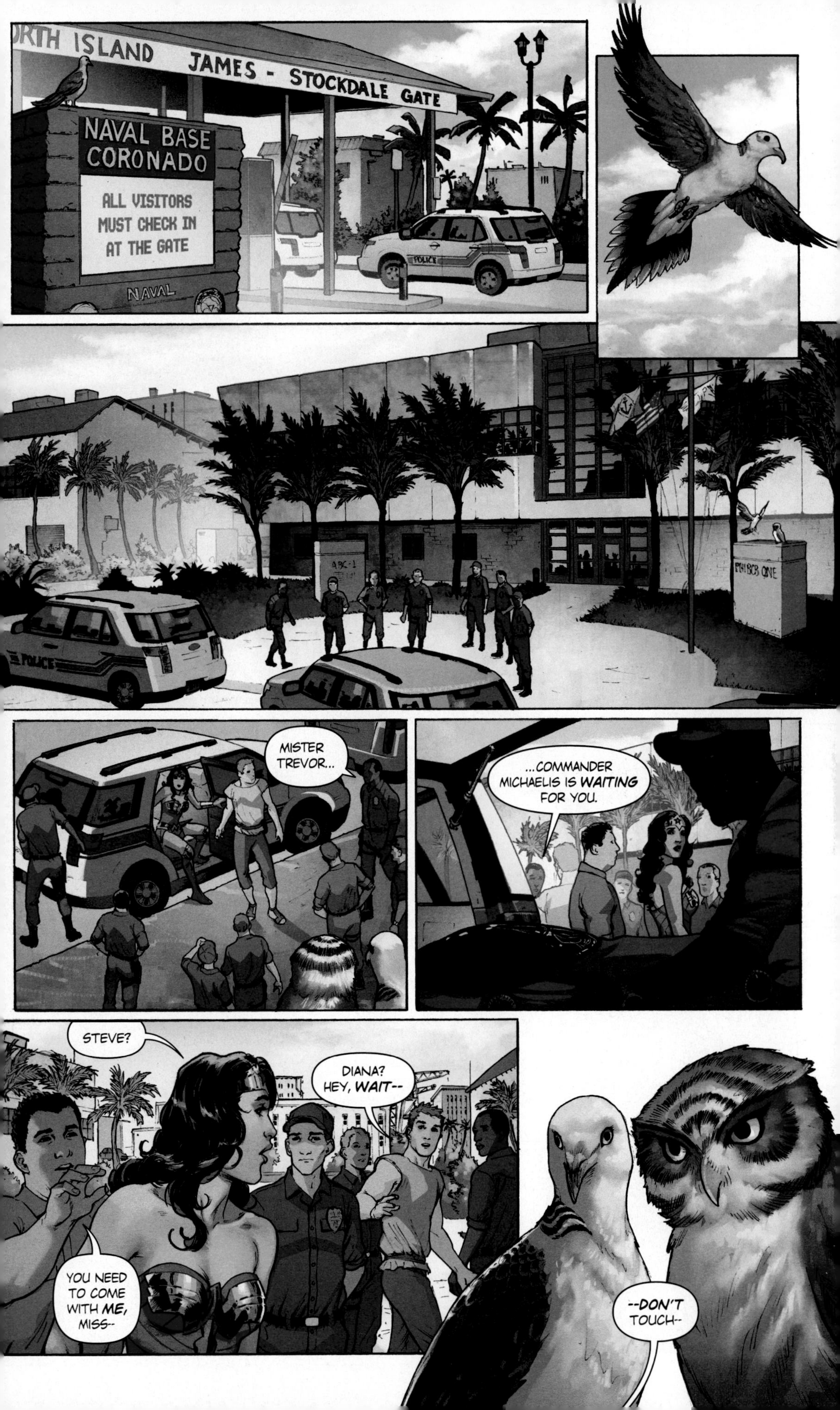
RTH ISLAND JAMES - STOCKDALE GATE
NAVAL BASE CORONADO
ALL VISITORS MUST CHECK IN AT THE GATE
NAVAL
POLICE
POLICE
MISTER TREVOR...
...COMMANDER MICHAELIS IS WAITING FOR YOU.
STEVE?
DIANA? HEY, WAIT--
YOU NEED TO COME WITH ME, MISS--
--DON'T TOUCH--

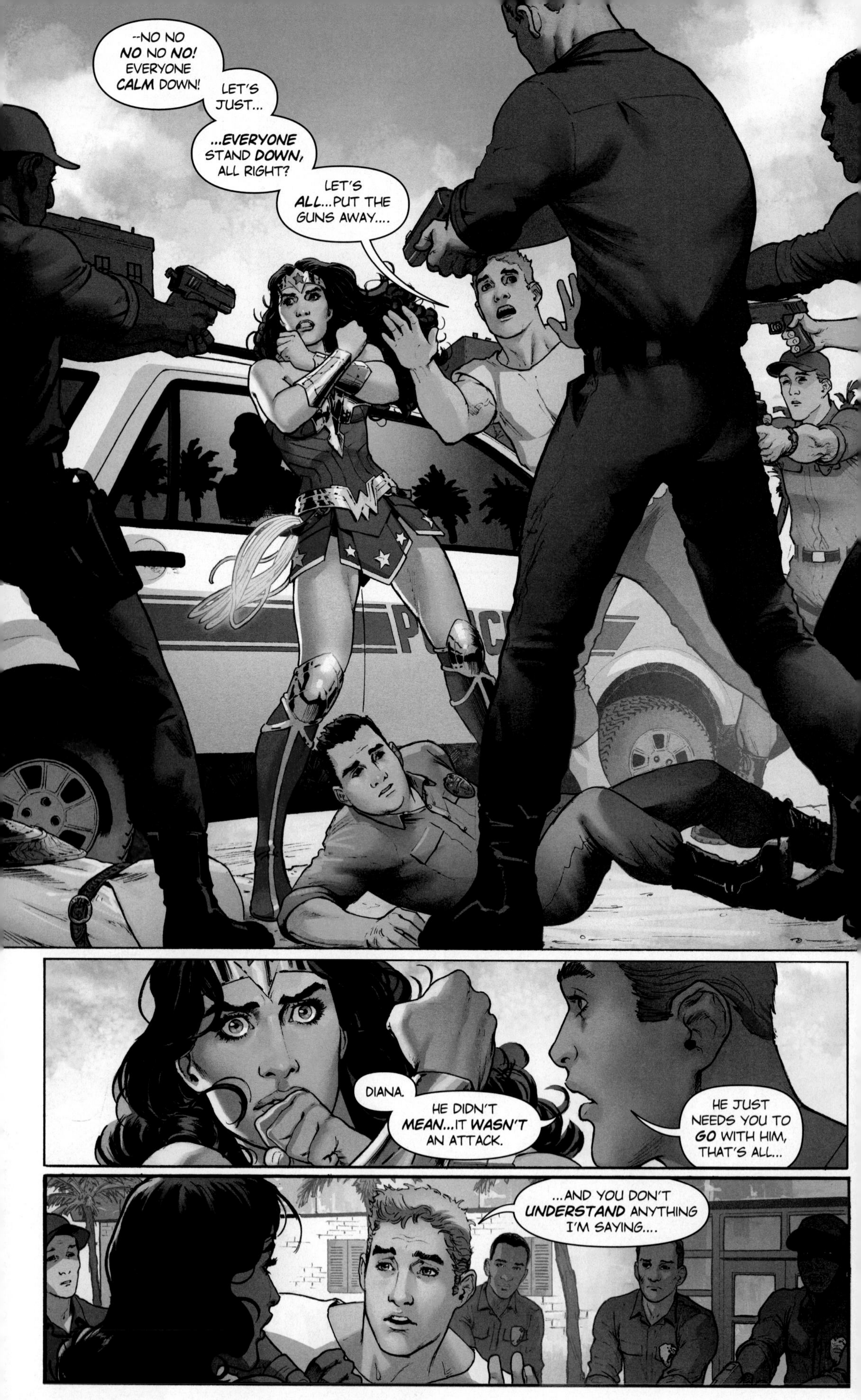
--NO NO **NO** NO **NO!** EVERYONE **CALM** DOWN!
LET'S JUST...
...**EVERYONE** STAND **DOWN,** ALL RIGHT?
LET'S **ALL**...PUT THE GUNS AWAY....
DIANA.
HE DIDN'T **MEAN**...IT **WASN'T** AN ATTACK.
HE JUST NEEDS YOU TO **GO** WITH HIM, THAT'S ALL...
...AND YOU DON'T **UNDERSTAND** ANYTHING I'M SAYING....

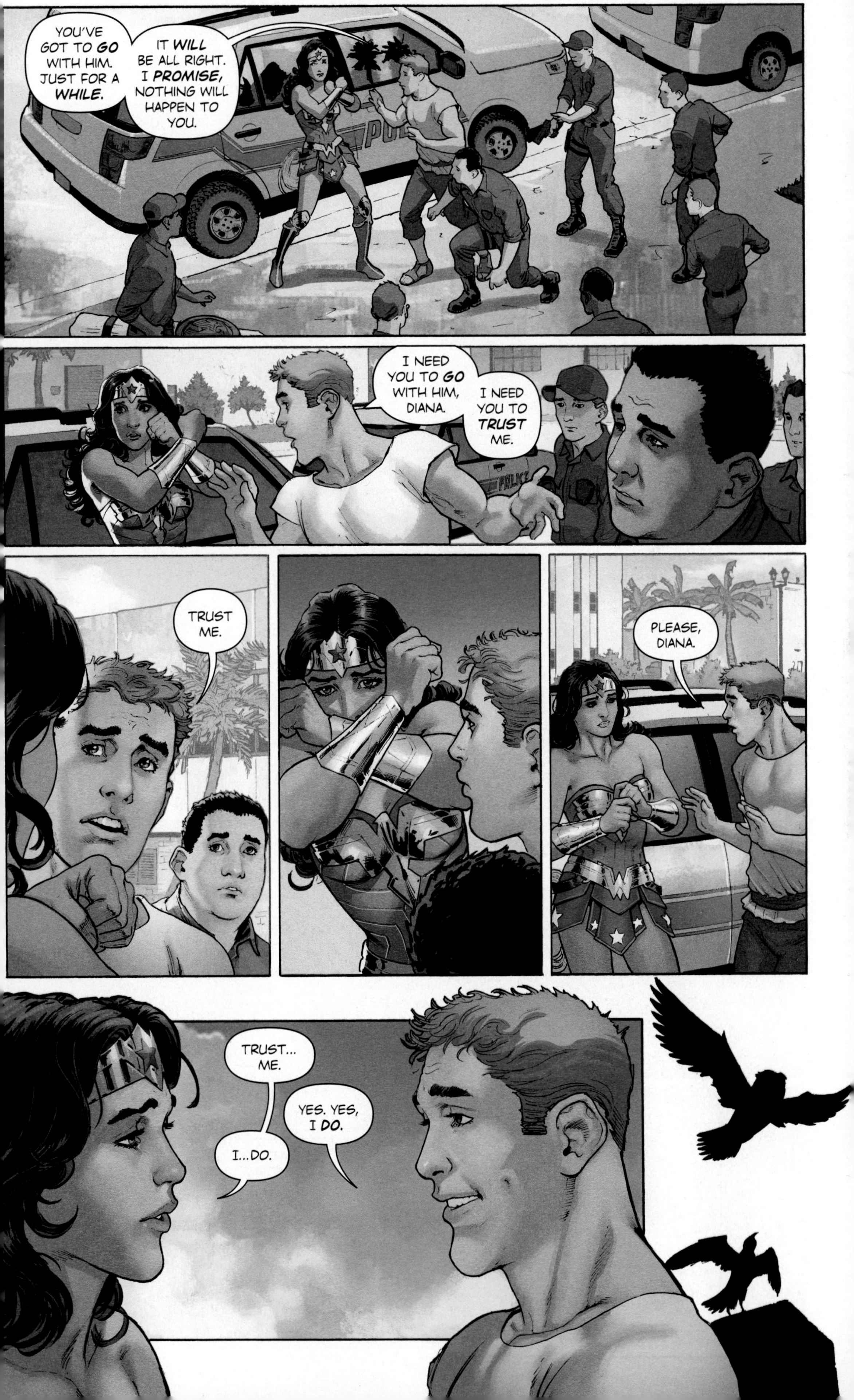
YOU'VE GOT TO **GO** WITH HIM. JUST FOR A **WHILE.**
IT **WILL** BE ALL RIGHT. I **PROMISE,** NOTHING WILL HAPPEN TO YOU.
POLICE
I NEED YOU TO **GO** WITH HIM, DIANA.
I NEED YOU TO **TRUST** ME.
POLICE
TRUST ME.
PLEASE, DIANA.
TRUST... ME.
I...DO.
YES. YES, I **DO.**

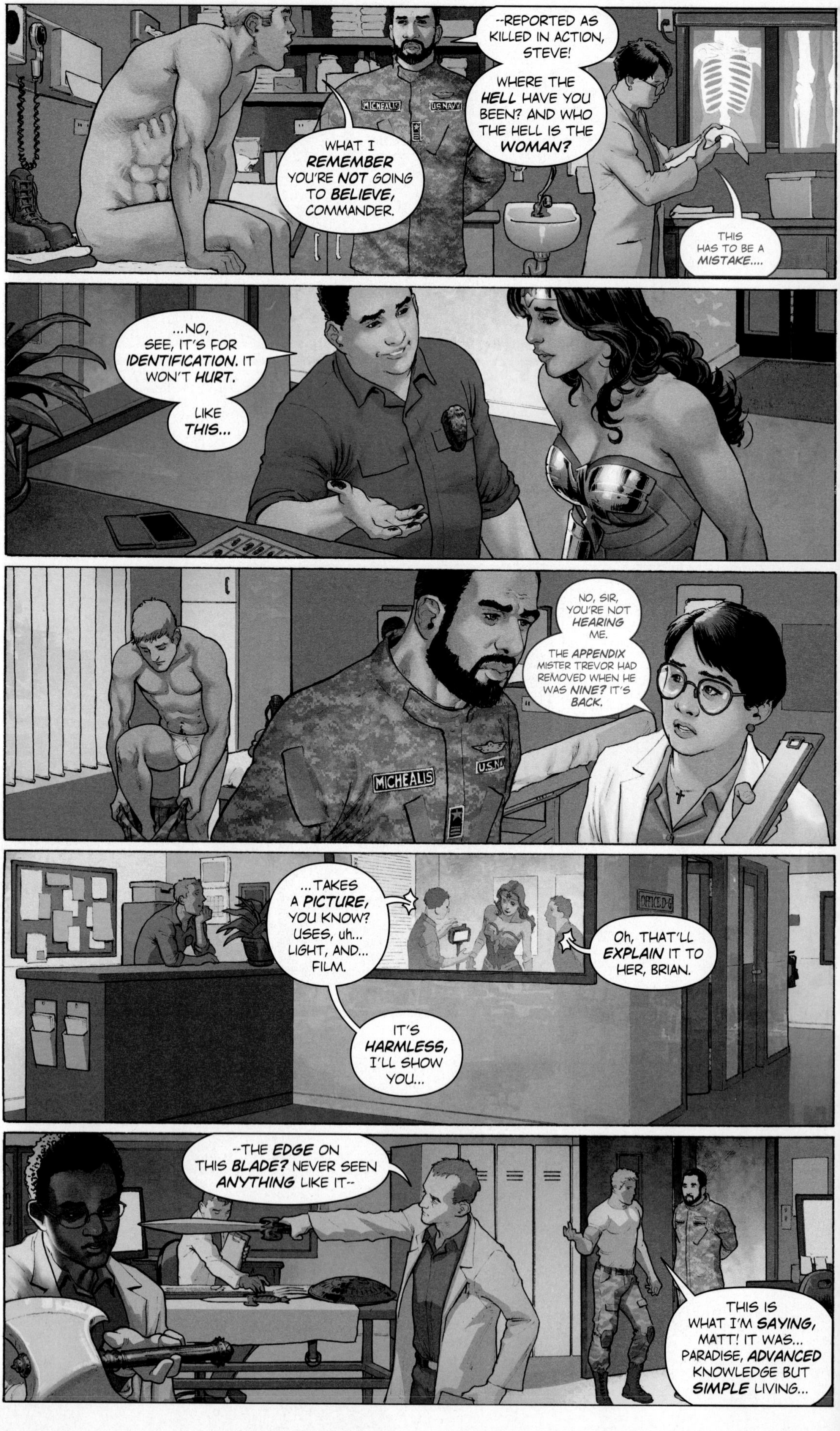
--REPORTED AS KILLED IN ACTION, STEVE!
WHERE THE HELL HAVE YOU BEEN? AND WHO THE HELL IS THE WOMAN?
WHAT I REMEMBER YOU'RE NOT GOING TO BELIEVE, COMMANDER.
MICHEALIS
U.S. NAVY
THIS HAS TO BE A MISTAKE....
...NO, SEE, IT'S FOR IDENTIFICATION. IT WON'T HURT.
LIKE THIS...
NO, SIR, YOU'RE NOT HEARING ME.
THE APPENDIX MISTER TREVOR HAD REMOVED WHEN HE WAS NINE? IT'S BACK.
MICHEALIS
U.S. NAVY
...TAKES A PICTURE, YOU KNOW? USES, uh... LIGHT, AND... FILM.
IT'S HARMLESS, I'LL SHOW YOU...
Oh, THAT'LL EXPLAIN IT TO HER, BRIAN.
--THE EDGE ON THIS BLADE? NEVER SEEN ANYTHING LIKE IT--
THIS IS WHAT I'M SAYING, MATT! IT WAS... PARADISE, ADVANCED KNOWLEDGE BUT SIMPLE LIVING...

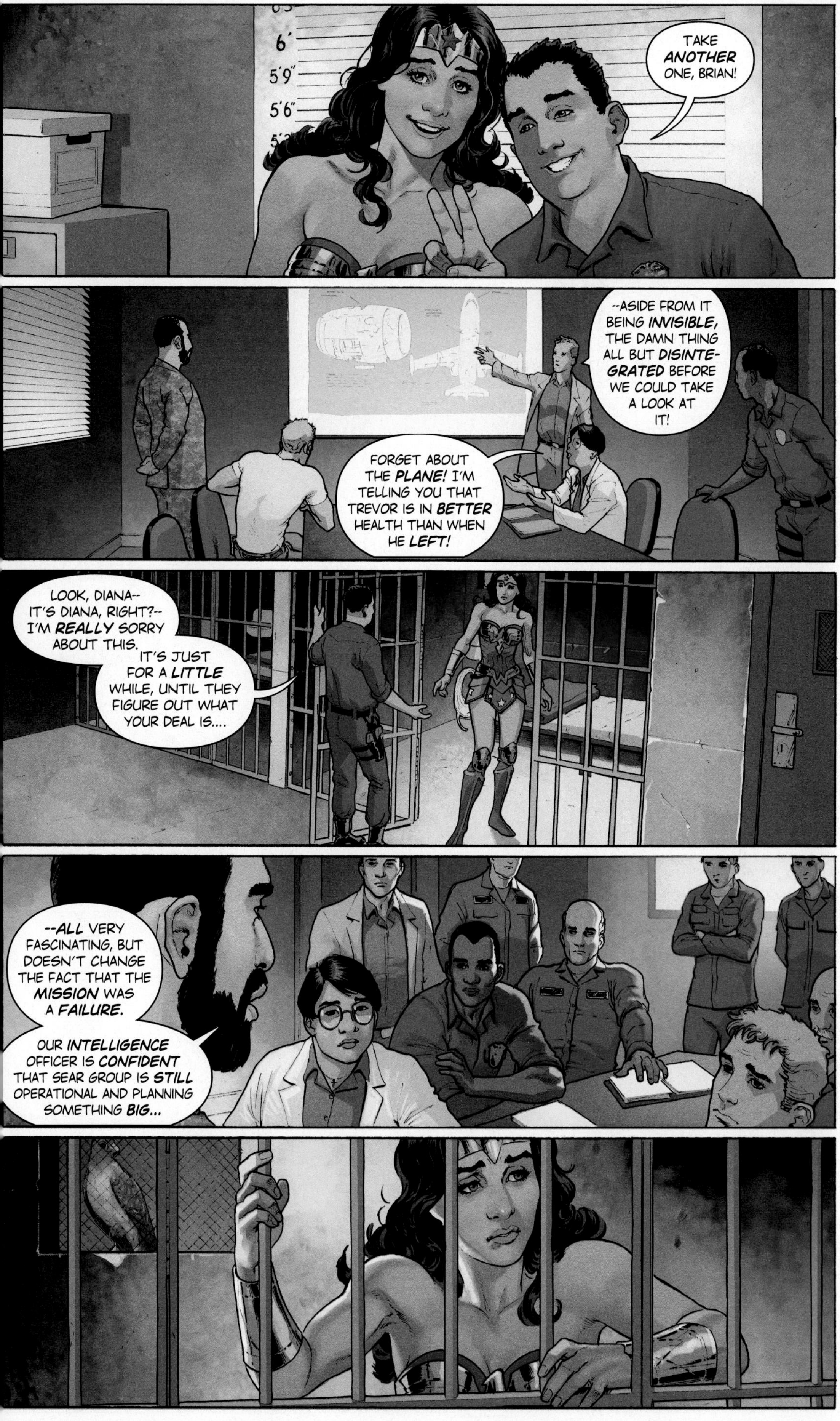

6'
5'9"
5'6"
TAKE ANOTHER ONE, BRIAN!
--ASIDE FROM IT BEING INVISIBLE, THE DAMN THING ALL BUT DISINTEGRATED BEFORE WE COULD TAKE A LOOK AT IT!
FORGET ABOUT THE PLANE! I'M TELLING YOU THAT TREVOR IS IN BETTER HEALTH THAN WHEN HE LEFT!
LOOK, DIANA-- IT'S DIANA, RIGHT?-- I'M REALLY SORRY ABOUT THIS.
IT'S JUST FOR A LITTLE WHILE, UNTIL THEY FIGURE OUT WHAT YOUR DEAL IS....
--ALL VERY FASCINATING, BUT DOESN'T CHANGE THE FACT THAT THE MISSION WAS A FAILURE.
OUR INTELLIGENCE OFFICER IS CONFIDENT THAT SEAR GROUP IS STILL OPERATIONAL AND PLANNING SOMETHING BIG...

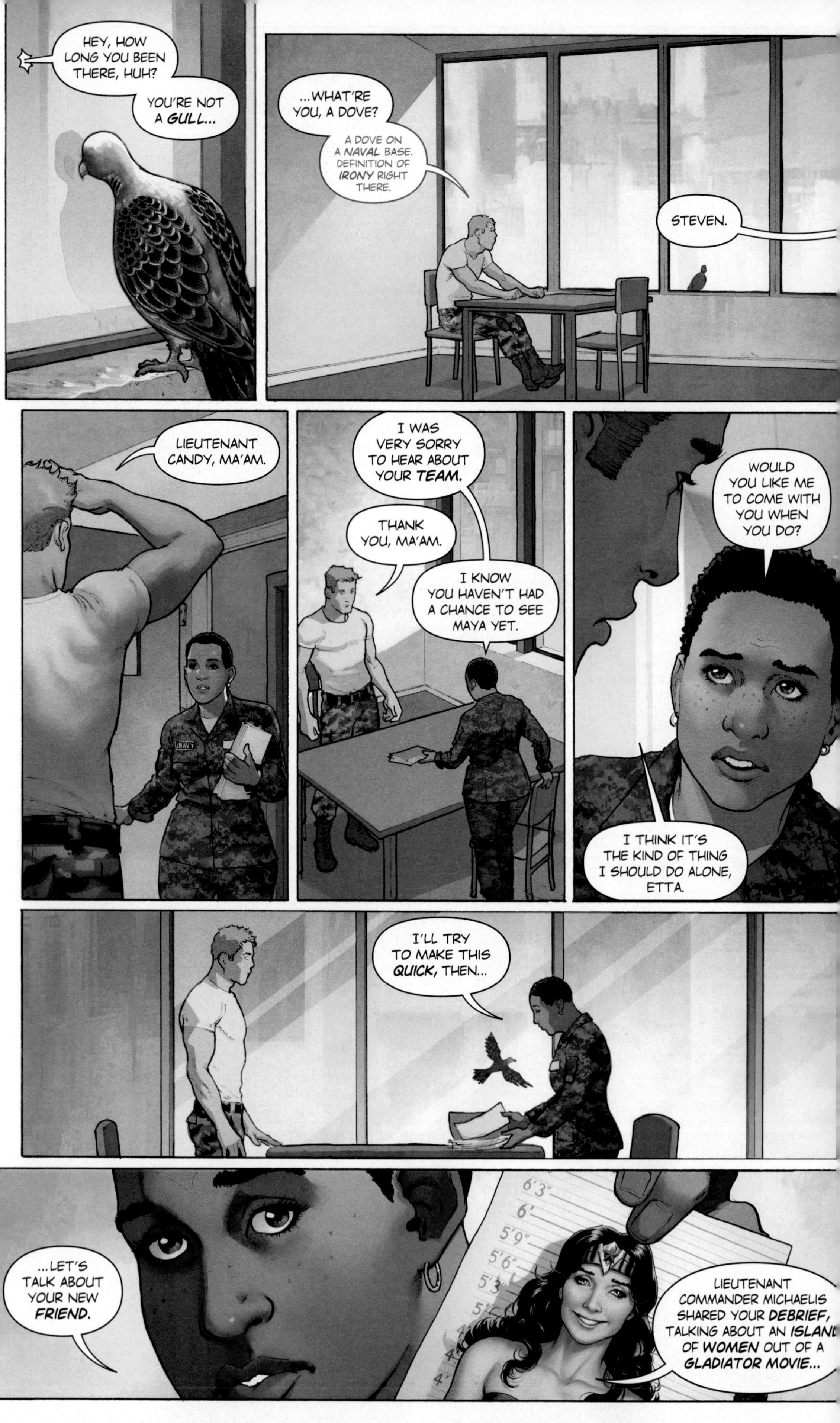
HEY, HOW LONG YOU BEEN THERE, HUH?
YOU'RE NOT A GULL...
...WHAT'RE YOU, A DOVE?
A DOVE ON A NAVAL BASE. DEFINITION OF IRONY RIGHT THERE.
STEVEN.
LIEUTENANT CANDY, MA'AM.
I WAS VERY SORRY TO HEAR ABOUT YOUR TEAM.
THANK YOU, MA'AM.
I KNOW YOU HAVEN'T HAD A CHANCE TO SEE MAYA YET.
WOULD YOU LIKE ME TO COME WITH YOU WHEN YOU DO?
I THINK IT'S THE KIND OF THING I SHOULD DO ALONE, ETTA.
I'LL TRY TO MAKE THIS QUICK, THEN...
...LET'S TALK ABOUT YOUR NEW FRIEND.
6'3"
6'
5'9"
5'6"
5'3"
4'
LIEUTENANT COMMANDER MICHAELIS SHARED YOUR DEBRIEF, TALKING ABOUT AN ISLAND OF WOMEN OUT OF A GLADIATOR MOVIE...

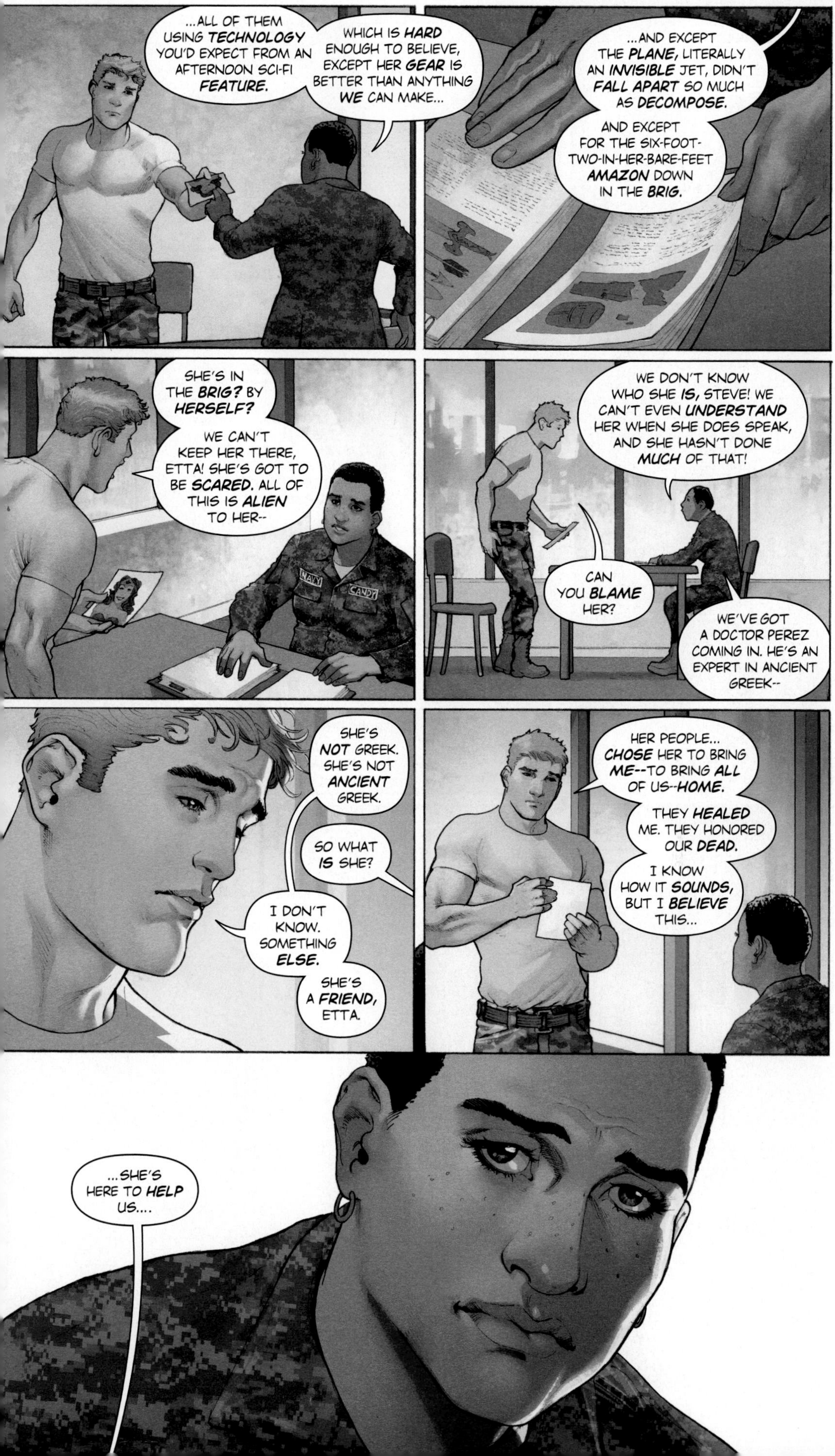
...ALL OF THEM USING TECHNOLOGY YOU'D EXPECT FROM AN AFTERNOON SCI-FI FEATURE.
WHICH IS HARD ENOUGH TO BELIEVE, EXCEPT HER GEAR IS BETTER THAN ANYTHING WE CAN MAKE...
...AND EXCEPT THE PLANE, LITERALLY AN INVISIBLE JET, DIDN'T FALL APART SO MUCH AS DECOMPOSE.
AND EXCEPT FOR THE SIX-FOOT-TWO-IN-HER-BARE-FEET AMAZON DOWN IN THE BRIG.
SHE'S IN THE BRIG? BY HERSELF?
WE CAN'T KEEP HER THERE, ETTA! SHE'S GOT TO BE SCARED. ALL OF THIS IS ALIEN TO HER--
NAVY
CANDY
WE DON'T KNOW WHO SHE IS, STEVE! WE CAN'T EVEN UNDERSTAND HER WHEN SHE DOES SPEAK, AND SHE HASN'T DONE MUCH OF THAT!
CAN YOU BLAME HER?
WE'VE GOT A DOCTOR PEREZ COMING IN. HE'S AN EXPERT IN ANCIENT GREEK--
SHE'S NOT GREEK. SHE'S NOT ANCIENT GREEK.
SO WHAT IS SHE?
I DON'T KNOW. SOMETHING ELSE.
SHE'S A FRIEND, ETTA.
HER PEOPLE... CHOSE HER TO BRING ME--TO BRING ALL OF US--HOME.
THEY HEALED ME. THEY HONORED OUR DEAD.
I KNOW HOW IT SOUNDS, BUT I BELIEVE THIS...
...SHE'S HERE TO HELP US....

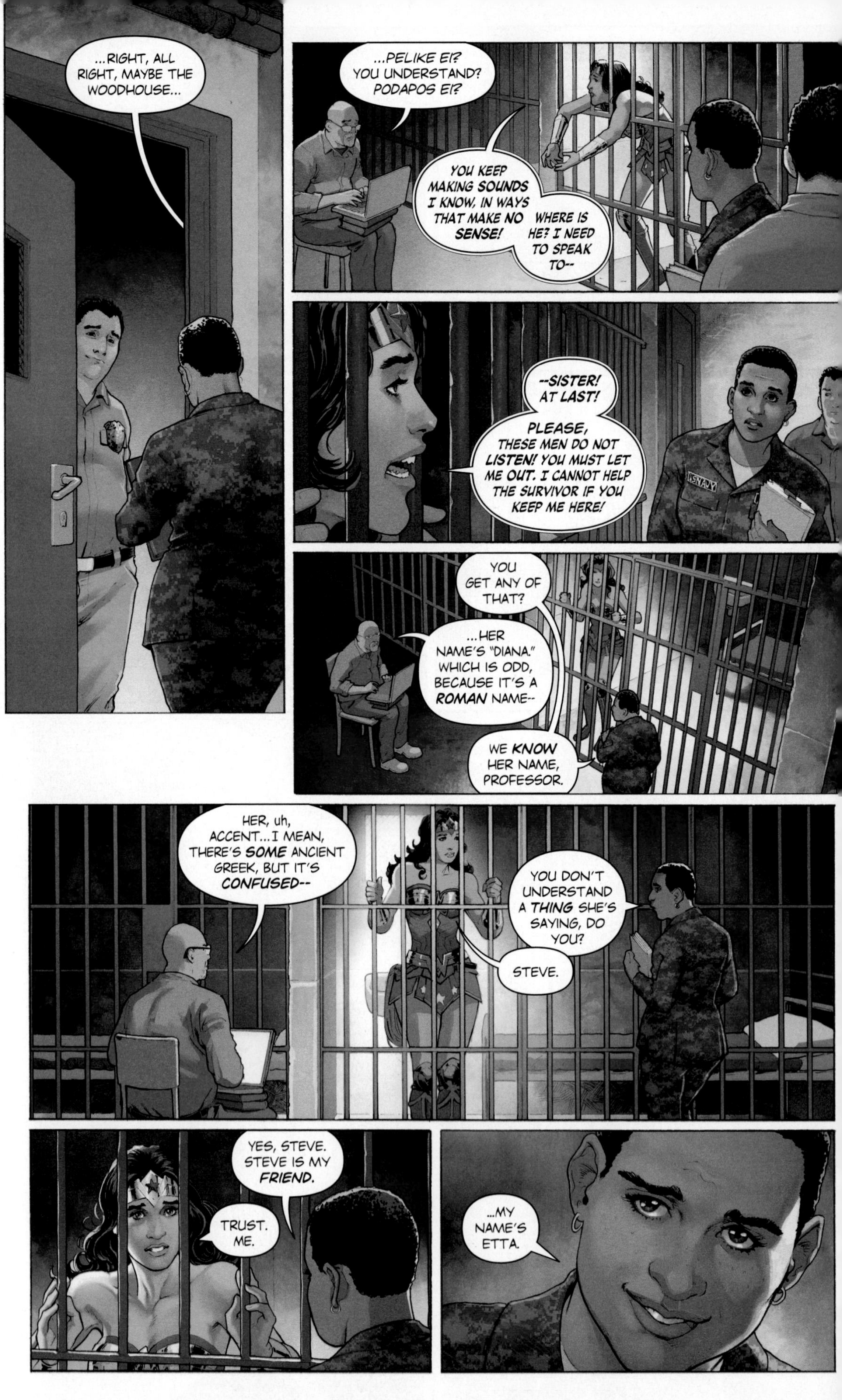
...RIGHT, ALL RIGHT, MAYBE THE WOODHOUSE...
...PELIKE EI? YOU UNDERSTAND? PODAPOS EI?
YOU KEEP MAKING SOUNDS I KNOW, IN WAYS THAT MAKE NO SENSE!
WHERE IS HE? I NEED TO SPEAK TO--
--SISTER! AT LAST!
PLEASE, THESE MEN DO NOT LISTEN! YOU MUST LET ME OUT. I CANNOT HELP THE SURVIVOR IF YOU KEEP ME HERE!
YOU GET ANY OF THAT?
...HER NAME'S "DIANA." WHICH IS ODD, BECAUSE IT'S A ROMAN NAME--
WE KNOW HER NAME, PROFESSOR.
HER, uh, ACCENT...I MEAN, THERE'S SOME ANCIENT GREEK, BUT IT'S CONFUSED--
YOU DON'T UNDERSTAND A THING SHE'S SAYING, DO YOU?
STEVE.
YES, STEVE. STEVE IS MY FRIEND.
TRUST. ME.
...MY NAME'S ETTA.

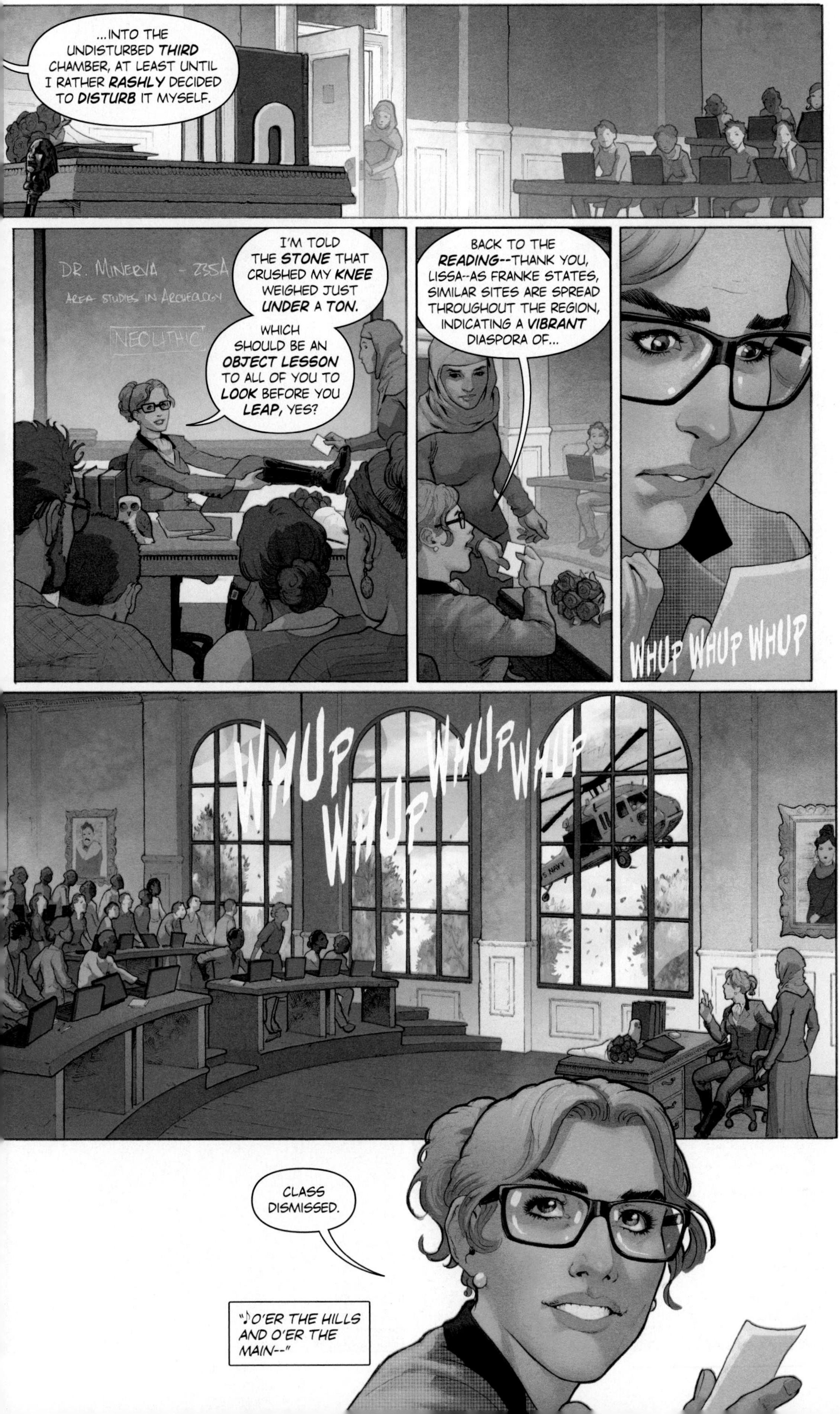
...INTO THE UNDISTURBED THIRD CHAMBER, AT LEAST UNTIL I RATHER RASHLY DECIDED TO DISTURB IT MYSELF.
DR. MINERVA - 235A
AREA STUDIES IN ARCHEOLOGY
NEOLITHIC
I'M TOLD THE STONE THAT CRUSHED MY KNEE WEIGHED JUST UNDER A TON.
WHICH SHOULD BE AN OBJECT LESSON TO ALL OF YOU TO LOOK BEFORE YOU LEAP, YES?
BACK TO THE READING--THANK YOU, LISSA--AS FRANKE STATES, SIMILAR SITES ARE SPREAD THROUGHOUT THE REGION, INDICATING A VIBRANT DIASPORA OF...
WHUP WHUP WHUP
WHUP WHUP WHUP WHUP
CLASS DISMISSED.
"♪O'ER THE HILLS AND O'ER THE MAIN--"

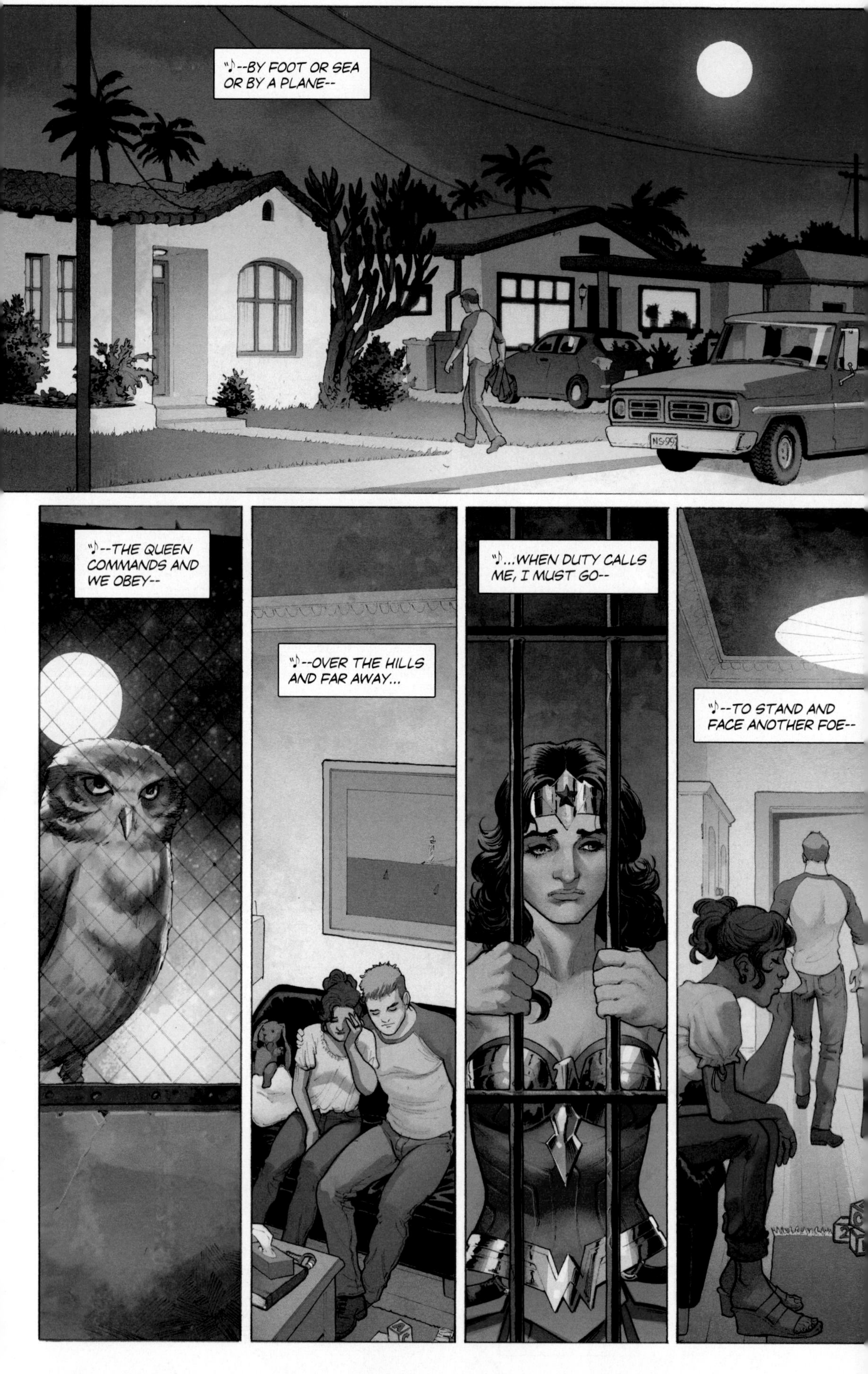
"♪--BY FOOT OR SEA OR BY A PLANE--
"♪--THE QUEEN COMMANDS AND WE OBEY--
"♪--OVER THE HILLS AND FAR AWAY...
"♪...WHEN DUTY CALLS ME, I MUST GO--
"♪--TO STAND AND FACE ANOTHER FOE--

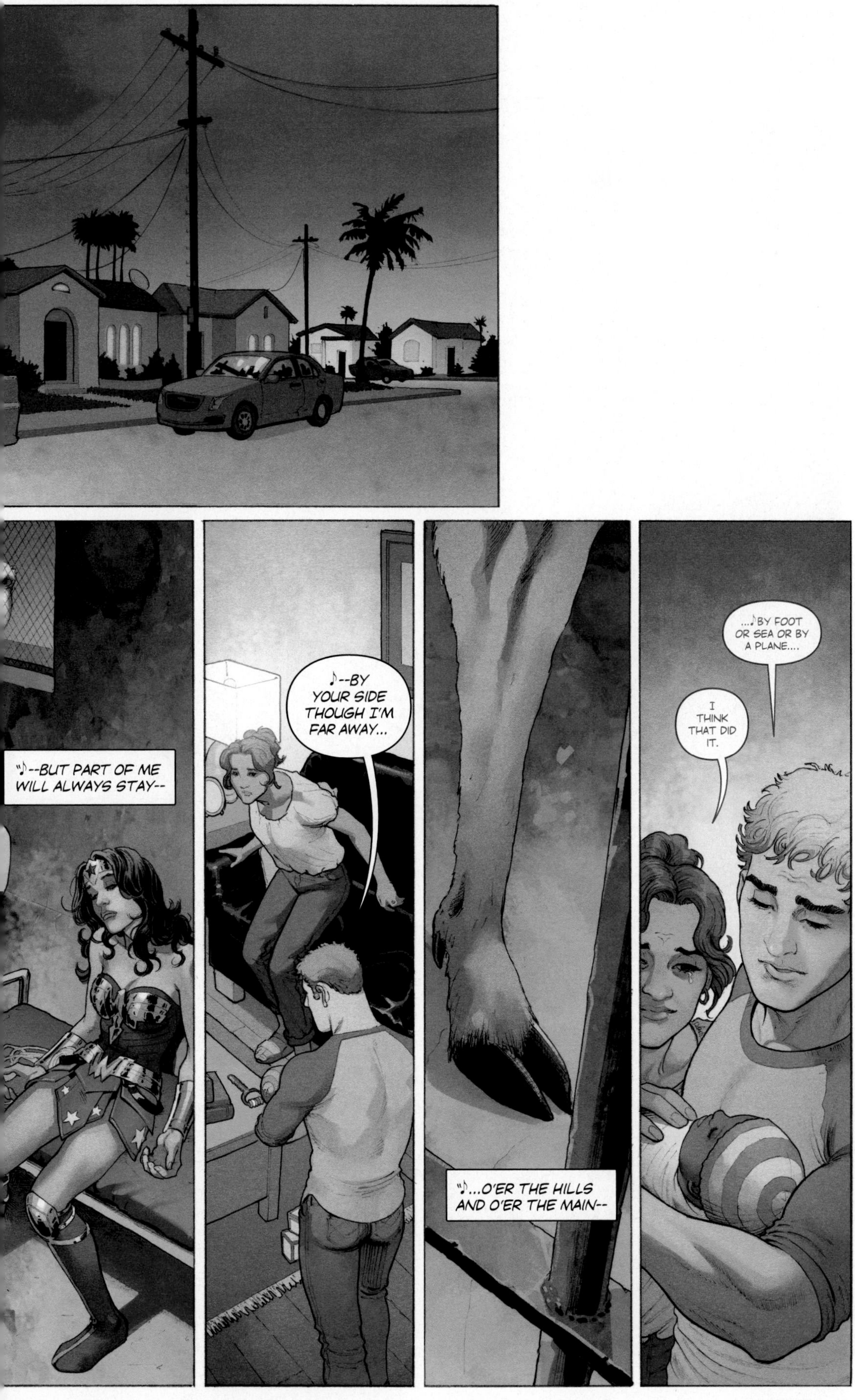
"♪--BUT PART OF ME WILL ALWAYS STAY--
♪--BY YOUR SIDE THOUGH I'M FAR AWAY...
"♪...O'ER THE HILLS AND O'ER THE MAIN--
...♪BY FOOT OR SEA OR BY A PLANE....
I THINK THAT DID IT.

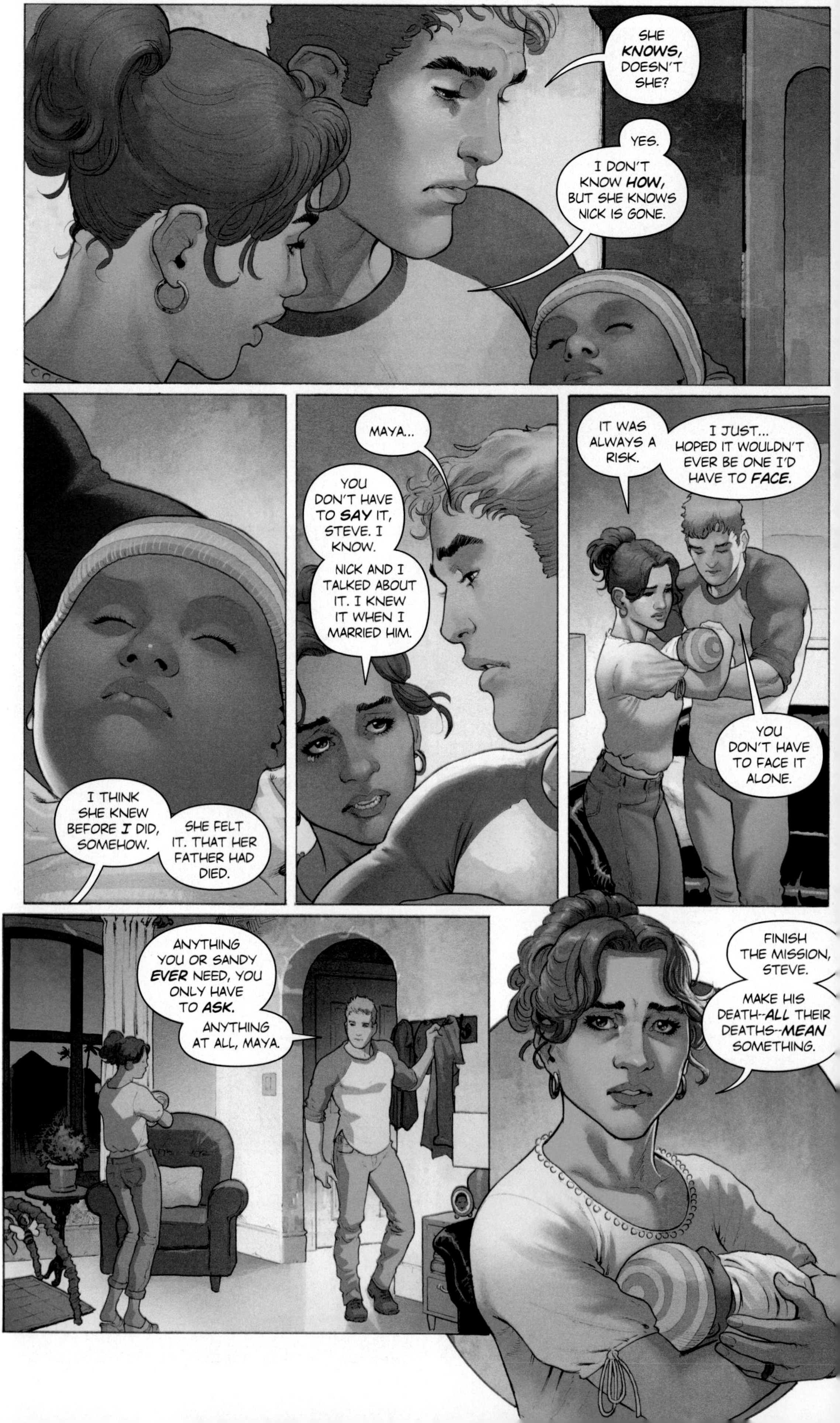
SHE KNOWS, DOESN'T SHE?
YES.
I DON'T KNOW HOW, BUT SHE KNOWS NICK IS GONE.
I THINK SHE KNEW BEFORE I DID, SOMEHOW.
SHE FELT IT. THAT HER FATHER HAD DIED.
MAYA...
YOU DON'T HAVE TO SAY IT, STEVE. I KNOW.
NICK AND I TALKED ABOUT IT. I KNEW IT WHEN I MARRIED HIM.
IT WAS ALWAYS A RISK.
I JUST... HOPED IT WOULDN'T EVER BE ONE I'D HAVE TO FACE.
YOU DON'T HAVE TO FACE IT ALONE.
ANYTHING YOU OR SANDY EVER NEED, YOU ONLY HAVE TO ASK.
ANYTHING AT ALL, MAYA.
FINISH THE MISSION, STEVE.
MAKE HIS DEATH--ALL THEIR DEATHS--MEAN SOMETHING.

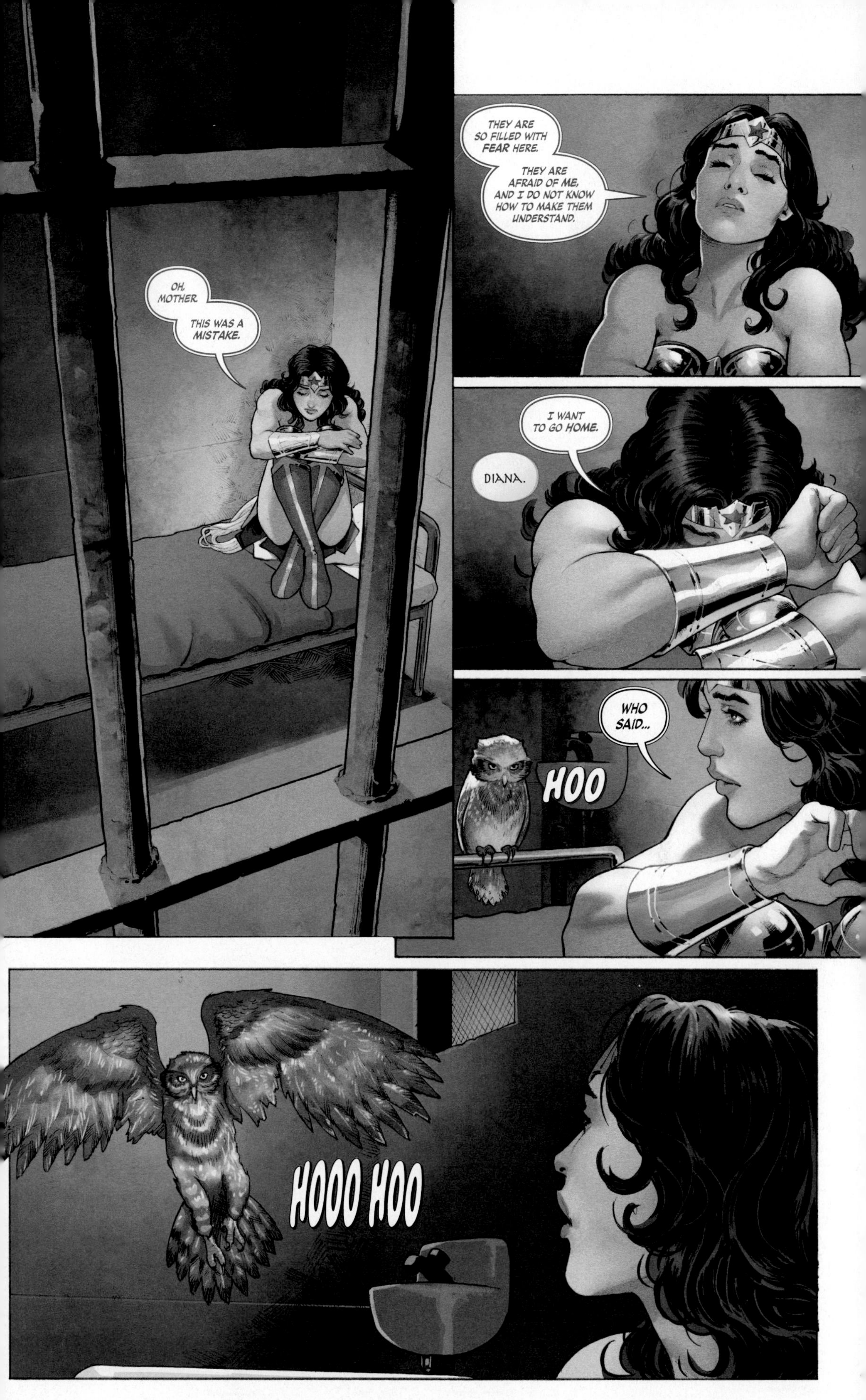
OH, MOTHER.
THIS WAS A MISTAKE.
THEY ARE SO FILLED WITH FEAR HERE.
THEY ARE AFRAID OF ME, AND I DO NOT KNOW HOW TO MAKE THEM UNDERSTAND.
I WANT TO GO HOME.
DIANA.
WHO SAID...
HOO
HOOO HOO

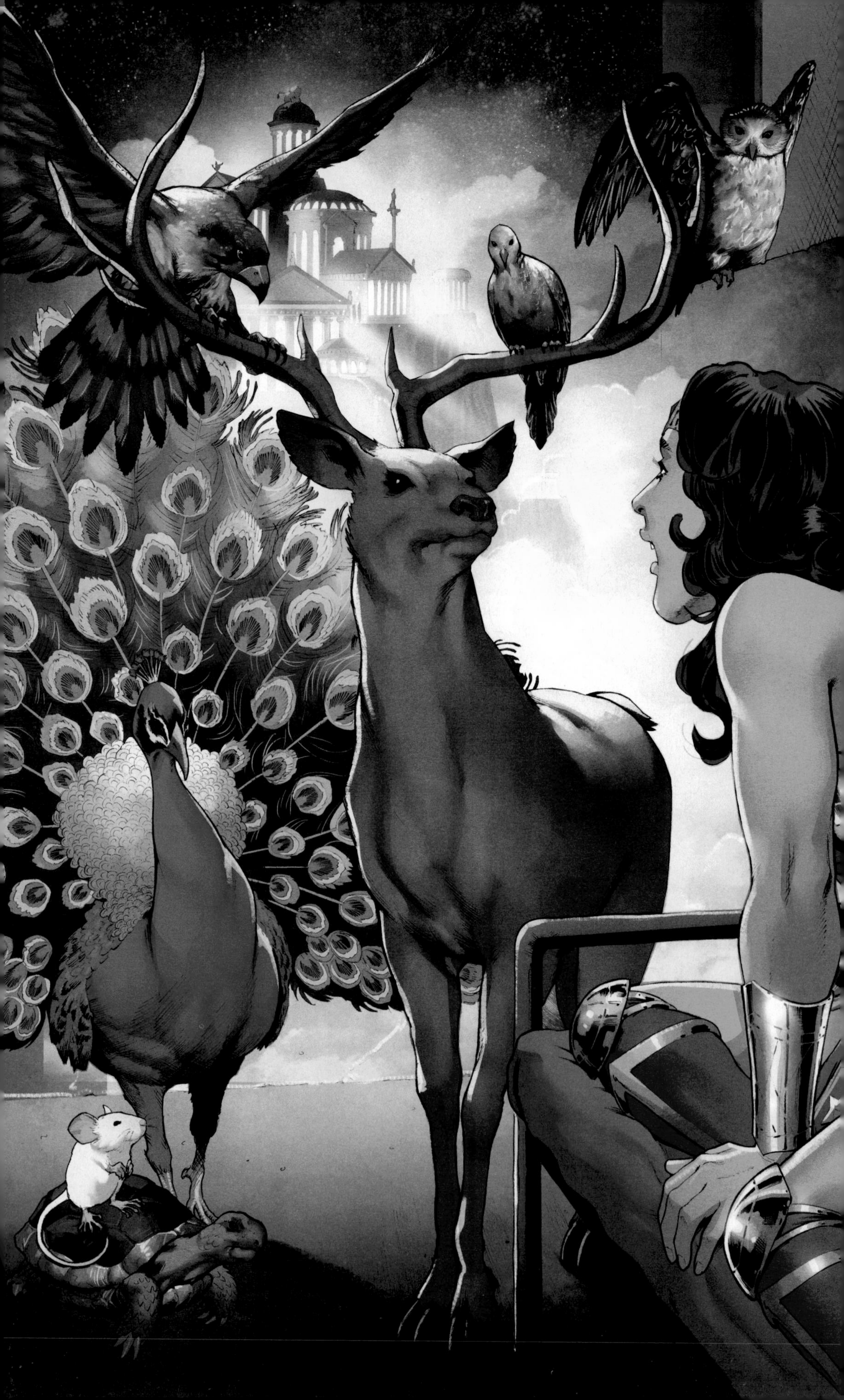

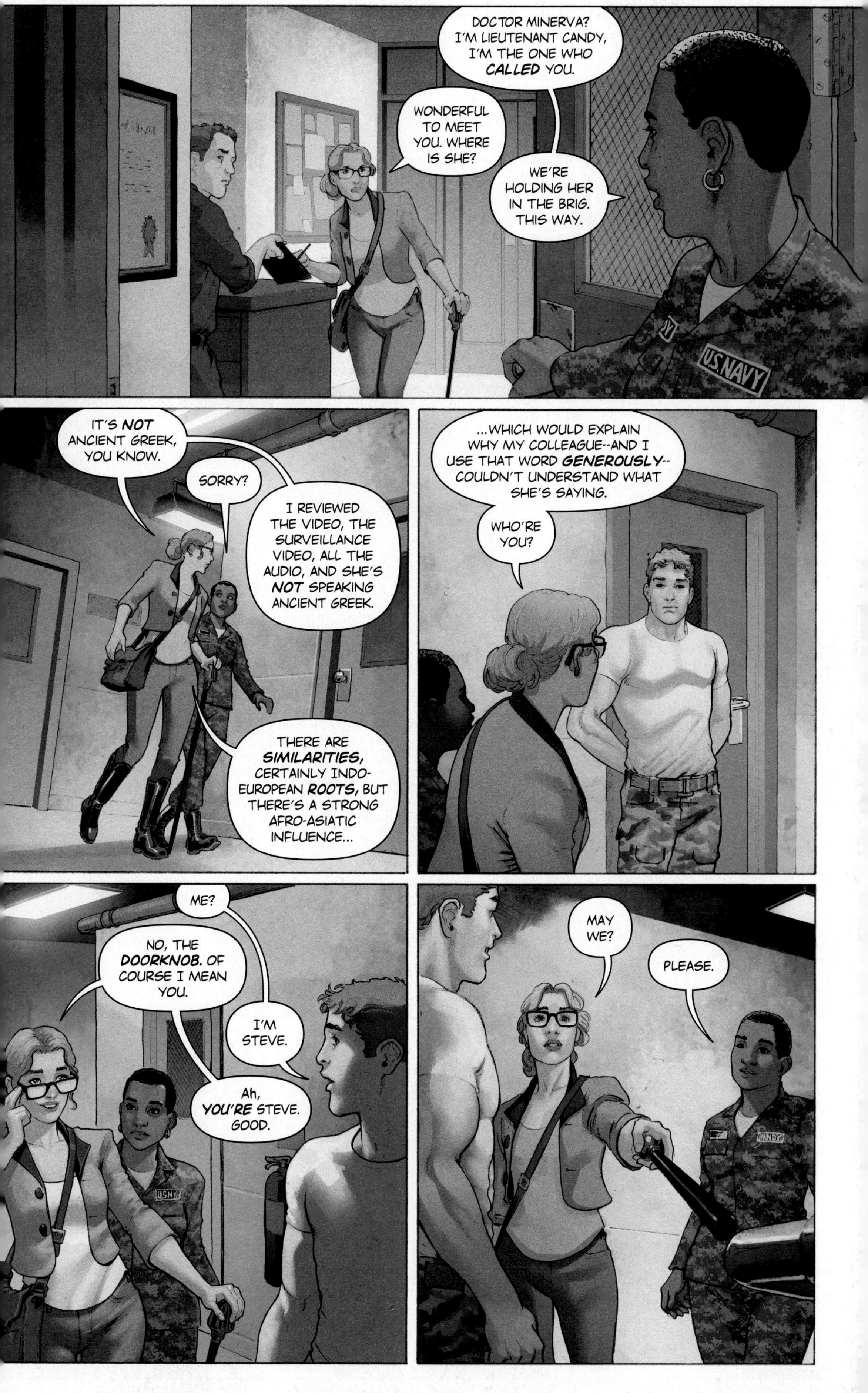
DOCTOR MINERVA? I'M LIEUTENANT CANDY, I'M THE ONE WHO CALLED YOU.
WONDERFUL TO MEET YOU. WHERE IS SHE?
WE'RE HOLDING HER IN THE BRIG. THIS WAY.
U.S. NAVY
IT'S NOT ANCIENT GREEK, YOU KNOW.
SORRY?
I REVIEWED THE VIDEO, THE SURVEILLANCE VIDEO, ALL THE AUDIO, AND SHE'S NOT SPEAKING ANCIENT GREEK.
THERE ARE SIMILARITIES, CERTAINLY INDO-EUROPEAN ROOTS, BUT THERE'S A STRONG AFRO-ASIATIC INFLUENCE...
...WHICH WOULD EXPLAIN WHY MY COLLEAGUE--AND I USE THAT WORD GENEROUSLY--COULDN'T UNDERSTAND WHAT SHE'S SAYING.
WHO'RE YOU?
ME?
NO, THE DOORKNOB. OF COURSE I MEAN YOU.
I'M STEVE.
Ah, YOU'RE STEVE. GOOD.
MAY WE?
PLEASE.

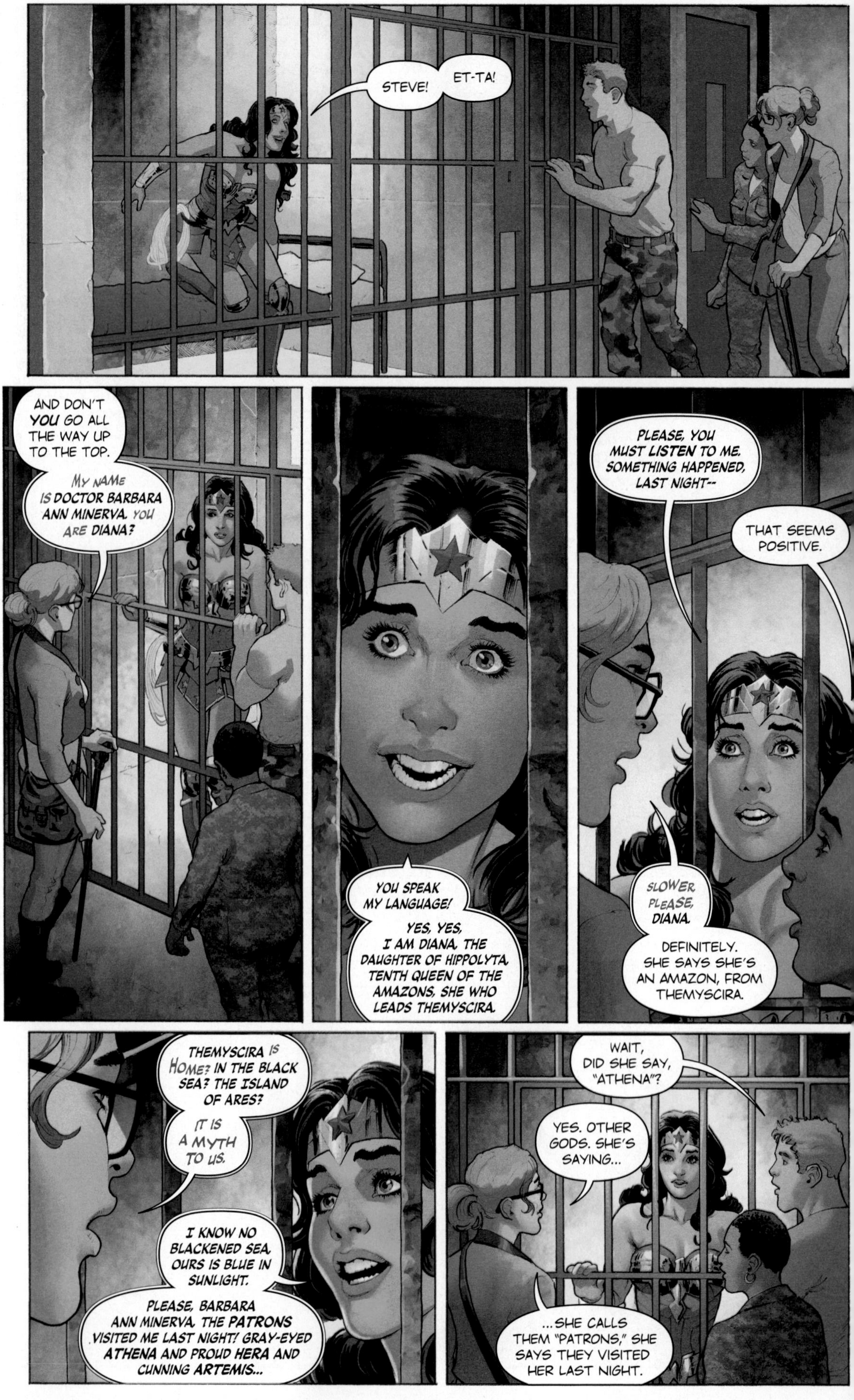

STEVE!
ET-TA!
AND DON'T YOU GO ALL THE WAY UP TO THE TOP.
MY NAME IS DOCTOR BARBARA ANN MINERVA. YOU ARE DIANA?
YOU SPEAK MY LANGUAGE!
YES, YES, I AM DIANA, THE DAUGHTER OF HIPPOLYTA, TENTH QUEEN OF THE AMAZONS, SHE WHO LEADS THEMYSCIRA.
PLEASE, YOU MUST LISTEN TO ME. SOMETHING HAPPENED, LAST NIGHT--
THAT SEEMS POSITIVE.
SLOWER, PLEASE, DIANA.
DEFINITELY. SHE SAYS SHE'S AN AMAZON, FROM THEMYSCIRA.
THEMYSCIRA IS HOME? IN THE BLACK SEA? THE ISLAND OF ARES?
IT IS A MYTH TO US.
I KNOW NO BLACKENED SEA, OURS IS BLUE IN SUNLIGHT.
PLEASE, BARBARA ANN MINERVA, THE PATRONS VISITED ME LAST NIGHT! GRAY-EYED ATHENA AND PROUD HERA AND CUNNING ARTEMIS...
WAIT, DID SHE SAY, "ATHENA"?
YES. OTHER GODS. SHE'S SAYING...
...SHE CALLS THEM "PATRONS," SHE SAYS THEY VISITED HER LAST NIGHT.

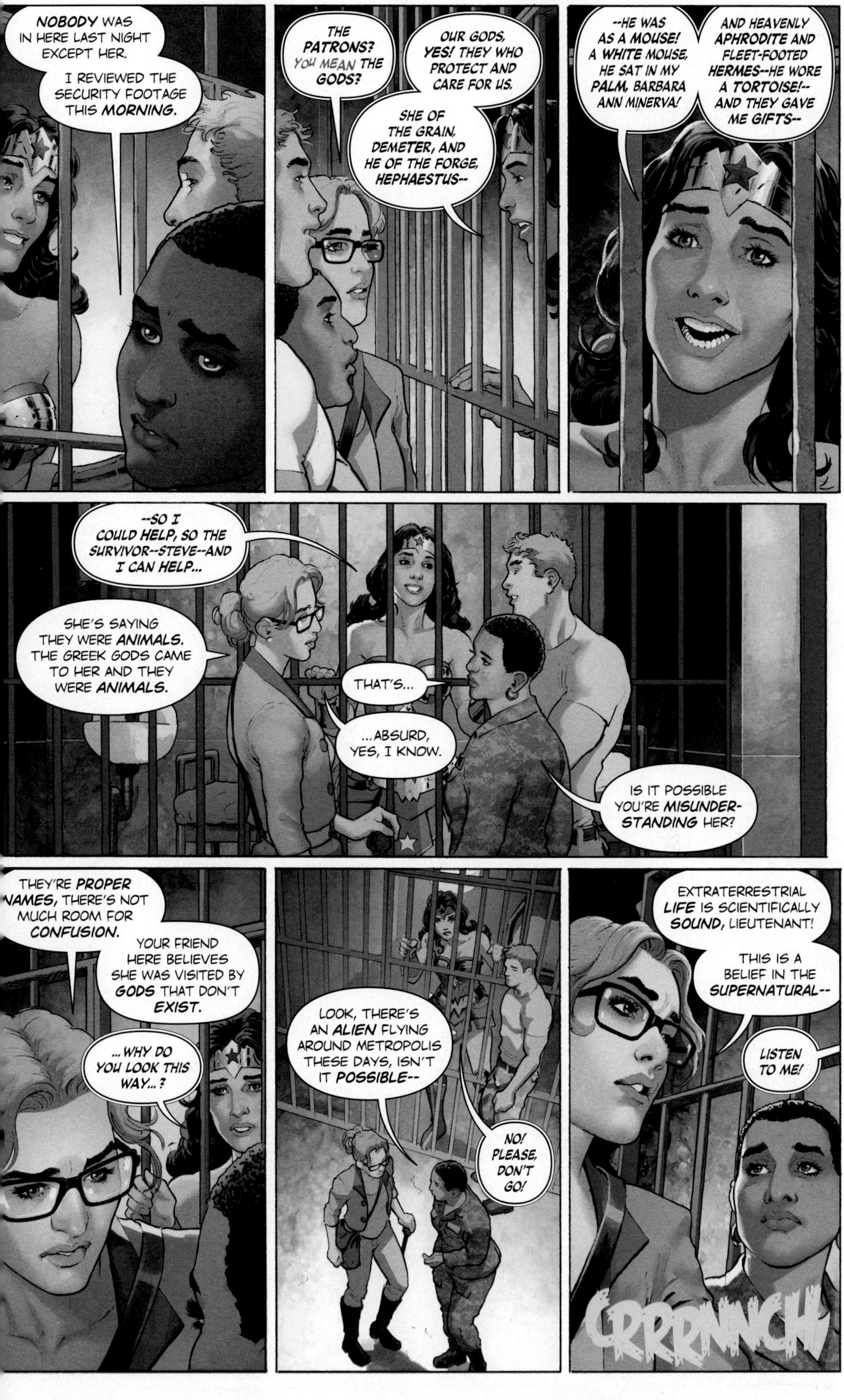
NOBODY WAS IN HERE LAST NIGHT EXCEPT HER.
I REVIEWED THE SECURITY FOOTAGE THIS MORNING.
THE PATRONS? YOU MEAN THE GODS?
OUR GODS, YES! THEY WHO PROTECT AND CARE FOR US.
SHE OF THE GRAIN, DEMETER, AND HE OF THE FORGE, HEPHAESTUS--
--HE WAS AS A MOUSE! A WHITE MOUSE, HE SAT IN MY PALM, BARBARA ANN MINERVA!
AND HEAVENLY APHRODITE AND FLEET-FOOTED HERMES--HE WORE A TORTOISE!--AND THEY GAVE ME GIFTS--
--SO I COULD HELP, SO THE SURVIVOR--STEVE--AND I CAN HELP...
SHE'S SAYING THEY WERE ANIMALS. THE GREEK GODS CAME TO HER AND THEY WERE ANIMALS.
THAT'S...
...ABSURD, YES, I KNOW.
IS IT POSSIBLE YOU'RE MISUNDER-STANDING HER?
THEY'RE PROPER NAMES, THERE'S NOT MUCH ROOM FOR CONFUSION.
YOUR FRIEND HERE BELIEVES SHE WAS VISITED BY GODS THAT DON'T EXIST.
...WHY DO YOU LOOK THIS WAY...?
LOOK, THERE'S AN ALIEN FLYING AROUND METROPOLIS THESE DAYS, ISN'T IT POSSIBLE--
NO! PLEASE, DON'T GO!
EXTRATERRESTRIAL LIFE IS SCIENTIFICALLY SOUND, LIEUTENANT!
THIS IS A BELIEF IN THE SUPERNATURAL--
LISTEN TO ME!
CRRRNNCH!

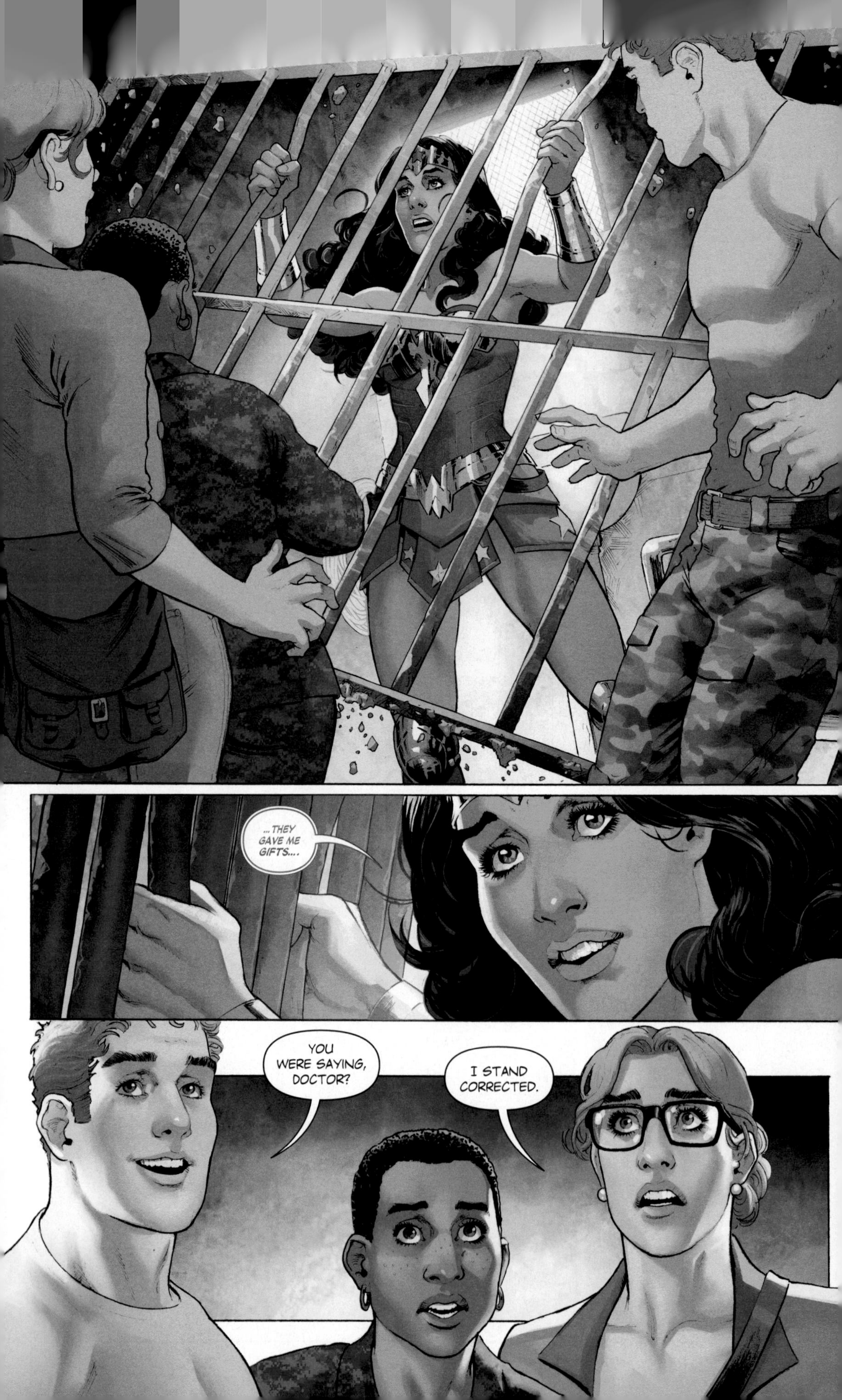
...THEY GAVE ME GIFTS....
YOU WERE SAYING, DOCTOR?
I STAND CORRECTED.

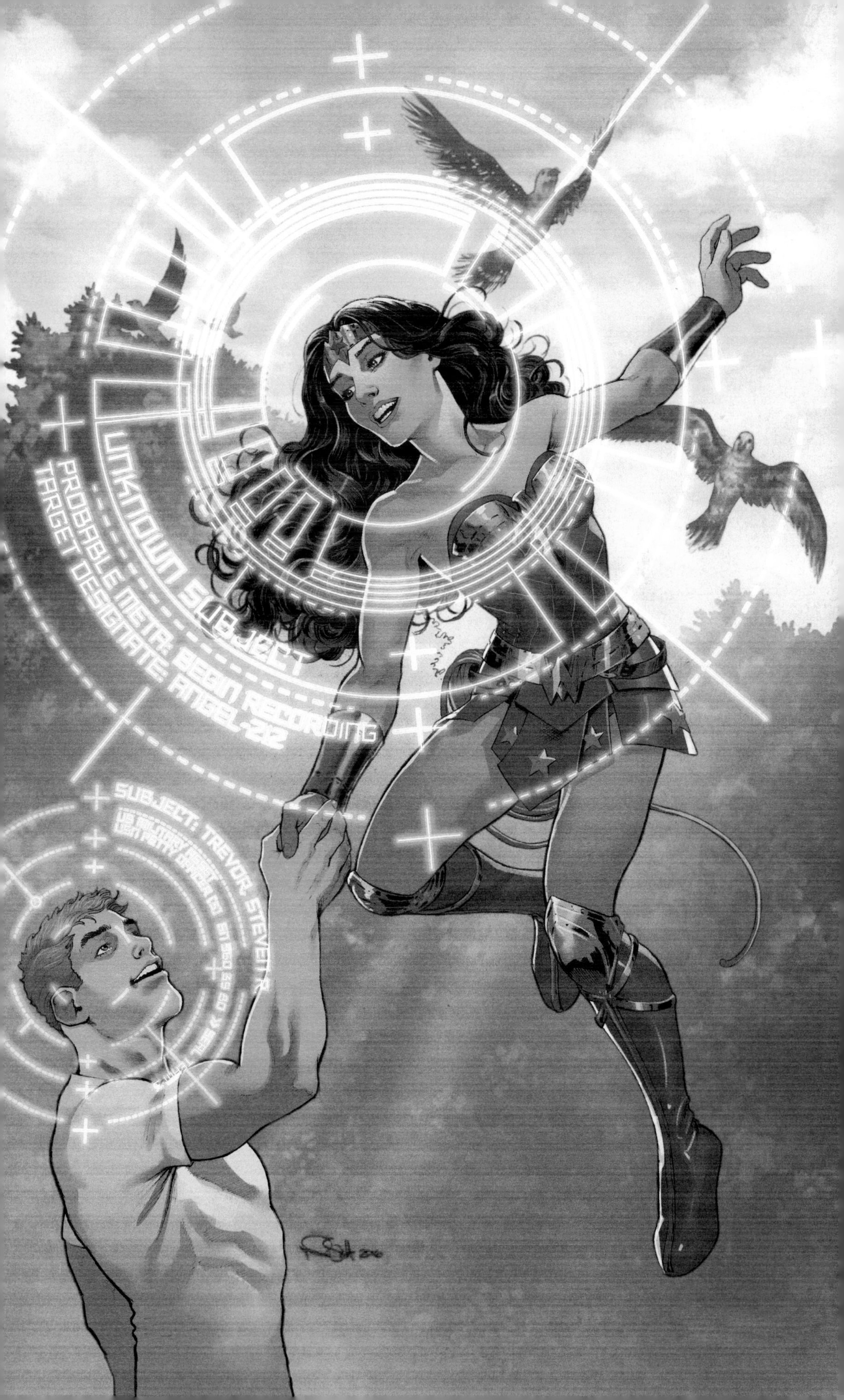
UNKNOWN SUBJECT
PROBABLE META: BEGIN RECORDING
TARGET DESIGNATE: ANGEL-212
SUBJECT: TREVOR, STEVE R
US MILITARY ASSET

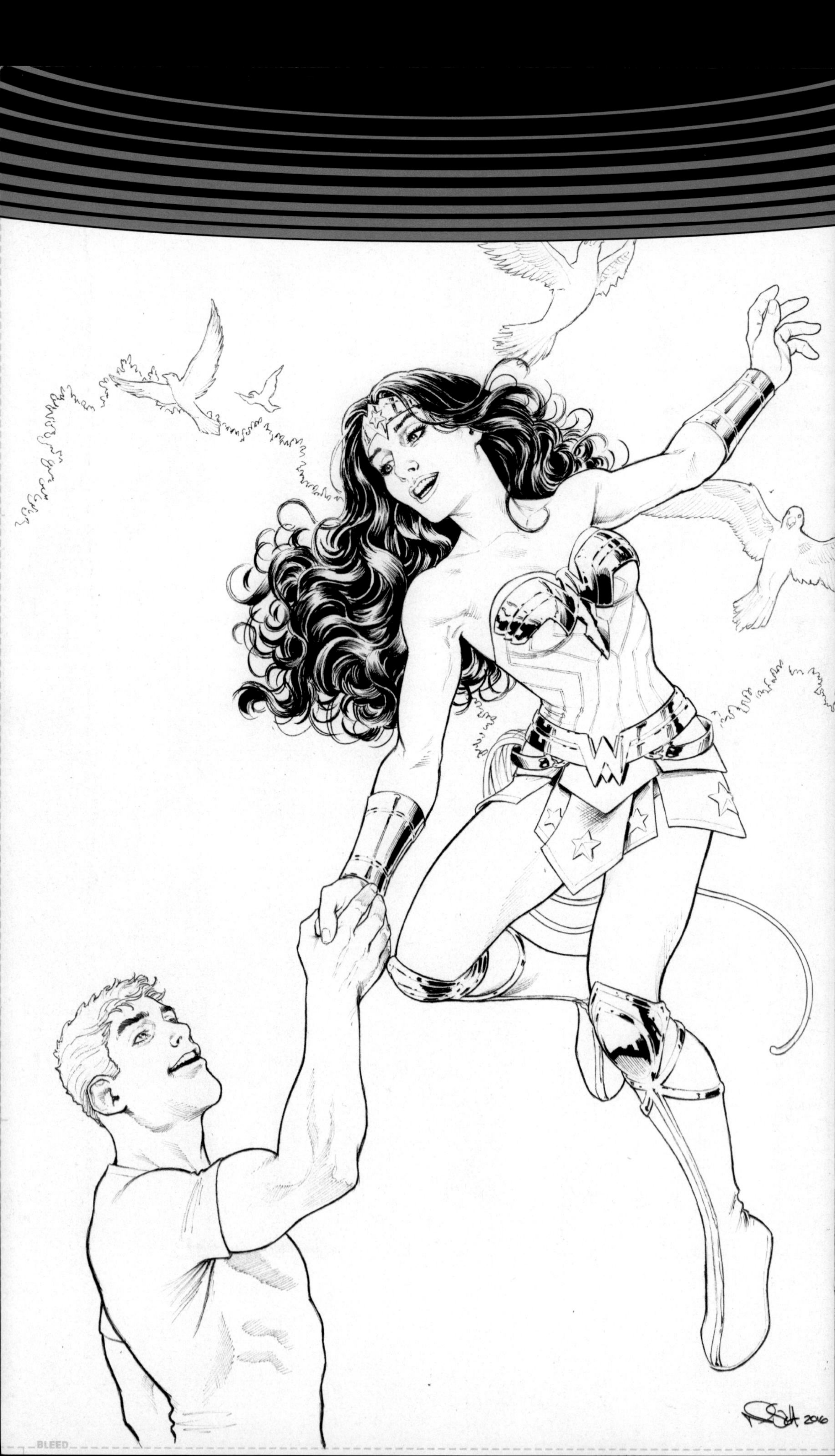

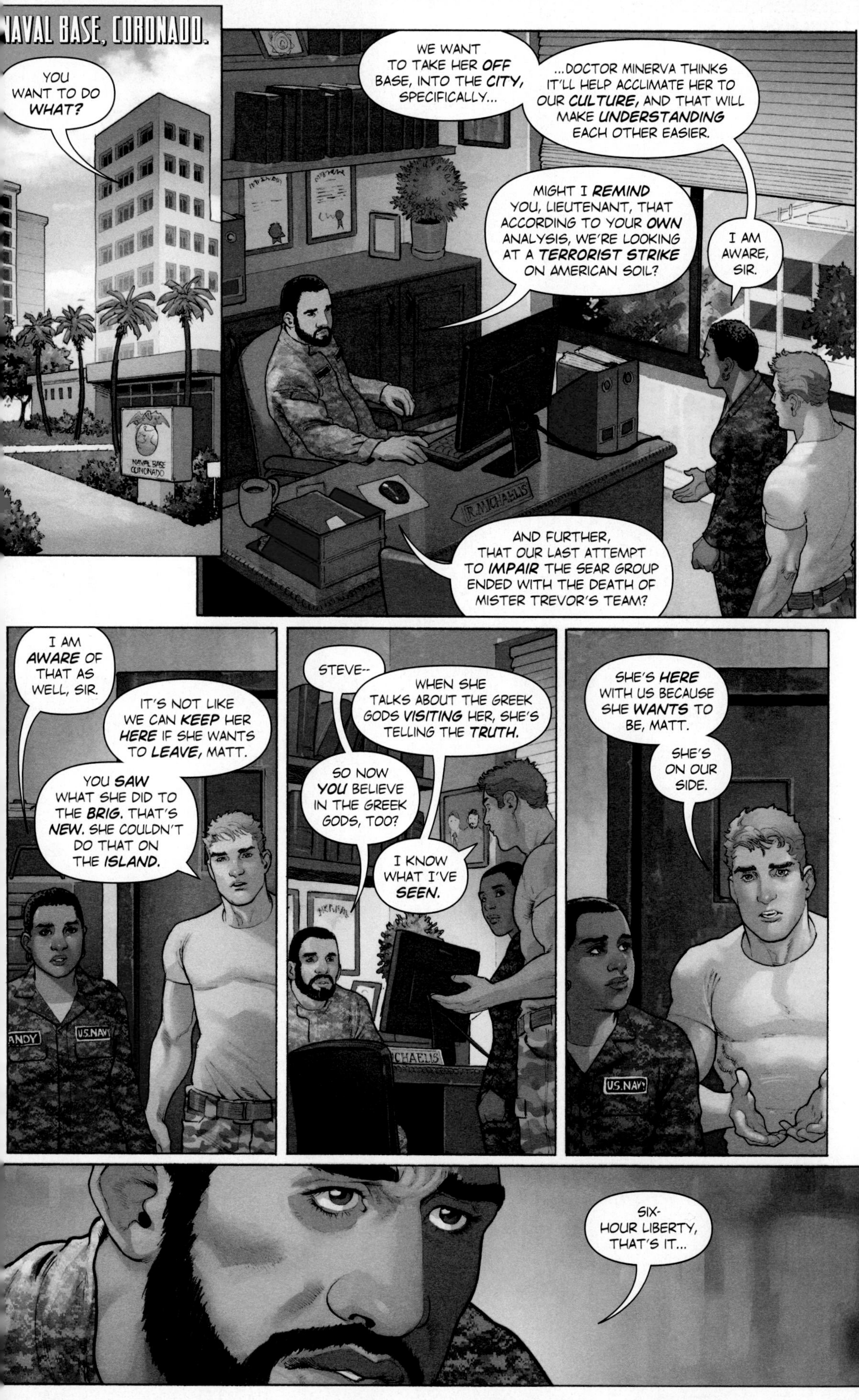
NAVAL BASE, CORONADO.
YOU WANT TO DO WHAT?
NAVAL BASE CORONADO
WE WANT TO TAKE HER OFF BASE, INTO THE CITY, SPECIFICALLY...
...DOCTOR MINERVA THINKS IT'LL HELP ACCLIMATE HER TO OUR CULTURE, AND THAT WILL MAKE UNDERSTANDING EACH OTHER EASIER.
MIGHT I REMIND YOU, LIEUTENANT, THAT ACCORDING TO YOUR OWN ANALYSIS, WE'RE LOOKING AT A TERRORIST STRIKE ON AMERICAN SOIL?
I AM AWARE, SIR.
R. MICHAELIS
AND FURTHER, THAT OUR LAST ATTEMPT TO IMPAIR THE SEAR GROUP ENDED WITH THE DEATH OF MISTER TREVOR'S TEAM?
I AM AWARE OF THAT AS WELL, SIR.
IT'S NOT LIKE WE CAN KEEP HER HERE IF SHE WANTS TO LEAVE, MATT.
YOU SAW WHAT SHE DID TO THE BRIG. THAT'S NEW. SHE COULDN'T DO THAT ON THE ISLAND.
U.S.NAVY
STEVE--
WHEN SHE TALKS ABOUT THE GREEK GODS VISITING HER, SHE'S TELLING THE TRUTH.
SO NOW YOU BELIEVE IN THE GREEK GODS, TOO?
I KNOW WHAT I'VE SEEN.
SHE'S HERE WITH US BECAUSE SHE WANTS TO BE, MATT.
SHE'S ON OUR SIDE.
U.S.NAVY
SIX-HOUR LIBERTY, THAT'S IT...

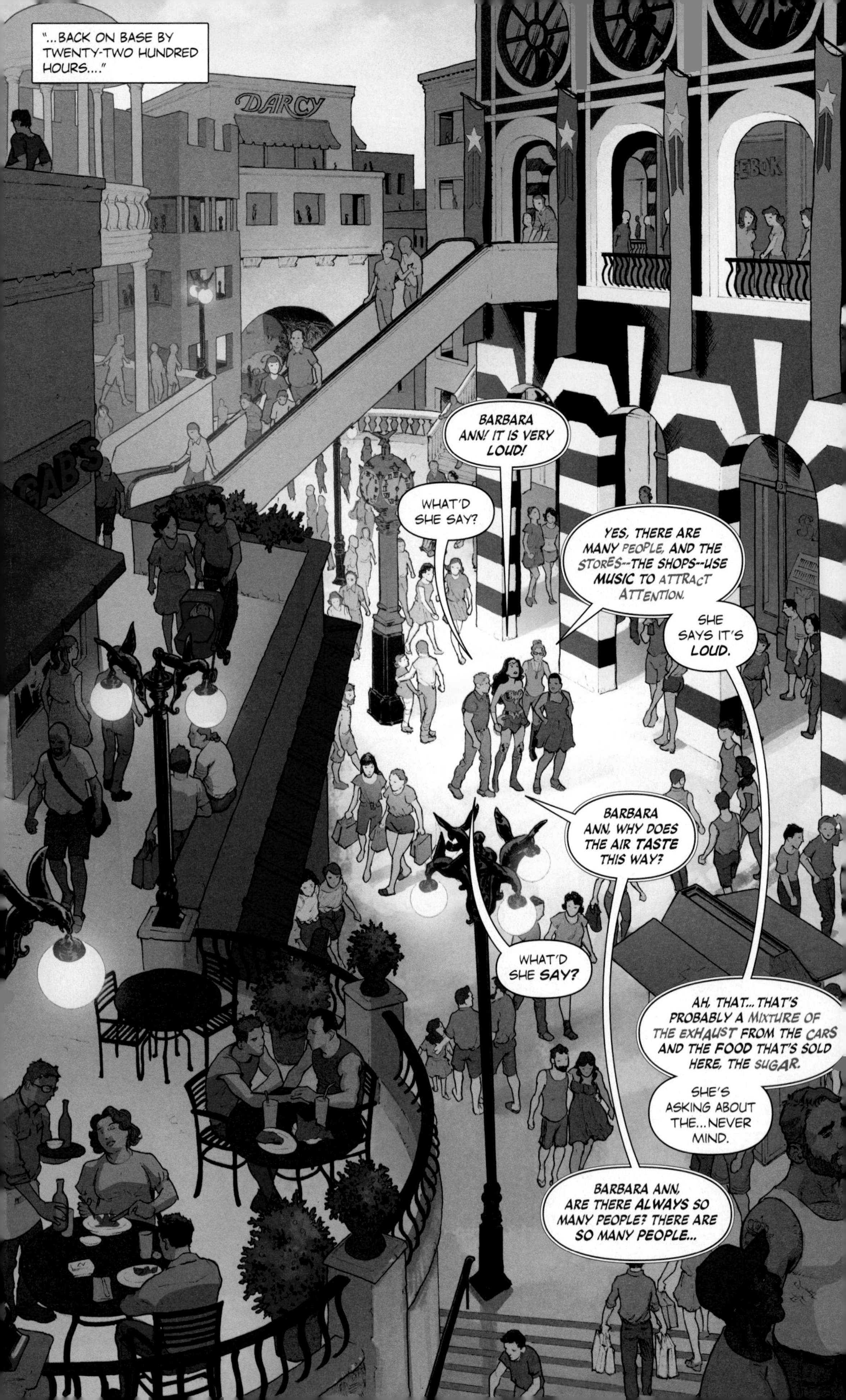
"...BACK ON BASE BY TWENTY-TWO HUNDRED HOURS...."
DARCY
BARBARA ANN! IT IS VERY LOUD!
WHAT'D SHE SAY?
YES, THERE ARE MANY PEOPLE, AND THE STORES--THE SHOPS--USE MUSIC TO ATTRACT ATTENTION.
SHE SAYS IT'S LOUD.
BARBARA ANN, WHY DOES THE AIR TASTE THIS WAY?
WHAT'D SHE SAY?
AH, THAT... THAT'S PROBABLY A MIXTURE OF THE EXHAUST FROM THE CARS AND THE FOOD THAT'S SOLD HERE, THE SUGAR.
SHE'S ASKING ABOUT THE... NEVER MIND.
BARBARA ANN, ARE THERE ALWAYS SO MANY PEOPLE? THERE ARE SO MANY PEOPLE...

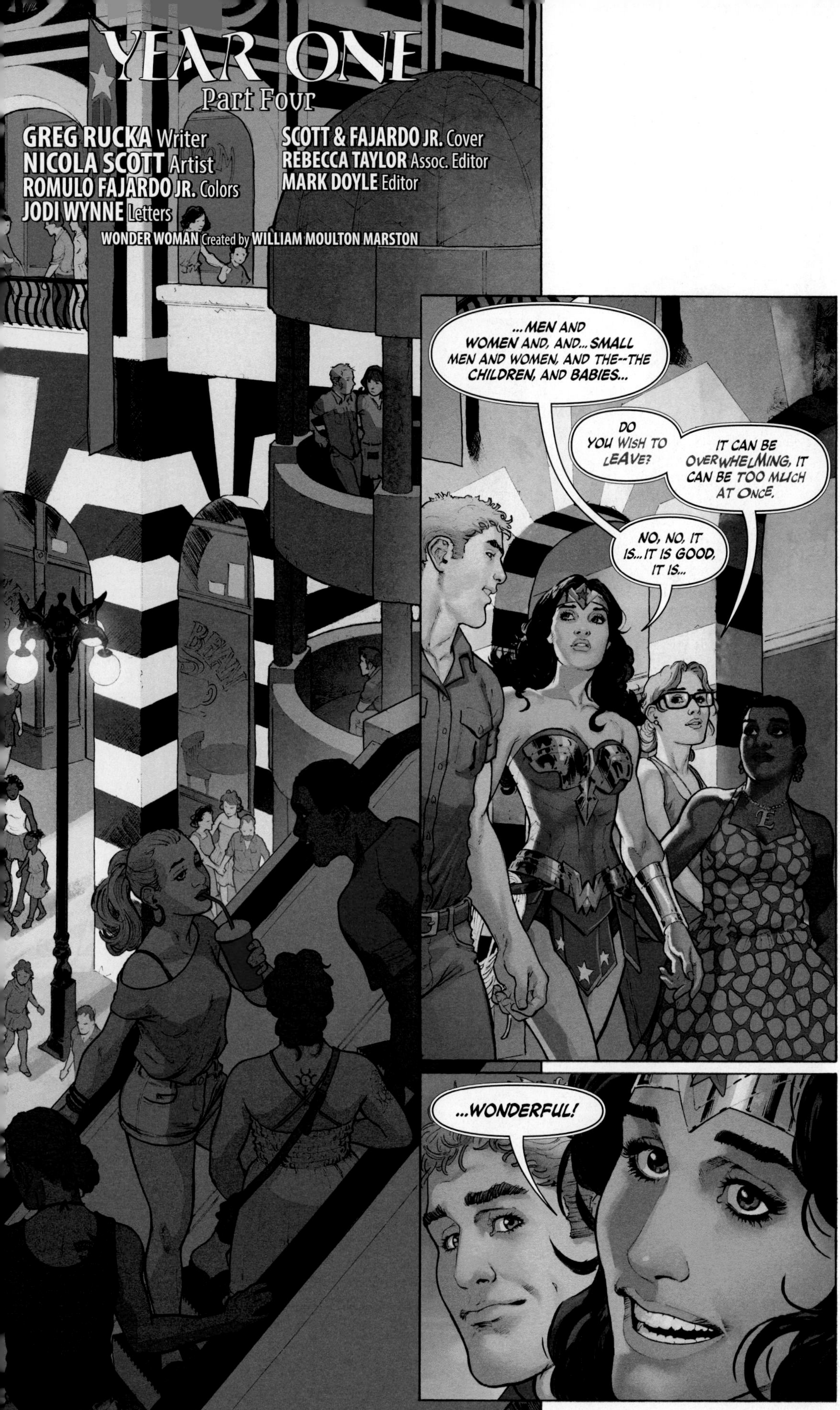
YEAR ONE
Part Four
GREG RUCKA Writer
NICOLA SCOTT Artist
ROMULO FAJARDO JR. Colors
JODI WYNNE Letters
SCOTT & FAJARDO JR. Cover
REBECCA TAYLOR Assoc. Editor
MARK DOYLE Editor
WONDER WOMAN Created by WILLIAM MOULTON MARSTON
...MEN AND WOMEN AND, AND...SMALL MEN AND WOMEN, AND THE--THE CHILDREN, AND BABIES...
DO YOU WISH TO LEAVE?
IT CAN BE OVERWHELMING, IT CAN BE TOO MUCH AT ONCE.
NO, NO, IT IS...IT IS GOOD, IT IS...
...WONDERFUL!

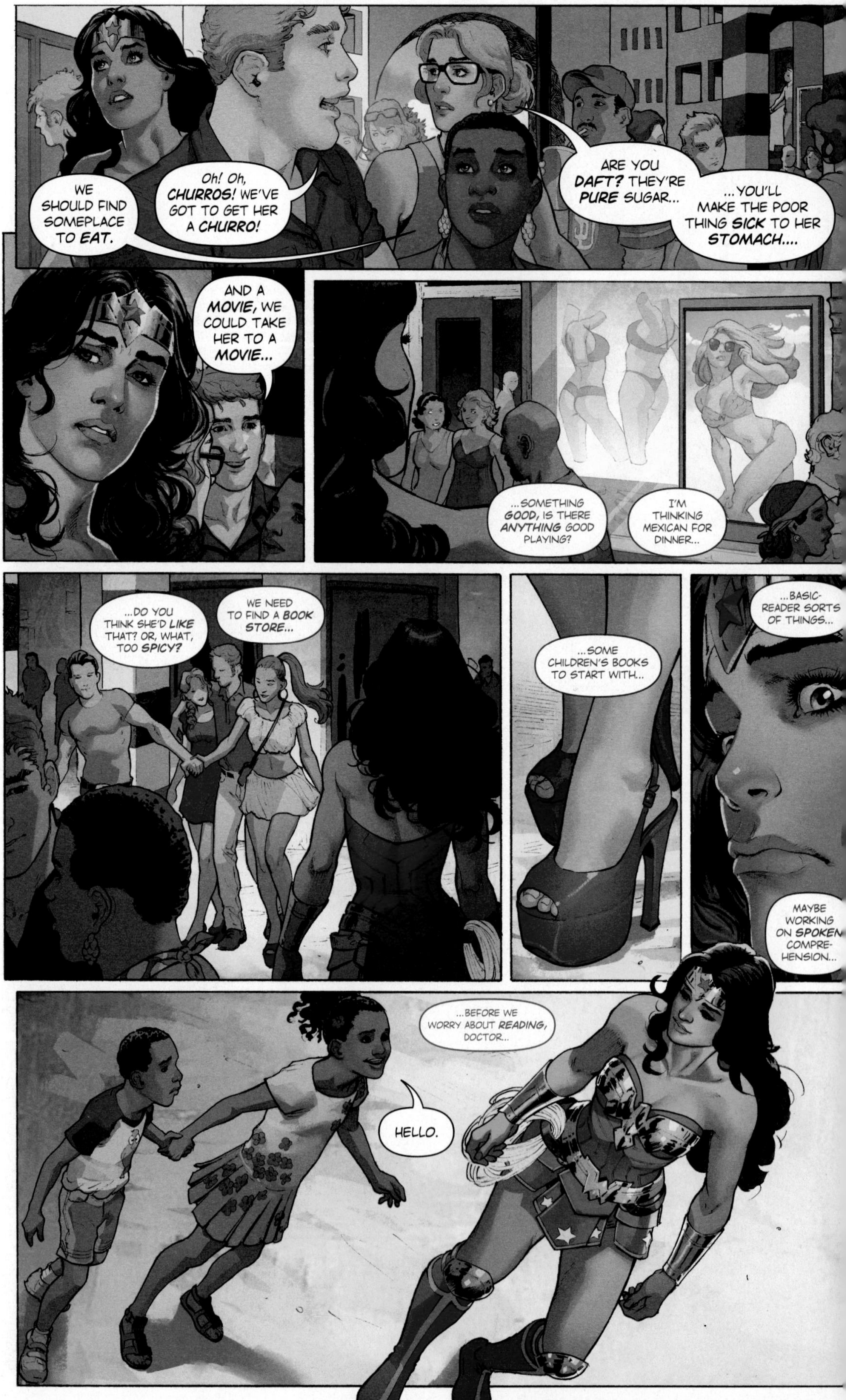
WE SHOULD FIND SOMEPLACE TO EAT.
Oh! Oh, CHURROS! WE'VE GOT TO GET HER A CHURRO!
ARE YOU DAFT? THEY'RE PURE SUGAR...
...YOU'LL MAKE THE POOR THING SICK TO HER STOMACH....
AND A MOVIE, WE COULD TAKE HER TO A MOVIE...
...SOMETHING GOOD, IS THERE ANYTHING GOOD PLAYING?
I'M THINKING MEXICAN FOR DINNER...
...DO YOU THINK SHE'D LIKE THAT? OR, WHAT, TOO SPICY?
WE NEED TO FIND A BOOK STORE...
...SOME CHILDREN'S BOOKS TO START WITH...
...BASIC-READER SORTS OF THINGS...
MAYBE WORKING ON SPOKEN COMPRE-HENSION...
...BEFORE WE WORRY ABOUT READING, DOCTOR...
HELLO.

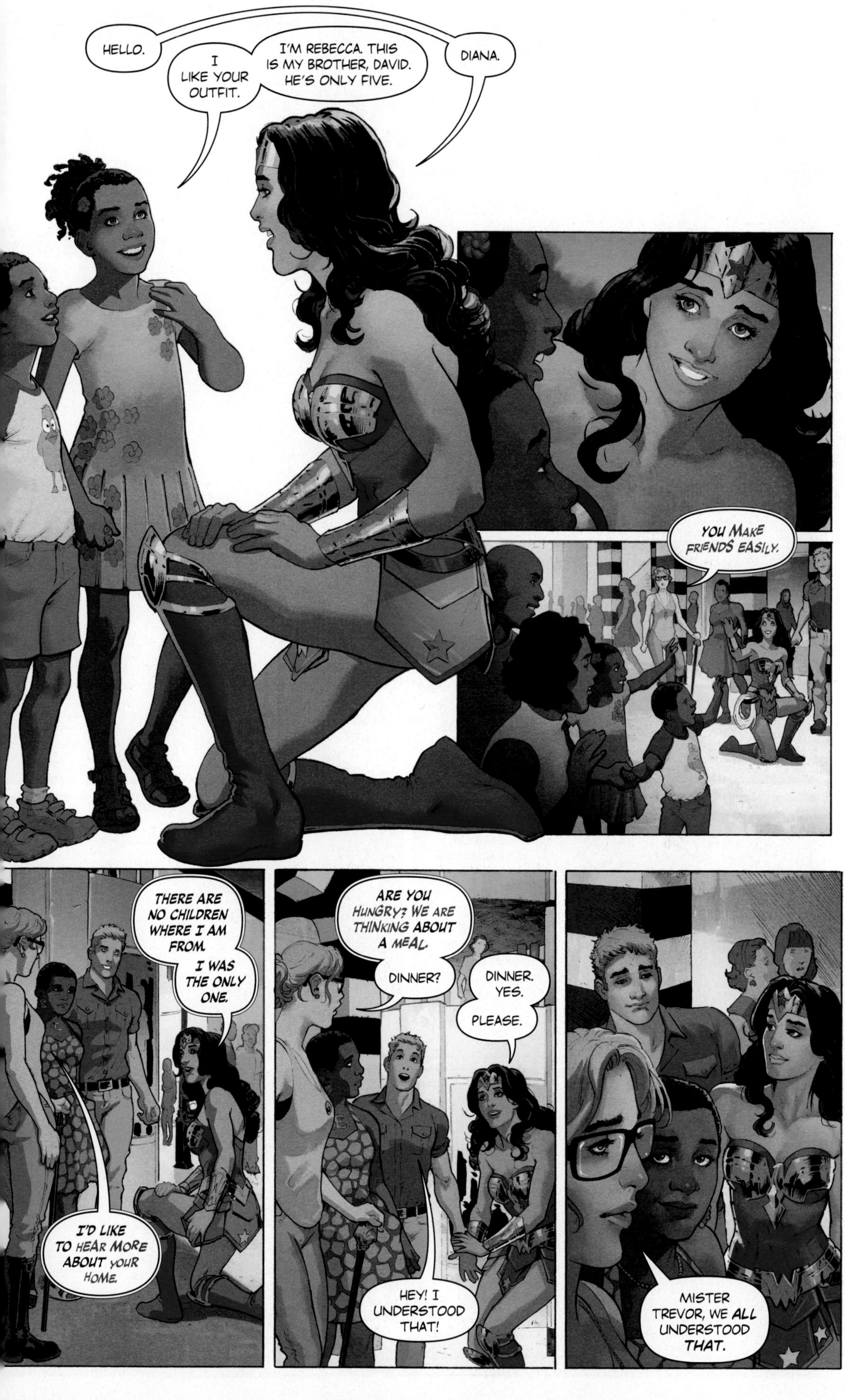
HELLO.
I LIKE YOUR OUTFIT.
I'M REBECCA. THIS IS MY BROTHER, DAVID. HE'S ONLY FIVE.
DIANA.
YOU MAKE FRIENDS EASILY.
THERE ARE NO CHILDREN WHERE I AM FROM.
I WAS THE ONLY ONE.
I'D LIKE TO HEAR MORE ABOUT YOUR HOME.
ARE YOU HUNGRY? WE ARE THINKING ABOUT A MEAL.
DINNER?
DINNER. YES.
PLEASE.
HEY! I UNDERSTOOD THAT!
MISTER TREVOR, WE ALL UNDERSTOOD THAT.

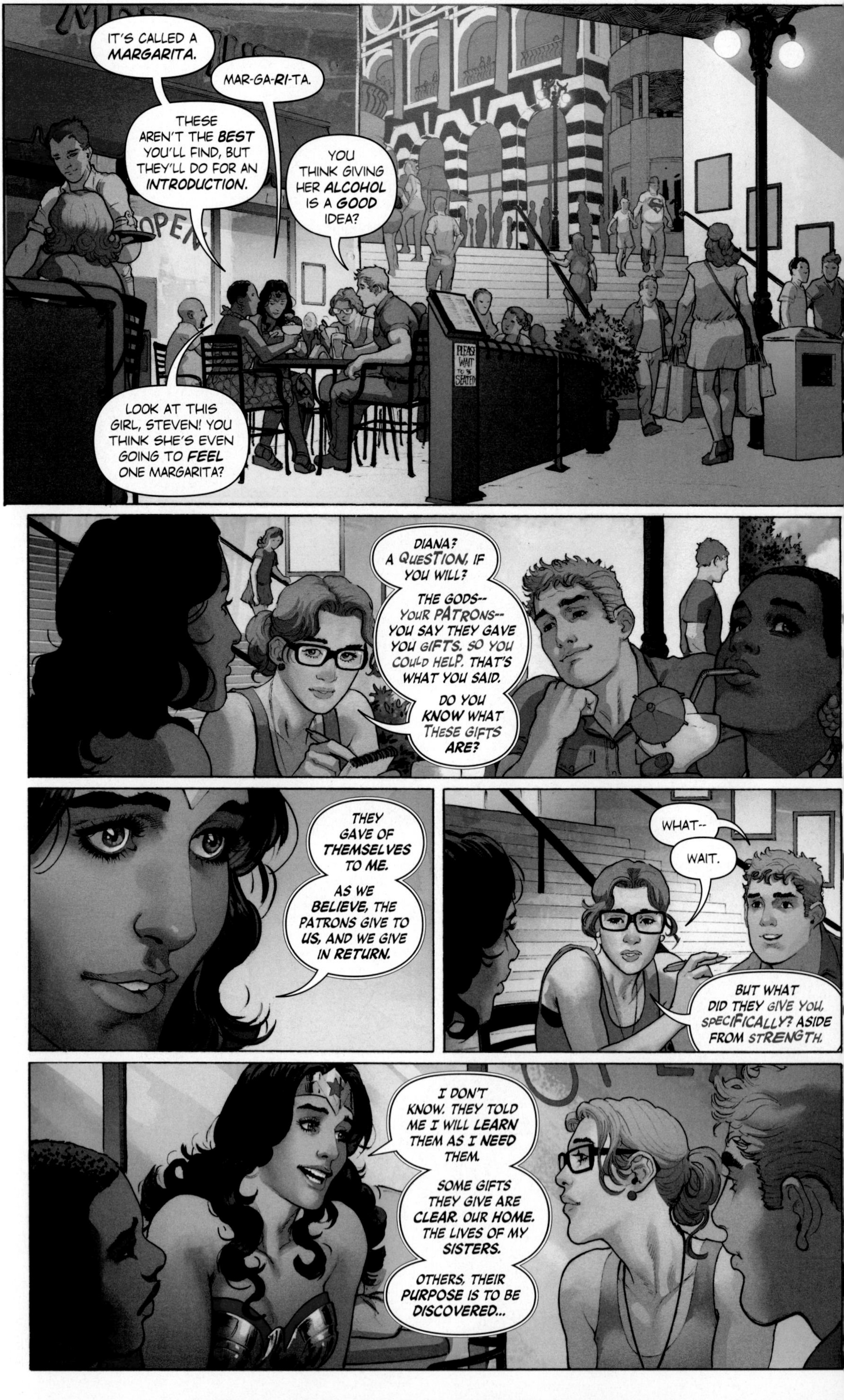
IT'S CALLED A MARGARITA.
MAR-GA-RI-TA.
THESE AREN'T THE BEST YOU'LL FIND, BUT THEY'LL DO FOR AN INTRODUCTION.
YOU THINK GIVING HER ALCOHOL IS A GOOD IDEA?
LOOK AT THIS GIRL, STEVEN! YOU THINK SHE'S EVEN GOING TO FEEL ONE MARGARITA?
OPEN
PLEASE WAIT TO BE SEATED
DIANA? A QUESTION, IF YOU WILL?
THE GODS-- YOUR PATRONS-- YOU SAY THEY GAVE YOU GIFTS. SO YOU COULD HELP. THAT'S WHAT YOU SAID.
DO YOU KNOW WHAT THESE GIFTS ARE?
THEY GAVE OF THEMSELVES TO ME.
AS WE BELIEVE, THE PATRONS GIVE TO US, AND WE GIVE IN RETURN.
WHAT--
WAIT.
BUT WHAT DID THEY GIVE YOU, SPECIFICALLY? ASIDE FROM STRENGTH.
I DON'T KNOW. THEY TOLD ME I WILL LEARN THEM AS I NEED THEM.
SOME GIFTS THEY GIVE ARE CLEAR. OUR HOME. THE LIVES OF MY SISTERS.
OTHERS, THEIR PURPOSE IS TO BE DISCOVERED...

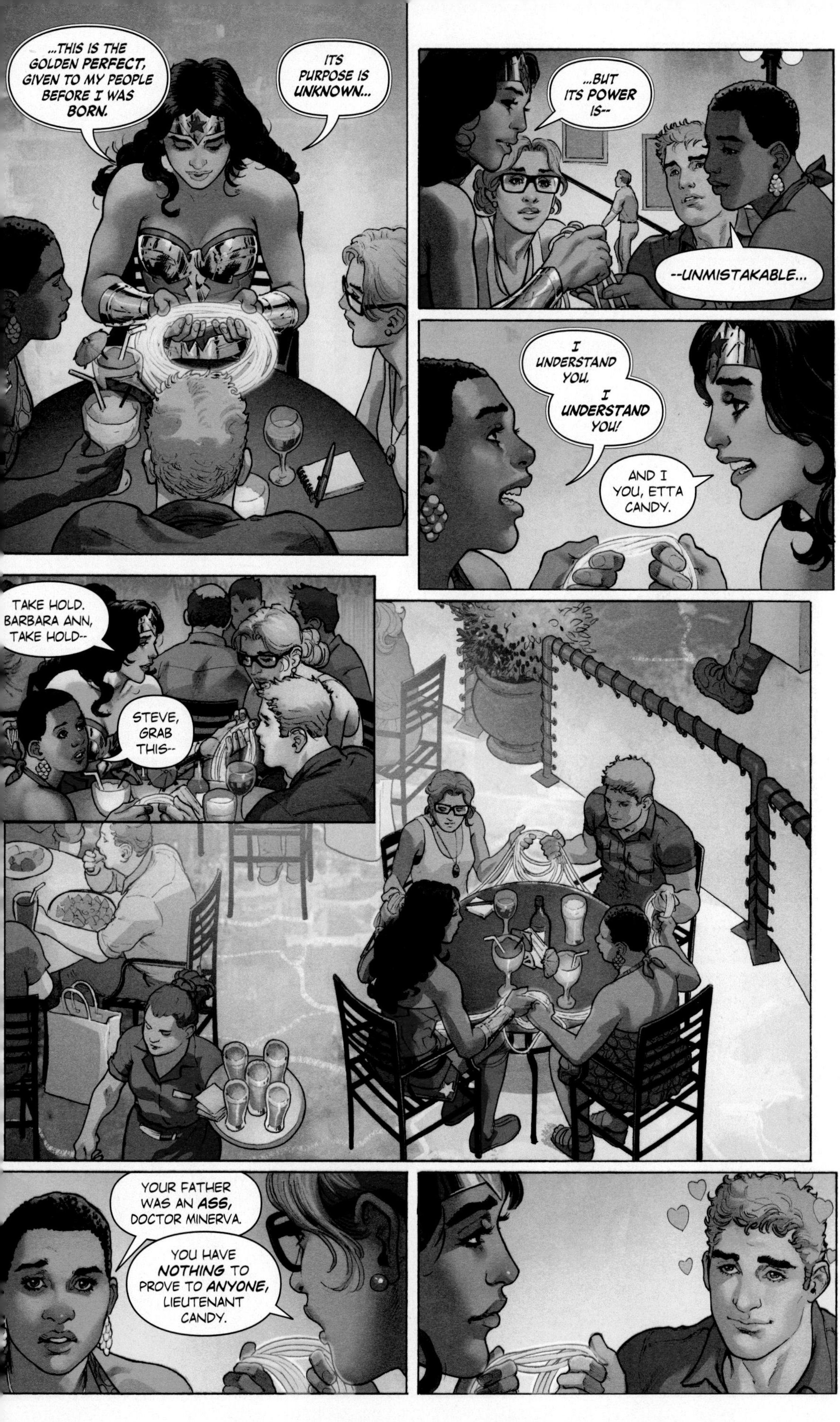
...THIS IS THE GOLDEN PERFECT, GIVEN TO MY PEOPLE BEFORE I WAS BORN.
ITS PURPOSE IS UNKNOWN...
...BUT ITS POWER IS--
--UNMISTAKABLE...
I UNDERSTAND YOU.
I UNDERSTAND YOU!
AND I YOU, ETTA CANDY.
TAKE HOLD. BARBARA ANN, TAKE HOLD--
STEVE, GRAB THIS--
YOUR FATHER WAS AN ASS, DOCTOR MINERVA.
YOU HAVE NOTHING TO PROVE TO ANYONE, LIEUTENANT CANDY.

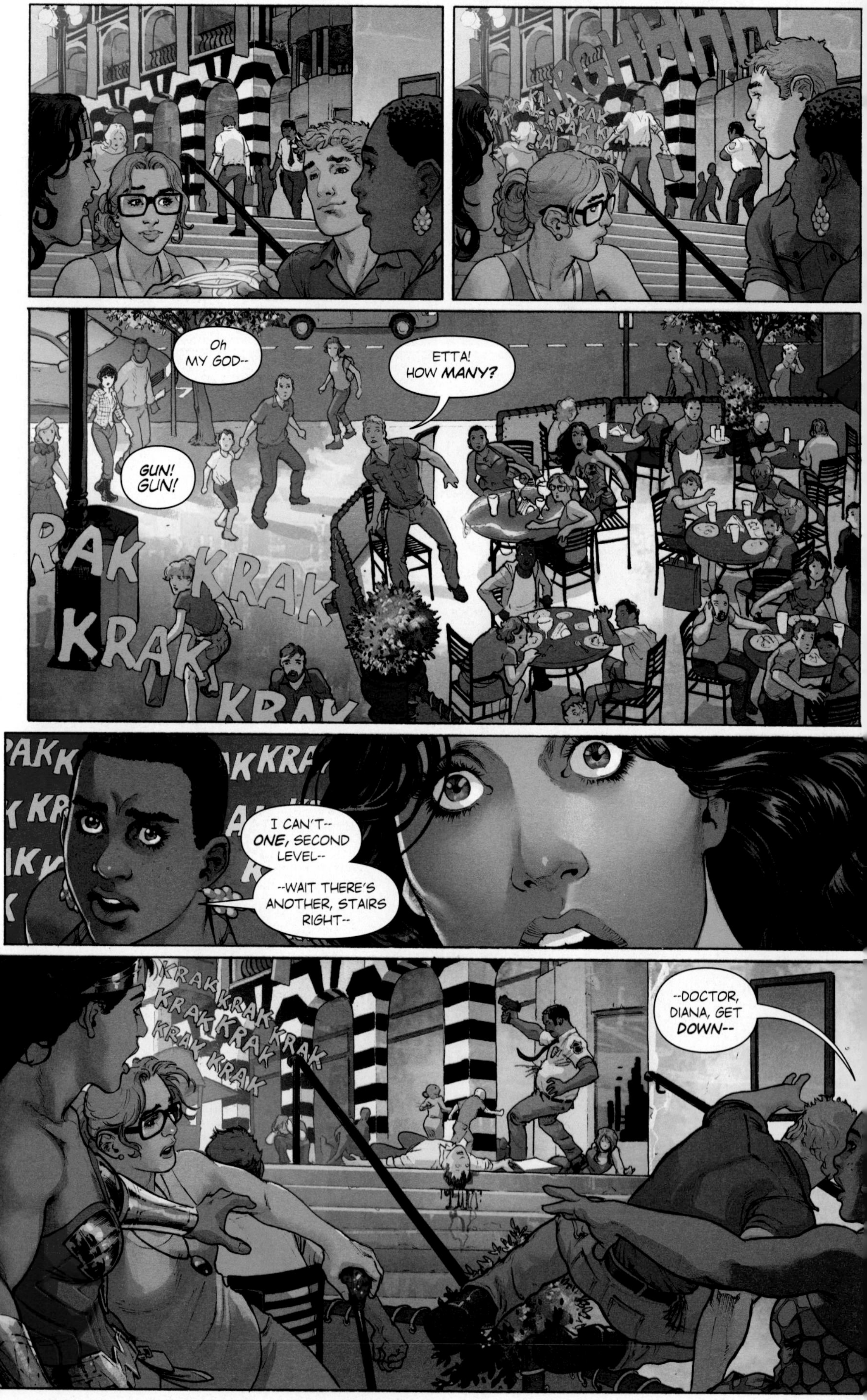
Oh MY GOD--
ETTA! HOW MANY?
GUN! GUN!
KRAK
KRAK
KRAK
I CAN'T-- ONE, SECOND LEVEL--
--WAIT THERE'S ANOTHER, STAIRS RIGHT--
KRAK KRAK KRAK KRAK KRAK KRAK KRAK KRAK
--DOCTOR, DIANA, GET DOWN--

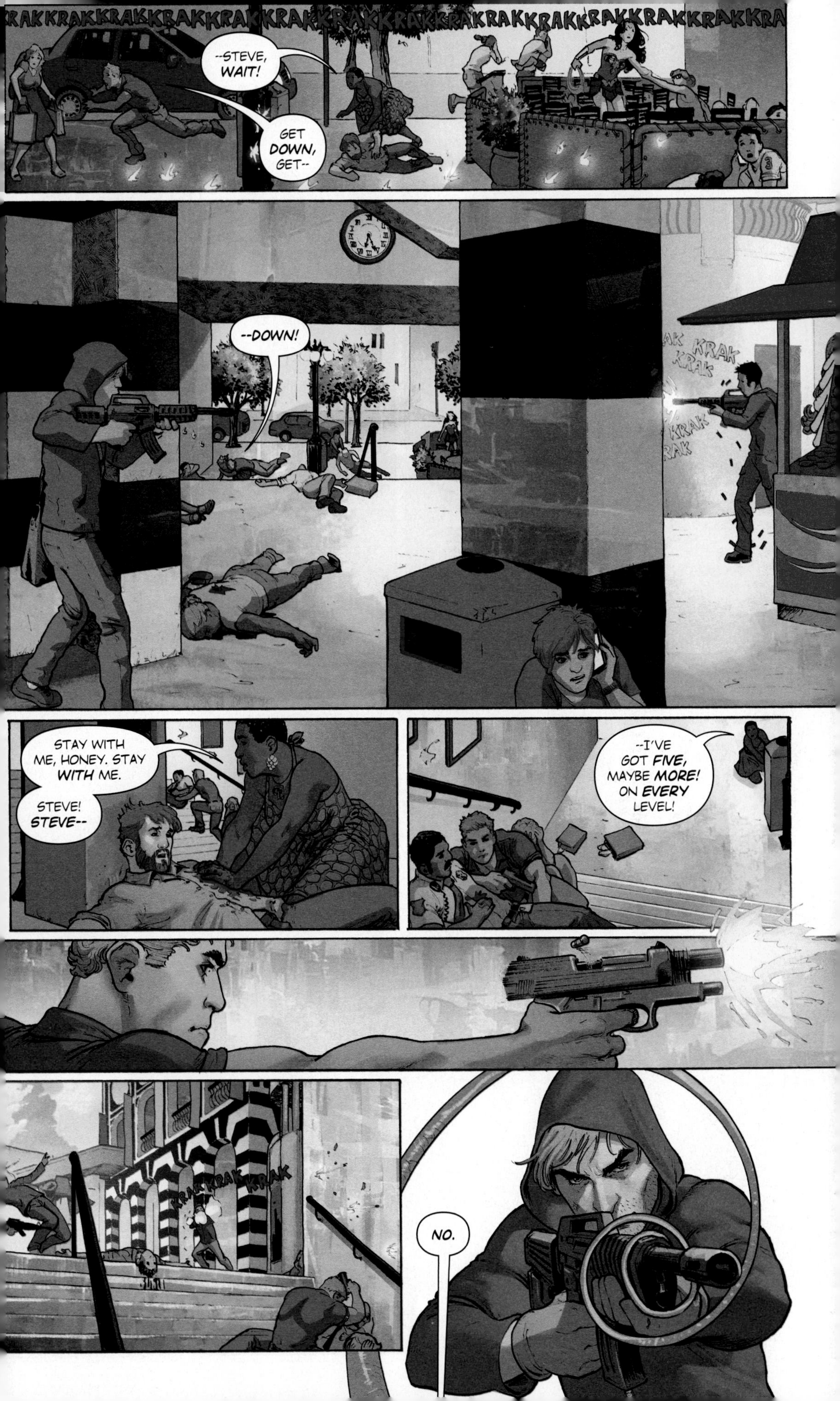

KRAK KRAK KRAK KRAK KRAK KRAK KRAK KRAK KRAK KRAK KRAK KRAK KRAK KRAK KRAK
--STEVE, WAIT!
GET DOWN, GET--
--DOWN!
KRAK KRAK KRAK
KRAK KRAK
STAY WITH ME, HONEY. STAY WITH ME.
STEVE! STEVE--
--I'VE GOT FIVE, MAYBE MORE! ON EVERY LEVEL!
KRAK KRAK KRAK
NO.

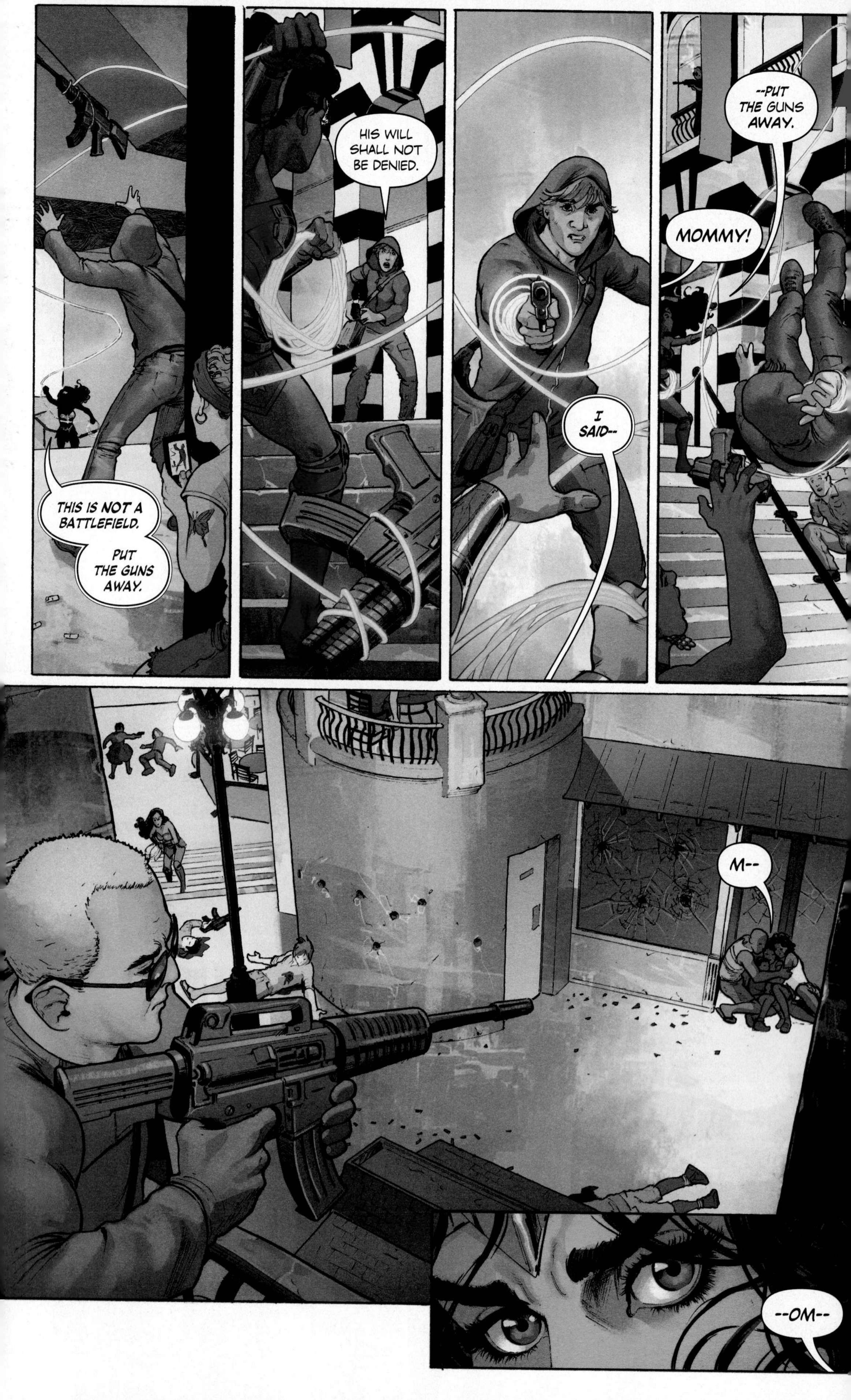
THIS IS NOT A BATTLEFIELD.
PUT THE GUNS AWAY.
HIS WILL SHALL NOT BE DENIED.
I SAID--
--PUT THE GUNS AWAY.
MOMMY!
M--
--OM--

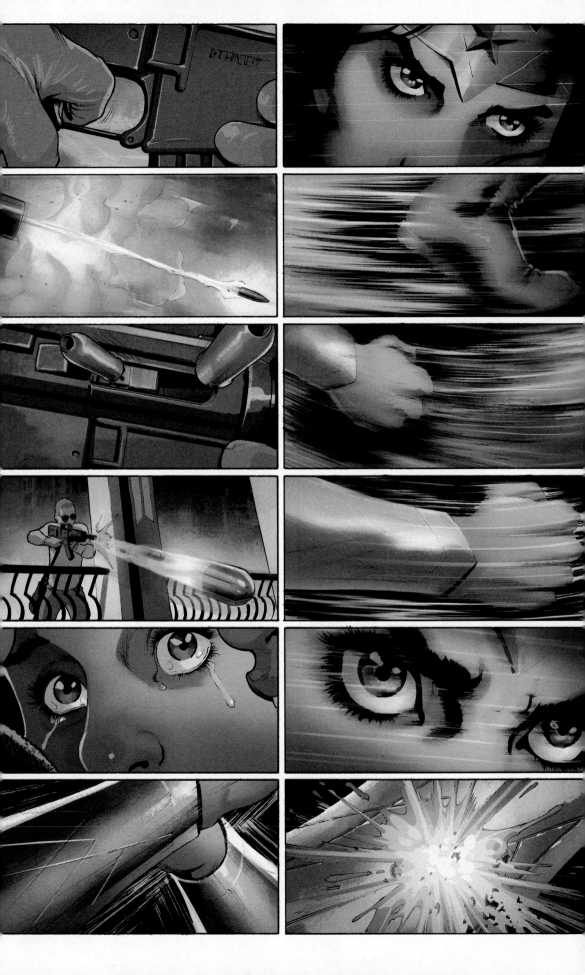

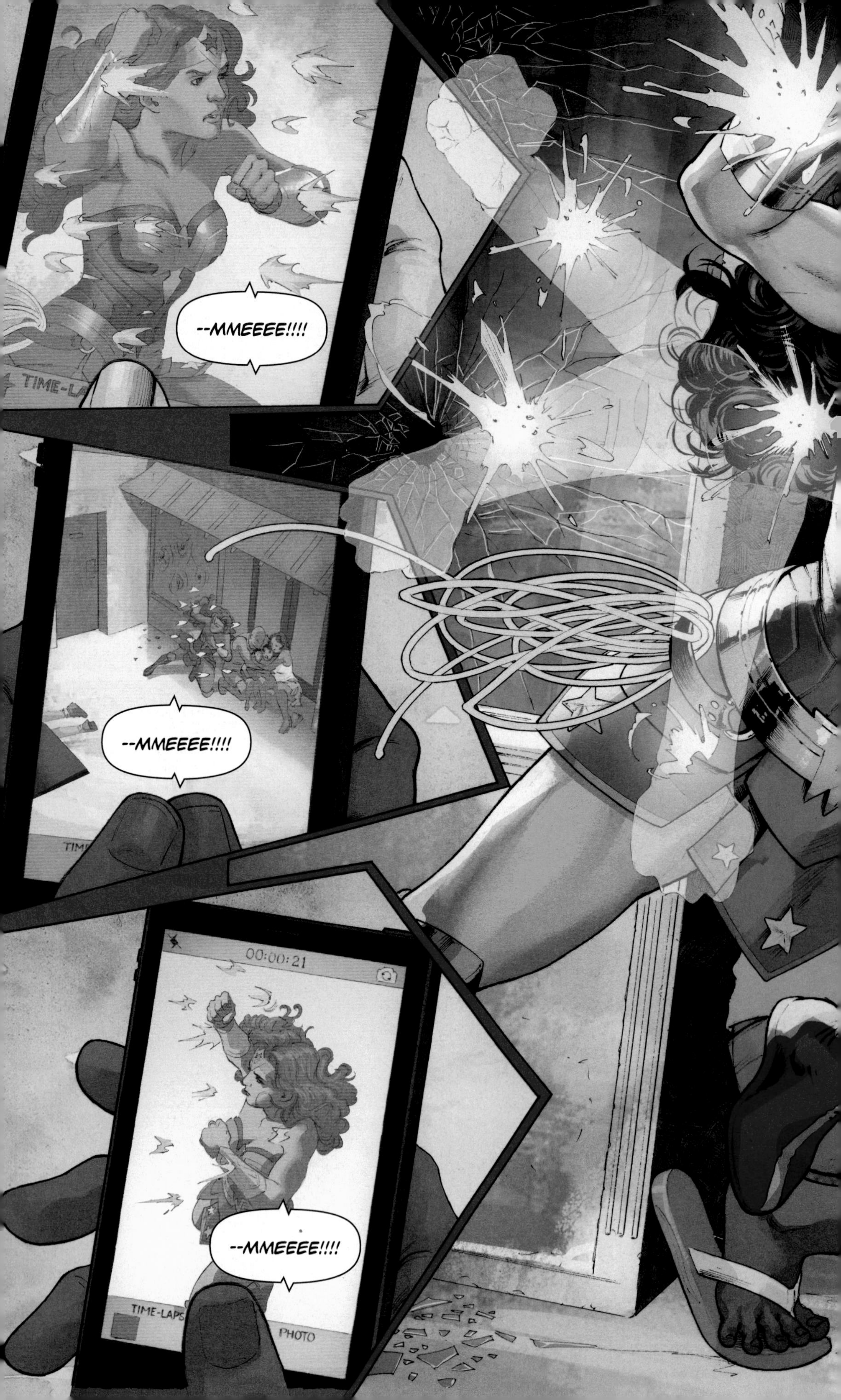
--MMEEEE!!!!
TIME-LA
--MMEEEE!!!!
TIME
00:00:21
--MMEEEE!!!!
TIME-LAPS
PHOTO

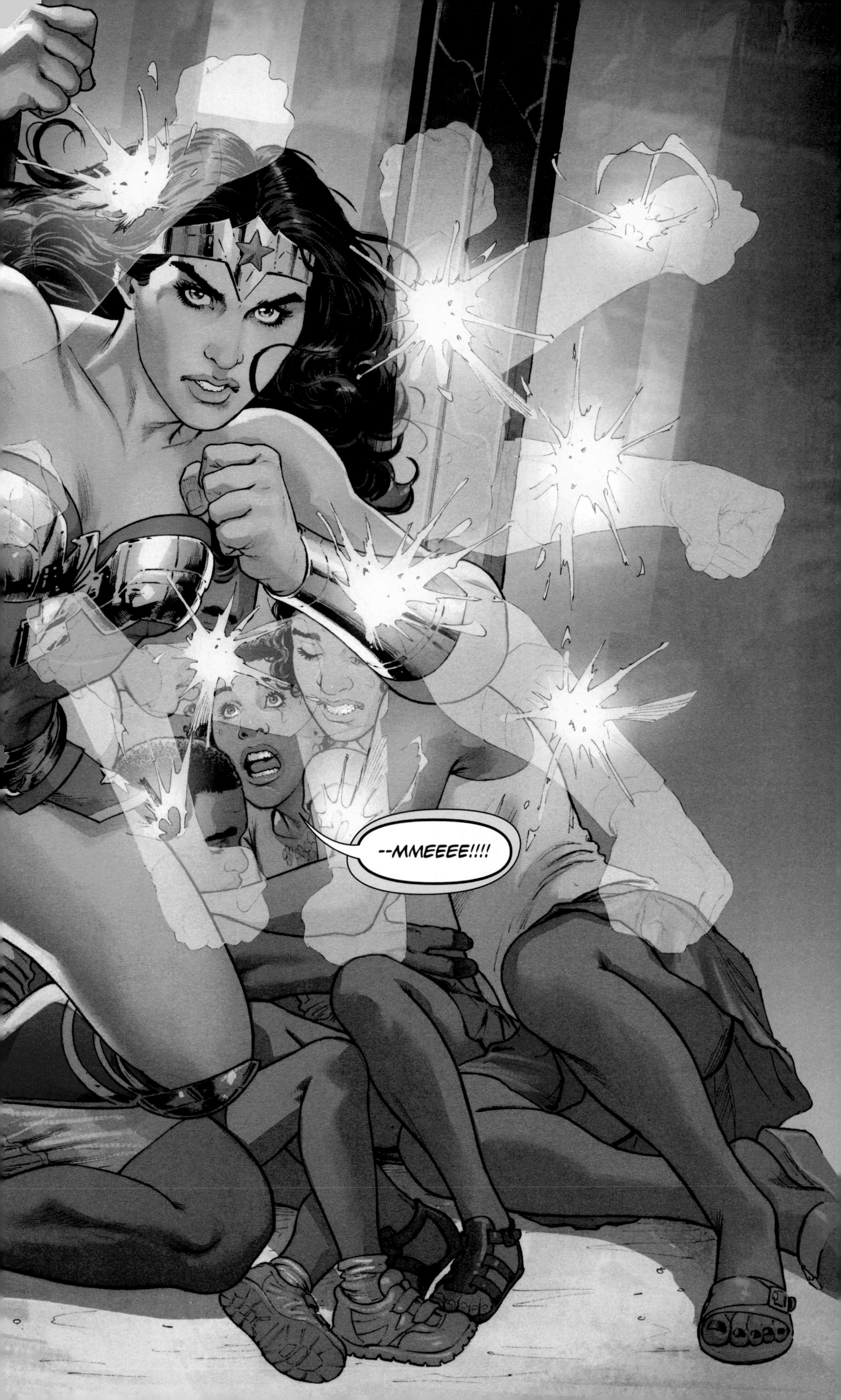
--MMEEEE!!!!

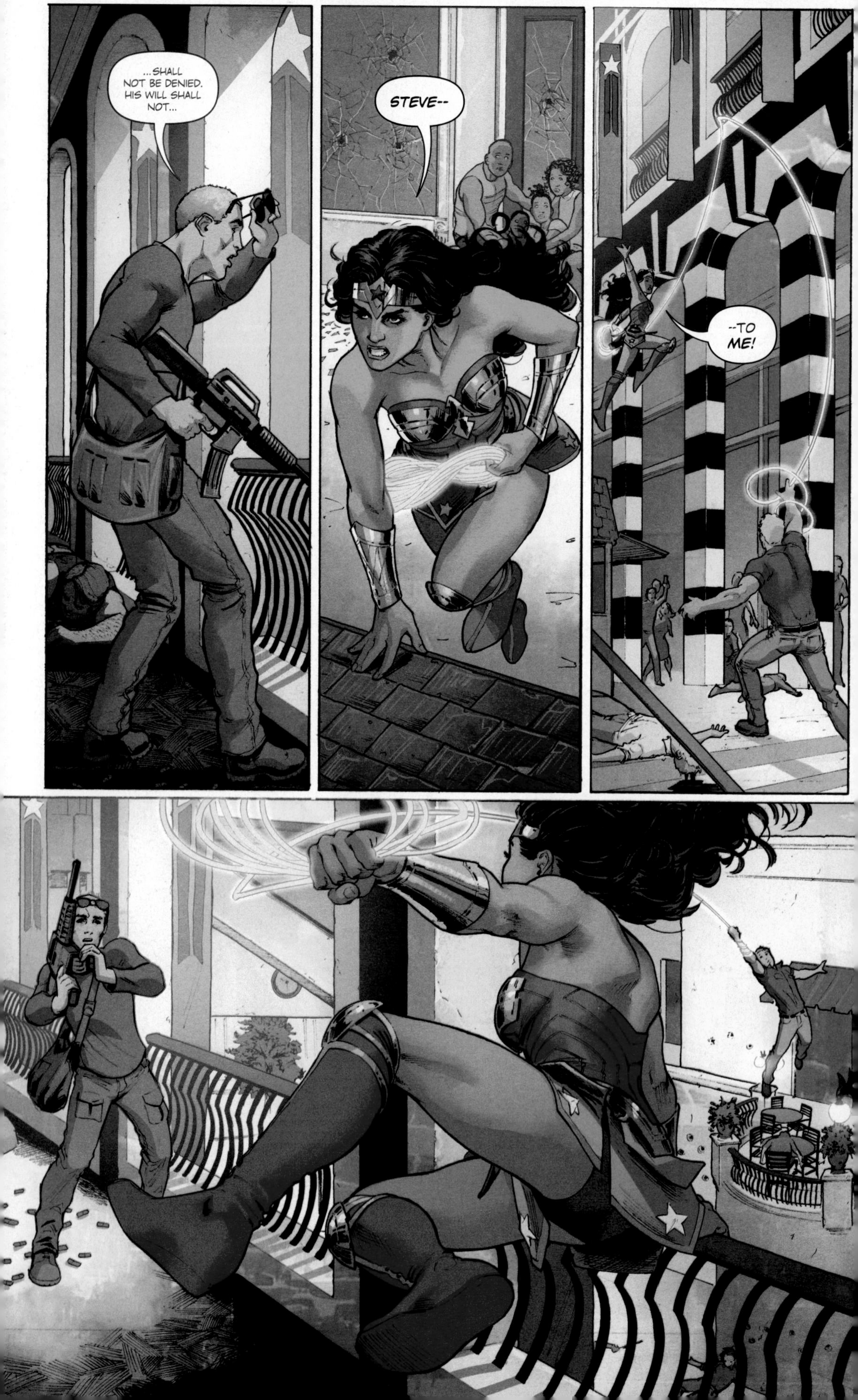
...SHALL NOT BE DENIED. HIS WILL SHALL NOT...
STEVE--
--TO ME!

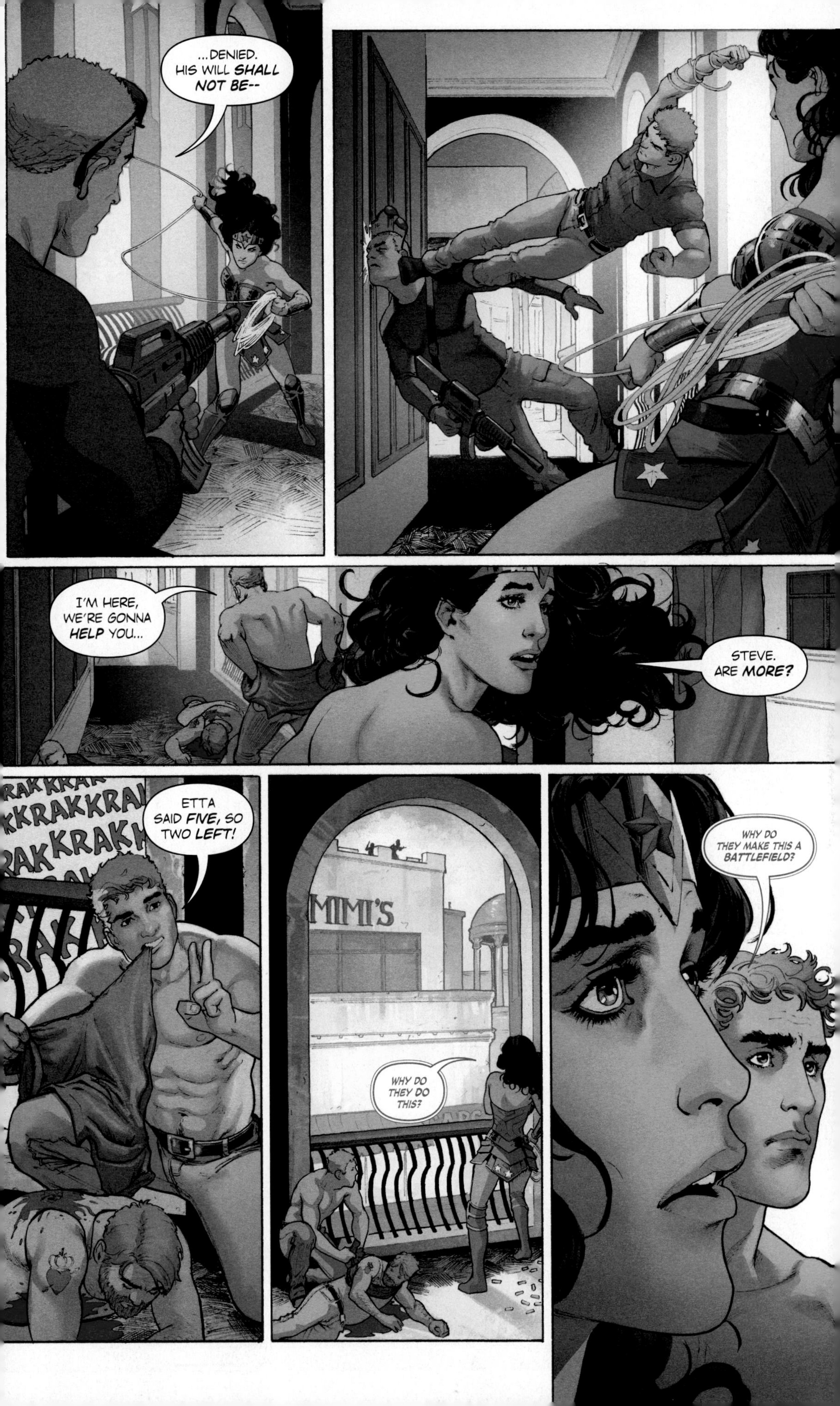
...DENIED. HIS WILL SHALL NOT BE--
I'M HERE, WE'RE GONNA HELP YOU...
STEVE. ARE MORE?
KRAKKRAKKRAKKRAK
ETTA SAID FIVE, SO TWO LEFT!
MIMI'S
WHY DO THEY DO THIS?
WHY DO THEY MAKE THIS A BATTLEFIELD?

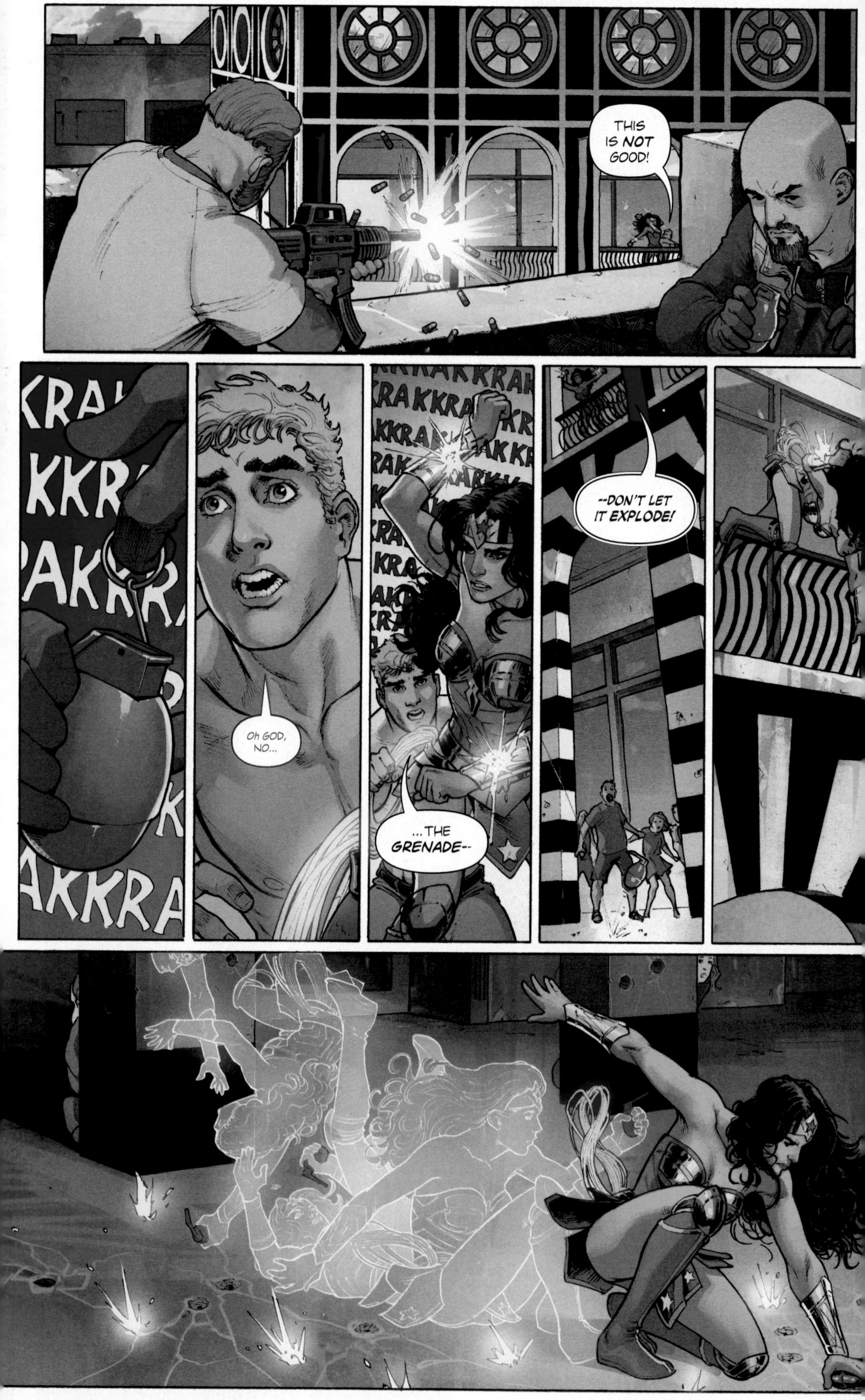
THIS IS NOT GOOD!
KRAKKRAKKRAKKRA
Oh GOD, NO...
...THE GRENADE--
--DON'T LET IT EXPLODE!

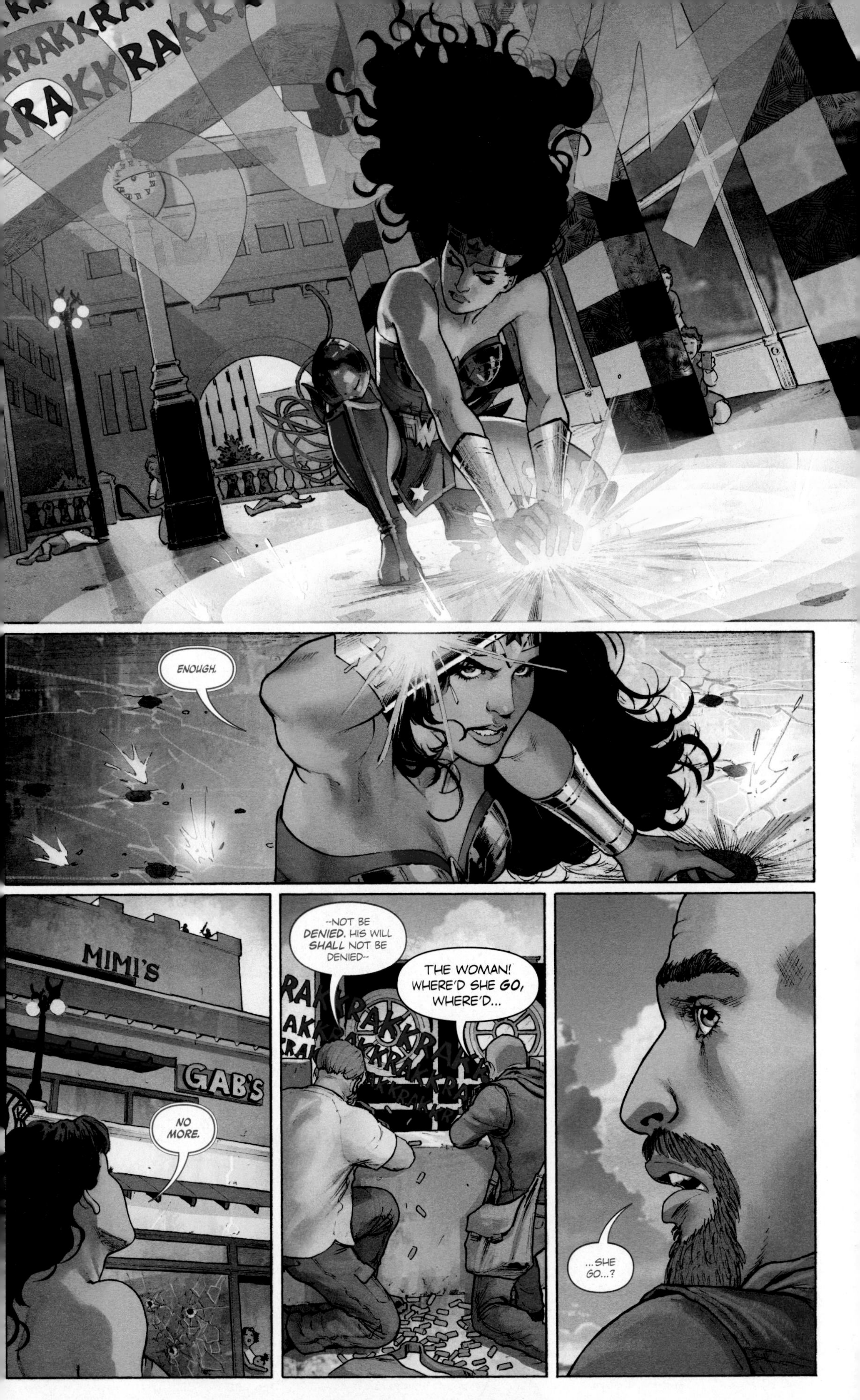
RAKKRAKKRAKKRAKK
ENOUGH.
MIMI'S
GAB'S
NO MORE.
--NOT BE DENIED. HIS WILL SHALL NOT BE DENIED--
THE WOMAN! WHERE'D SHE GO, WHERE'D...
RAKKRAKKRAKKRAKK
...SHE GO...?

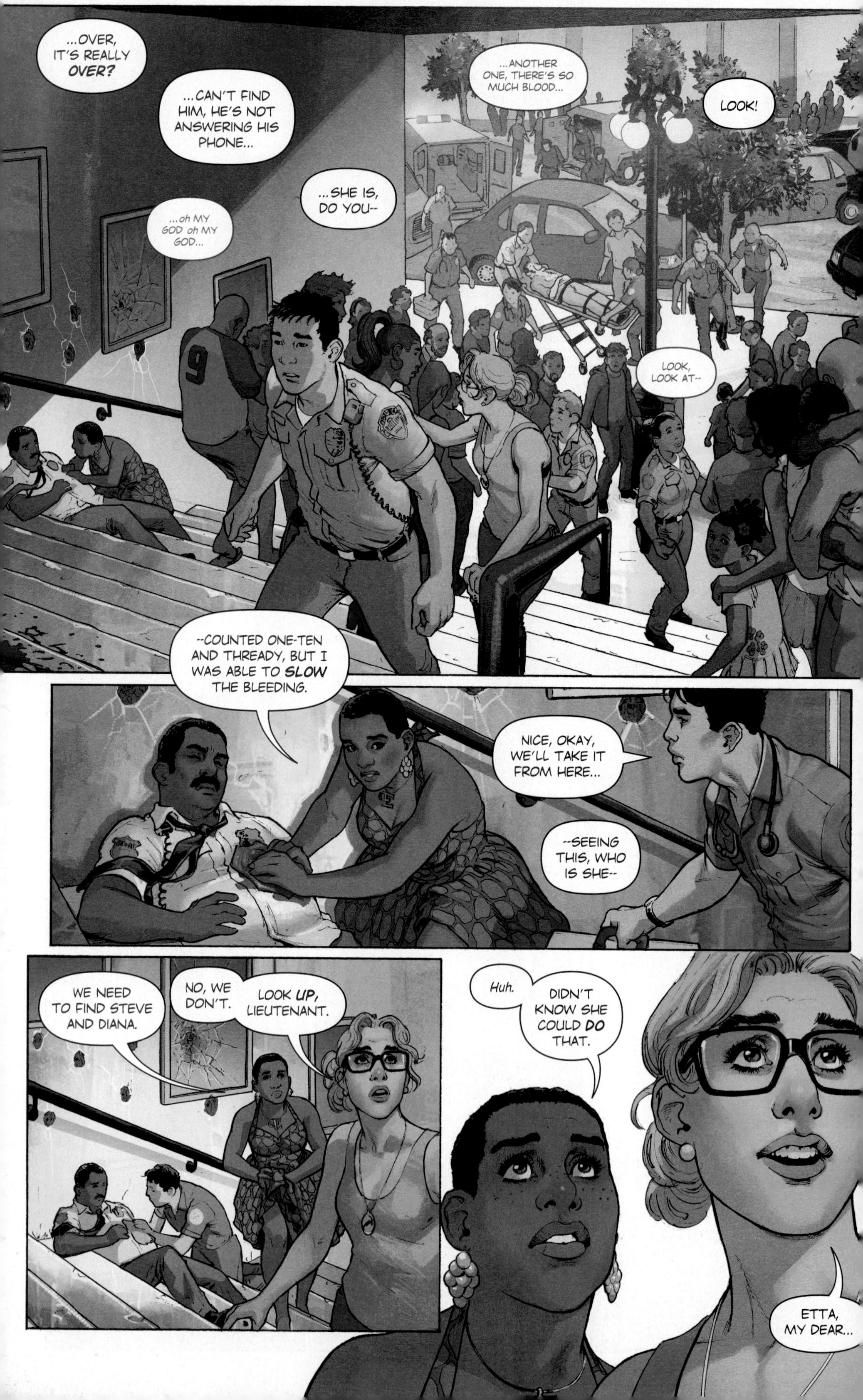
...OVER, IT'S REALLY **OVER?**
...CAN'T FIND HIM, HE'S NOT ANSWERING HIS PHONE...
...oh MY GOD oh MY GOD...
...SHE IS, DO YOU--
...ANOTHER ONE, THERE'S SO MUCH BLOOD...
LOOK!
LOOK, LOOK AT--
--COUNTED ONE-TEN AND THREADY, BUT I WAS ABLE TO **SLOW** THE BLEEDING.
NICE, OKAY, WE'LL TAKE IT FROM HERE...
--SEEING THIS, WHO IS SHE--
WE NEED TO FIND STEVE AND DIANA.
NO, WE DON'T.
LOOK **UP**, LIEUTENANT.
Huh.
DIDN'T KNOW SHE COULD **DO** THAT.
ETTA, MY DEAR...

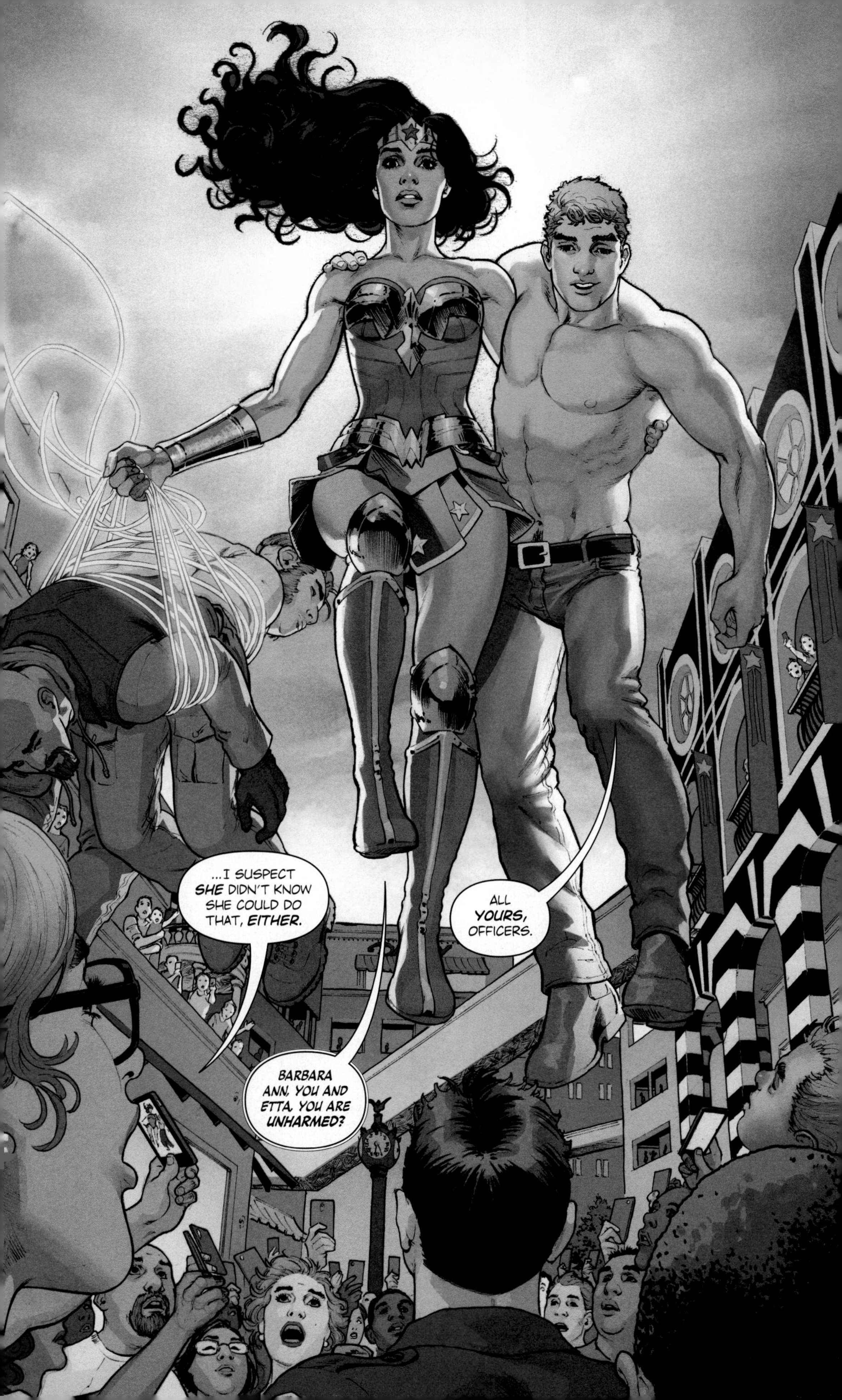
...I SUSPECT SHE DIDN'T KNOW SHE COULD DO THAT, EITHER.
ALL YOURS, OFFICERS.
BARBARA ANN, YOU AND ETTA, YOU ARE UNHARMED?

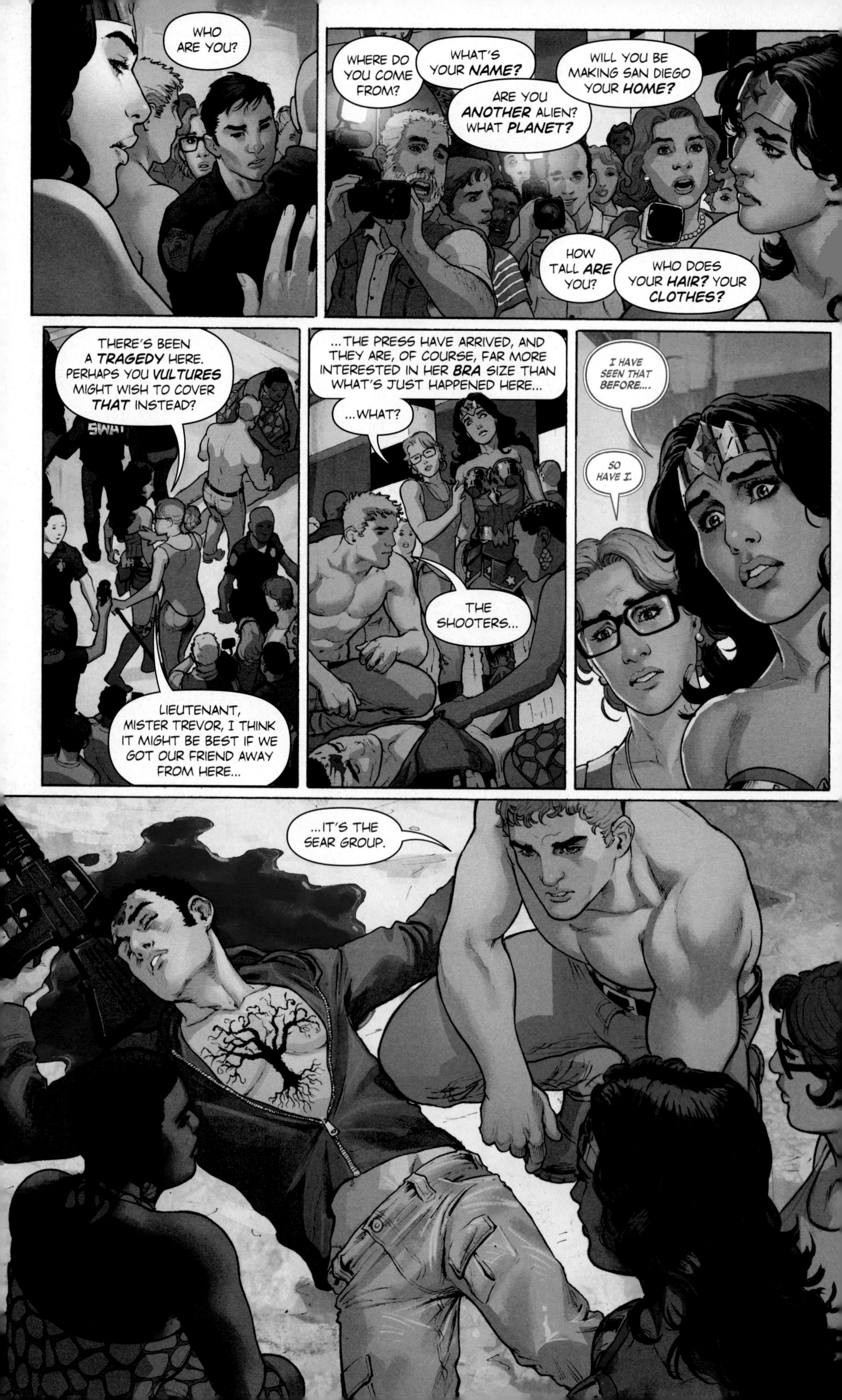
WHO ARE YOU?
WHERE DO YOU COME FROM?
WHAT'S YOUR NAME?
ARE YOU ANOTHER ALIEN? WHAT PLANET?
WILL YOU BE MAKING SAN DIEGO YOUR HOME?
HOW TALL ARE YOU?
WHO DOES YOUR HAIR? YOUR CLOTHES?
THERE'S BEEN A TRAGEDY HERE. PERHAPS YOU VULTURES MIGHT WISH TO COVER THAT INSTEAD?
LIEUTENANT, MISTER TREVOR, I THINK IT MIGHT BE BEST IF WE GOT OUR FRIEND AWAY FROM HERE...
...THE PRESS HAVE ARRIVED, AND THEY ARE, OF COURSE, FAR MORE INTERESTED IN HER BRA SIZE THAN WHAT'S JUST HAPPENED HERE...
...WHAT?
THE SHOOTERS...
I HAVE SEEN THAT BEFORE....
SO HAVE I.
...IT'S THE SEAR GROUP.

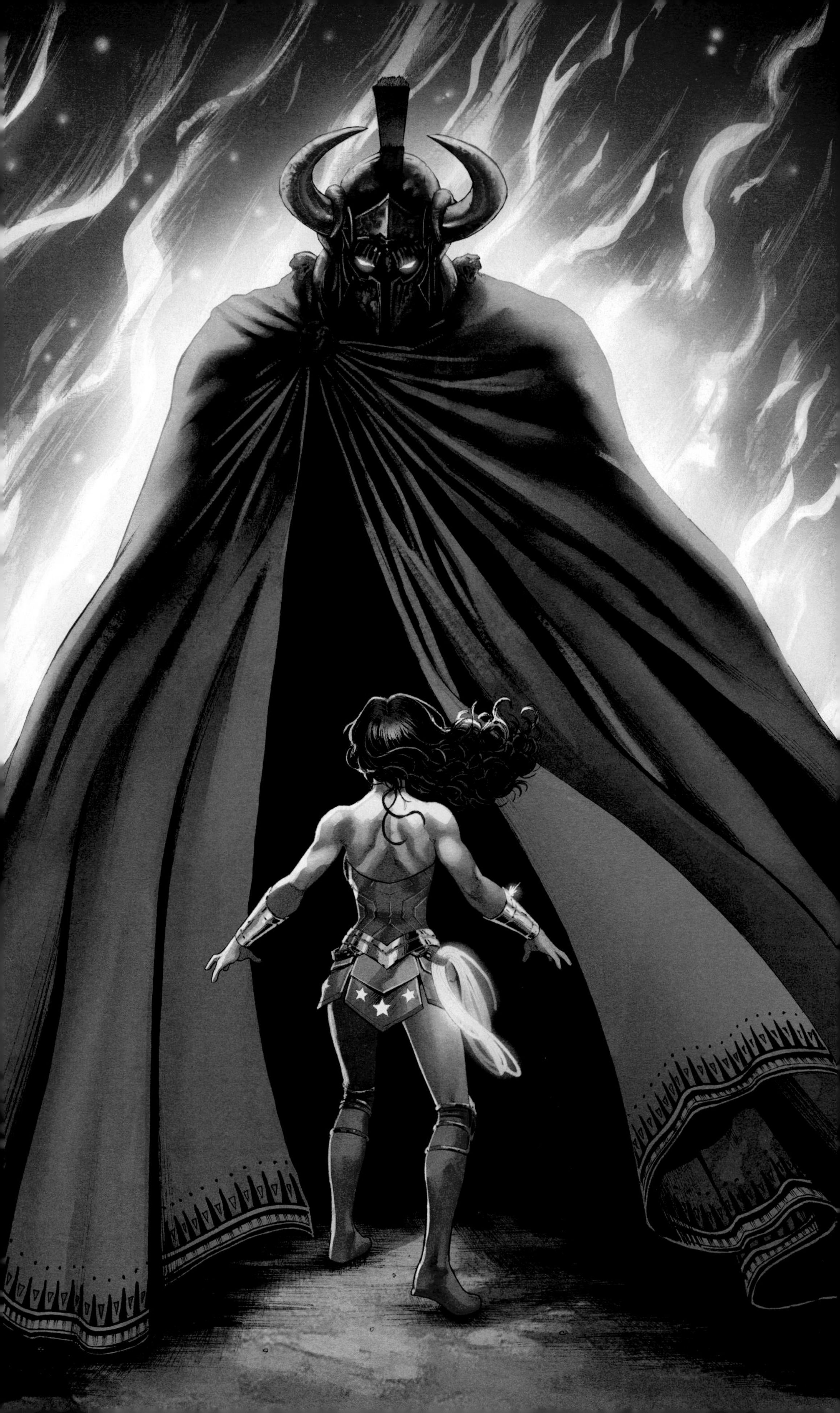

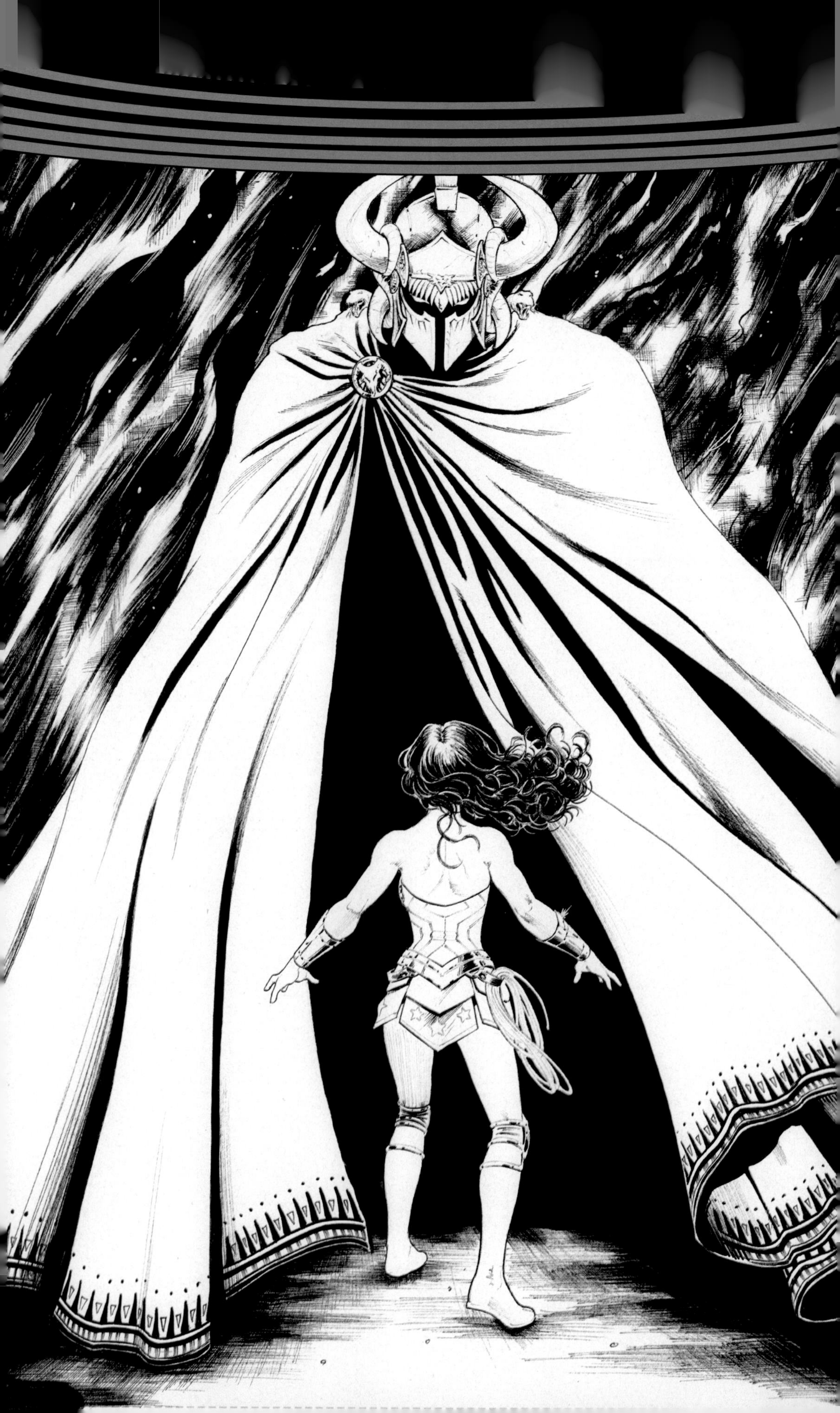

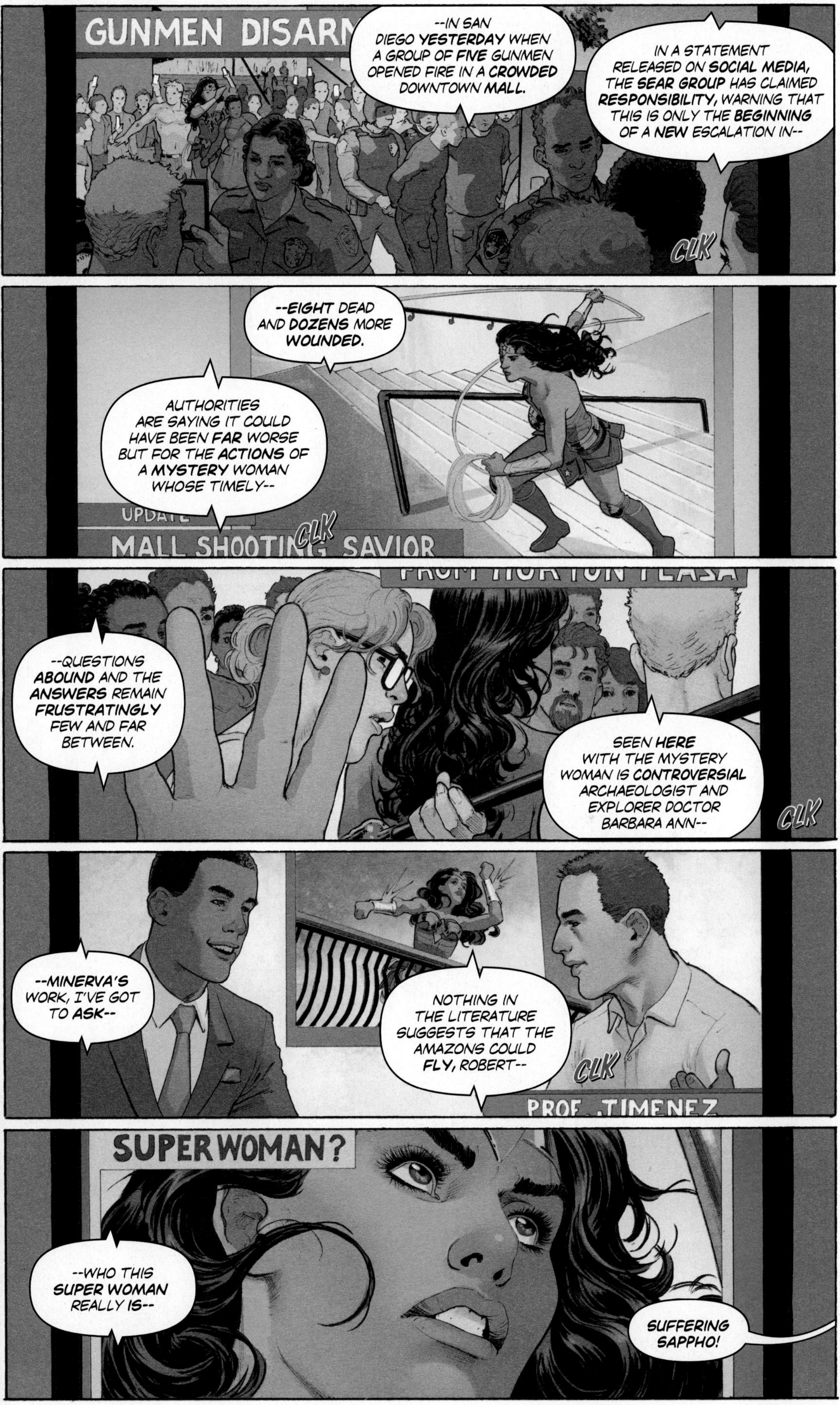
GUNMEN DISARM
--IN SAN DIEGO YESTERDAY WHEN A GROUP OF FIVE GUNMEN OPENED FIRE IN A CROWDED DOWNTOWN MALL.
IN A STATEMENT RELEASED ON SOCIAL MEDIA, THE SEAR GROUP HAS CLAIMED RESPONSIBILITY, WARNING THAT THIS IS ONLY THE BEGINNING OF A NEW ESCALATION IN--
CLK
--EIGHT DEAD AND DOZENS MORE WOUNDED.
AUTHORITIES ARE SAYING IT COULD HAVE BEEN FAR WORSE BUT FOR THE ACTIONS OF A MYSTERY WOMAN WHOSE TIMELY--
UPDATE
MALL SHOOTING SAVIOR
CLK
--QUESTIONS ABOUND AND THE ANSWERS REMAIN FRUSTRATINGLY FEW AND FAR BETWEEN.
SEEN HERE WITH THE MYSTERY WOMAN IS CONTROVERSIAL ARCHAEOLOGIST AND EXPLORER DOCTOR BARBARA ANN--
CLK
--MINERVA'S WORK, I'VE GOT TO ASK--
NOTHING IN THE LITERATURE SUGGESTS THAT THE AMAZONS COULD FLY, ROBERT--
CLK
PROF. JIMENEZ
SUPERWOMAN?
--WHO THIS SUPER WOMAN REALLY IS--
SUFFERING SAPPHO!

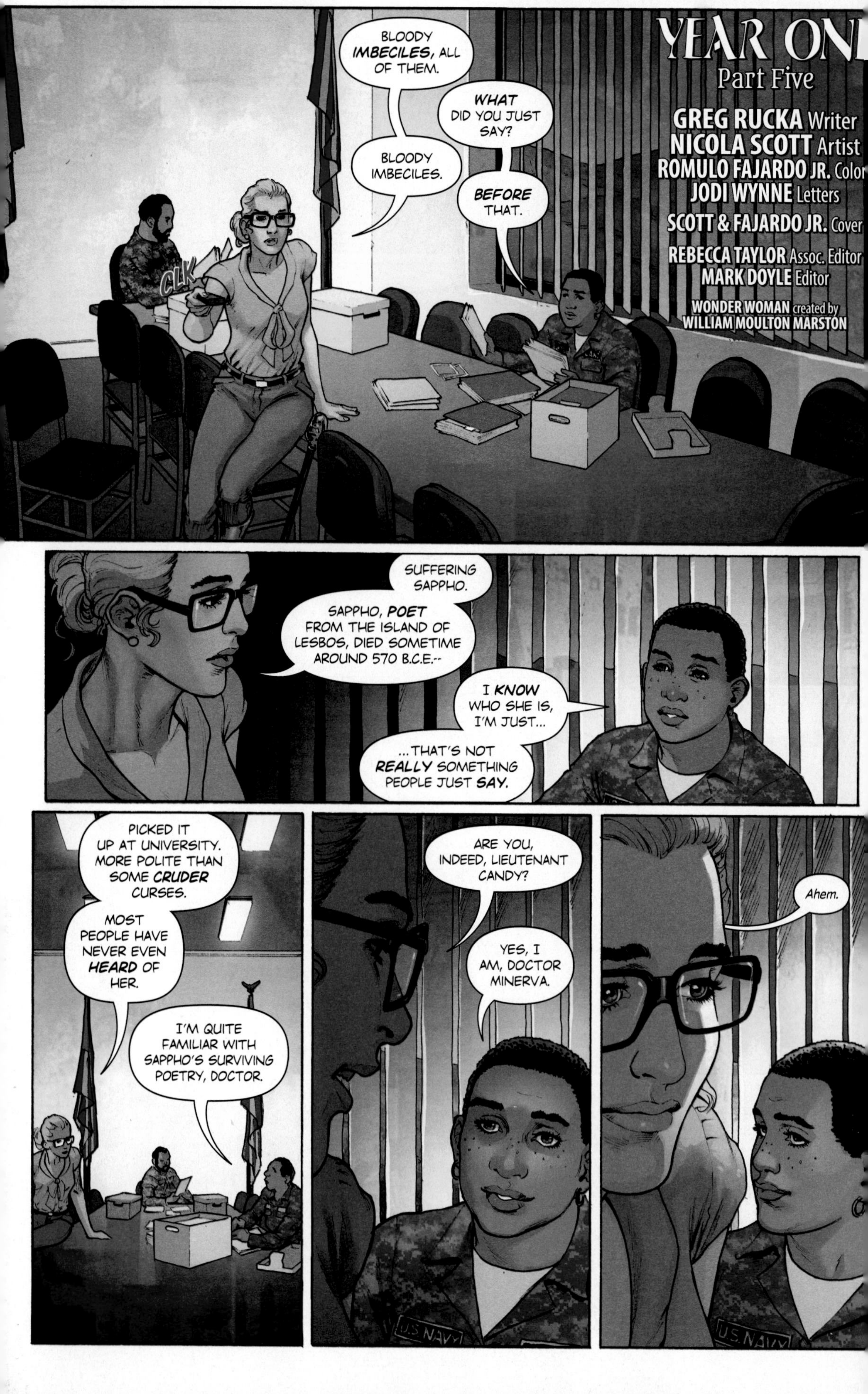
YEAR ONE
Part Five
GREG RUCKA Writer
NICOLA SCOTT Artist
ROMULO FAJARDO JR. Color
JODI WYNNE Letters
SCOTT & FAJARDO JR. Cover
REBECCA TAYLOR Assoc. Editor
MARK DOYLE Editor
WONDER WOMAN created by WILLIAM MOULTON MARSTON
CLK
BLOODY IMBECILES, ALL OF THEM.
WHAT DID YOU JUST SAY?
BLOODY IMBECILES.
BEFORE THAT.
SUFFERING SAPPHO.
SAPPHO, POET FROM THE ISLAND OF LESBOS, DIED SOMETIME AROUND 570 B.C.E.--
I KNOW WHO SHE IS, I'M JUST...
...THAT'S NOT REALLY SOMETHING PEOPLE JUST SAY.
PICKED IT UP AT UNIVERSITY. MORE POLITE THAN SOME CRUDER CURSES.
MOST PEOPLE HAVE NEVER EVEN HEARD OF HER.
I'M QUITE FAMILIAR WITH SAPPHO'S SURVIVING POETRY, DOCTOR.
ARE YOU, INDEED, LIEUTENANT CANDY?
YES, I AM, DOCTOR MINERVA.
Ahem.
U.S. NAVY
U.S. NAVY

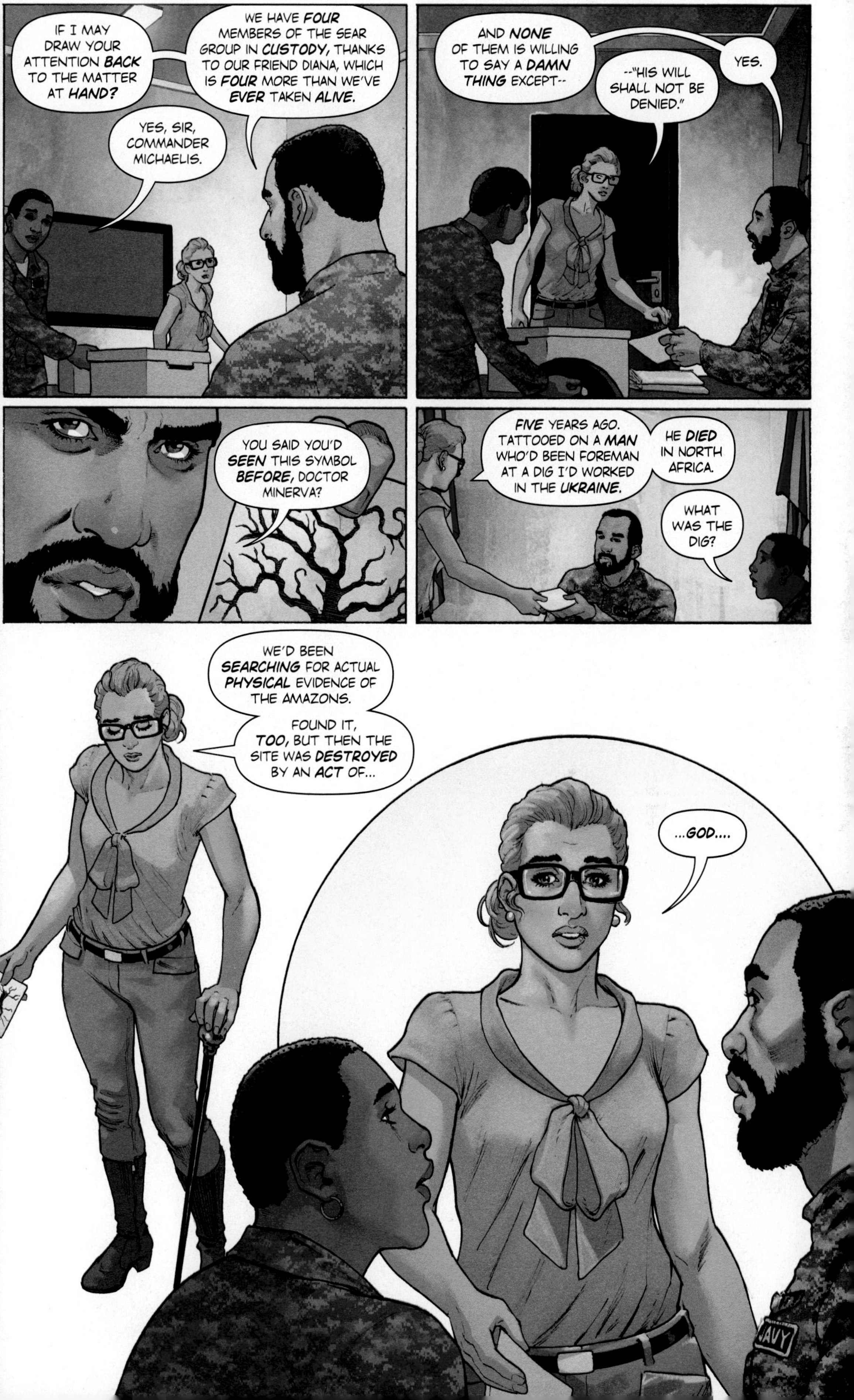
IF I MAY DRAW YOUR ATTENTION BACK TO THE MATTER AT HAND?
WE HAVE FOUR MEMBERS OF THE SEAR GROUP IN CUSTODY, THANKS TO OUR FRIEND DIANA, WHICH IS FOUR MORE THAN WE'VE EVER TAKEN ALIVE.
YES, SIR, COMMANDER MICHAELIS.
AND NONE OF THEM IS WILLING TO SAY A DAMN THING EXCEPT--
--"HIS WILL SHALL NOT BE DENIED."
YES.
YOU SAID YOU'D SEEN THIS SYMBOL BEFORE, DOCTOR MINERVA?
FIVE YEARS AGO. TATTOOED ON A MAN WHO'D BEEN FOREMAN AT A DIG I'D WORKED IN THE UKRAINE.
HE DIED IN NORTH AFRICA.
WHAT WAS THE DIG?
WE'D BEEN SEARCHING FOR ACTUAL PHYSICAL EVIDENCE OF THE AMAZONS.
FOUND IT, TOO, BUT THEN THE SITE WAS DESTROYED BY AN ACT OF...
...GOD....
NAVY

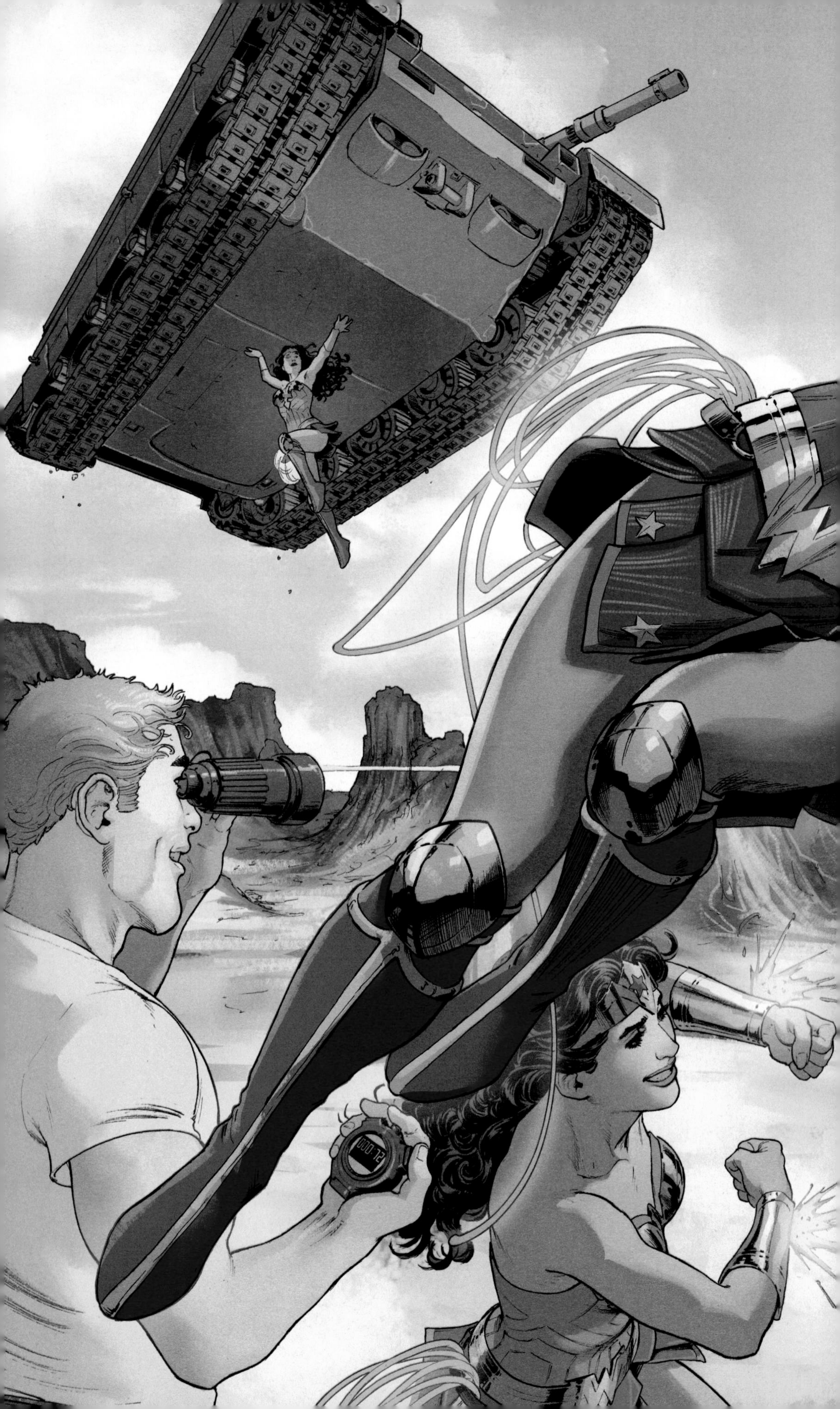

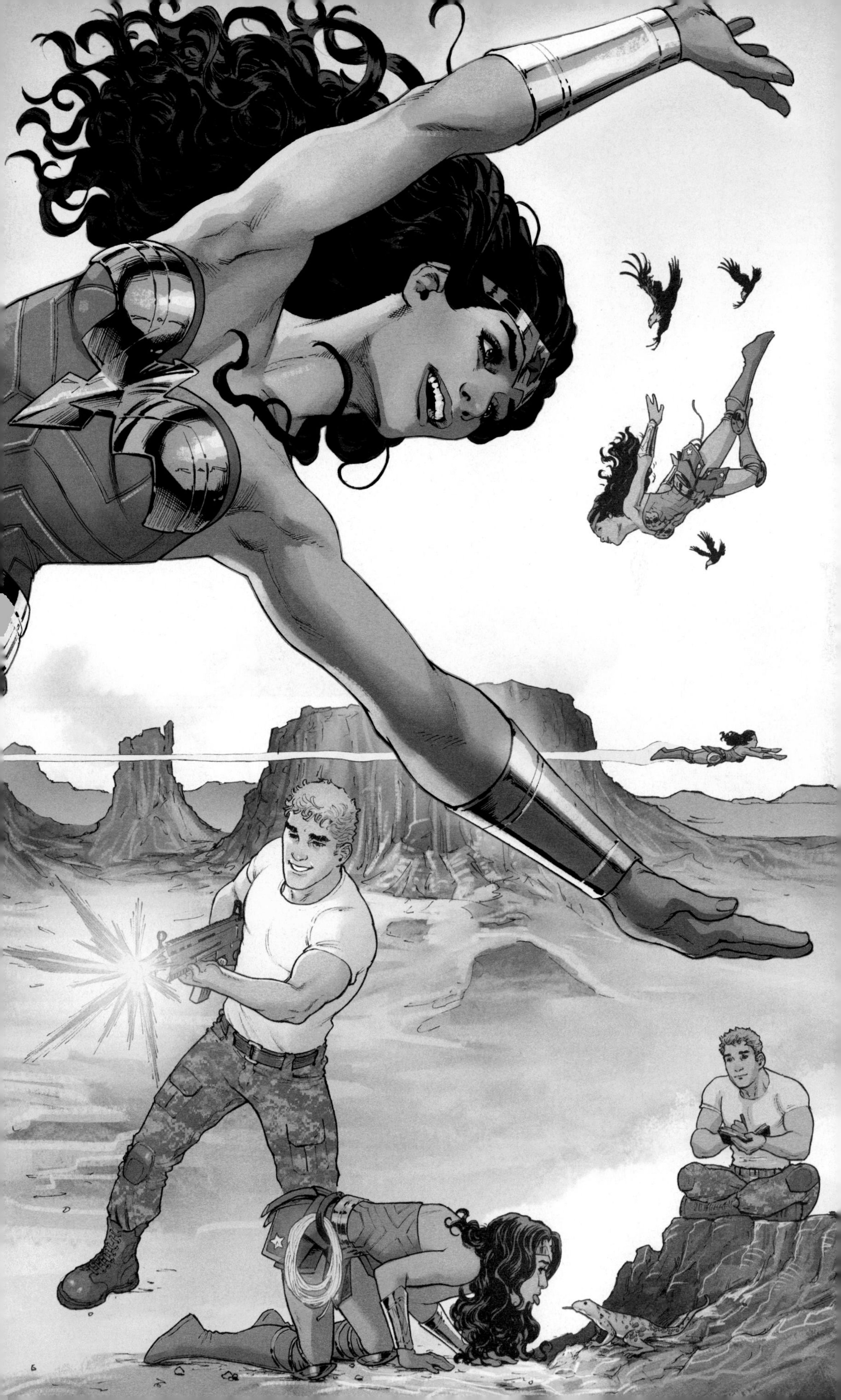

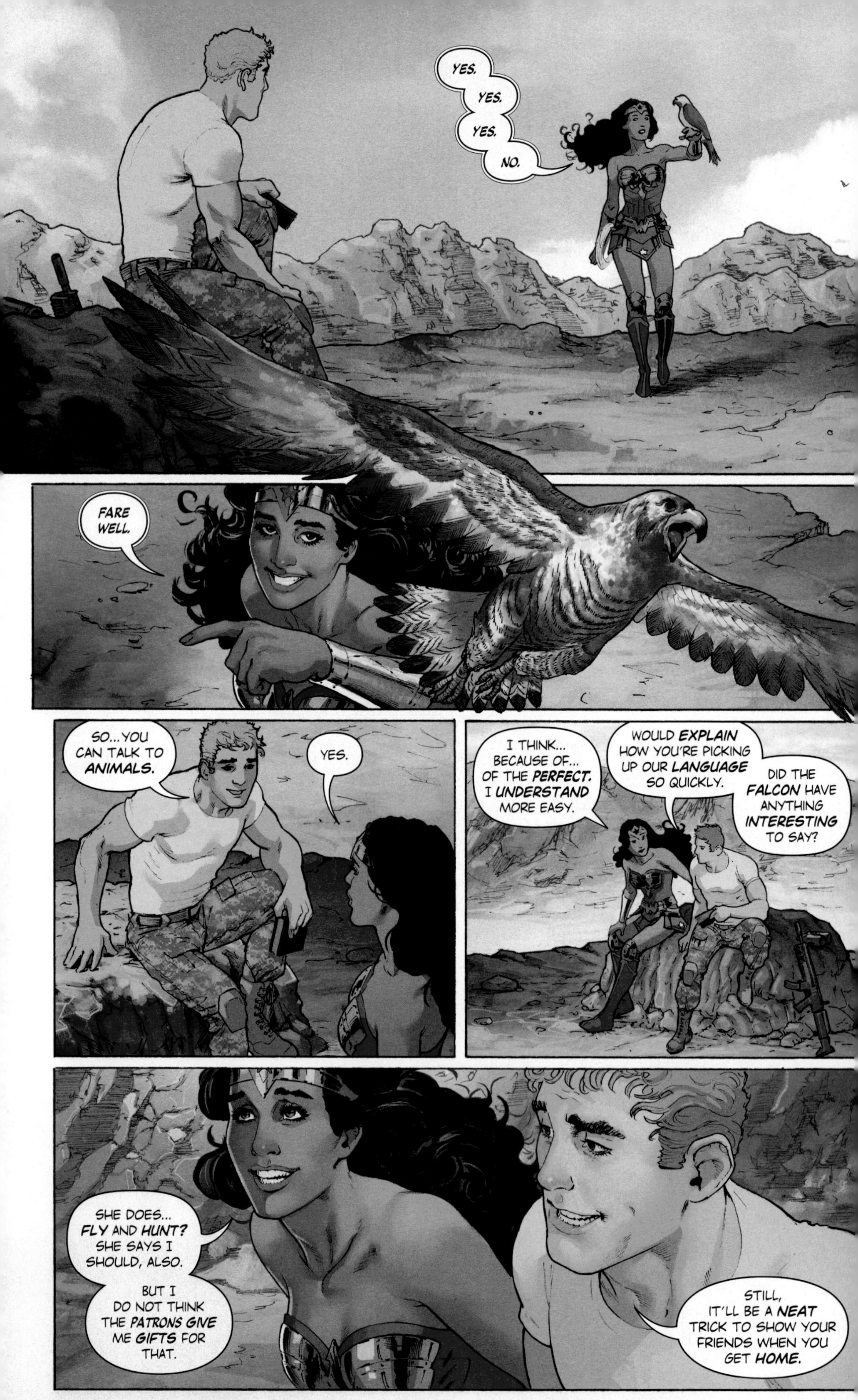
YES.
YES.
YES.
NO.
FARE WELL.
SO...YOU CAN TALK TO ANIMALS.
YES.
I THINK... BECAUSE OF... OF THE PERFECT. I UNDERSTAND MORE EASY.
WOULD EXPLAIN HOW YOU'RE PICKING UP OUR LANGUAGE SO QUICKLY.
DID THE FALCON HAVE ANYTHING INTERESTING TO SAY?
SHE DOES... FLY AND HUNT? SHE SAYS I SHOULD, ALSO.
BUT I DO NOT THINK THE PATRONS GIVE ME GIFTS FOR THAT.
STILL, IT'LL BE A NEAT TRICK TO SHOW YOUR FRIENDS WHEN YOU GET HOME.

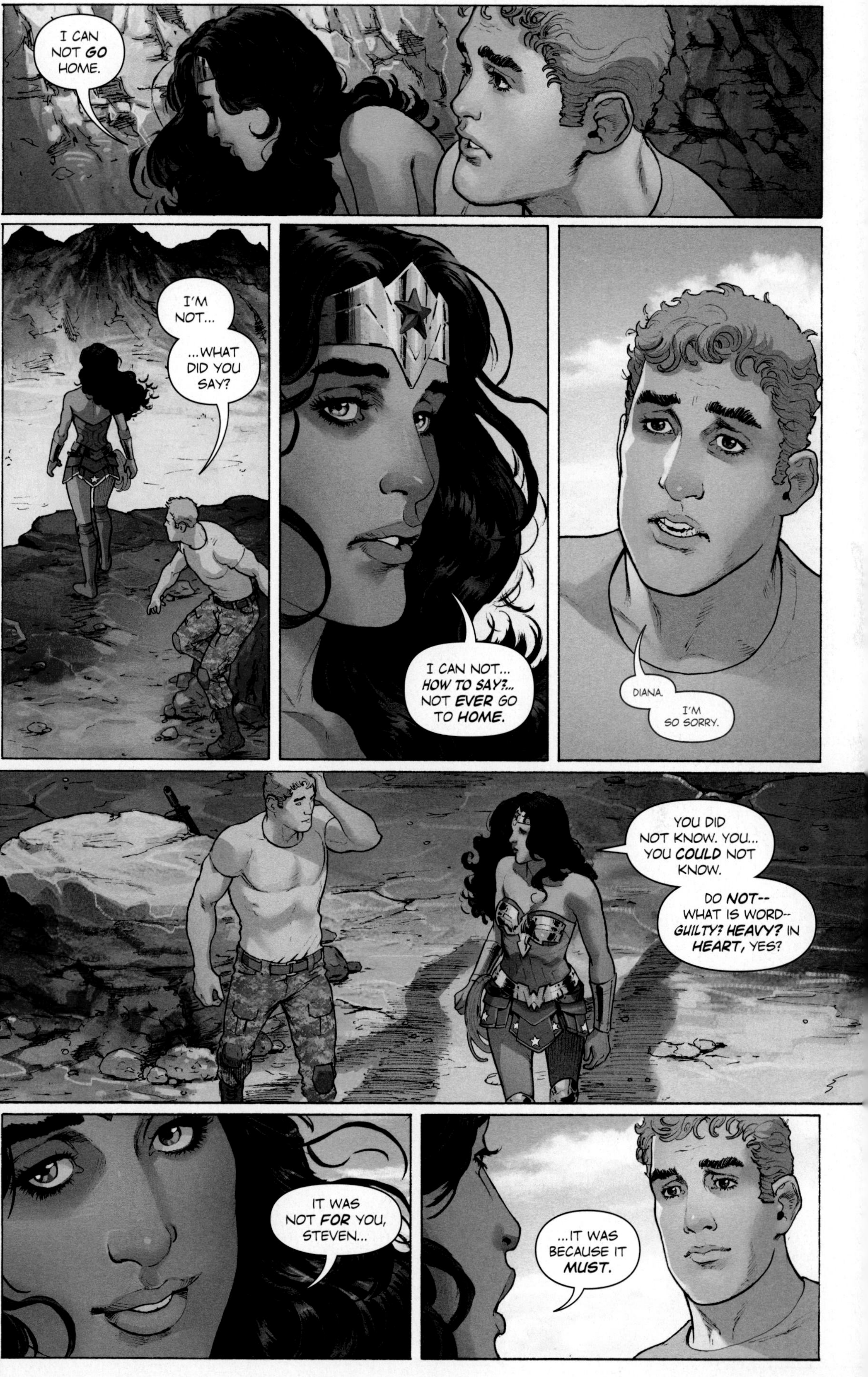
I CAN NOT GO HOME.
I'M NOT...
...WHAT DID YOU SAY?
I CAN NOT... HOW TO SAY?... NOT EVER GO TO HOME.
DIANA.
I'M SO SORRY.
YOU DID NOT KNOW. YOU... YOU COULD NOT KNOW.
DO NOT-- WHAT IS WORD-- GUILTY? HEAVY? IN HEART, YES?
IT WAS NOT FOR YOU, STEVEN...
...IT WAS BECAUSE IT MUST.

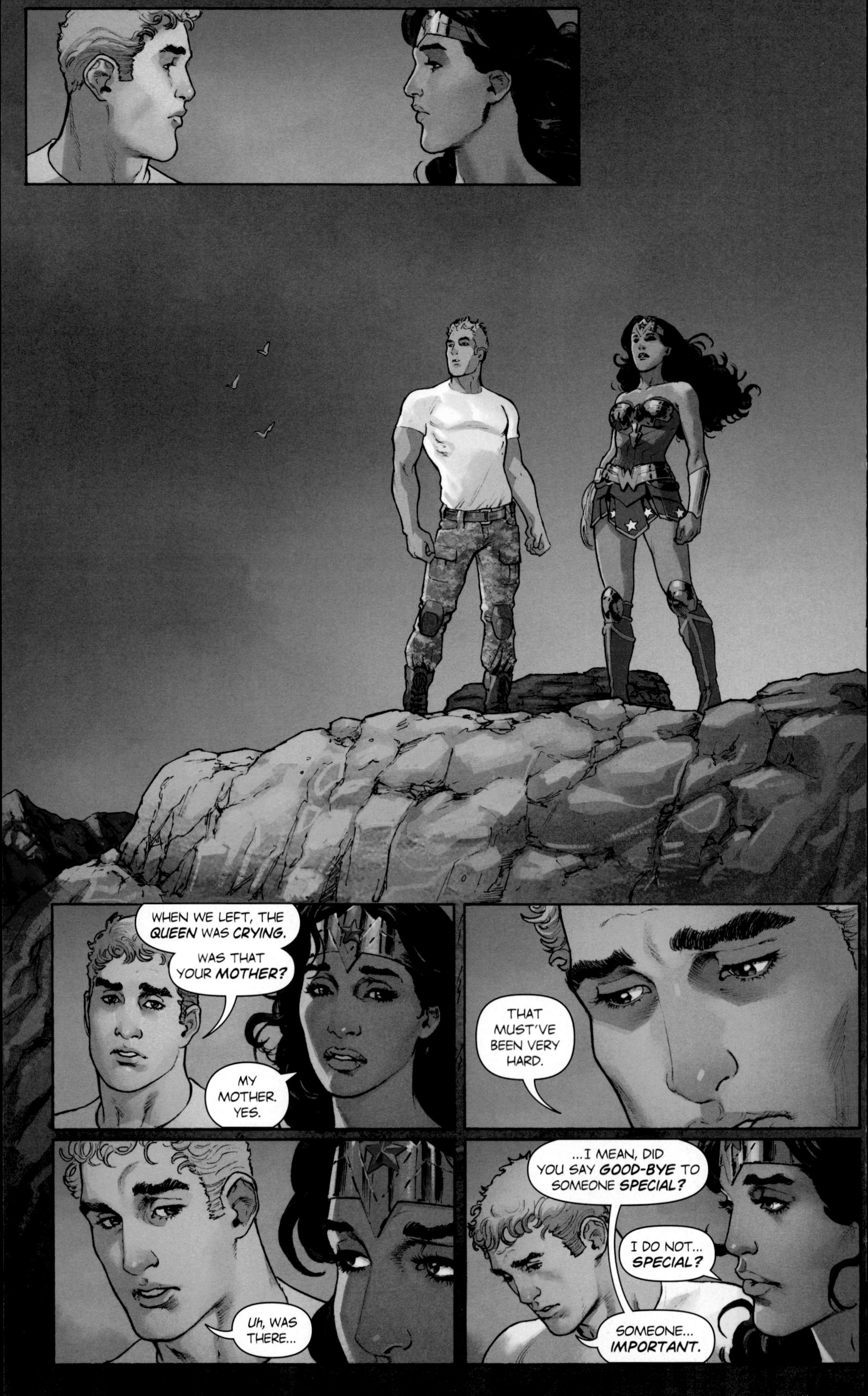
WHEN WE LEFT, THE QUEEN WAS CRYING.
WAS THAT YOUR MOTHER?
MY MOTHER. YES.
THAT MUST'VE BEEN VERY HARD.
Uh, WAS THERE...
...I MEAN, DID YOU SAY GOOD-BYE TO SOMEONE SPECIAL?
I DO NOT... SPECIAL?
SOMEONE... IMPORTANT.

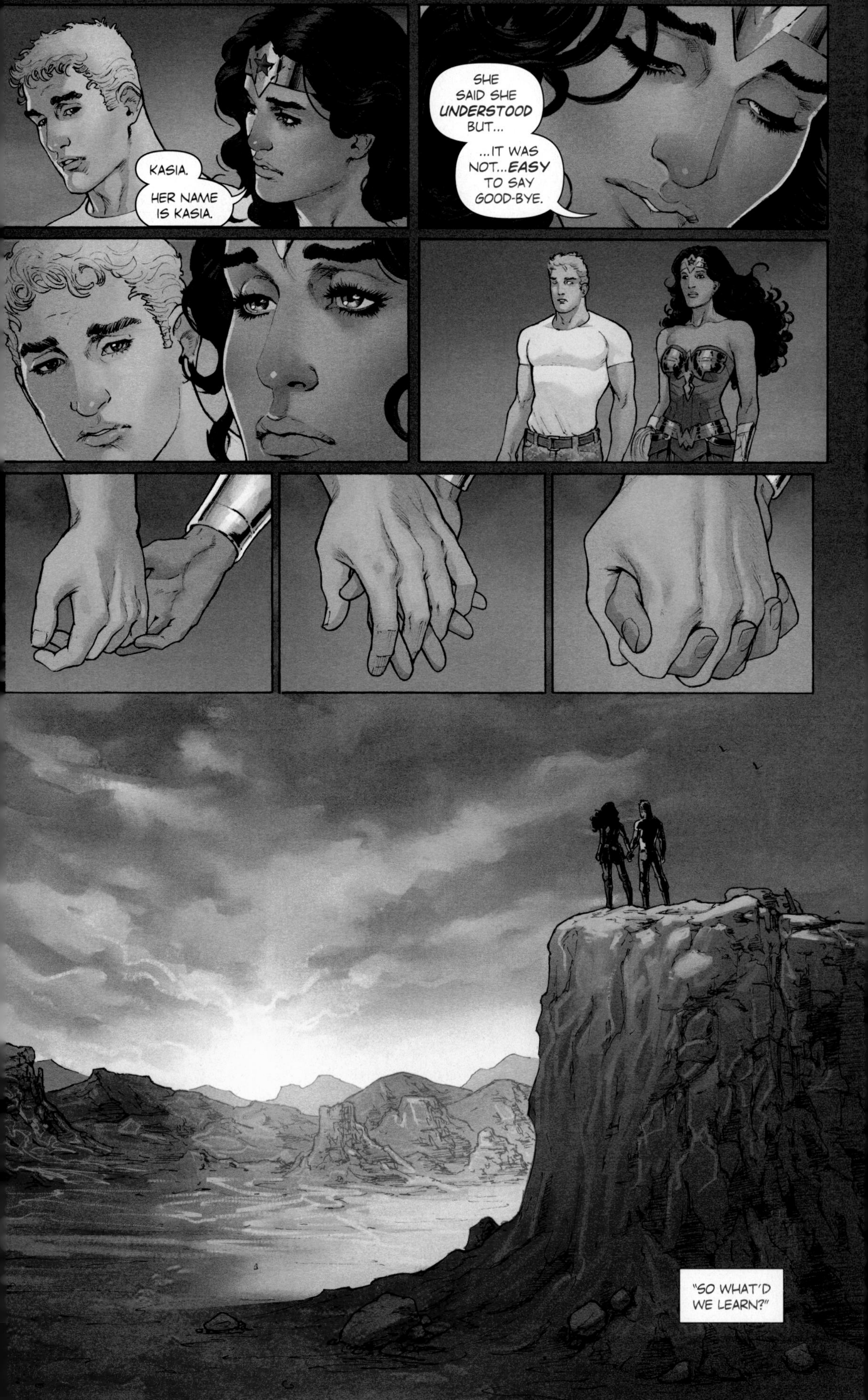
KASIA.
HER NAME IS KASIA.
SHE SAID SHE UNDERSTOOD BUT...
...IT WAS NOT...EASY TO SAY GOOD-BYE.
"SO WHAT'D WE LEARN?"

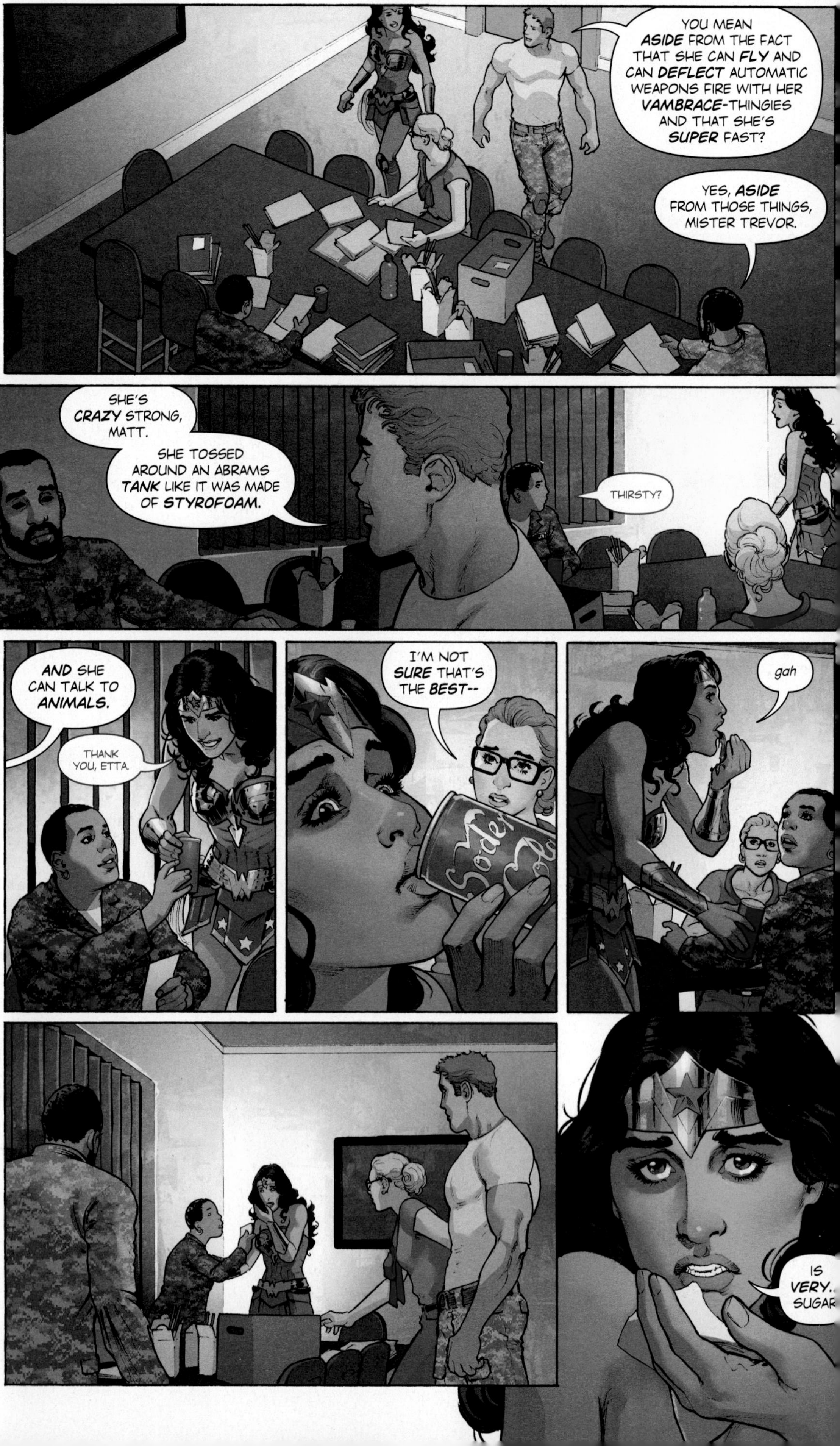
YOU MEAN ASIDE FROM THE FACT THAT SHE CAN FLY AND CAN DEFLECT AUTOMATIC WEAPONS FIRE WITH HER VAMBRACE-THINGIES AND THAT SHE'S SUPER FAST?
YES, ASIDE FROM THOSE THINGS, MISTER TREVOR.
SHE'S CRAZY STRONG, MATT.
SHE TOSSED AROUND AN ABRAMS TANK LIKE IT WAS MADE OF STYROFOAM.
THIRSTY?
AND SHE CAN TALK TO ANIMALS.
THANK YOU, ETTA.
I'M NOT SURE THAT'S THE BEST--
gah
IS VERY... SUGAR

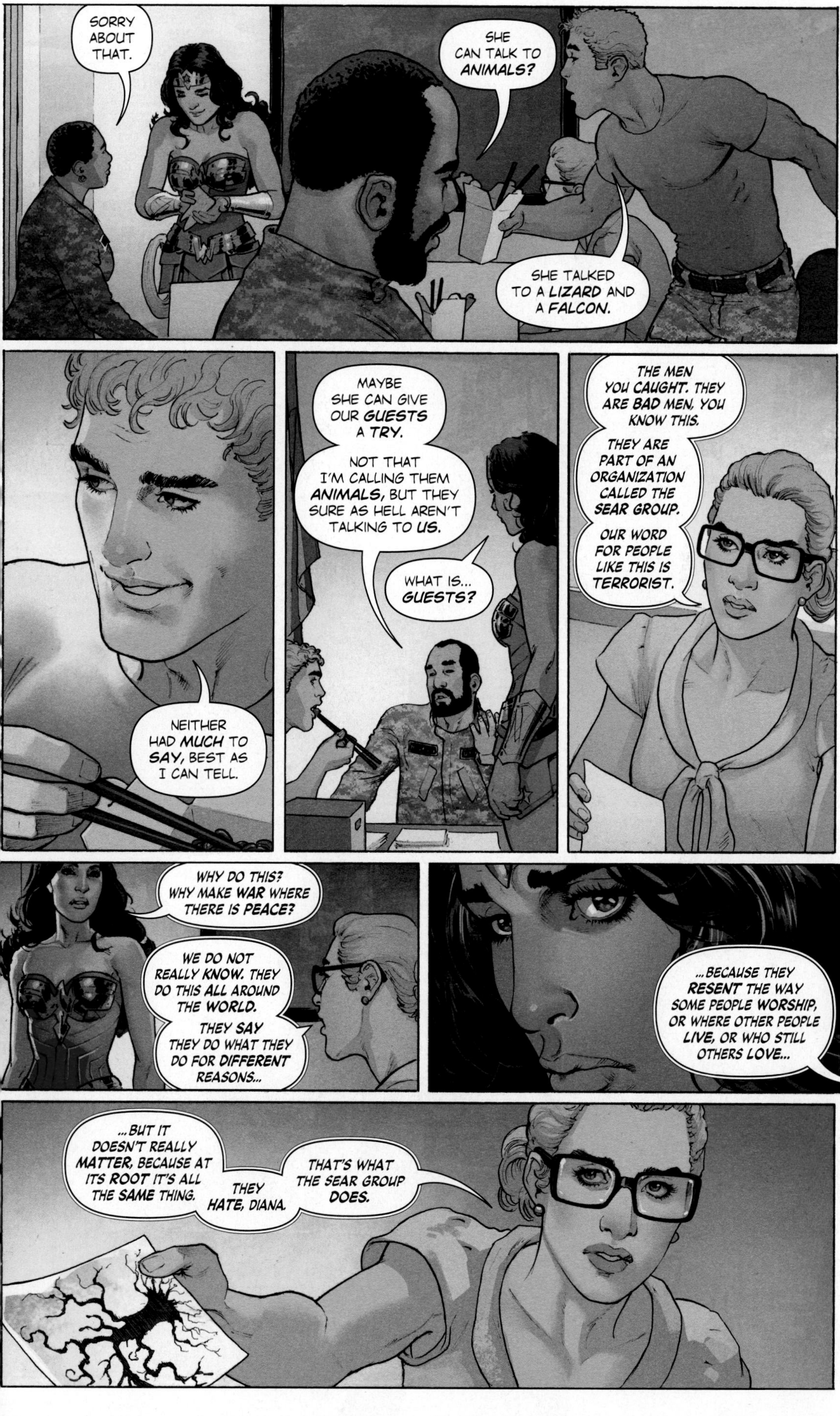

SORRY ABOUT THAT.
SHE CAN TALK TO ANIMALS?
SHE TALKED TO A LIZARD AND A FALCON.
NEITHER HAD MUCH TO SAY, BEST AS I CAN TELL.
MAYBE SHE CAN GIVE OUR GUESTS A TRY.
NOT THAT I'M CALLING THEM ANIMALS, BUT THEY SURE AS HELL AREN'T TALKING TO US.
WHAT IS... GUESTS?
THE MEN YOU CAUGHT. THEY ARE BAD MEN, YOU KNOW THIS.
THEY ARE PART OF AN ORGANIZATION CALLED THE SEAR GROUP.
OUR WORD FOR PEOPLE LIKE THIS IS TERRORIST.
WHY DO THIS? WHY MAKE WAR WHERE THERE IS PEACE?
WE DO NOT REALLY KNOW. THEY DO THIS ALL AROUND THE WORLD.
THEY SAY THEY DO WHAT THEY DO FOR DIFFERENT REASONS...
...BECAUSE THEY RESENT THE WAY SOME PEOPLE WORSHIP, OR WHERE OTHER PEOPLE LIVE, OR WHO STILL OTHERS LOVE...
...BUT IT DOESN'T REALLY MATTER, BECAUSE AT ITS ROOT IT'S ALL THE SAME THING.
THEY HATE, DIANA.
THAT'S WHAT THE SEAR GROUP DOES.

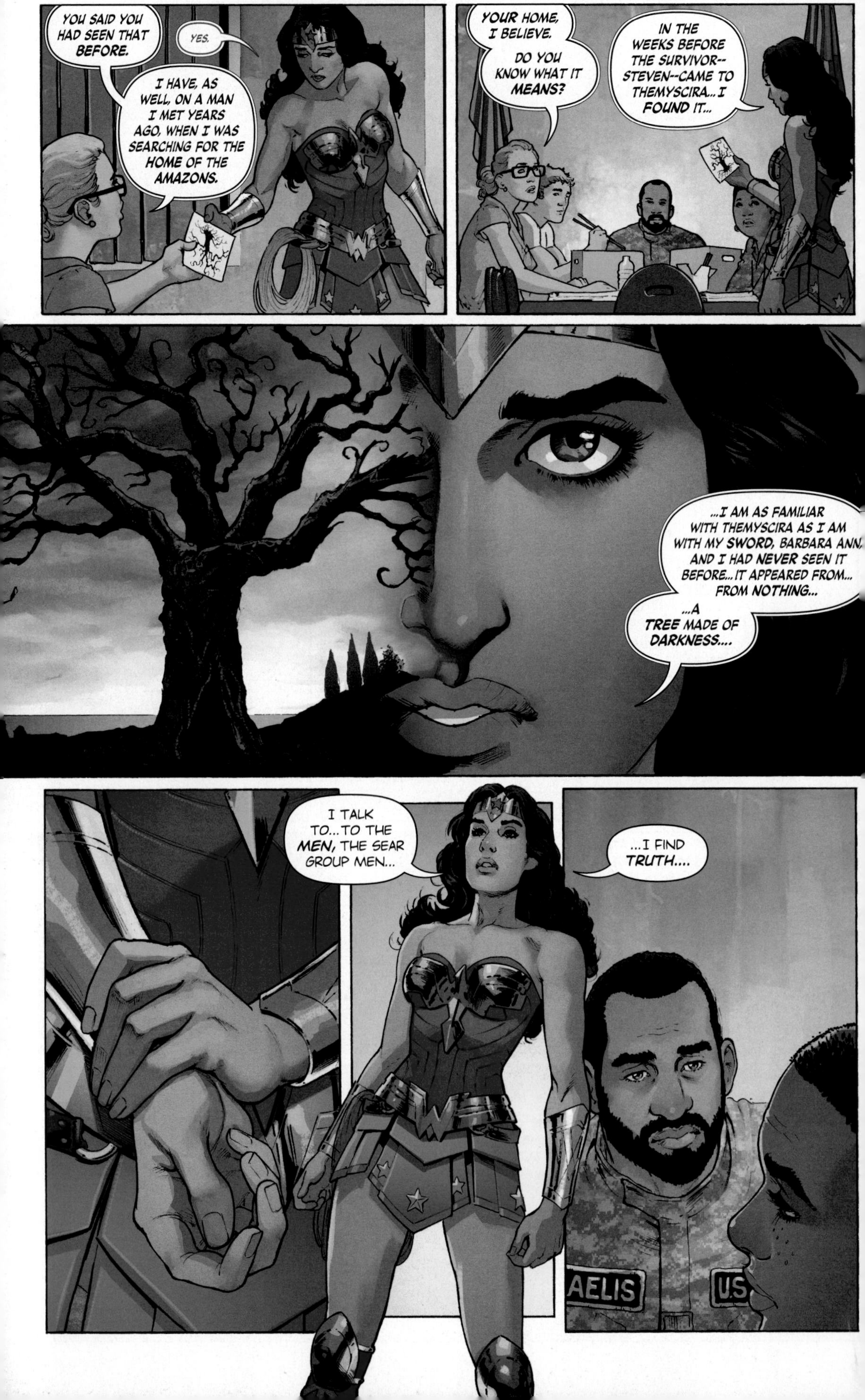

YOU SAID YOU HAD SEEN THAT BEFORE.
YES.
I HAVE, AS WELL, ON A MAN I MET YEARS AGO, WHEN I WAS SEARCHING FOR THE HOME OF THE AMAZONS.
YOUR HOME, I BELIEVE.
DO YOU KNOW WHAT IT MEANS?
IN THE WEEKS BEFORE THE SURVIVOR--STEVEN--CAME TO THEMYSCIRA... I FOUND IT...
...I AM AS FAMILIAR WITH THEMYSCIRA AS I AM WITH MY SWORD, BARBARA ANN, AND I HAD NEVER SEEN IT BEFORE... IT APPEARED FROM... FROM NOTHING...
...A TREE MADE OF DARKNESS....
I TALK TO... TO THE MEN, THE SEAR GROUP MEN...
...I FIND TRUTH....
AELIS
U.S

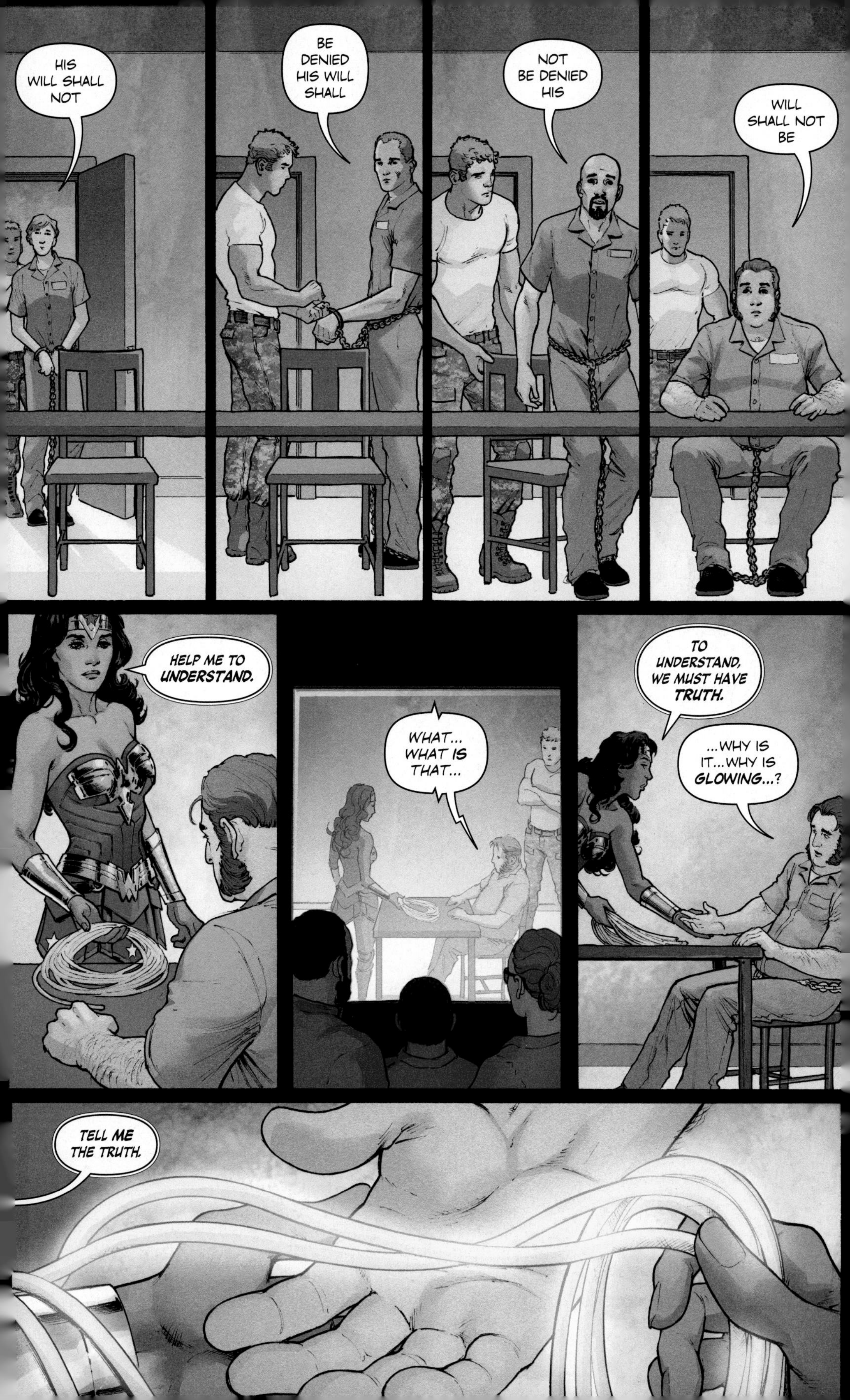
HIS WILL SHALL NOT
BE DENIED HIS WILL SHALL
NOT BE DENIED HIS
WILL SHALL NOT BE
HELP ME TO UNDERSTAND.
WHAT... WHAT IS THAT...
TO UNDERSTAND, WE MUST HAVE TRUTH.
...WHY IS IT...WHY IS GLOWING...?
TELL ME THE TRUTH.

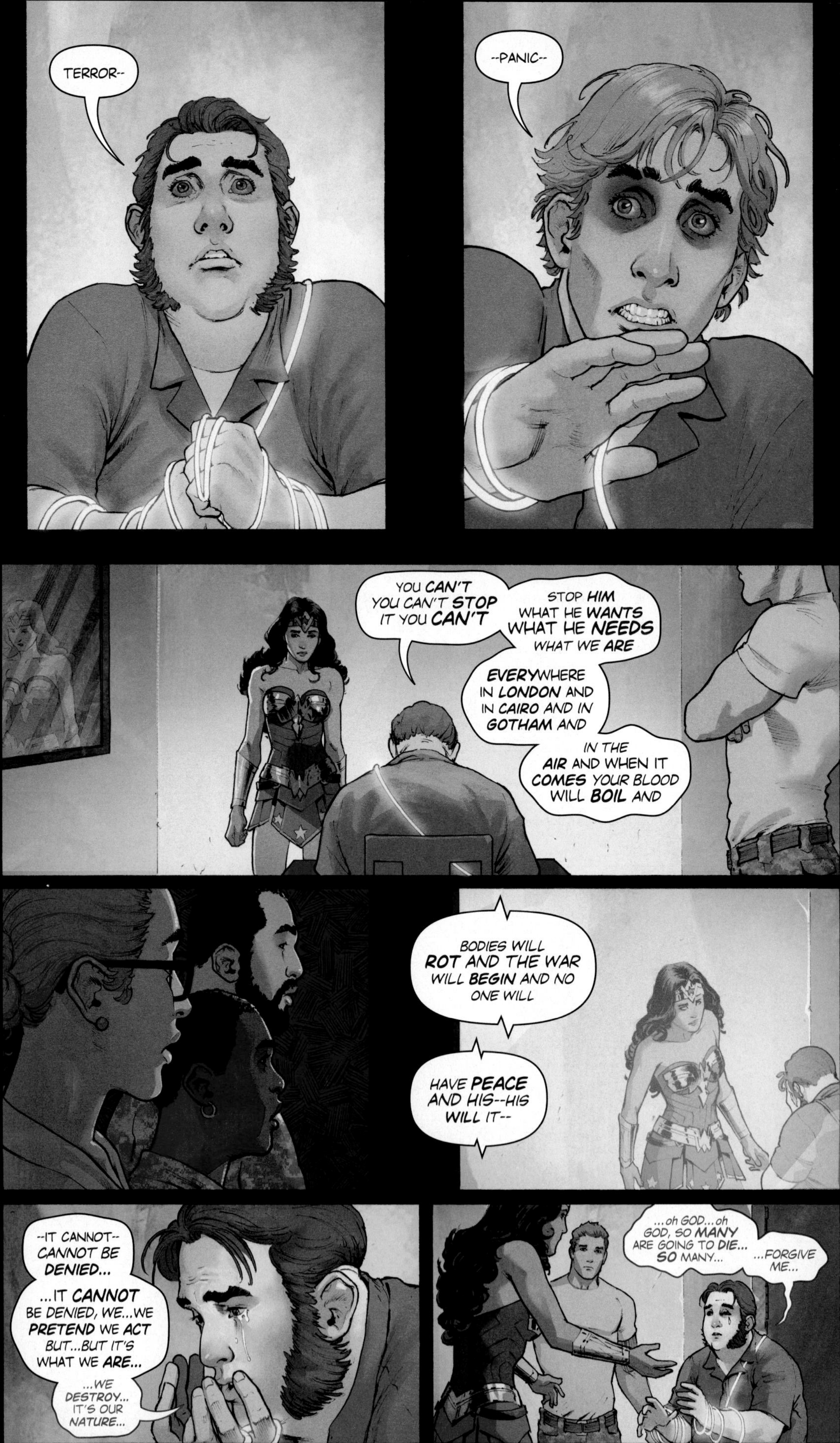
TERROR--
--PANIC--
YOU CAN'T YOU CAN'T STOP IT YOU CAN'T
STOP HIM WHAT HE WANTS WHAT HE NEEDS WHAT WE ARE
EVERYWHERE IN LONDON AND IN CAIRO AND IN GOTHAM AND
IN THE AIR AND WHEN IT COMES YOUR BLOOD WILL BOIL AND
BODIES WILL ROT AND THE WAR WILL BEGIN AND NO ONE WILL
HAVE PEACE AND HIS--HIS WILL IT--
--IT CANNOT-- CANNOT BE DENIED...
...IT CANNOT BE DENIED, WE...WE PRETEND WE ACT BUT...BUT IT'S WHAT WE ARE...
...WE DESTROY... IT'S OUR NATURE...
...oh GOD...oh GOD, SO MANY ARE GOING TO DIE... SO MANY...
...FORGIVE ME...

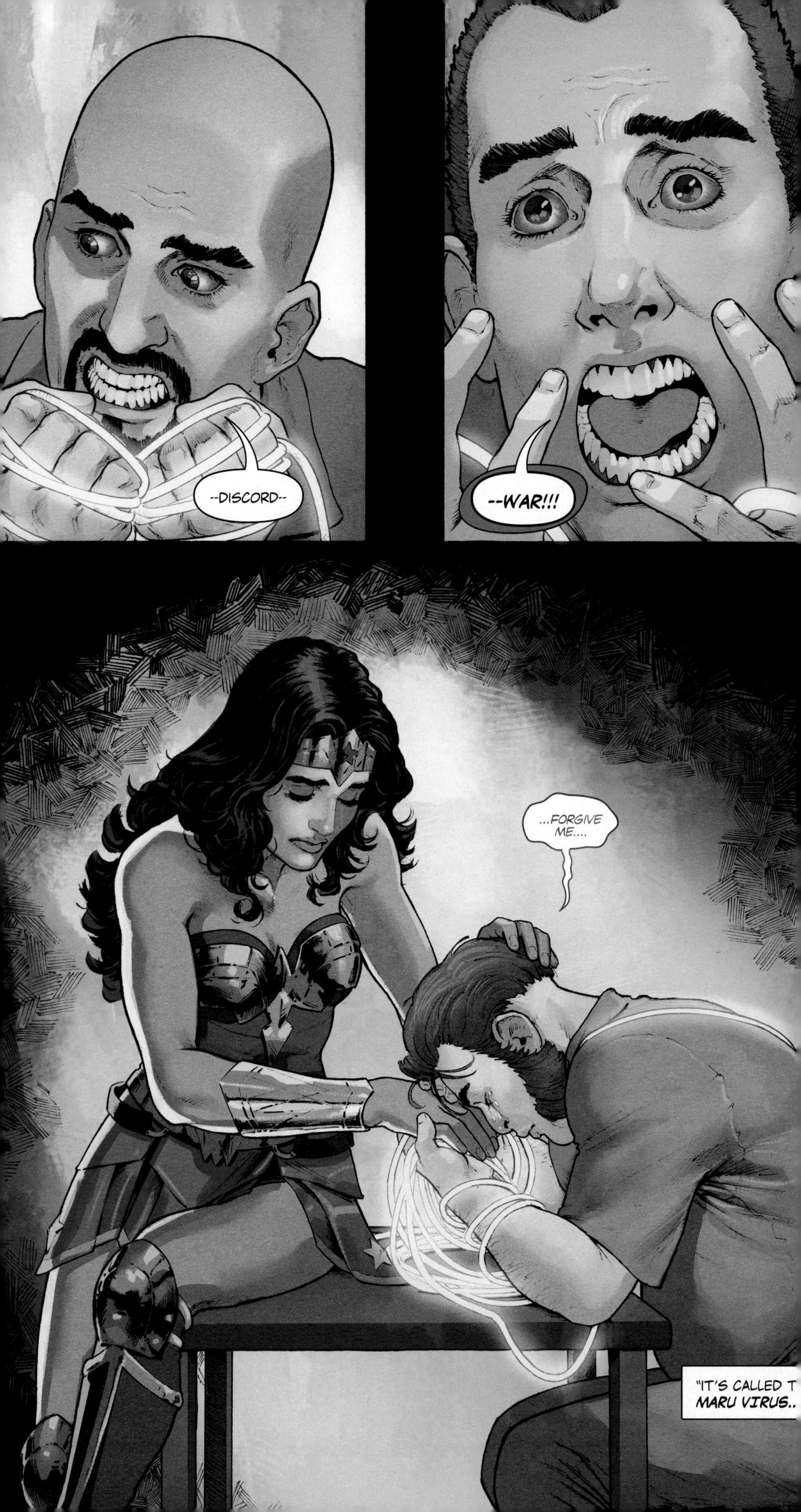

--DISCORD--
--WAR!!!
...FORGIVE ME....
"IT'S CALLED T
MARU VIRUS..

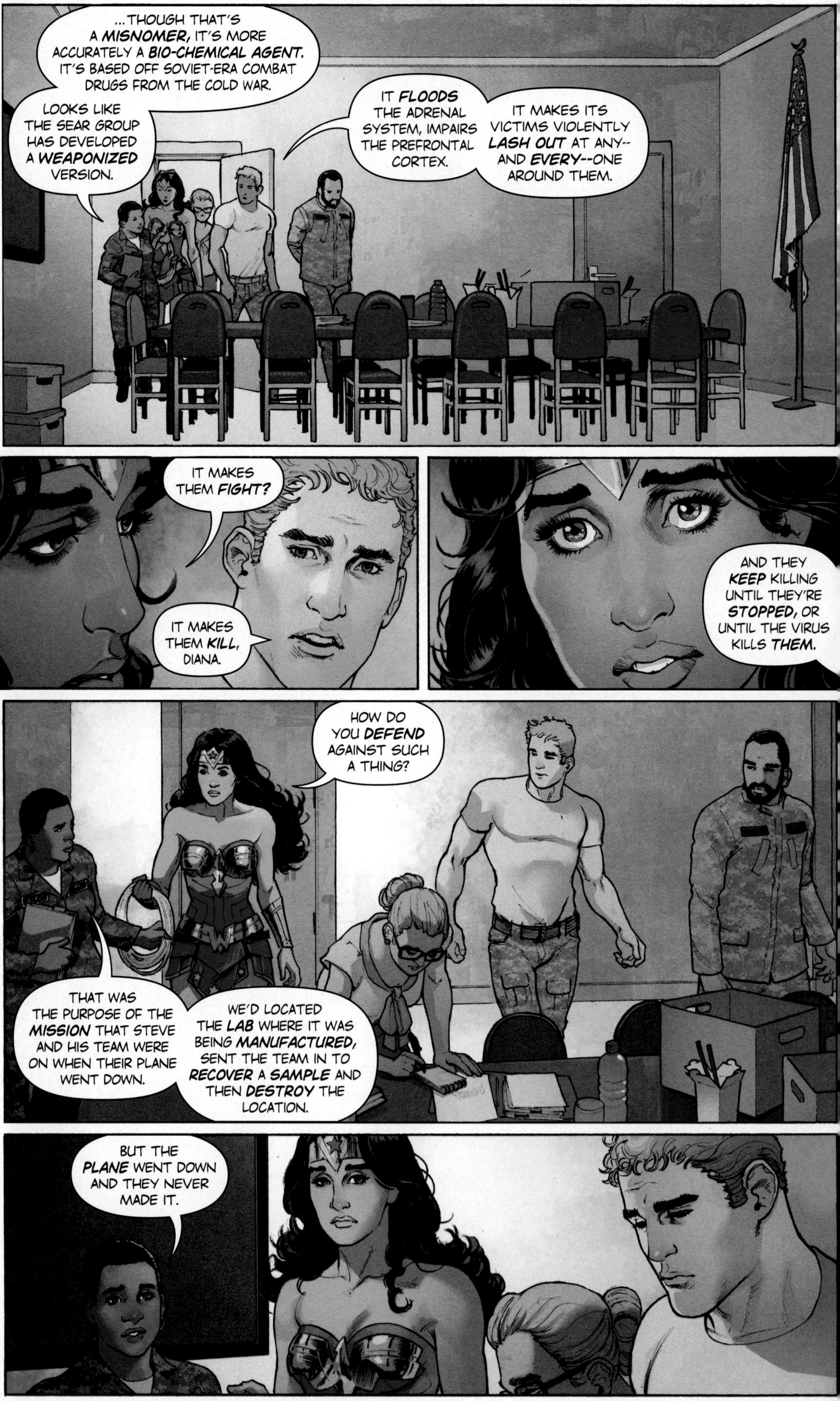
...THOUGH THAT'S A MISNOMER, IT'S MORE ACCURATELY A BIO-CHEMICAL AGENT. IT'S BASED OFF SOVIET-ERA COMBAT DRUGS FROM THE COLD WAR.
LOOKS LIKE THE SEAR GROUP HAS DEVELOPED A WEAPONIZED VERSION.
IT FLOODS THE ADRENAL SYSTEM, IMPAIRS THE PREFRONTAL CORTEX.
IT MAKES ITS VICTIMS VIOLENTLY LASH OUT AT ANY-- AND EVERY--ONE AROUND THEM.
IT MAKES THEM FIGHT?
IT MAKES THEM KILL, DIANA.
AND THEY KEEP KILLING UNTIL THEY'RE STOPPED, OR UNTIL THE VIRUS KILLS THEM.
HOW DO YOU DEFEND AGAINST SUCH A THING?
THAT WAS THE PURPOSE OF THE MISSION THAT STEVE AND HIS TEAM WERE ON WHEN THEIR PLANE WENT DOWN.
WE'D LOCATED THE LAB WHERE IT WAS BEING MANUFACTURED, SENT THE TEAM IN TO RECOVER A SAMPLE AND THEN DESTROY THE LOCATION.
BUT THE PLANE WENT DOWN AND THEY NEVER MADE IT.

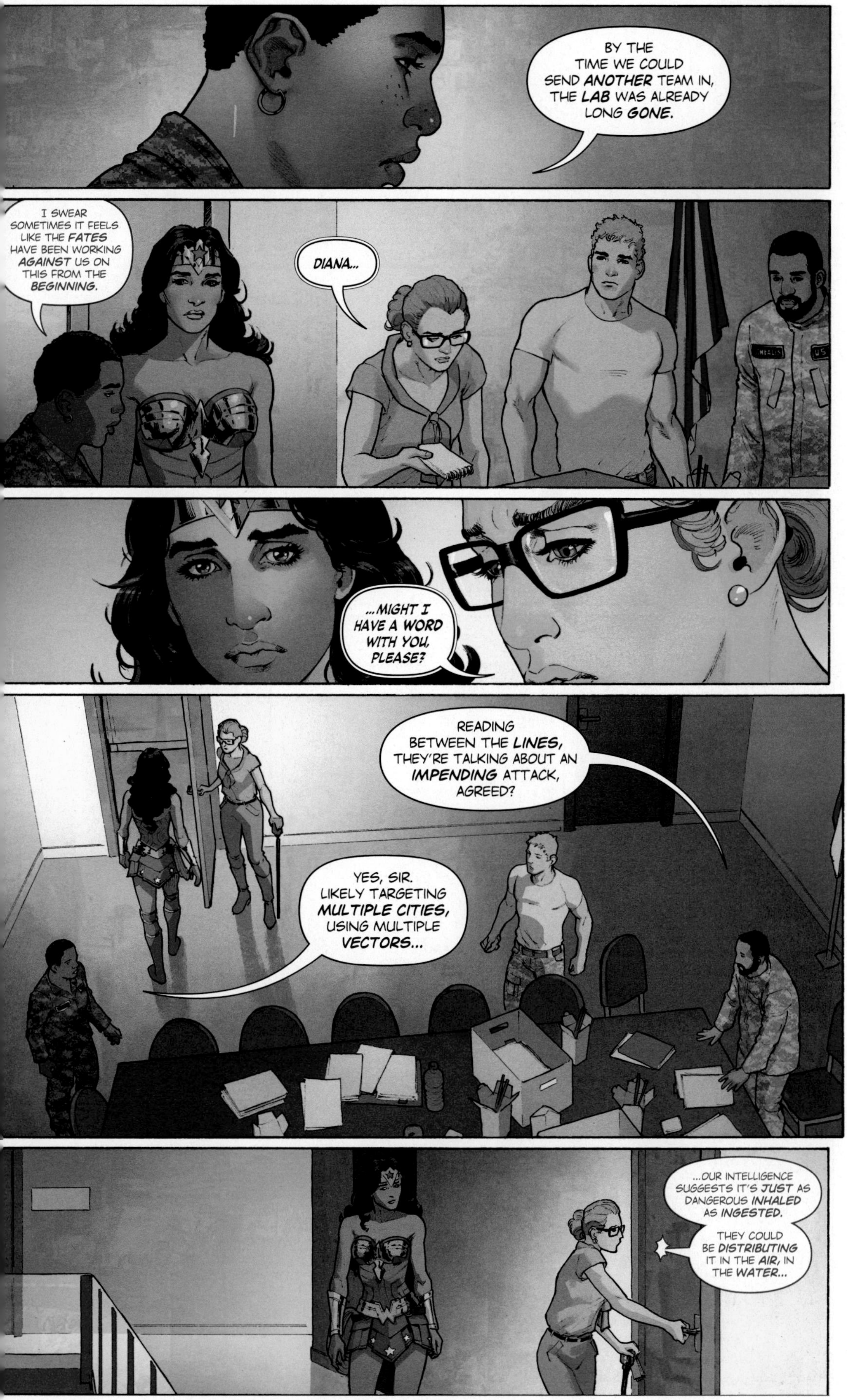
BY THE TIME WE COULD SEND ANOTHER TEAM IN, THE LAB WAS ALREADY LONG GONE.
I SWEAR SOMETIMES IT FEELS LIKE THE FATES HAVE BEEN WORKING AGAINST US ON THIS FROM THE BEGINNING.
DIANA...
...MIGHT I HAVE A WORD WITH YOU, PLEASE?
READING BETWEEN THE LINES, THEY'RE TALKING ABOUT AN IMPENDING ATTACK, AGREED?
YES, SIR. LIKELY TARGETING MULTIPLE CITIES, USING MULTIPLE VECTORS...
...OUR INTELLIGENCE SUGGESTS IT'S JUST AS DANGEROUS INHALED AS INGESTED.
THEY COULD BE DISTRIBUTING IT IN THE AIR, IN THE WATER...

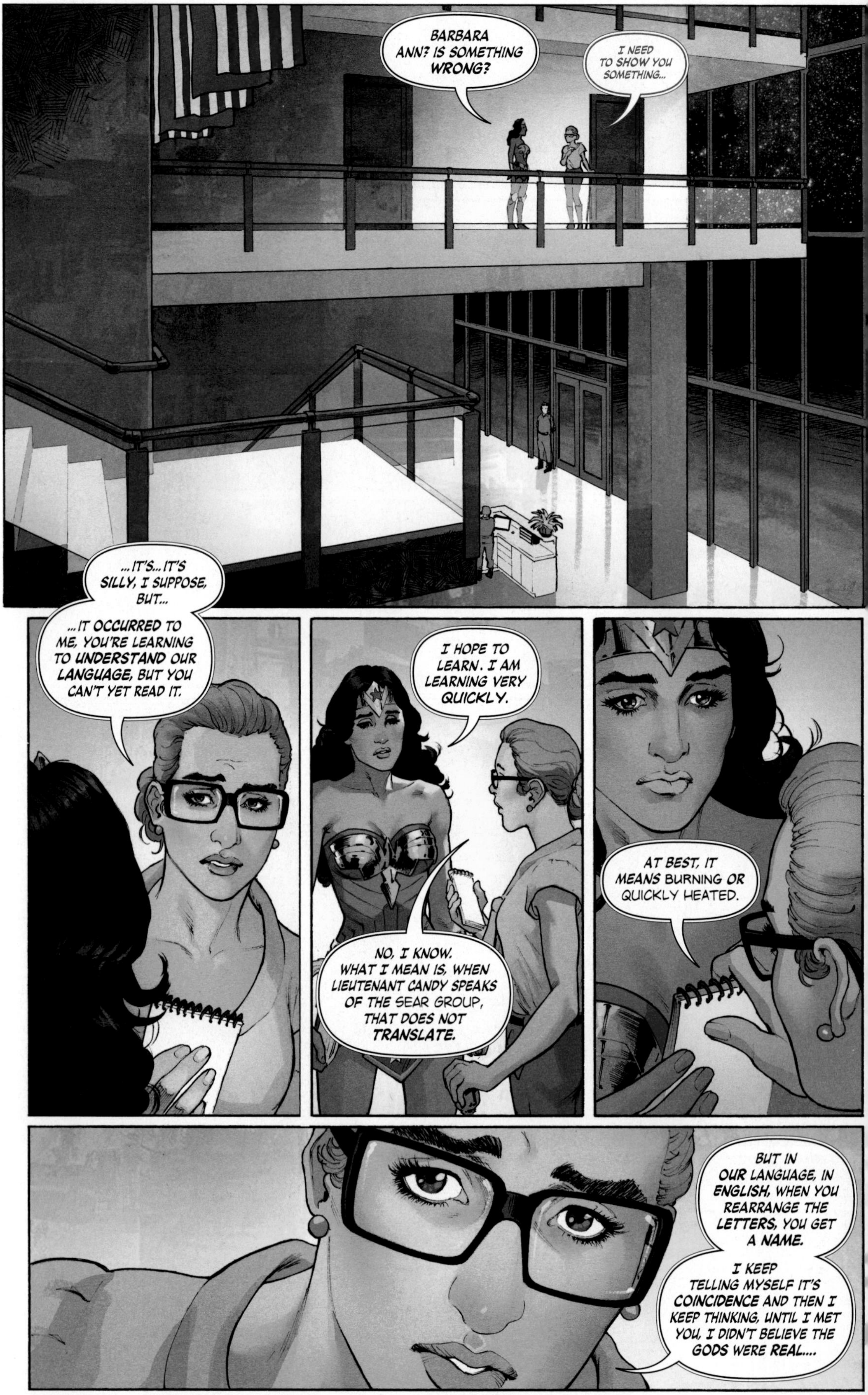
BARBARA ANN? IS SOMETHING WRONG?
I NEED TO SHOW YOU SOMETHING...
...IT'S... IT'S SILLY, I SUPPOSE, BUT...
...IT OCCURRED TO ME, YOU'RE LEARNING TO UNDERSTAND OUR LANGUAGE, BUT YOU CAN'T YET READ IT.
I HOPE TO LEARN. I AM LEARNING VERY QUICKLY.
NO, I KNOW. WHAT I MEAN IS, WHEN LIEUTENANT CANDY SPEAKS OF THE SEAR GROUP, THAT DOES NOT TRANSLATE.
AT BEST, IT MEANS BURNING OR QUICKLY HEATED.
BUT IN OUR LANGUAGE, IN ENGLISH, WHEN YOU REARRANGE THE LETTERS, YOU GET A NAME.
I KEEP TELLING MYSELF IT'S COINCIDENCE AND THEN I KEEP THINKING, UNTIL I MET YOU, I DIDN'T BELIEVE THE GODS WERE REAL....

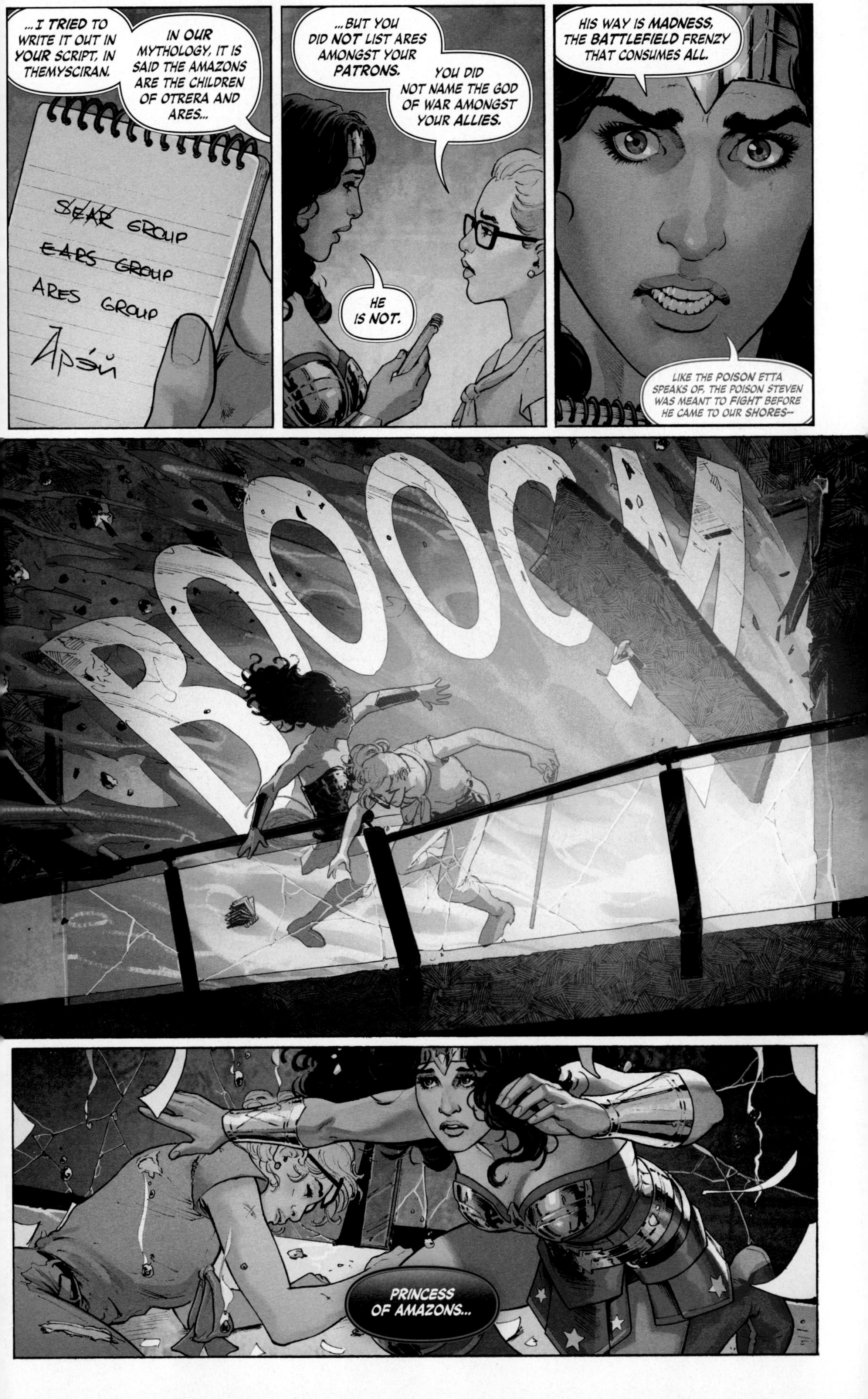
...I TRIED TO WRITE IT OUT IN YOUR SCRIPT, IN THEMYSCIRAN.
IN OUR MYTHOLOGY, IT IS SAID THE AMAZONS ARE THE CHILDREN OF OTRERA AND ARES...
SEAR GROUP
EARS GROUP
ARES GROUP
Άρέω
...BUT YOU DID NOT LIST ARES AMONGST YOUR PATRONS.
YOU DID NOT NAME THE GOD OF WAR AMONGST YOUR ALLIES.
HE IS NOT.
HIS WAY IS MADNESS, THE BATTLEFIELD FRENZY THAT CONSUMES ALL.
LIKE THE POISON ETTA SPEAKS OF, THE POISON STEVEN WAS MEANT TO FIGHT BEFORE HE CAME TO OUR SHORES--
BOOOOM
PRINCESS OF AMAZONS...

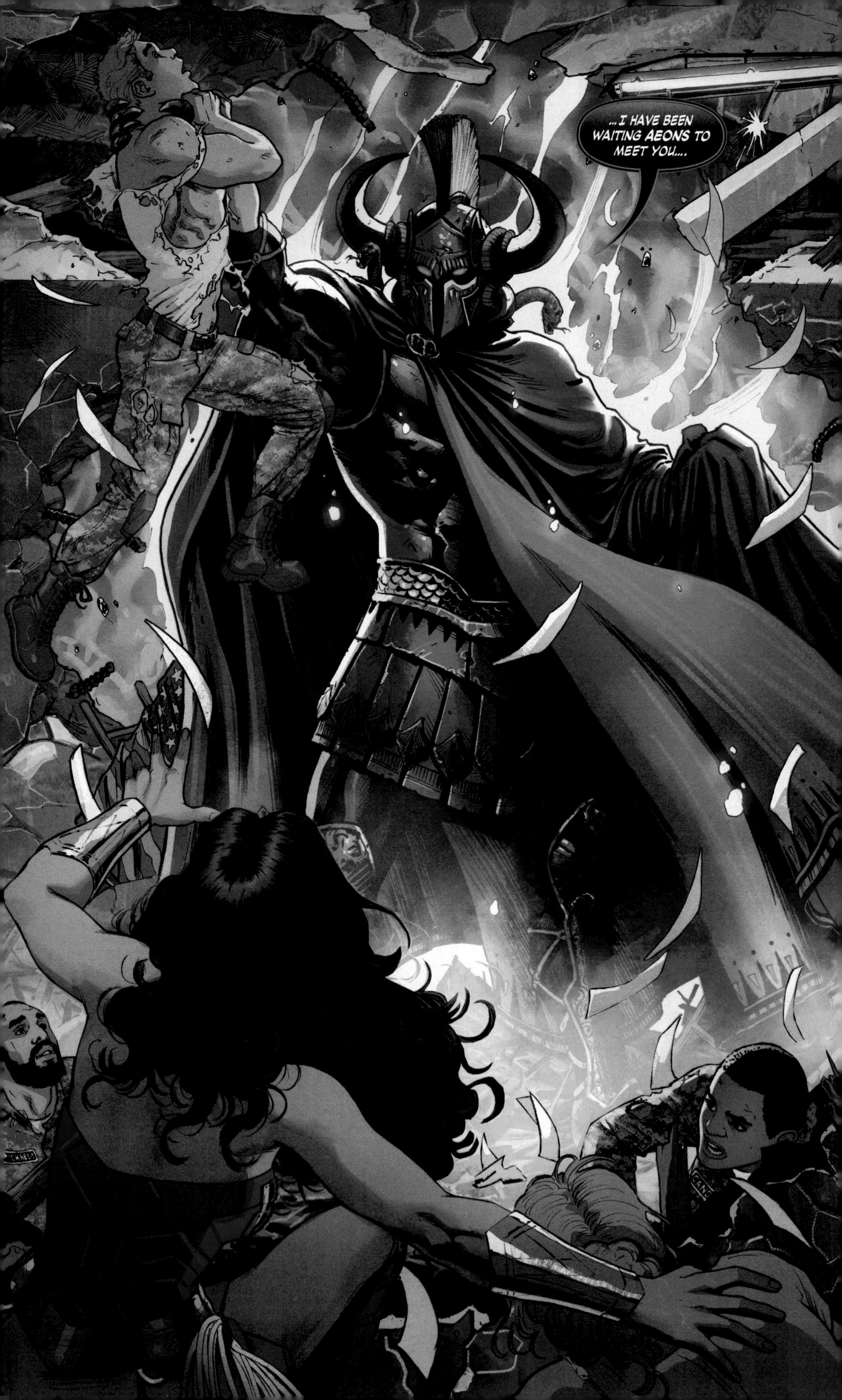
...I HAVE BEEN WAITING AEONS TO MEET YOU....

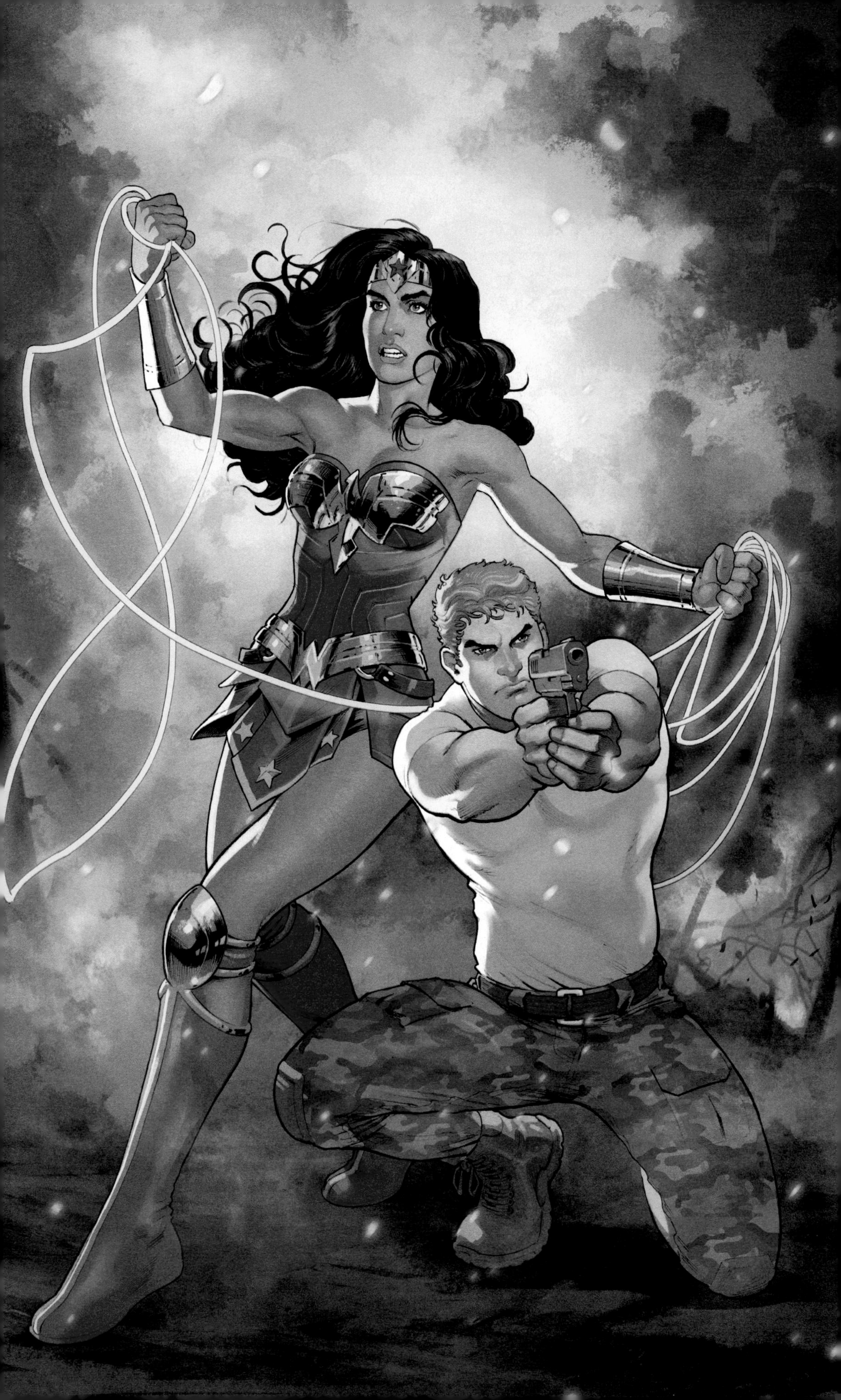

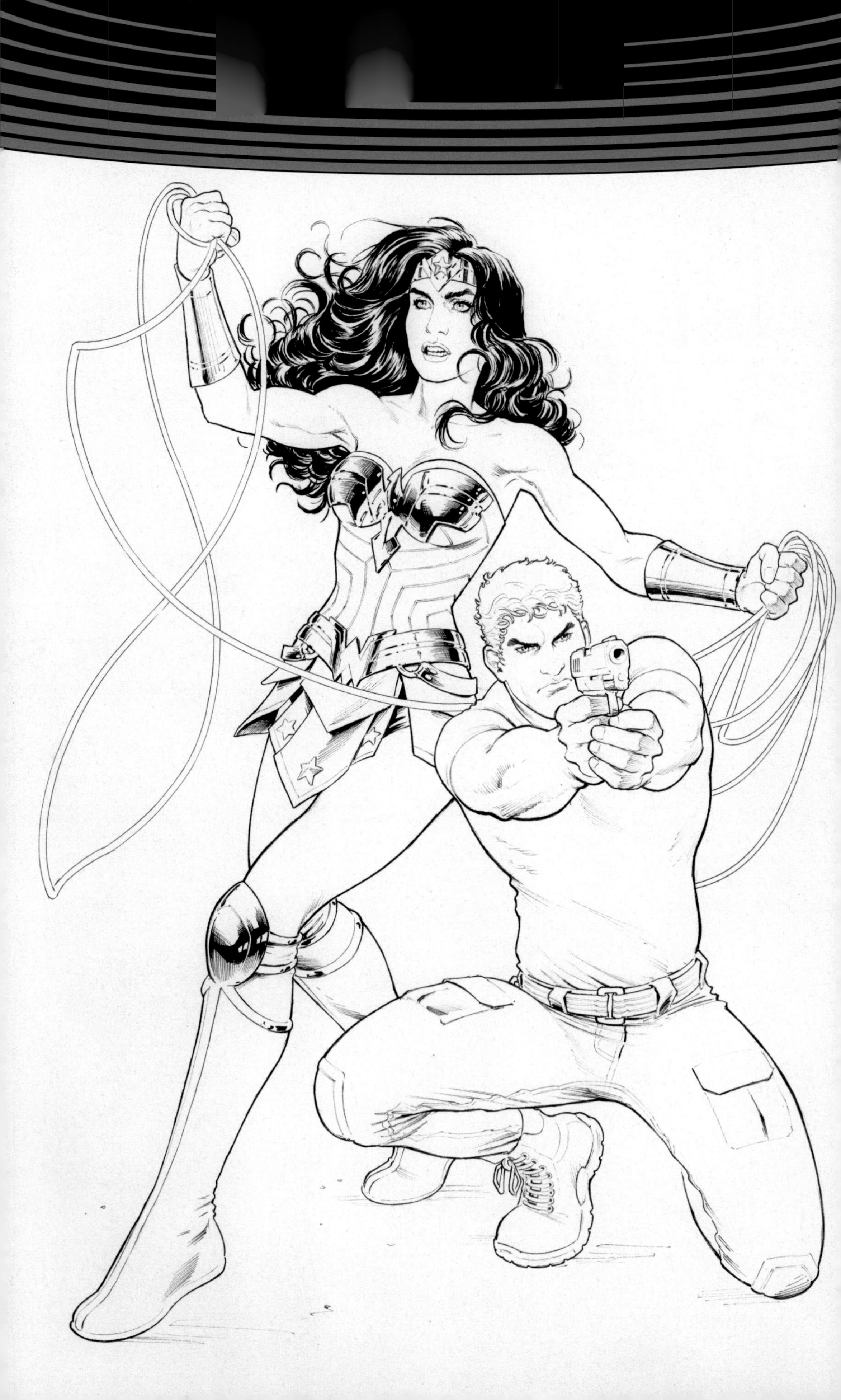

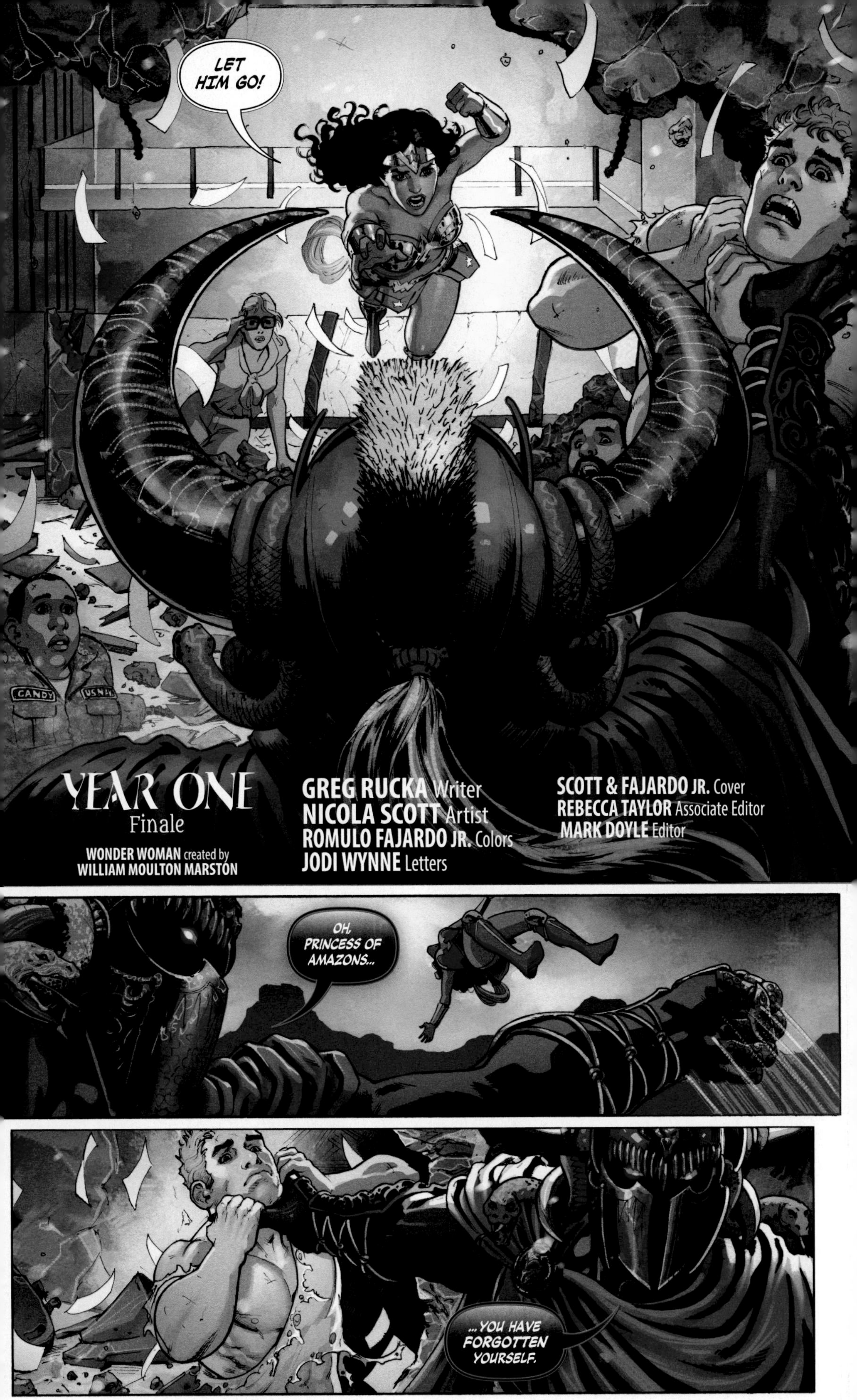
LET HIM GO!
CANDY
US NAVY
YEAR ONE
Finale
WONDER WOMAN created by
WILLIAM MOULTON MARSTON
GREG RUCKA Writer
NICOLA SCOTT Artist
ROMULO FAJARDO JR. Colors
JODI WYNNE Letters
SCOTT & FAJARDO JR. Cover
REBECCA TAYLOR Associate Editor
MARK DOYLE Editor
OH, PRINCESS OF AMAZONS...
...YOU HAVE FORGOTTEN YOURSELF.

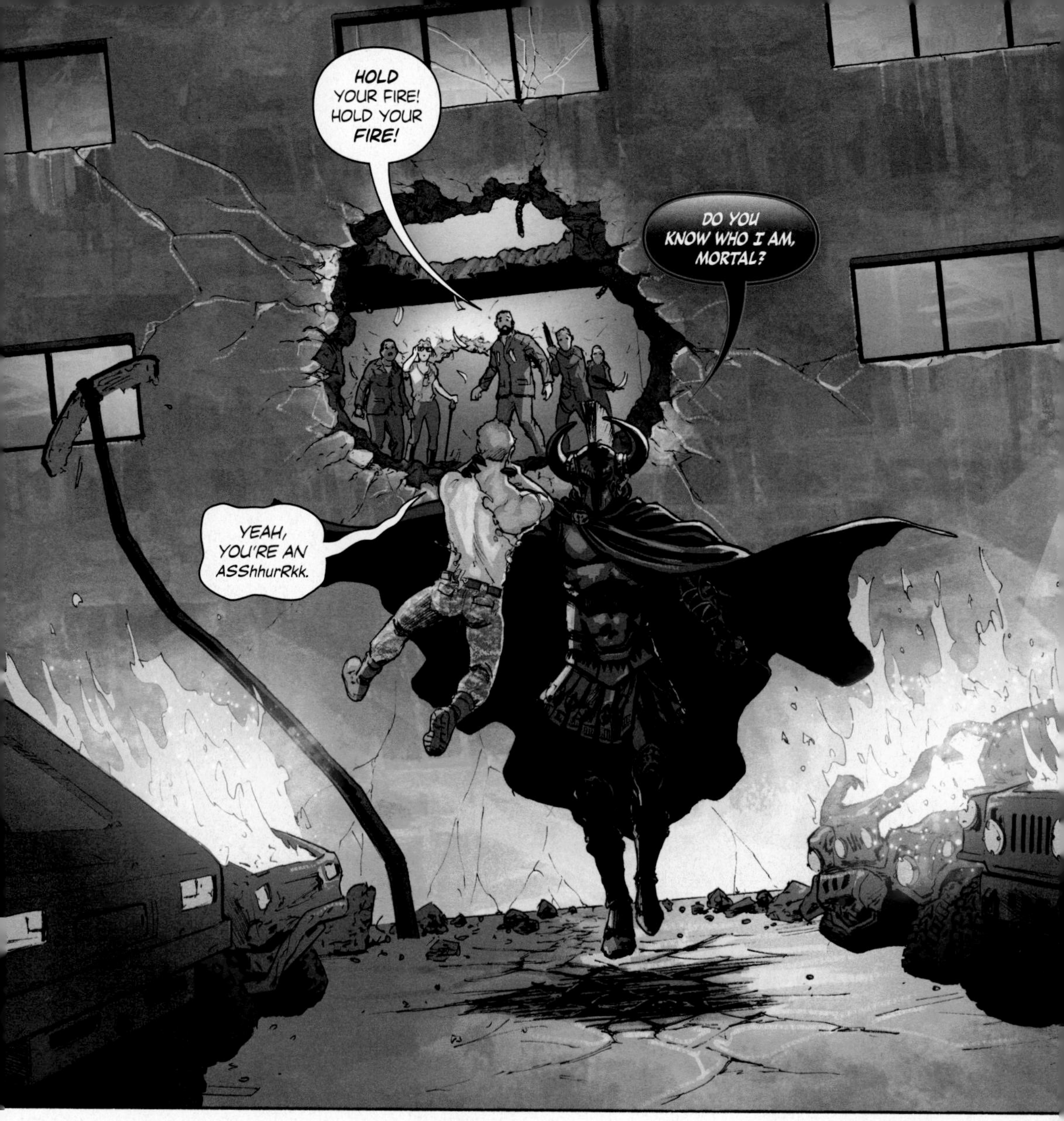
HOLD YOUR FIRE! HOLD YOUR FIRE!
DO YOU KNOW WHO I AM, MORTAL?
YEAH, YOU'RE AN ASShhurRkk.

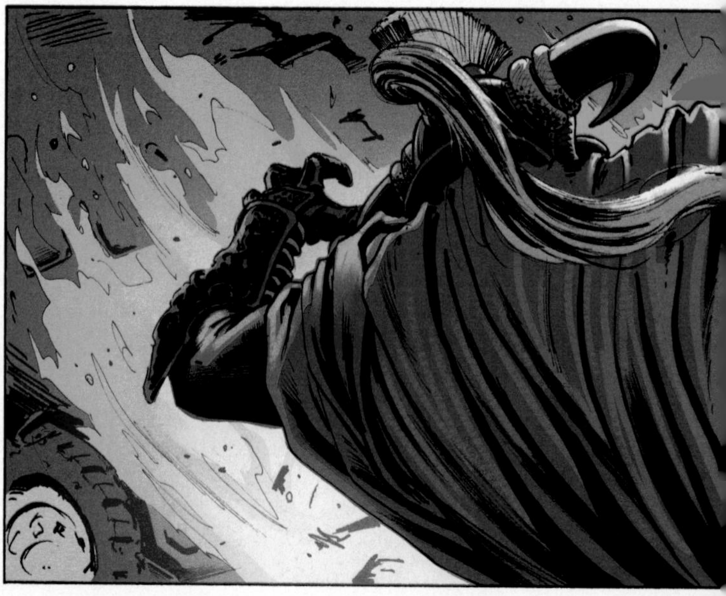

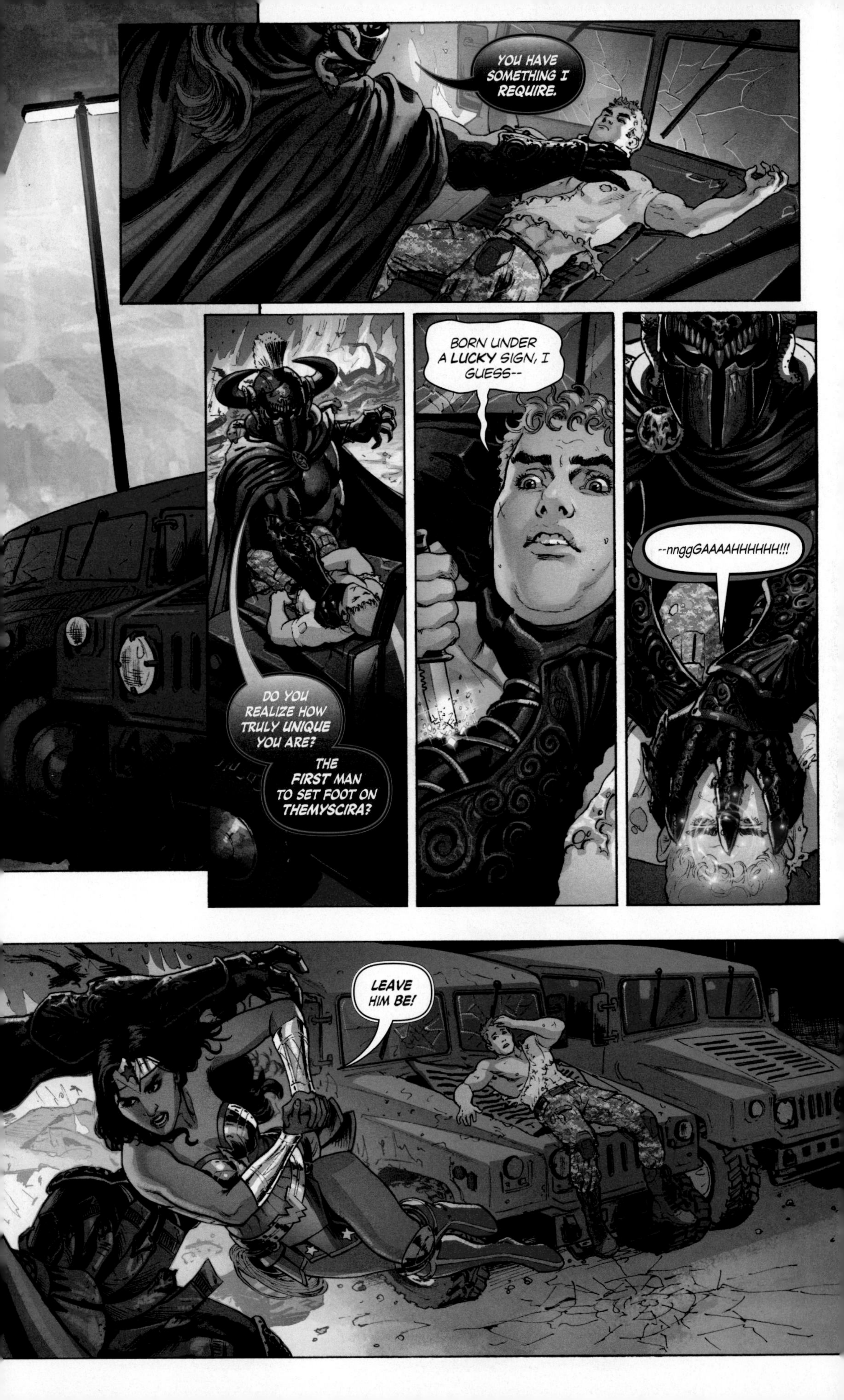
YOU HAVE SOMETHING I REQUIRE.
DO YOU REALIZE HOW TRULY UNIQUE YOU ARE?
THE FIRST MAN TO SET FOOT ON THEMYSCIRA?
BORN UNDER A LUCKY SIGN, I GUESS--
--nnggGAAAAHHHHHH!!!
LEAVE HIM BE!

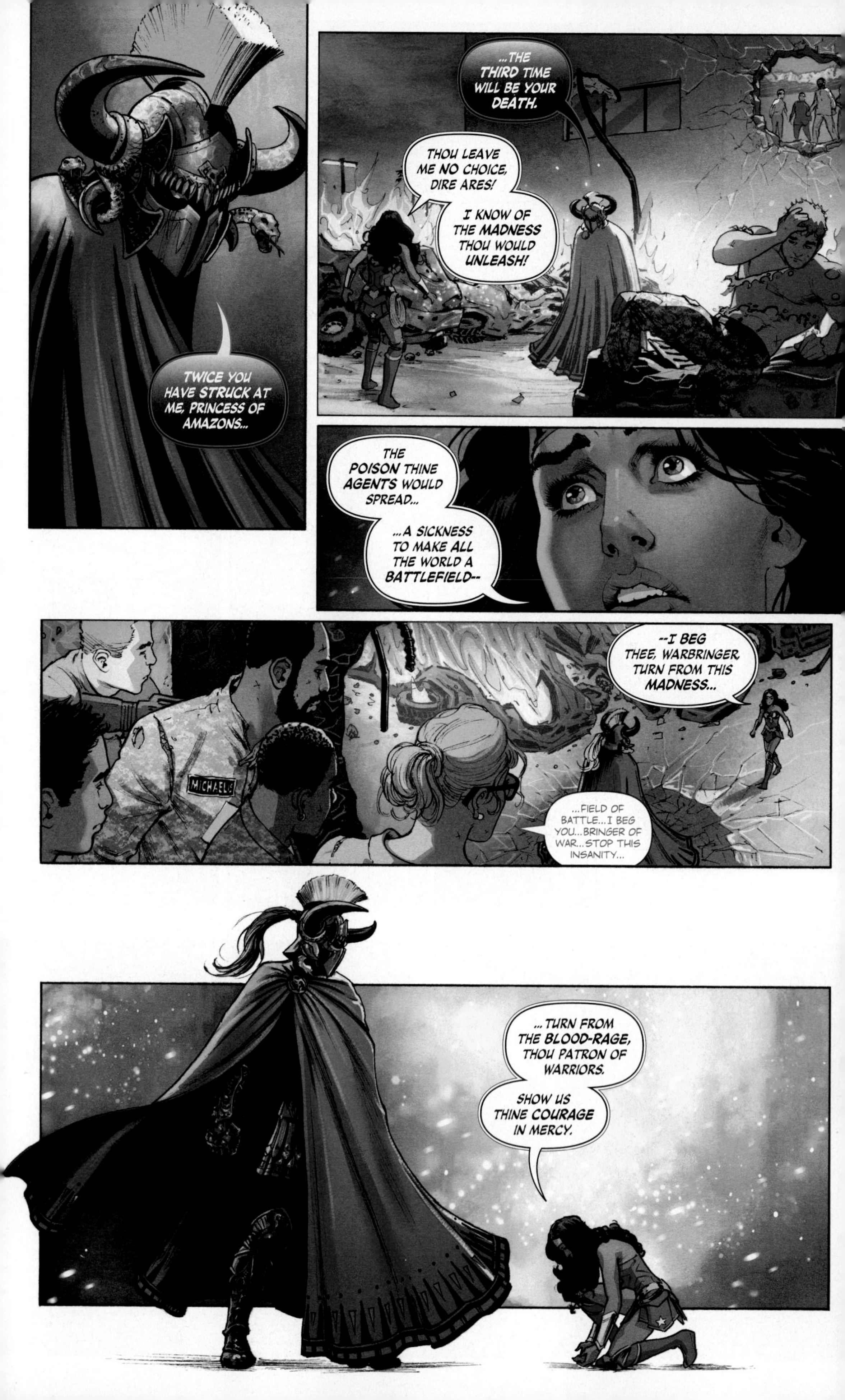
TWICE YOU HAVE STRUCK AT ME, PRINCESS OF AMAZONS...
...THE THIRD TIME WILL BE YOUR DEATH.
THOU LEAVE ME NO CHOICE, DIRE ARES!
I KNOW OF THE MADNESS THOU WOULD UNLEASH!
THE POISON THINE AGENTS WOULD SPREAD...
...A SICKNESS TO MAKE ALL THE WORLD A BATTLEFIELD--
--I BEG THEE, WARBRINGER, TURN FROM THIS MADNESS...
MICHAELS
...FIELD OF BATTLE...I BEG YOU...BRINGER OF WAR...STOP THIS INSANITY...
... TURN FROM THE BLOOD-RAGE, THOU PATRON OF WARRIORS.
SHOW US THINE COURAGE IN MERCY.

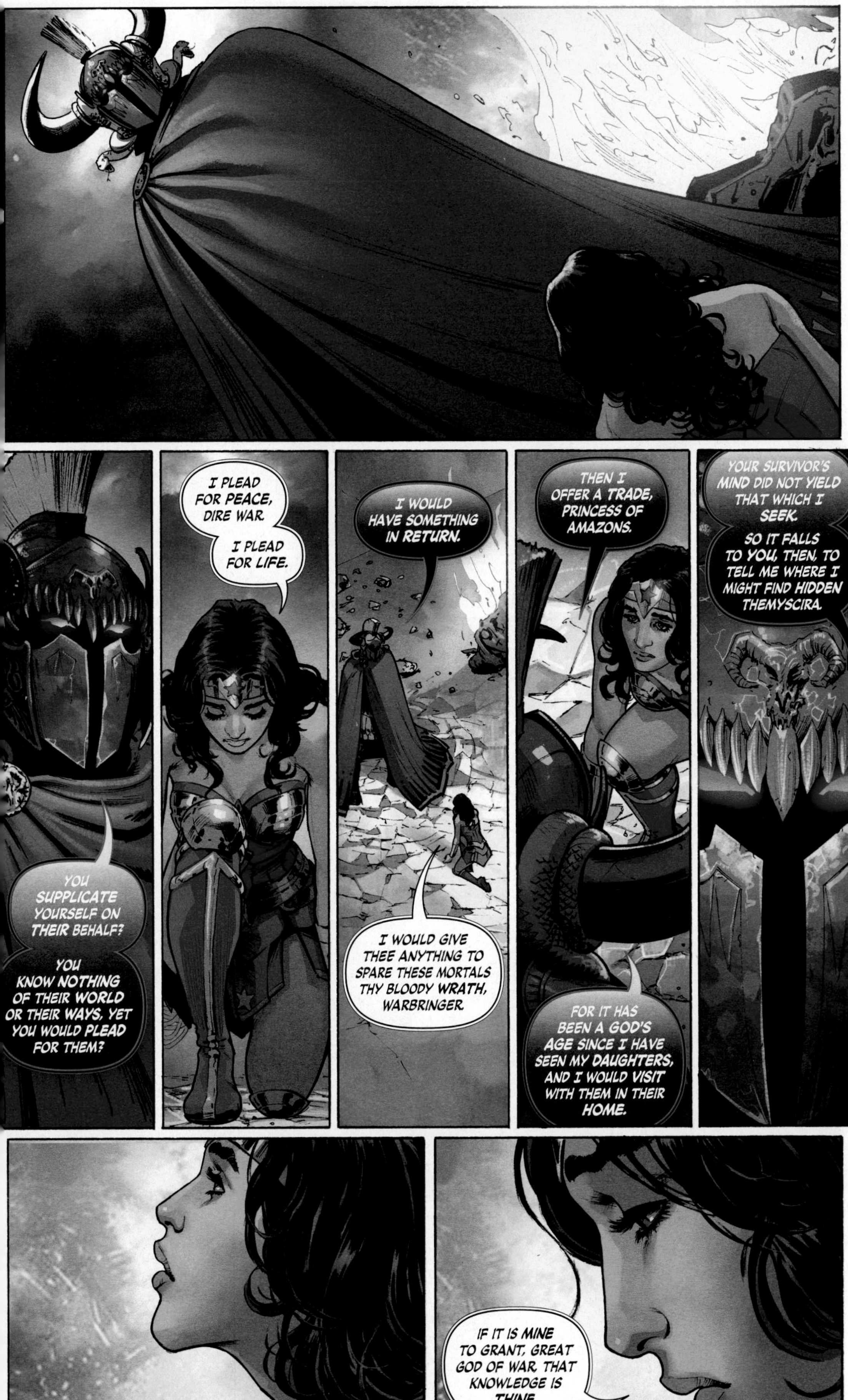

YOU SUPPLICATE YOURSELF ON THEIR BEHALF?
YOU KNOW NOTHING OF THEIR WORLD OR THEIR WAYS, YET YOU WOULD PLEAD FOR THEM?
I PLEAD FOR PEACE, DIRE WAR.
I PLEAD FOR LIFE.
I WOULD HAVE SOMETHING IN RETURN.
I WOULD GIVE THEE ANYTHING TO SPARE THESE MORTALS THY BLOODY WRATH, WARBRINGER.
THEN I OFFER A TRADE, PRINCESS OF AMAZONS.
FOR IT HAS BEEN A GOD'S AGE SINCE I HAVE SEEN MY DAUGHTERS, AND I WOULD VISIT WITH THEM IN THEIR HOME.
YOUR SURVIVOR'S MIND DID NOT YIELD THAT WHICH I SEEK.
SO IT FALLS TO YOU, THEN, TO TELL ME WHERE I MIGHT FIND HIDDEN THEMYSCIRA.
IF IT IS MINE TO GRANT, GREAT GOD OF WAR, THAT KNOWLEDGE IS THINE.

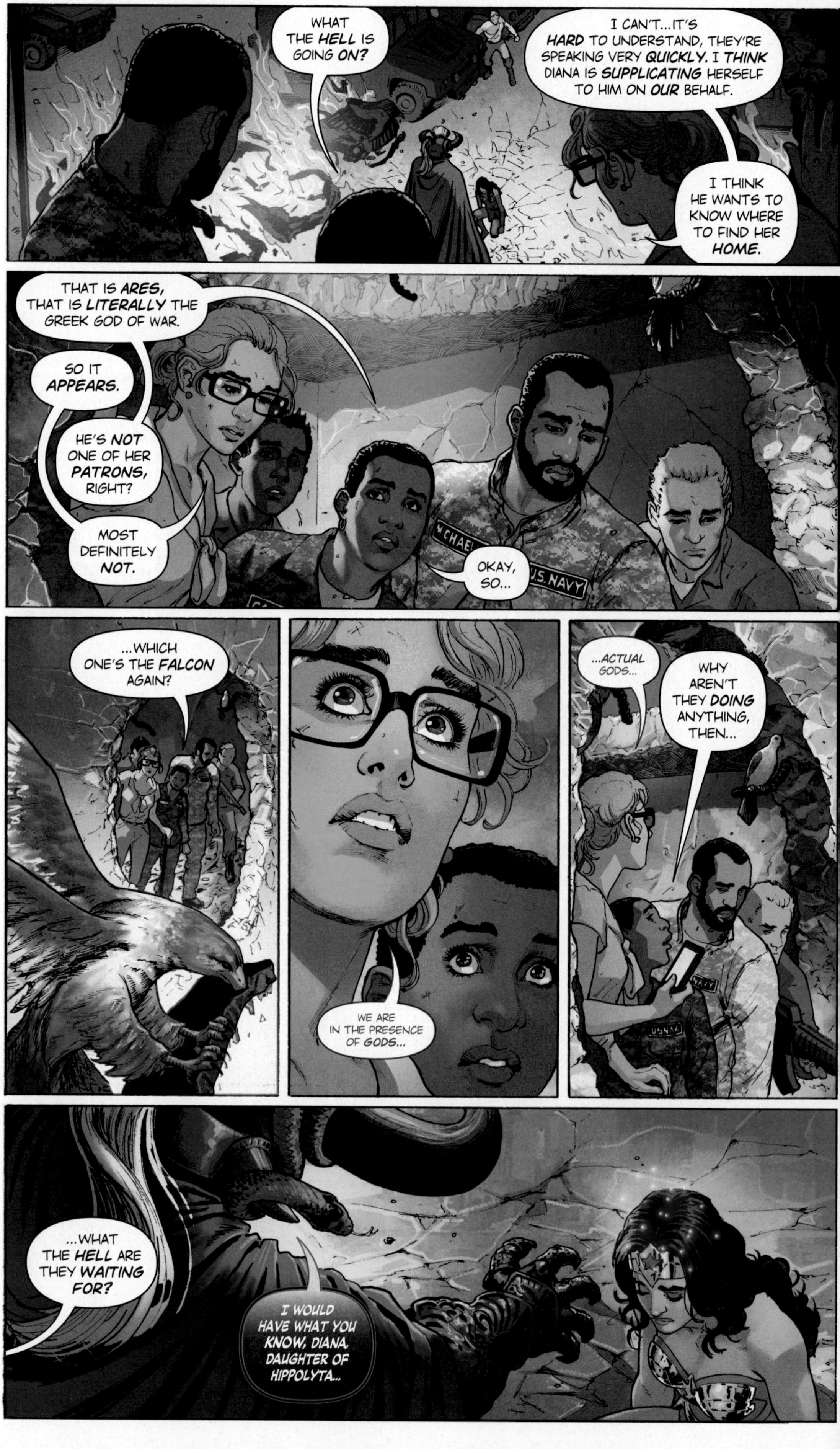
WHAT THE HELL IS GOING ON?
I CAN'T...IT'S HARD TO UNDERSTAND, THEY'RE SPEAKING VERY QUICKLY. I THINK DIANA IS SUPPLICATING HERSELF TO HIM ON OUR BEHALF.
I THINK HE WANTS TO KNOW WHERE TO FIND HER HOME.
THAT IS ARES, THAT IS LITERALLY THE GREEK GOD OF WAR.
SO IT APPEARS.
HE'S NOT ONE OF HER PATRONS, RIGHT?
MOST DEFINITELY NOT.
OKAY, SO...
MICHAEL
U.S. NAVY
...WHICH ONE'S THE FALCON AGAIN?
WE ARE IN THE PRESENCE OF GODS...
...ACTUAL GODS...
WHY AREN'T THEY DOING ANYTHING, THEN...
...WHAT THE HELL ARE THEY WAITING FOR?
I WOULD HAVE WHAT YOU KNOW, DIANA, DAUGHTER OF HIPPOLYTA...

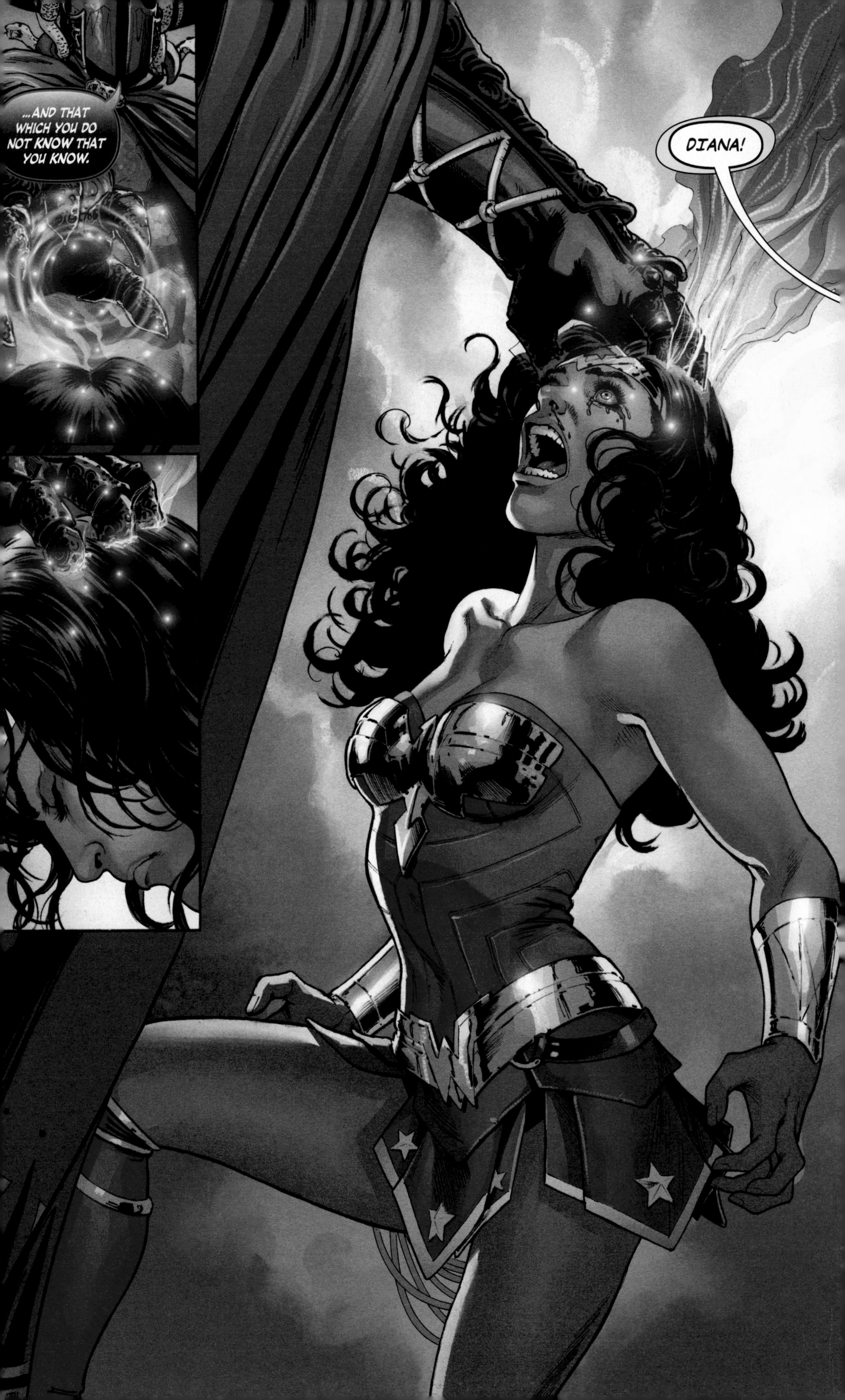
...AND THAT WHICH YOU DO NOT KNOW THAT YOU KNOW.
DIANA!

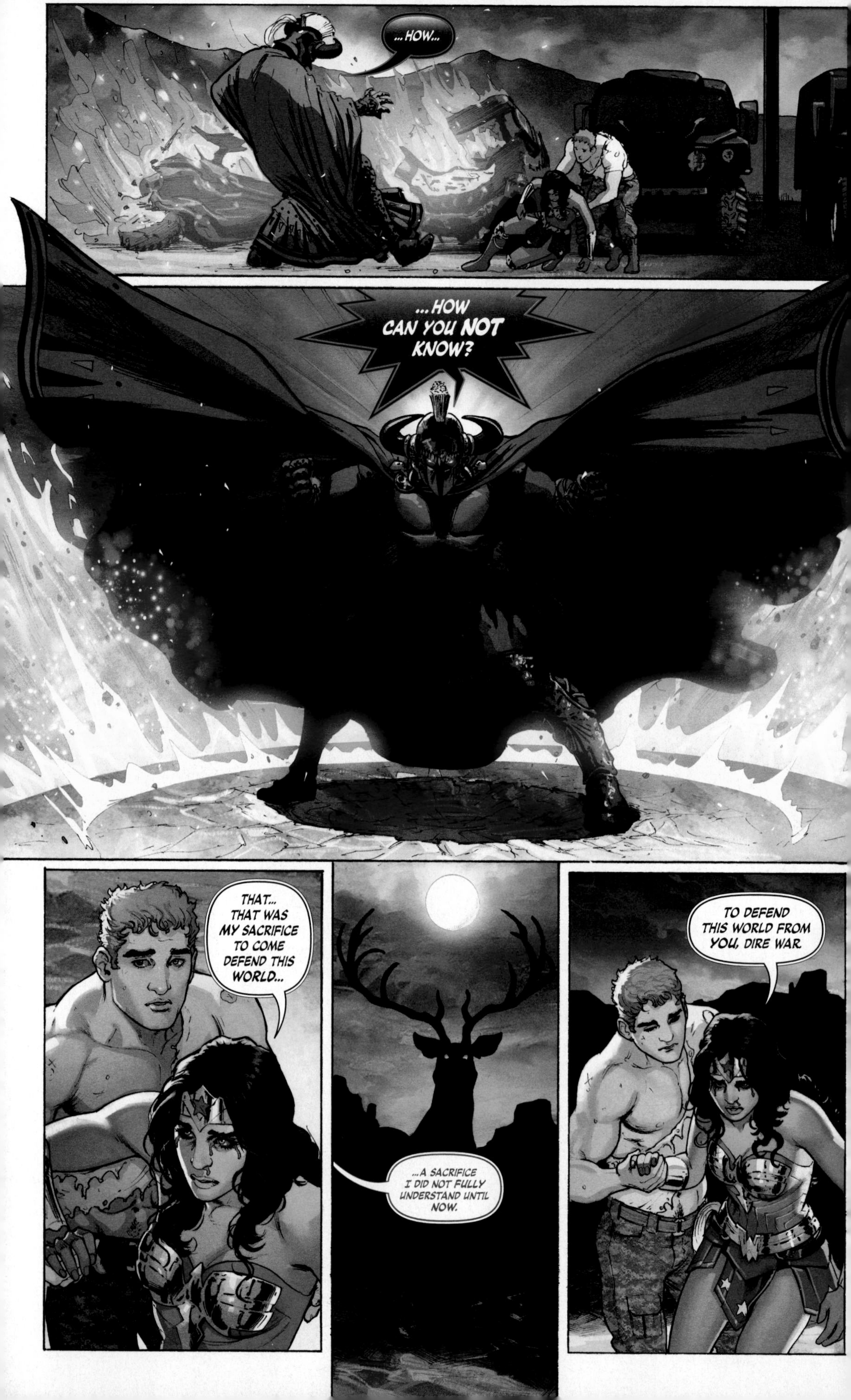
...HOW...
...HOW CAN YOU NOT KNOW?
THAT... THAT WAS MY SACRIFICE TO COME DEFEND THIS WORLD...
...A SACRIFICE I DID NOT FULLY UNDERSTAND UNTIL NOW.
TO DEFEND THIS WORLD FROM YOU, DIRE WAR.

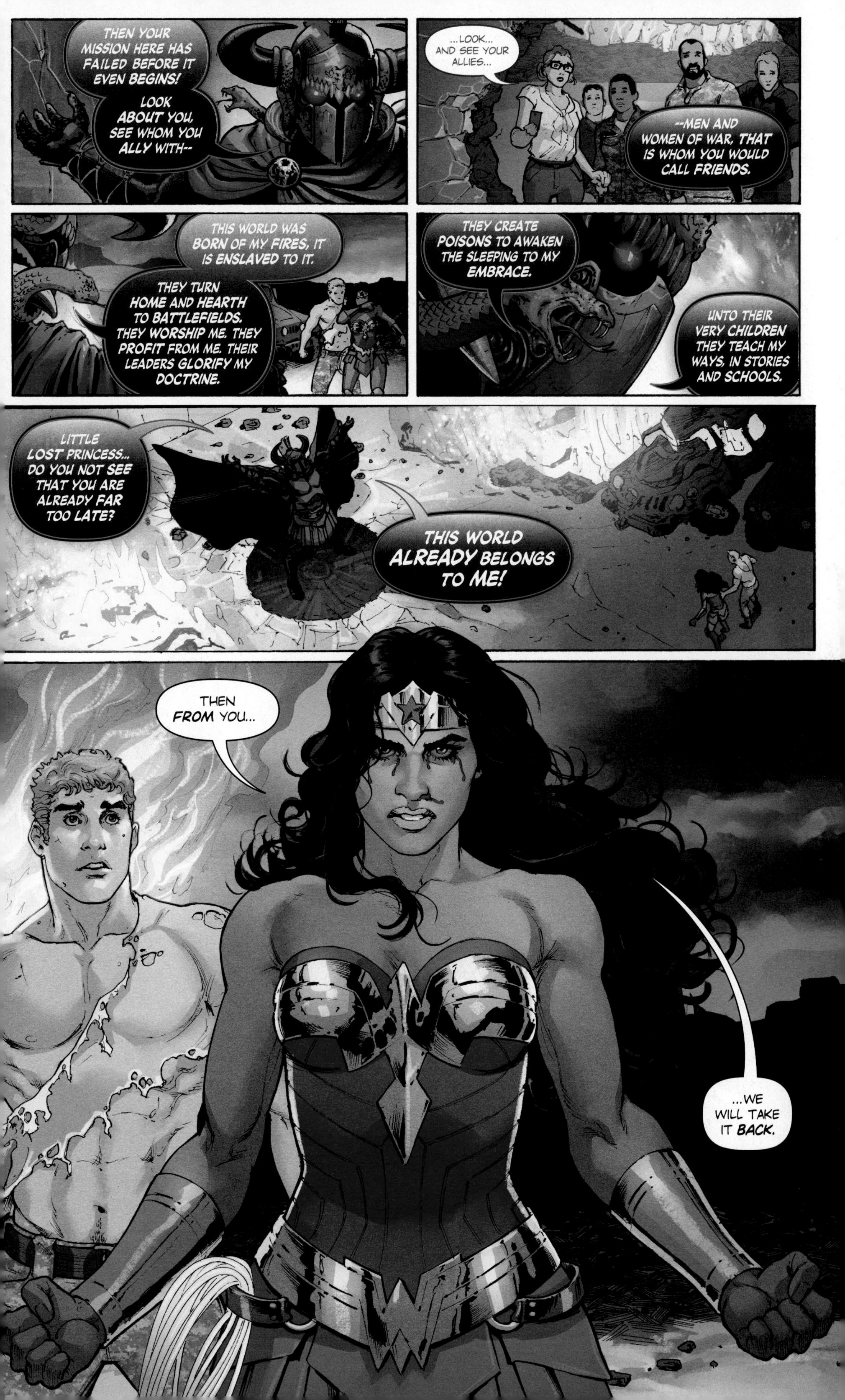
THEN YOUR MISSION HERE HAS FAILED BEFORE IT EVEN BEGINS!
LOOK ABOUT YOU, SEE WHOM YOU ALLY WITH--
...LOOK... AND SEE YOUR ALLIES...
--MEN AND WOMEN OF WAR, THAT IS WHOM YOU WOULD CALL FRIENDS.
THIS WORLD WAS BORN OF MY FIRES, IT IS ENSLAVED TO IT.
THEY TURN HOME AND HEARTH TO BATTLEFIELDS. THEY WORSHIP ME. THEY PROFIT FROM ME. THEIR LEADERS GLORIFY MY DOCTRINE.
THEY CREATE POISONS TO AWAKEN THE SLEEPING TO MY EMBRACE.
UNTO THEIR VERY CHILDREN THEY TEACH MY WAYS, IN STORIES AND SCHOOLS.
LITTLE LOST PRINCESS... DO YOU NOT SEE THAT YOU ARE ALREADY FAR TOO LATE?
THIS WORLD ALREADY BELONGS TO ME!
THEN FROM YOU...
...WE WILL TAKE IT BACK.

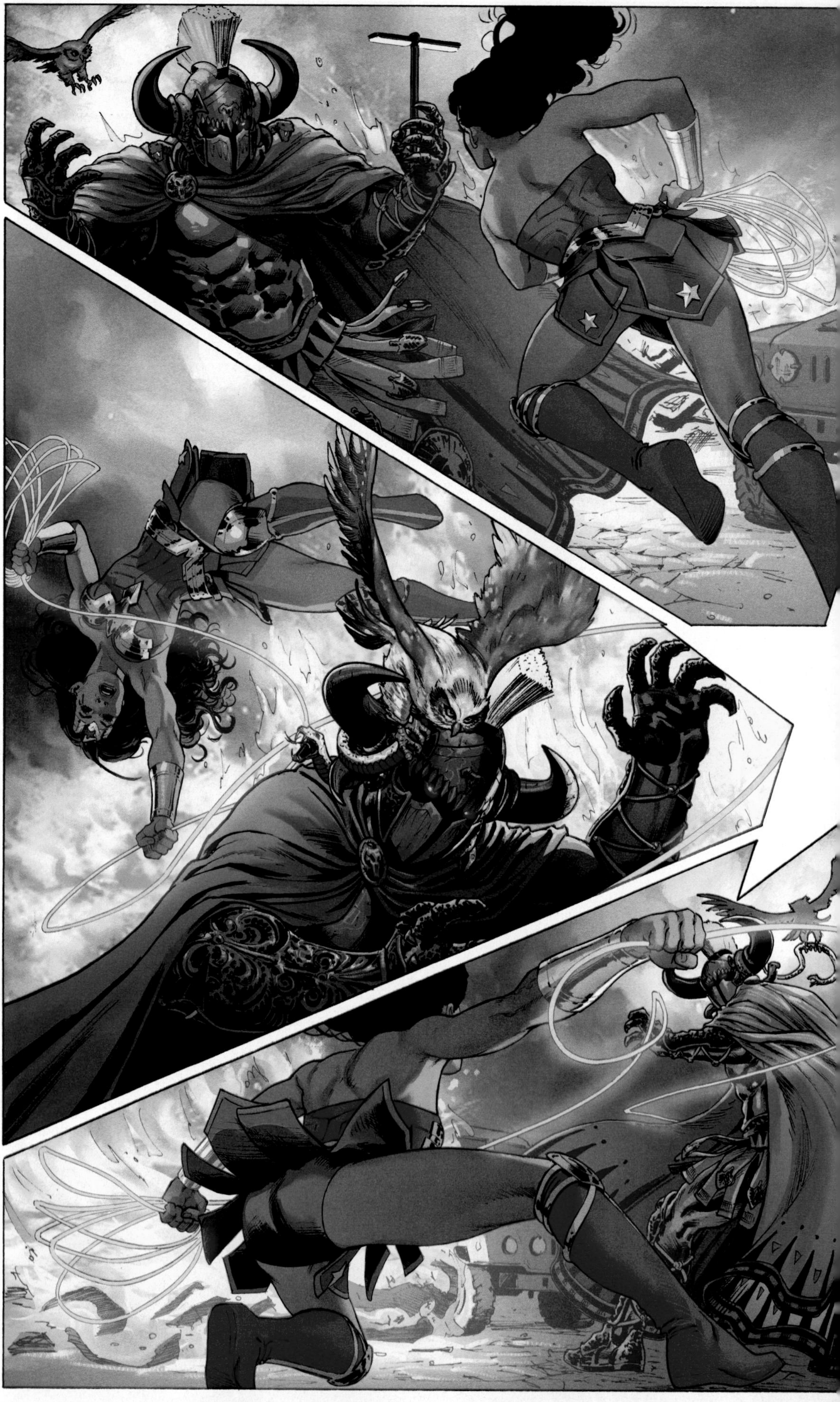

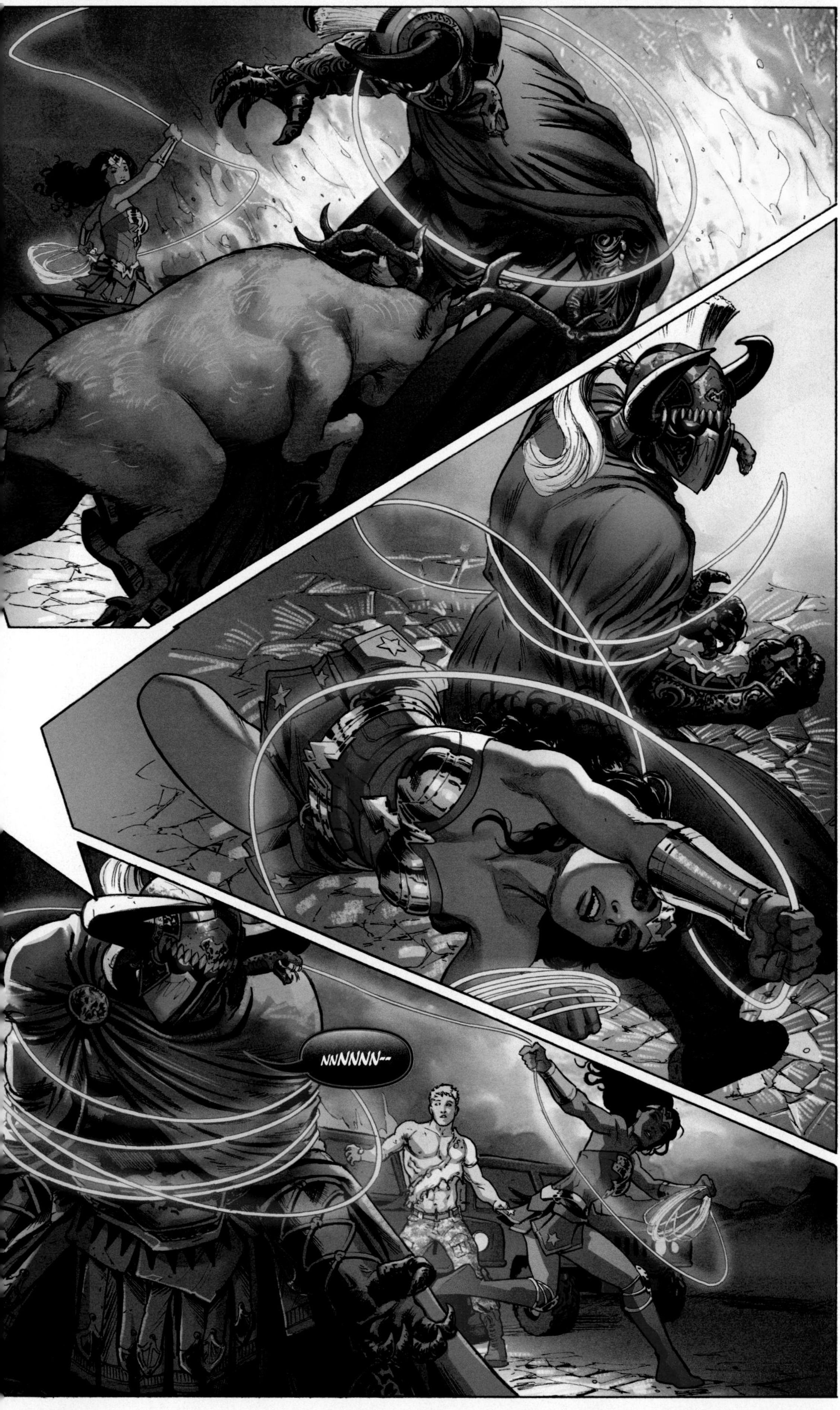
NNNNNN--

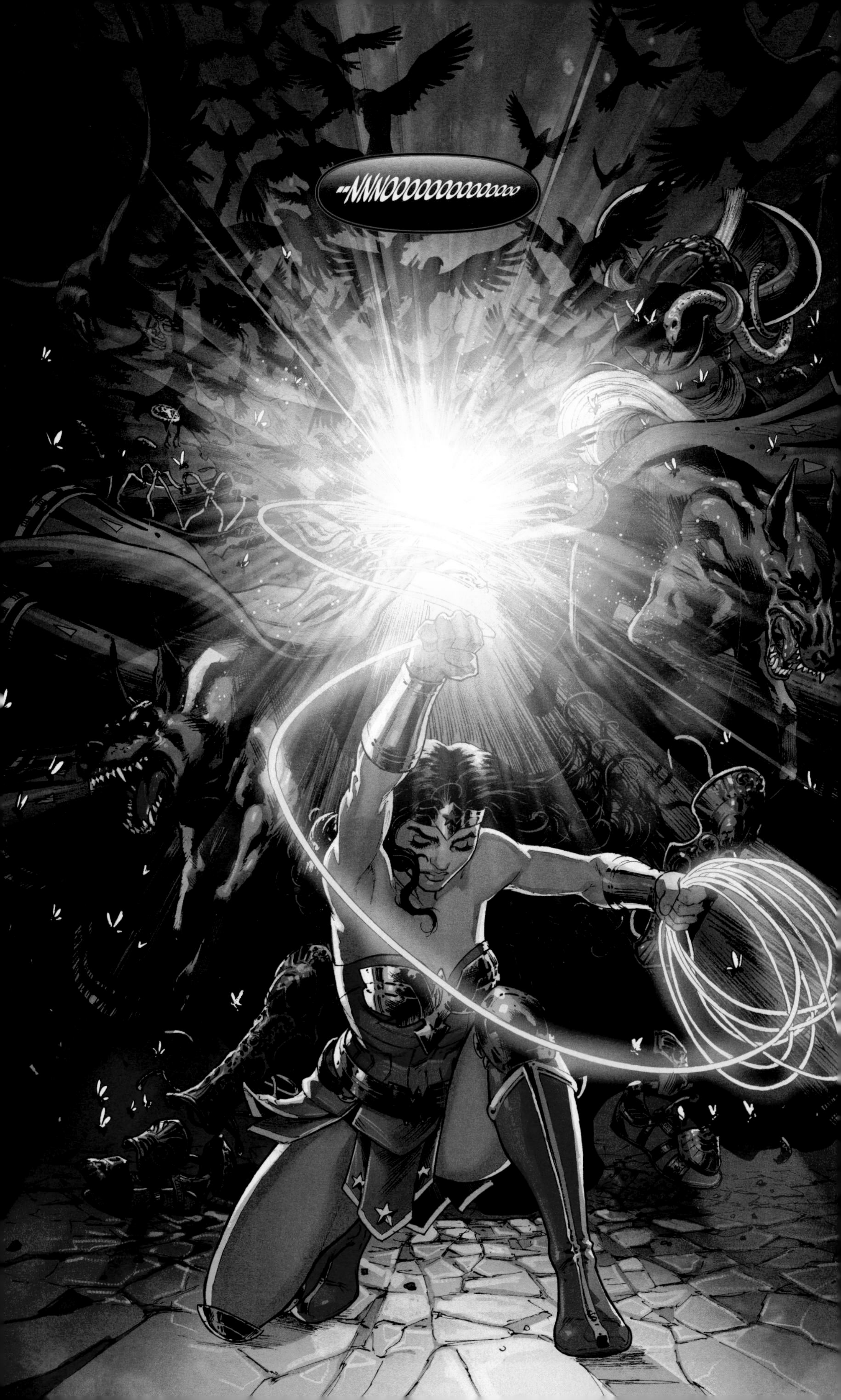
--NNNOOOOOOOOOOOoo

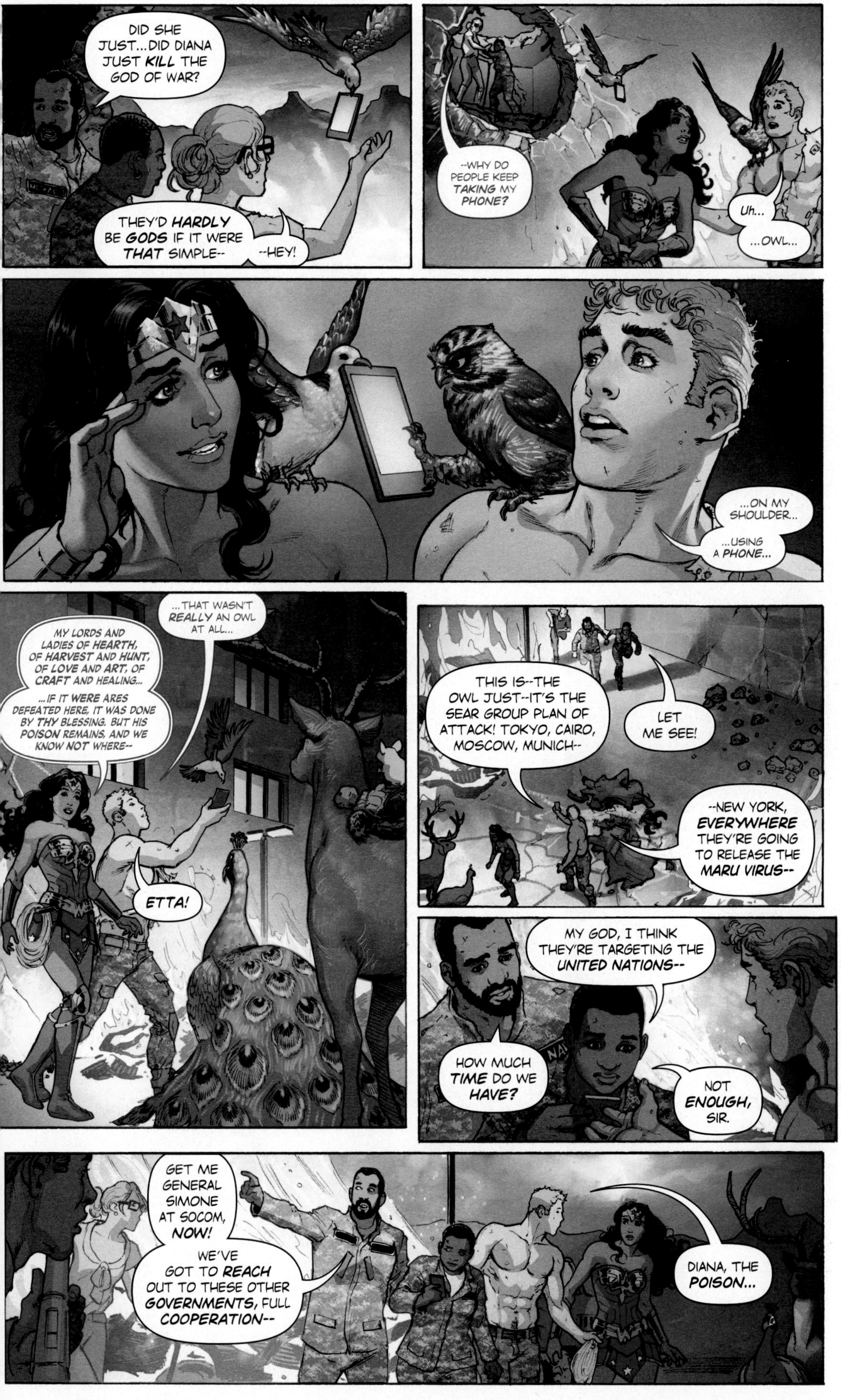
DID SHE JUST...DID DIANA JUST KILL THE GOD OF WAR?
THEY'D HARDLY BE GODS IF IT WERE THAT SIMPLE--
--HEY!
--WHY DO PEOPLE KEEP TAKING MY PHONE?
Uh...
...OWL...
...ON MY SHOULDER...
...USING A PHONE...
...THAT WASN'T REALLY AN OWL AT ALL...
MY LORDS AND LADIES OF HEARTH, OF HARVEST AND HUNT, OF LOVE AND ART, OF CRAFT AND HEALING...
...IF IT WERE ARES DEFEATED HERE, IT WAS DONE BY THY BLESSING. BUT HIS POISON REMAINS, AND WE KNOW NOT WHERE--
ETTA!
THIS IS--THE OWL JUST--IT'S THE SEAR GROUP PLAN OF ATTACK! TOKYO, CAIRO, MOSCOW, MUNICH--
LET ME SEE!
--NEW YORK, EVERYWHERE THEY'RE GOING TO RELEASE THE MARU VIRUS--
MY GOD, I THINK THEY'RE TARGETING THE UNITED NATIONS--
HOW MUCH TIME DO WE HAVE?
NOT ENOUGH, SIR.
GET ME GENERAL SIMONE AT SOCOM, NOW!
WE'VE GOT TO REACH OUT TO THESE OTHER GOVERNMENTS, FULL COOPERATION--
DIANA, THE POISON...

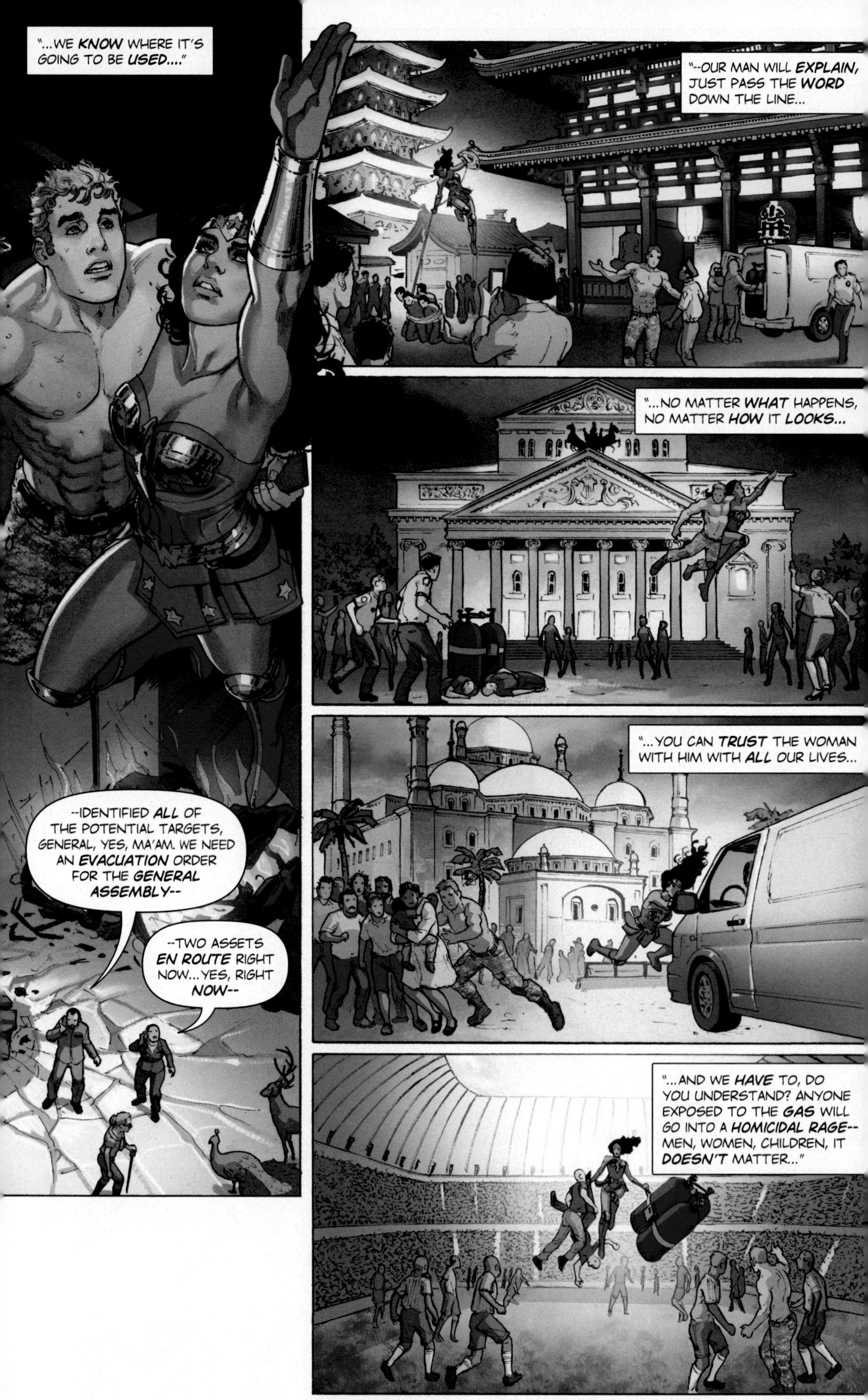
"...WE KNOW WHERE IT'S GOING TO BE USED...."
"--OUR MAN WILL EXPLAIN, JUST PASS THE WORD DOWN THE LINE...
"...NO MATTER WHAT HAPPENS, NO MATTER HOW IT LOOKS...
"...YOU CAN TRUST THE WOMAN WITH HIM WITH ALL OUR LIVES...
--IDENTIFIED ALL OF THE POTENTIAL TARGETS, GENERAL, YES, MA'AM. WE NEED AN EVACUATION ORDER FOR THE GENERAL ASSEMBLY--
--TWO ASSETS EN ROUTE RIGHT NOW...YES, RIGHT NOW--
"...AND WE HAVE TO, DO YOU UNDERSTAND? ANYONE EXPOSED TO THE GAS WILL GO INTO A HOMICIDAL RAGE--MEN, WOMEN, CHILDREN, IT DOESN'T MATTER..."

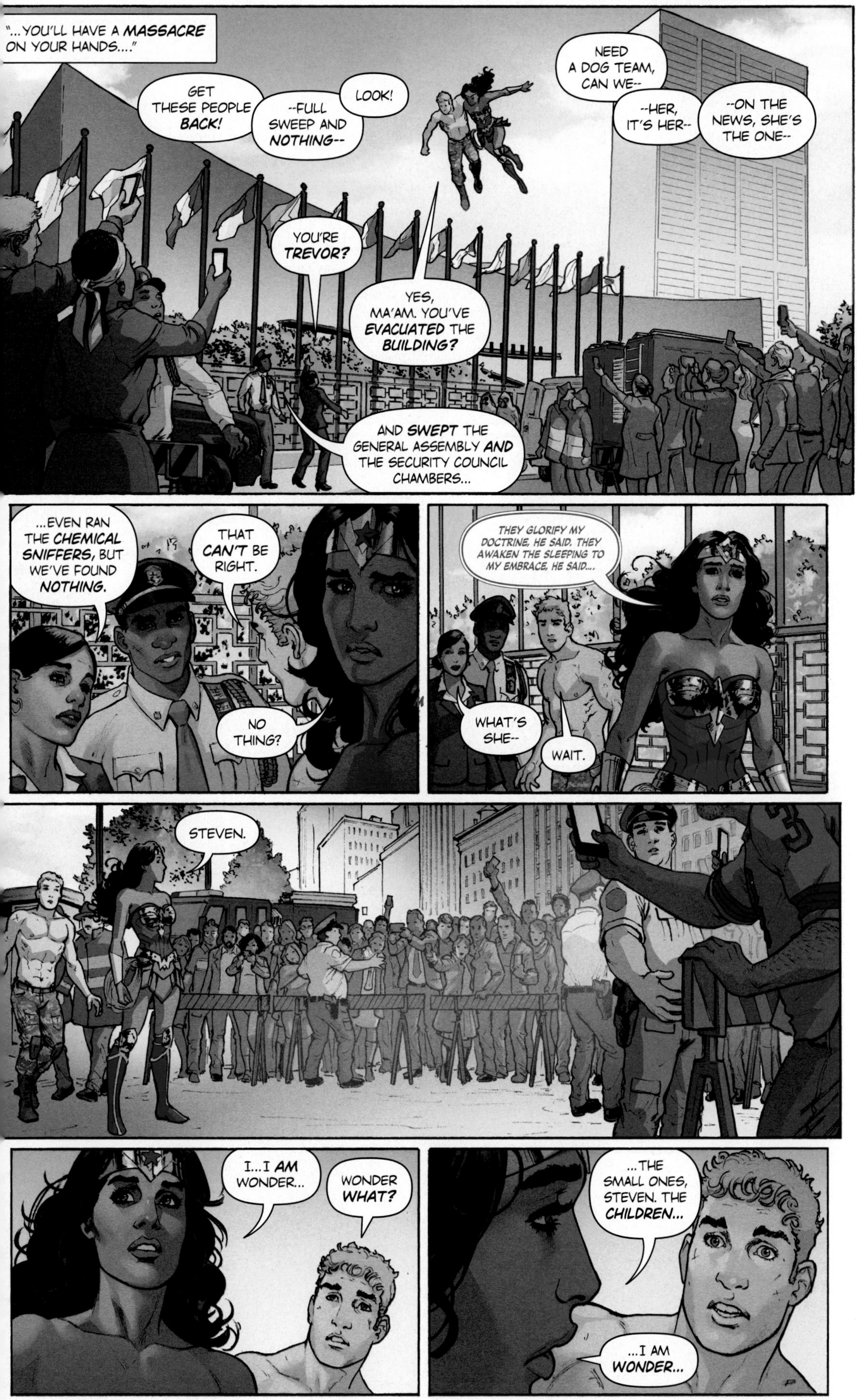
"...YOU'LL HAVE A MASSACRE ON YOUR HANDS...."
GET THESE PEOPLE BACK!
--FULL SWEEP AND NOTHING--
LOOK!
NEED A DOG TEAM, CAN WE--
--HER, IT'S HER--
--ON THE NEWS, SHE'S THE ONE--
YOU'RE TREVOR?
YES, MA'AM. YOU'VE EVACUATED THE BUILDING?
AND SWEPT THE GENERAL ASSEMBLY AND THE SECURITY COUNCIL CHAMBERS...
...EVEN RAN THE CHEMICAL SNIFFERS, BUT WE'VE FOUND NOTHING.
THAT CAN'T BE RIGHT.
NO THING?
THEY GLORIFY MY DOCTRINE, HE SAID. THEY AWAKEN THE SLEEPING TO MY EMBRACE, HE SAID....
WHAT'S SHE--
WAIT.
STEVEN.
I...I AM WONDER...
WONDER WHAT?
...THE SMALL ONES, STEVEN. THE CHILDREN...
...I AM WONDER...

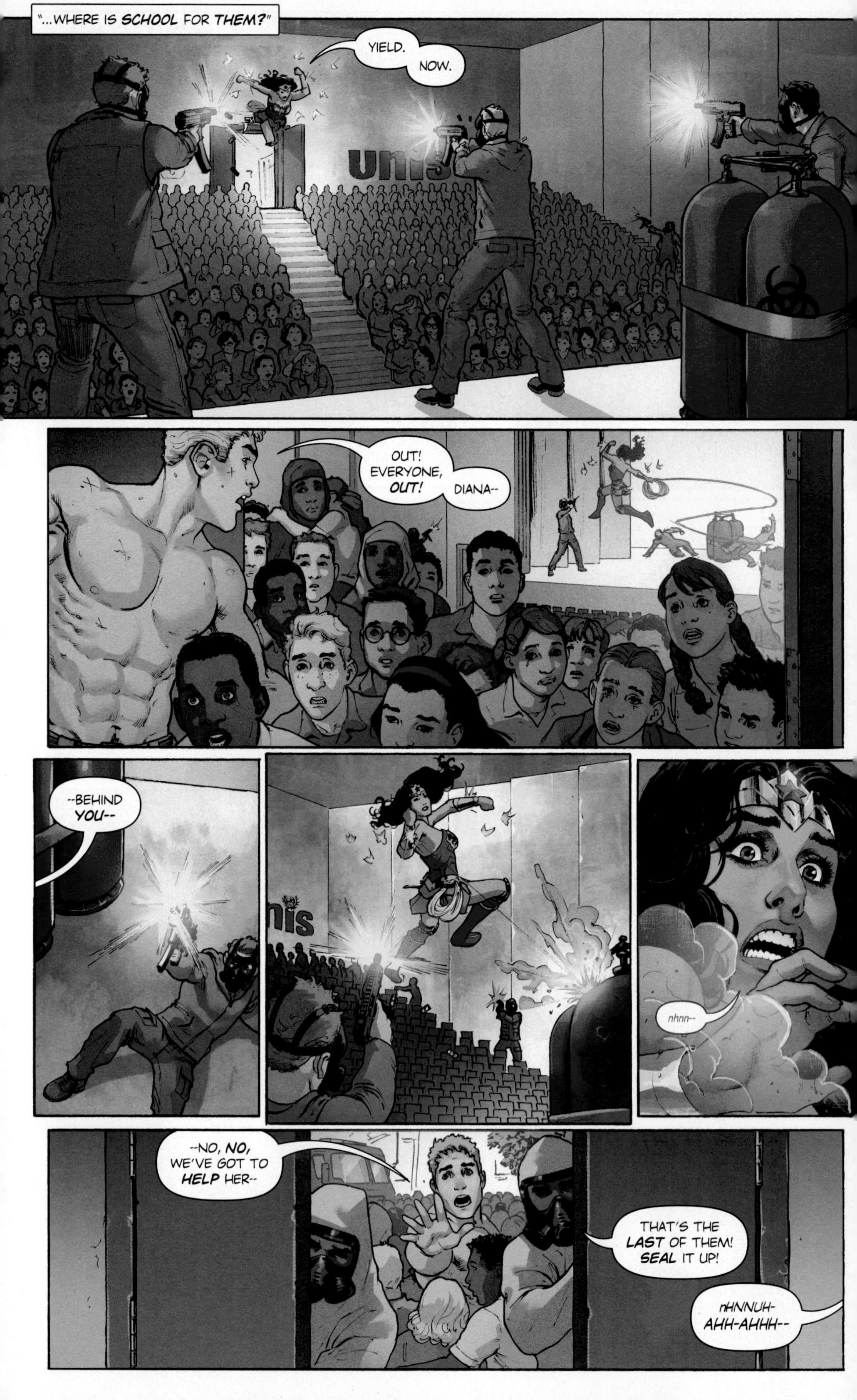
"...WHERE IS SCHOOL FOR THEM?"
YIELD. NOW.
OUT! EVERYONE, OUT!
DIANA--
--BEHIND YOU--
nhnn--
--NO, NO, WE'VE GOT TO HELP HER--
THAT'S THE LAST OF THEM! SEAL IT UP!
nHNNUH-AHH-AHHH--

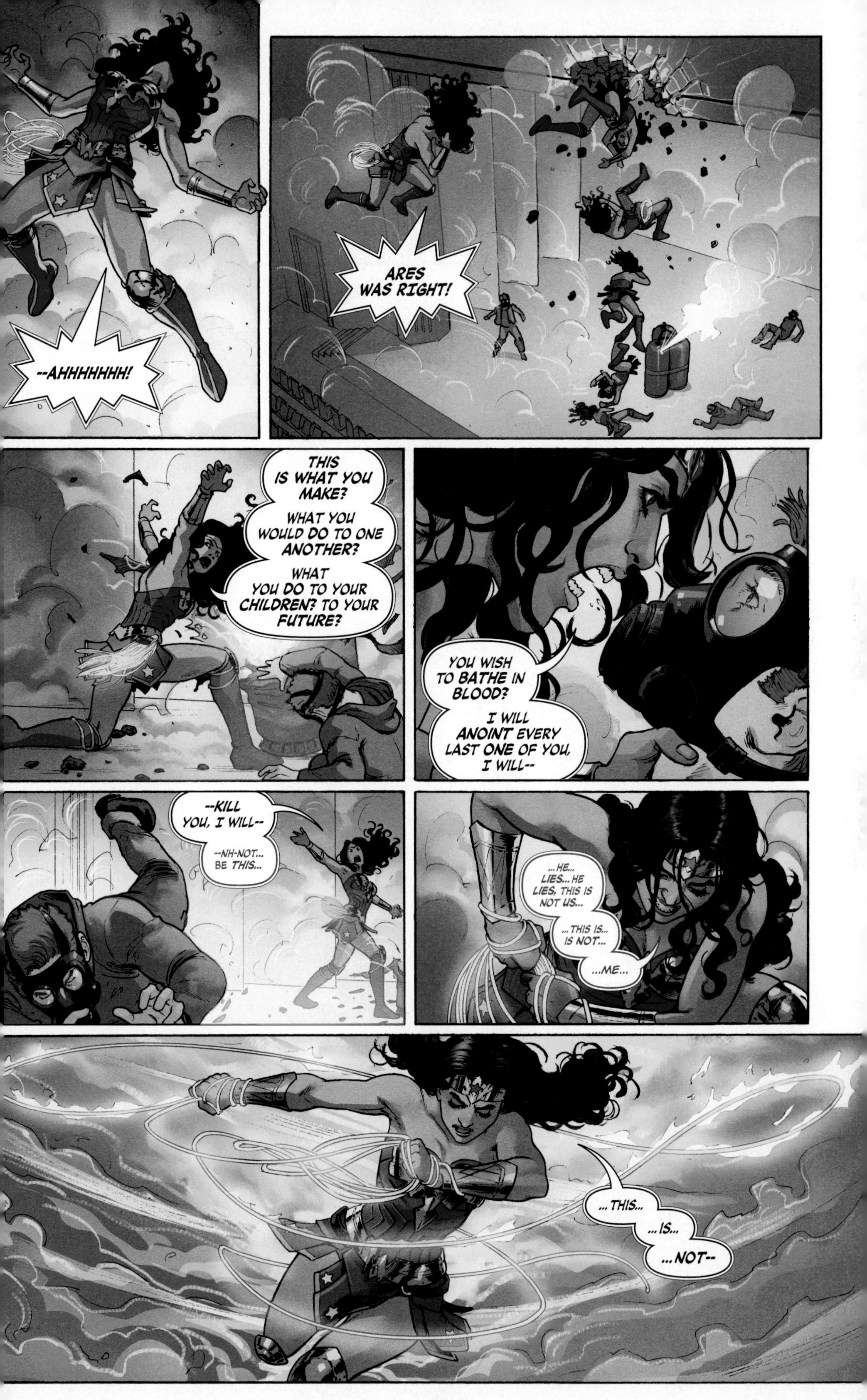
--AHHHHHHH!
ARES WAS RIGHT!
THIS IS WHAT YOU MAKE?
WHAT YOU WOULD DO TO ONE ANOTHER?
WHAT YOU DO TO YOUR CHILDREN? TO YOUR FUTURE?
YOU WISH TO BATHE IN BLOOD?
I WILL ANOINT EVERY LAST ONE OF YOU, I WILL--
--KILL YOU, I WILL--
--NH-NOT... BE THIS...
...HE... LIES... HE LIES, THIS IS NOT US...
...THIS IS... IS NOT...
...ME...
...THIS...
...IS...
...NOT--

--TRUE!

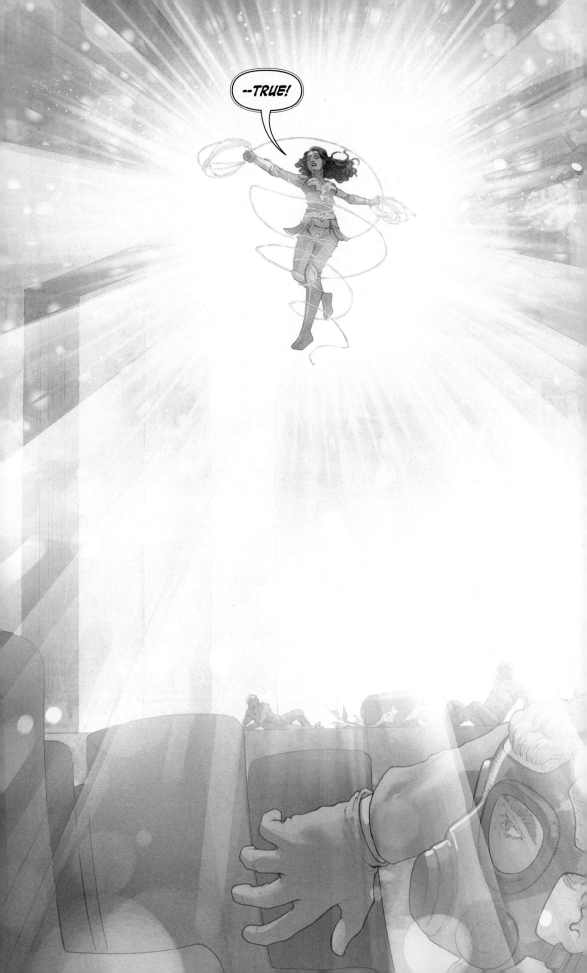

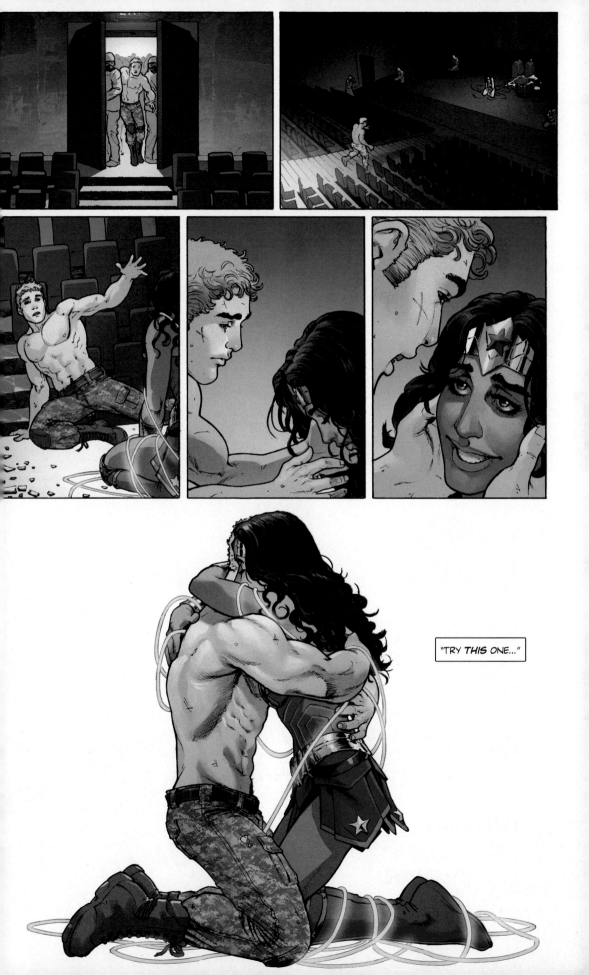

"TRY **THIS** ONE..."

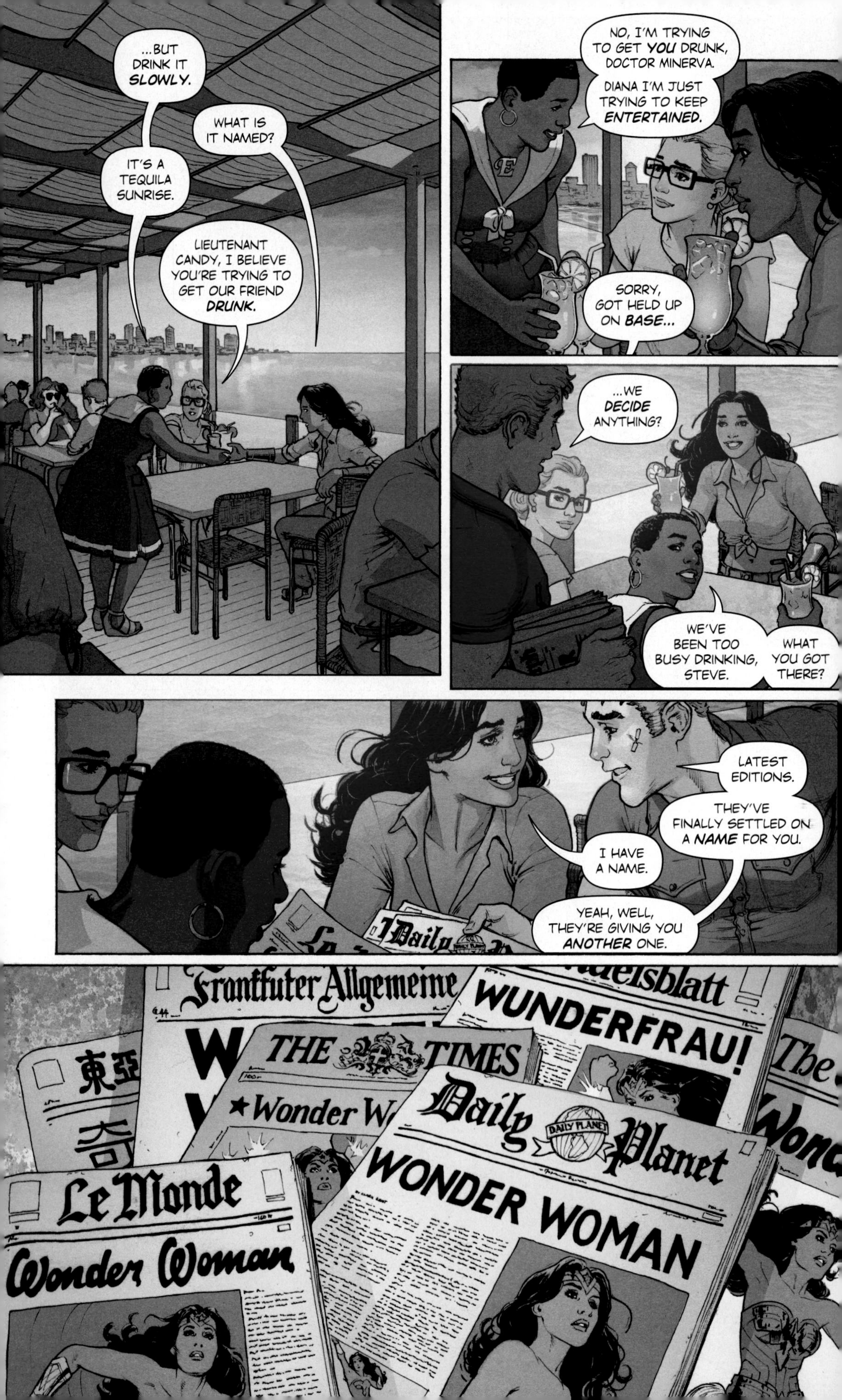

WHAT IS IT NAMED?
IT'S A TEQUILA SUNRISE.
...BUT DRINK IT SLOWLY.
LIEUTENANT CANDY, I BELIEVE YOU'RE TRYING TO GET OUR FRIEND DRUNK.
NO, I'M TRYING TO GET YOU DRUNK, DOCTOR MINERVA.
DIANA I'M JUST TRYING TO KEEP ENTERTAINED.
SORRY, GOT HELD UP ON BASE...
...WE DECIDE ANYTHING?
WE'VE BEEN TOO BUSY DRINKING, STEVE.
WHAT YOU GOT THERE?
LATEST EDITIONS.
THEY'VE FINALLY SETTLED ON A NAME FOR YOU.
I HAVE A NAME.
YEAH, WELL, THEY'RE GIVING YOU ANOTHER ONE.
Frankfuter Allgemeine
WUNDERFRAU!
THE TIMES
★Wonder W
東亞
奇
Daily Planet
WONDER WOMAN
Le Monde
Wonder Woman

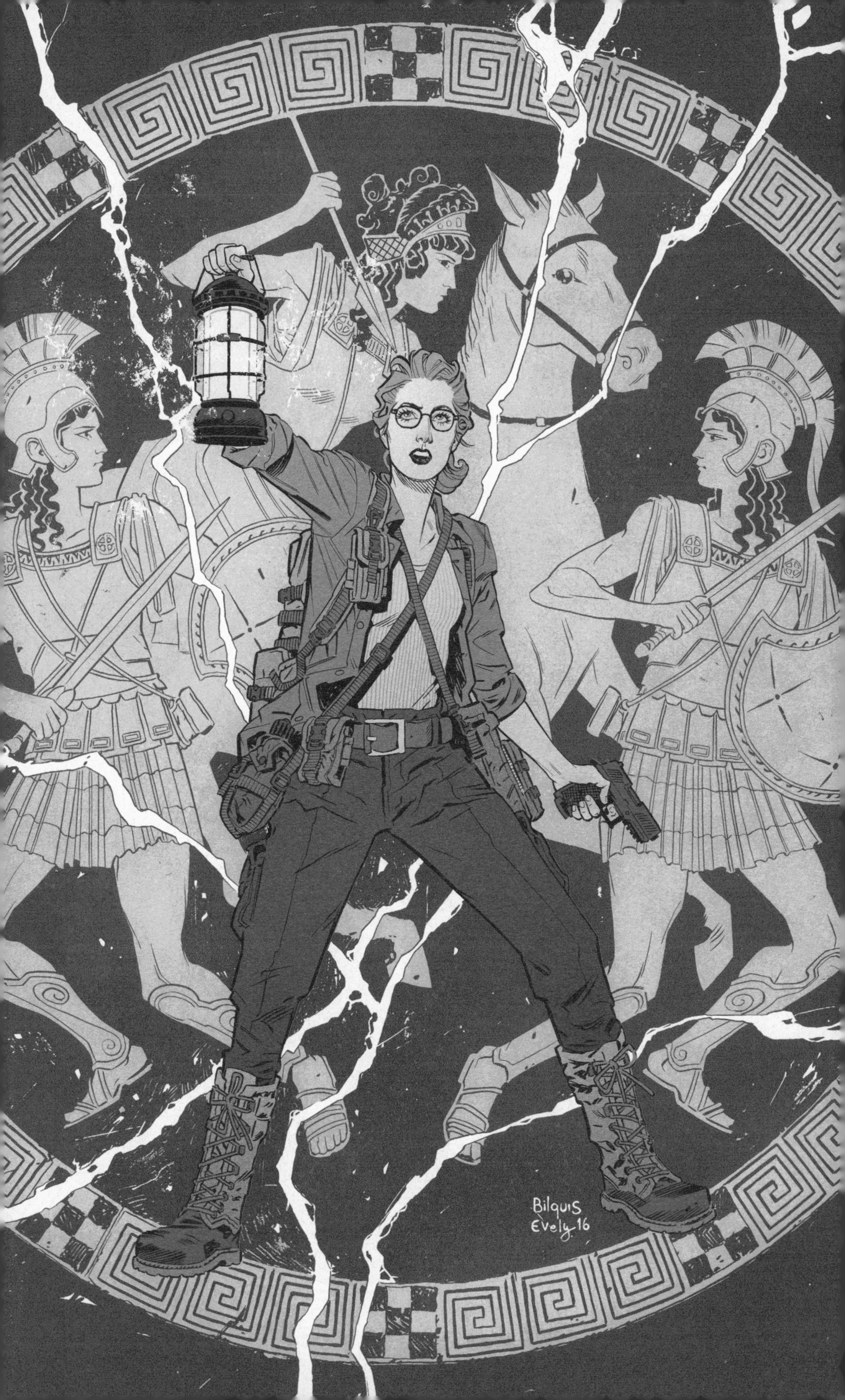
BILQUIS
EVELY 16

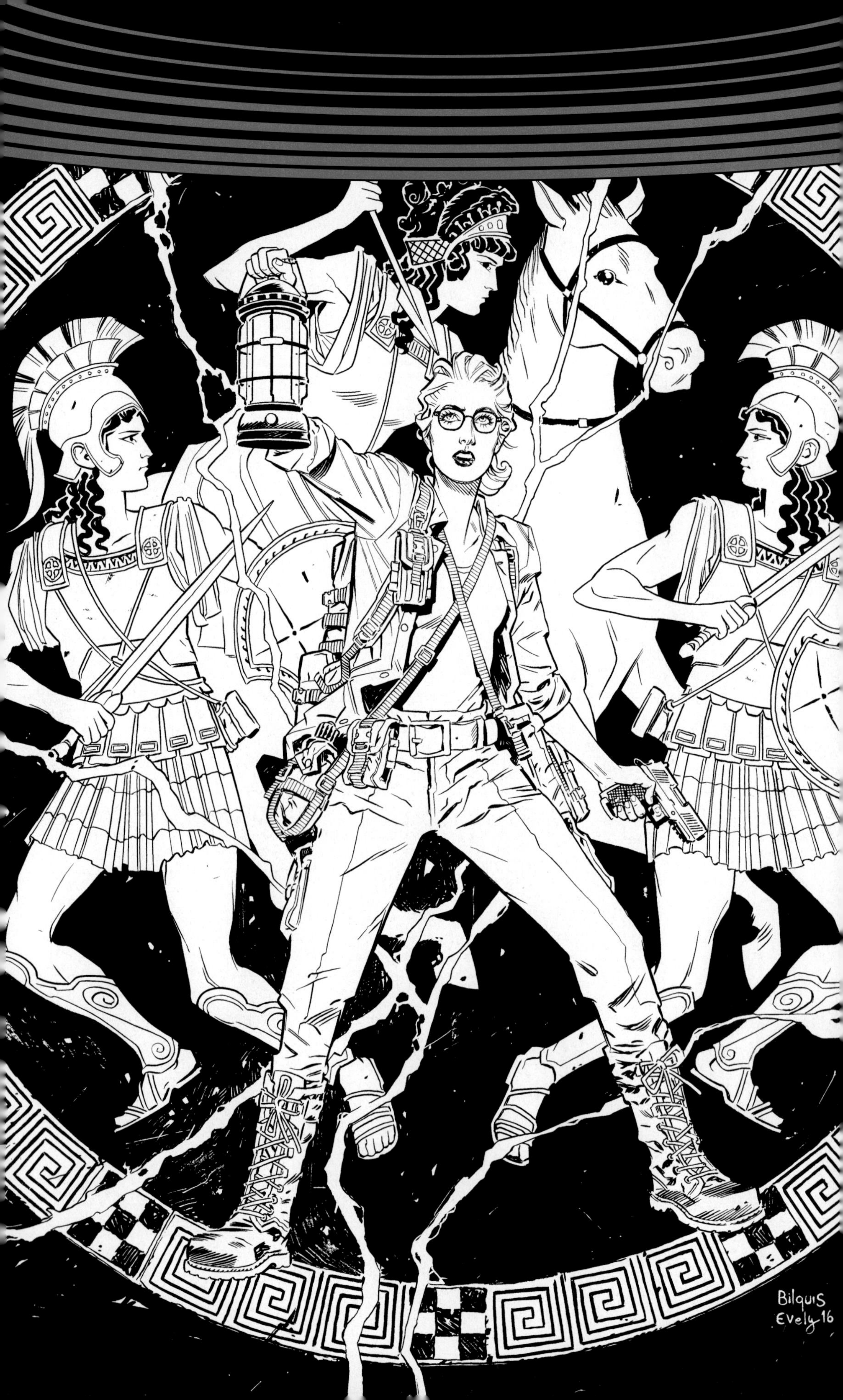
Bilquis
Evely 16

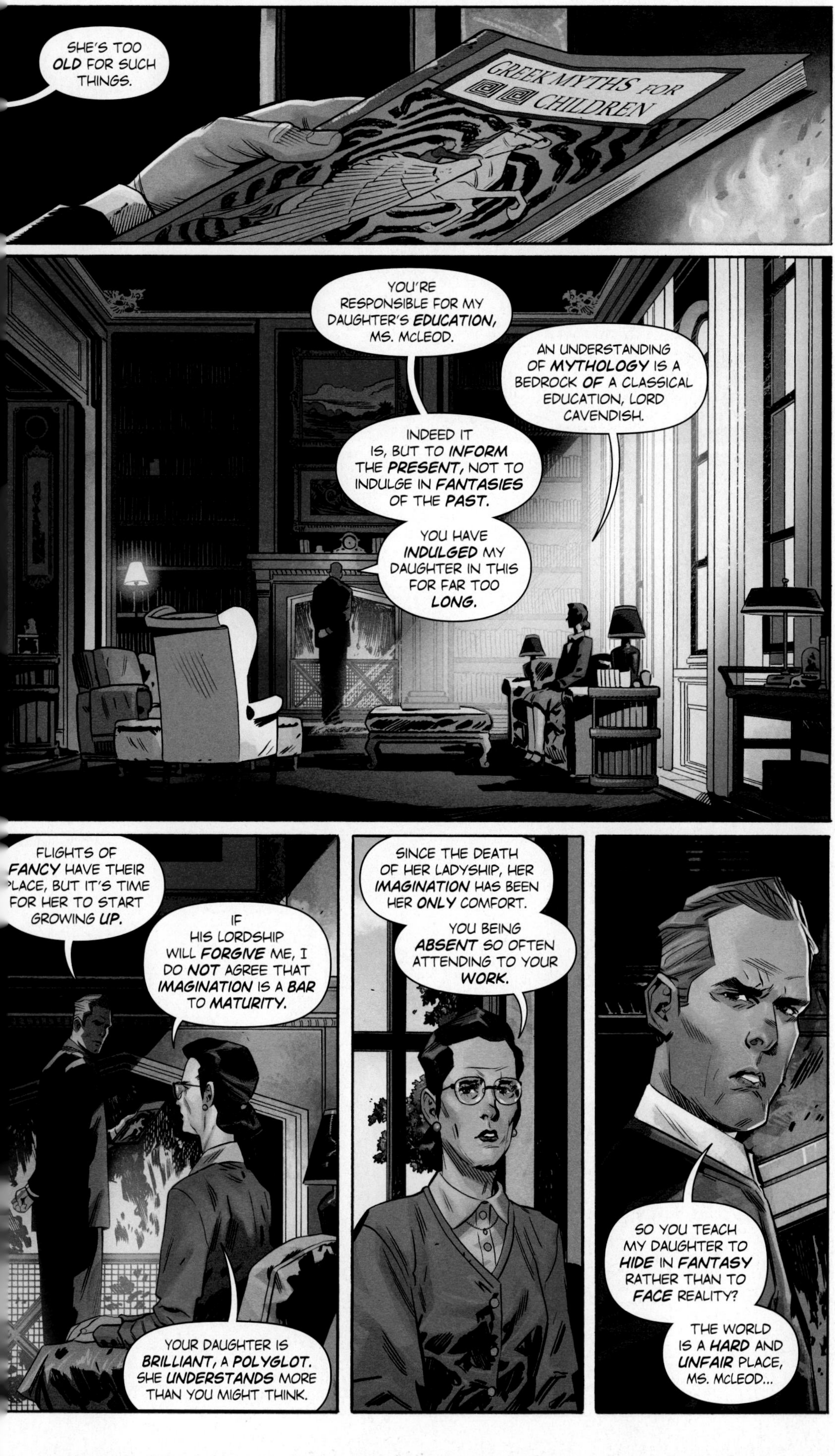
SHE'S TOO OLD FOR SUCH THINGS.
GREEK MYTHS FOR CHILDREN
YOU'RE RESPONSIBLE FOR MY DAUGHTER'S EDUCATION, MS. McLEOD.
AN UNDERSTANDING OF MYTHOLOGY IS A BEDROCK OF A CLASSICAL EDUCATION, LORD CAVENDISH.
INDEED IT IS, BUT TO INFORM THE PRESENT, NOT TO INDULGE IN FANTASIES OF THE PAST.
YOU HAVE INDULGED MY DAUGHTER IN THIS FOR FAR TOO LONG.
FLIGHTS OF FANCY HAVE THEIR PLACE, BUT IT'S TIME FOR HER TO START GROWING UP.
IF HIS LORDSHIP WILL FORGIVE ME, I DO NOT AGREE THAT IMAGINATION IS A BAR TO MATURITY.
YOUR DAUGHTER IS BRILLIANT, A POLYGLOT. SHE UNDERSTANDS MORE THAN YOU MIGHT THINK.
SINCE THE DEATH OF HER LADYSHIP, HER IMAGINATION HAS BEEN HER ONLY COMFORT.
YOU BEING ABSENT SO OFTEN ATTENDING TO YOUR WORK.
SO YOU TEACH MY DAUGHTER TO HIDE IN FANTASY RATHER THAN TO FACE REALITY?
THE WORLD IS A HARD AND UNFAIR PLACE, MS. McLEOD...

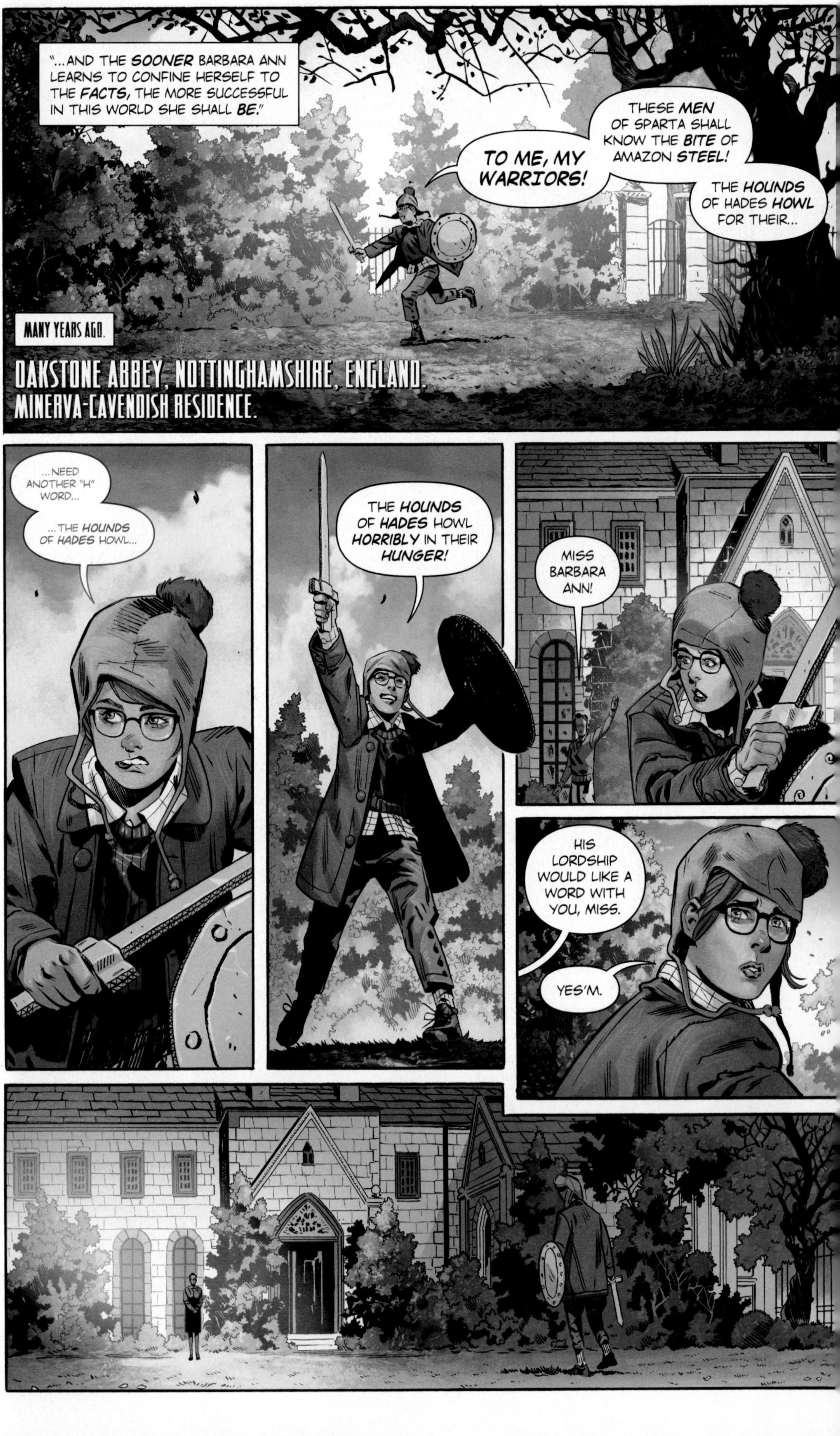
"...AND THE SOONER BARBARA ANN LEARNS TO CONFINE HERSELF TO THE FACTS, THE MORE SUCCESSFUL IN THIS WORLD SHE SHALL BE."
TO ME, MY WARRIORS!
THESE MEN OF SPARTA SHALL KNOW THE BITE OF AMAZON STEEL!
THE HOUNDS OF HADES HOWL FOR THEIR...
MANY YEARS AGO.
OAKSTONE ABBEY, NOTTINGHAMSHIRE, ENGLAND.
MINERVA-CAVENDISH RESIDENCE.
...NEED ANOTHER "H" WORD...
...THE HOUNDS OF HADES HOWL...
THE HOUNDS OF HADES HOWL HORRIBLY IN THEIR HUNGER!
MISS BARBARA ANN!
HIS LORDSHIP WOULD LIKE A WORD WITH YOU, MISS.
YES'M.

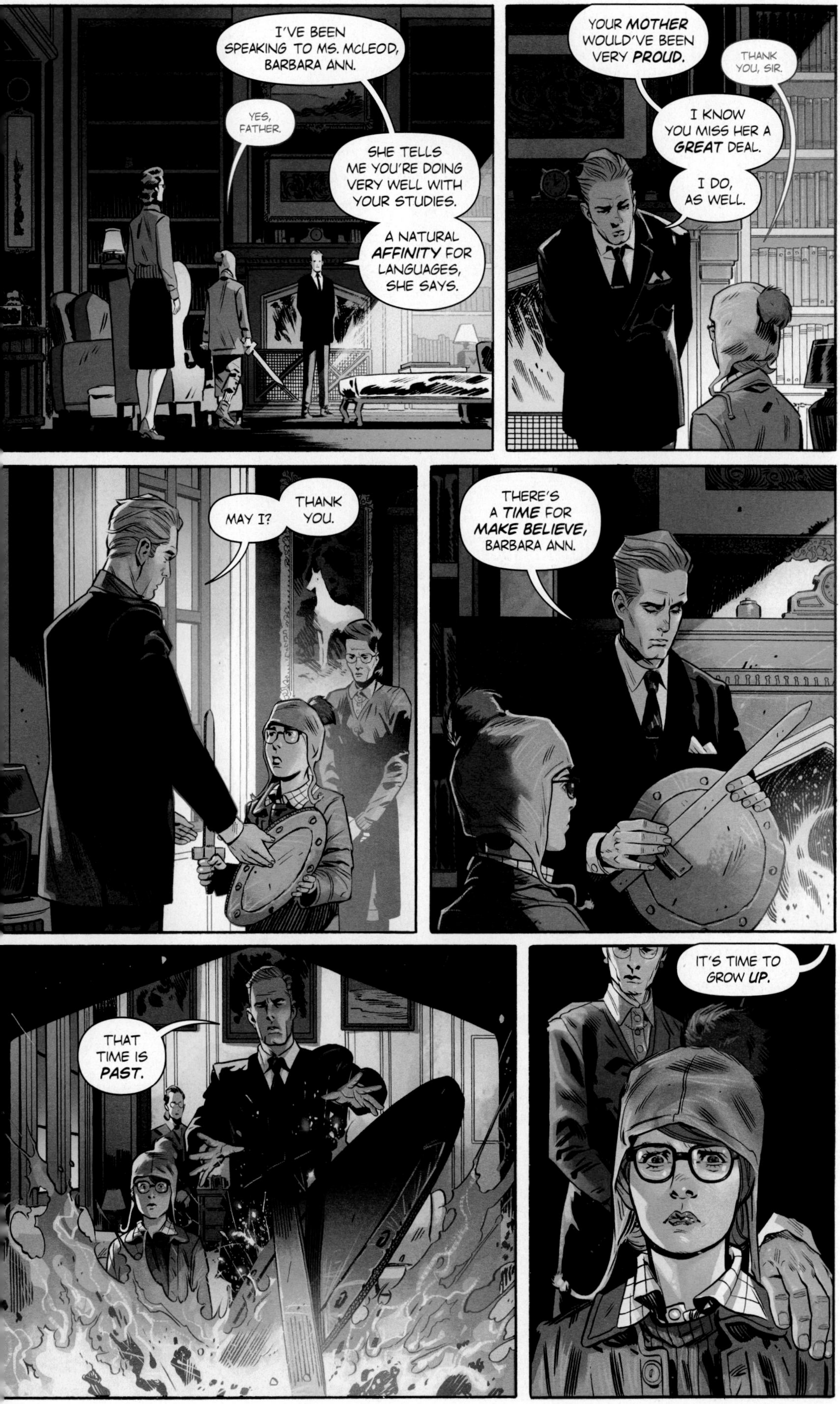
I'VE BEEN SPEAKING TO MS. McLEOD, BARBARA ANN.
YES, FATHER.
SHE TELLS ME YOU'RE DOING VERY WELL WITH YOUR STUDIES.
A NATURAL AFFINITY FOR LANGUAGES, SHE SAYS.
YOUR MOTHER WOULD'VE BEEN VERY PROUD.
THANK YOU, SIR.
I KNOW YOU MISS HER A GREAT DEAL.
I DO, AS WELL.
MAY I?
THANK YOU.
THERE'S A TIME FOR MAKE BELIEVE, BARBARA ANN.
THAT TIME IS PAST.
IT'S TIME TO GROW UP.

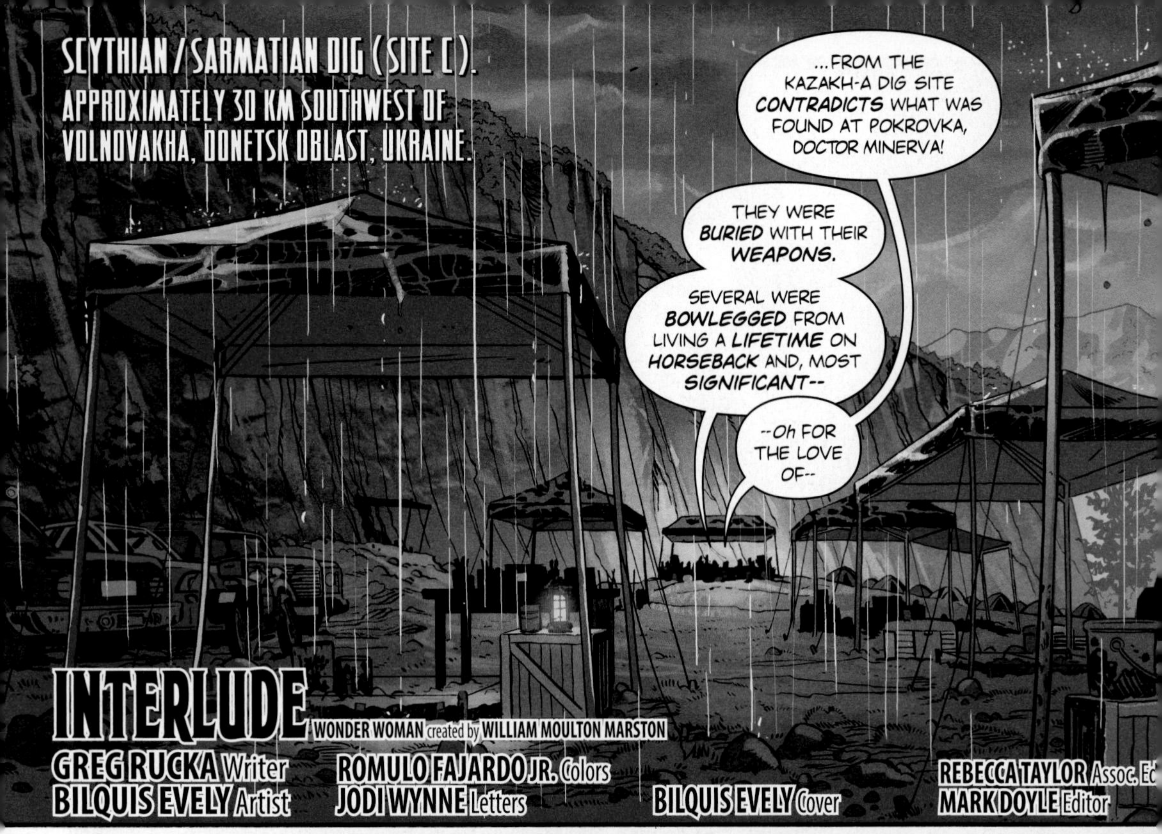
SCYTHIAN / SARMATIAN DIG (SITE C).
APPROXIMATELY 30 KM SOUTHWEST OF VOLNOVAKHA, DONETSK OBLAST, UKRAINE.
...FROM THE KAZAKH-A DIG SITE CONTRADICTS WHAT WAS FOUND AT POKROVKA, DOCTOR MINERVA!
THEY WERE BURIED WITH THEIR WEAPONS.
SEVERAL WERE BOWLEGGED FROM LIVING A LIFETIME ON HORSEBACK AND, MOST SIGNIFICANT--
--Oh FOR THE LOVE OF--
INTERLUDE
WONDER WOMAN created by WILLIAM MOULTON MARSTON
GREG RUCKA Writer
BILQUIS EVELY Artist
ROMULO FAJARDO JR. Colors
JODI WYNNE Letters
BILQUIS EVELY Cover
REBECCA TAYLOR Assoc. Ed
MARK DOYLE Editor

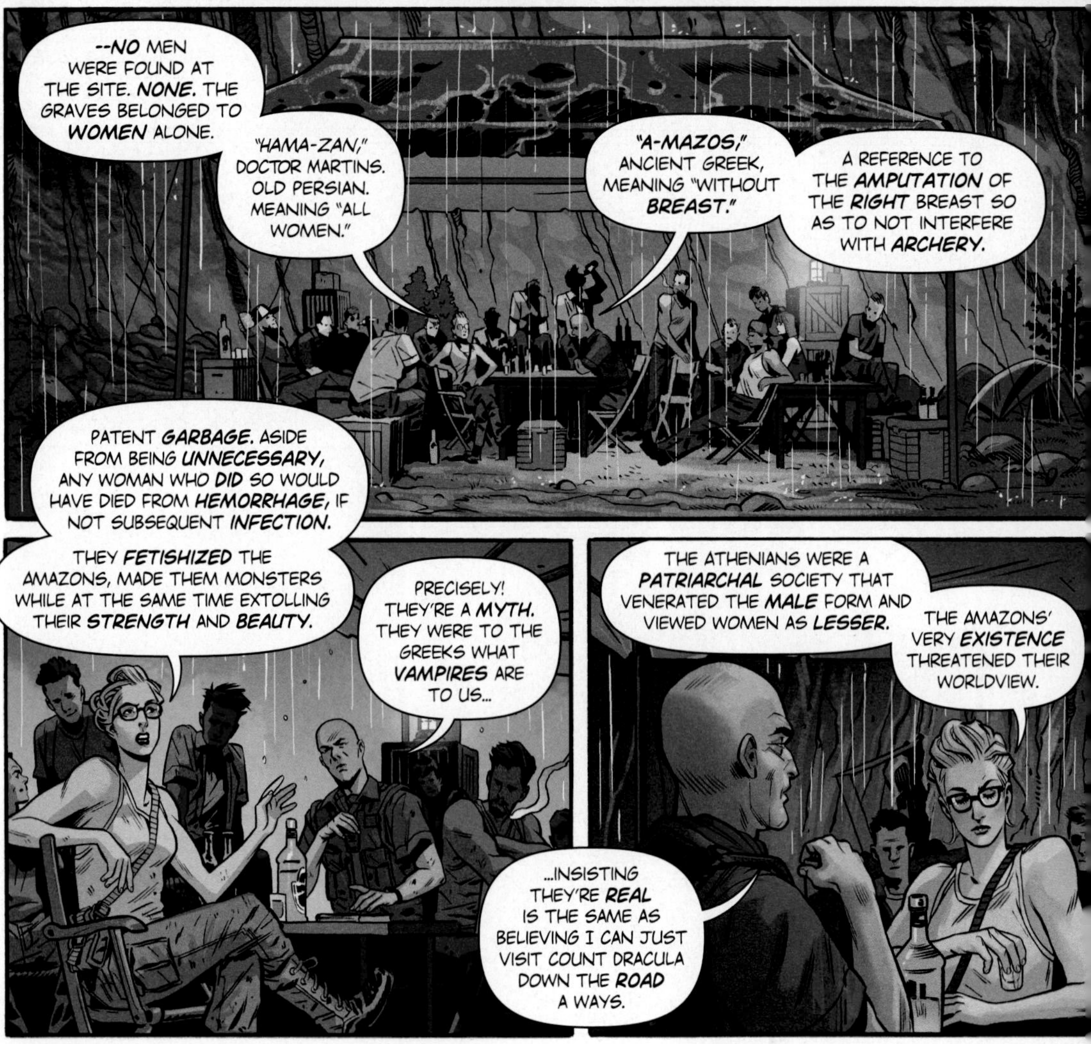
--NO MEN WERE FOUND AT THE SITE. NONE. THE GRAVES BELONGED TO WOMEN ALONE.
"HAMA-ZAN," DOCTOR MARTINS. OLD PERSIAN. MEANING "ALL WOMEN."
"A-MAZOS," ANCIENT GREEK, MEANING "WITHOUT BREAST."
A REFERENCE TO THE AMPUTATION OF THE RIGHT BREAST SO AS TO NOT INTERFERE WITH ARCHERY.
PATENT GARBAGE. ASIDE FROM BEING UNNECESSARY, ANY WOMAN WHO DID SO WOULD HAVE DIED FROM HEMORRHAGE, IF NOT SUBSEQUENT INFECTION.
THEY FETISHIZED THE AMAZONS, MADE THEM MONSTERS WHILE AT THE SAME TIME EXTOLLING THEIR STRENGTH AND BEAUTY.
PRECISELY! THEY'RE A MYTH. THEY WERE TO THE GREEKS WHAT VAMPIRES ARE TO US...
THE ATHENIANS WERE A PATRIARCHAL SOCIETY THAT VENERATED THE MALE FORM AND VIEWED WOMEN AS LESSER.
THE AMAZONS' VERY EXISTENCE THREATENED THEIR WORLDVIEW.
...INSISTING THEY'RE REAL IS THE SAME AS BELIEVING I CAN JUST VISIT COUNT DRACULA DOWN THE ROAD A WAYS.

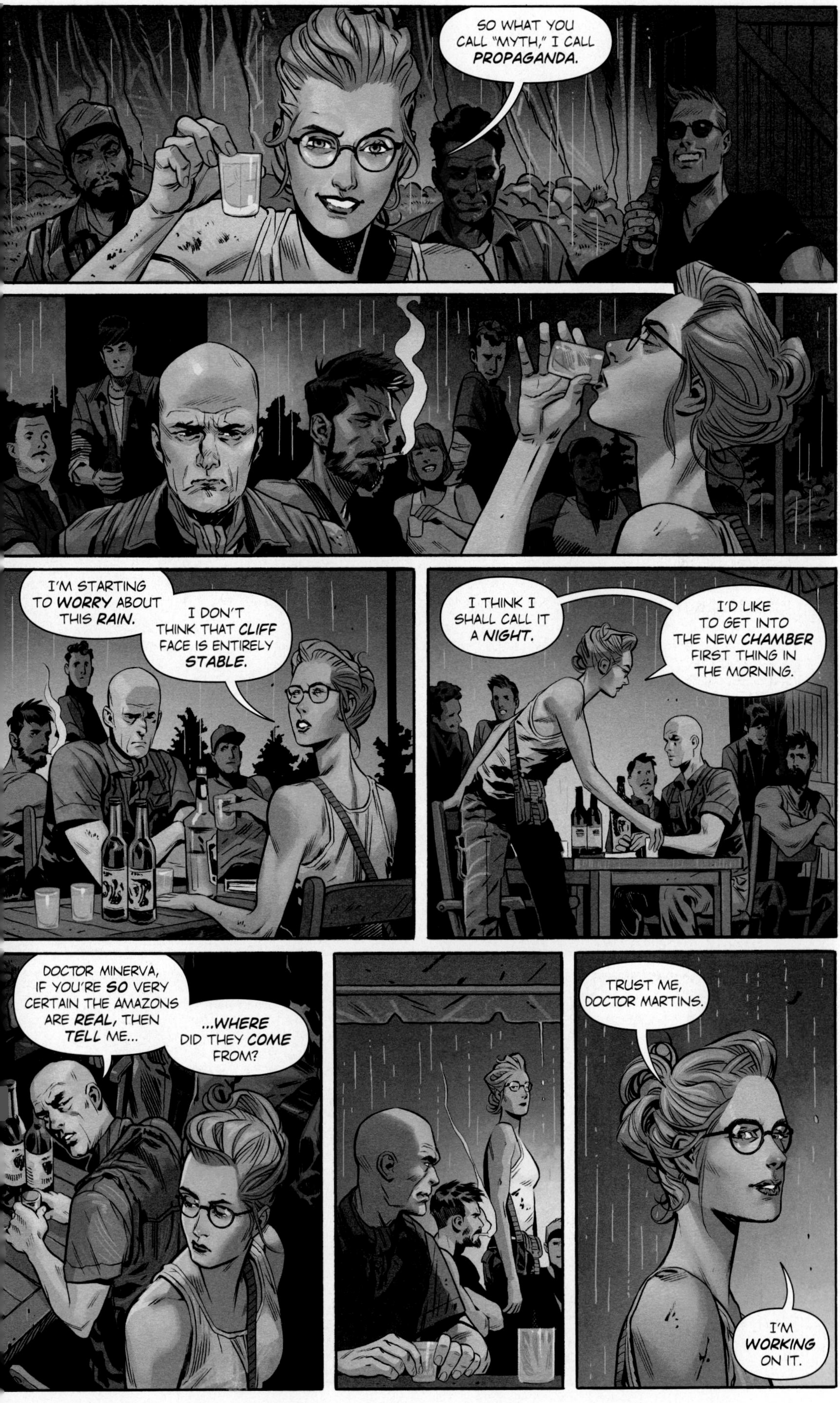
SO WHAT YOU CALL "MYTH," I CALL PROPAGANDA.
I'M STARTING TO WORRY ABOUT THIS RAIN.
I DON'T THINK THAT CLIFF FACE IS ENTIRELY STABLE.
I THINK I SHALL CALL IT A NIGHT.
I'D LIKE TO GET INTO THE NEW CHAMBER FIRST THING IN THE MORNING.
DOCTOR MINERVA, IF YOU'RE SO VERY CERTAIN THE AMAZONS ARE REAL, THEN TELL ME...
...WHERE DID THEY COME FROM?
TRUST ME, DOCTOR MARTINS.
I'M WORKING ON IT.

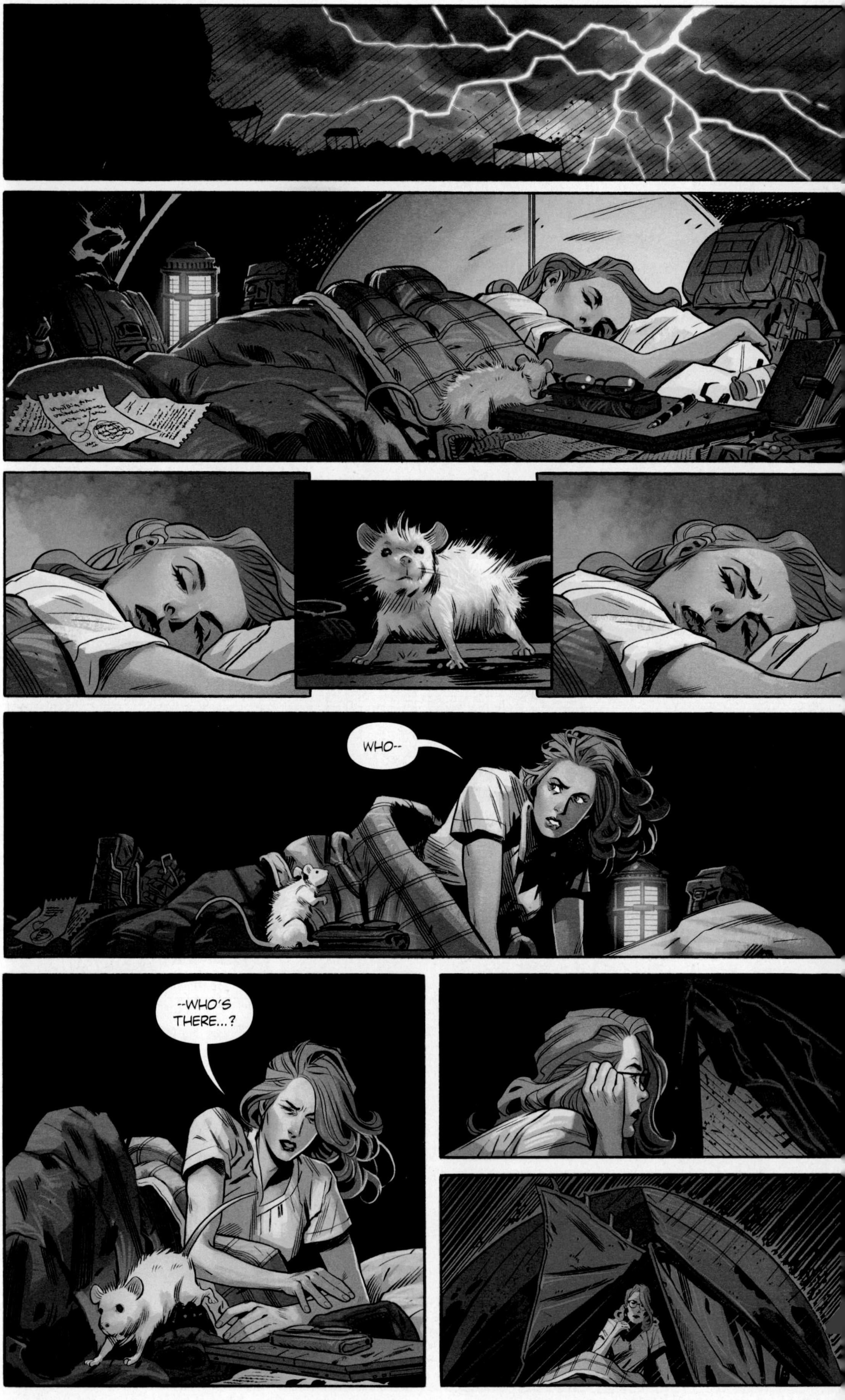
WHO--
--WHO'S THERE...?

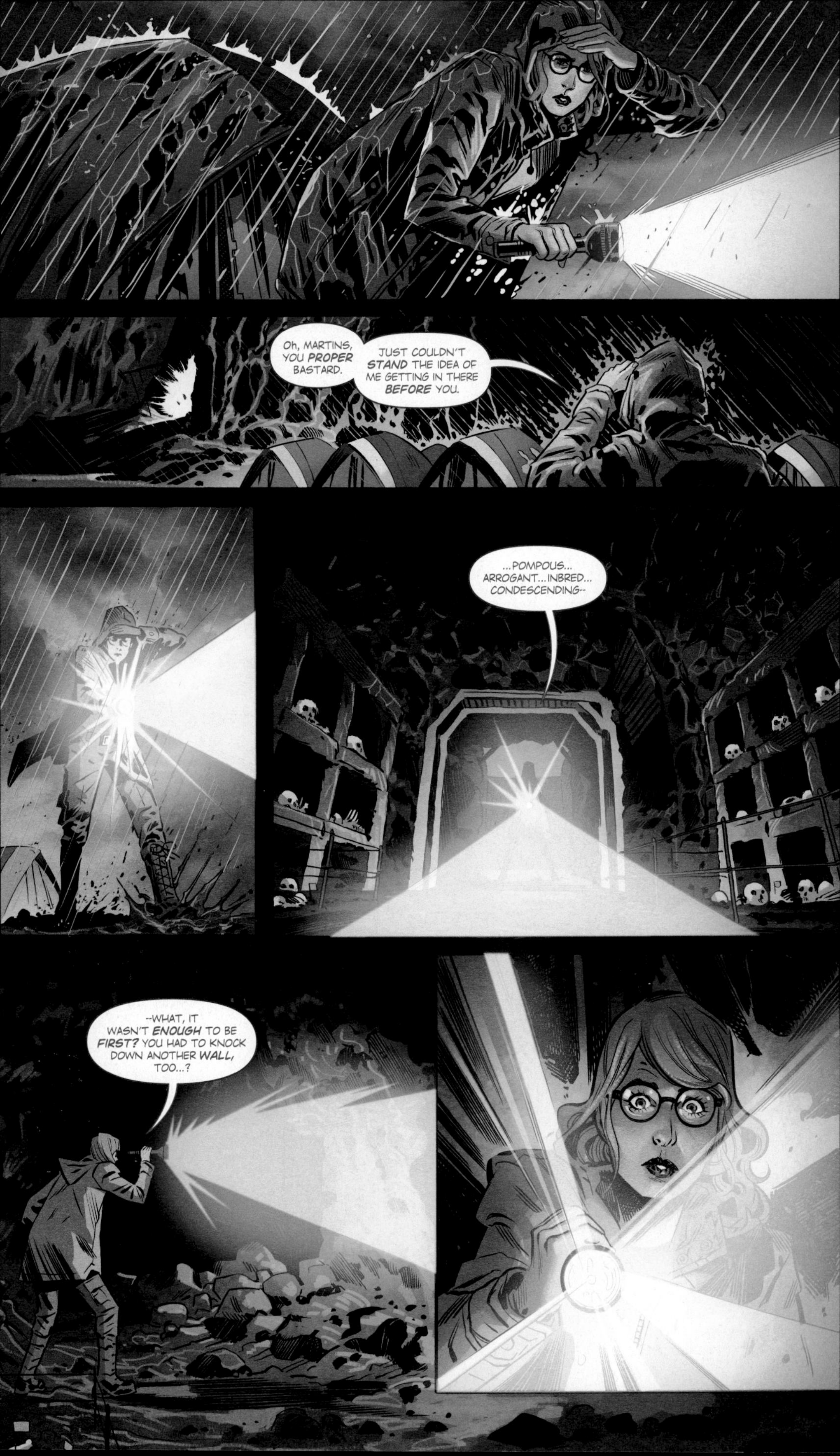
Oh, MARTINS, YOU PROPER BASTARD.
JUST COULDN'T STAND THE IDEA OF ME GETTING IN THERE BEFORE YOU.
...POMPOUS... ARROGANT...INBRED... CONDESCENDING--
--WHAT, IT WASN'T ENOUGH TO BE FIRST? YOU HAD TO KNOCK DOWN ANOTHER WALL, TOO...?

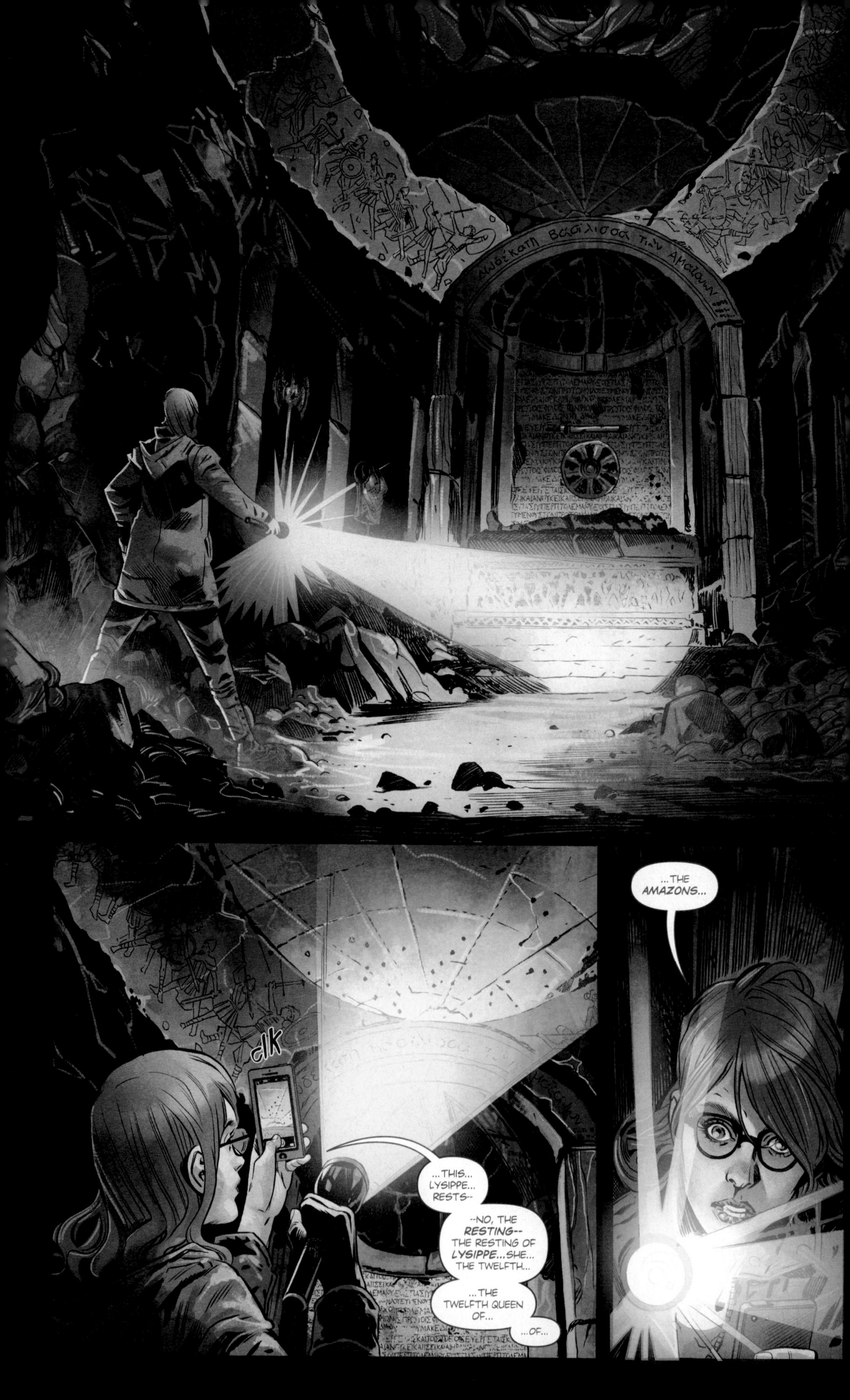
clk
...THIS... LYSIPPE... RESTS--
--NO, THE RESTING-- THE RESTING OF LYSIPPE...SHE... THE TWELFTH...
...THE TWELFTH QUEEN OF...
...OF...
...THE AMAZONS...

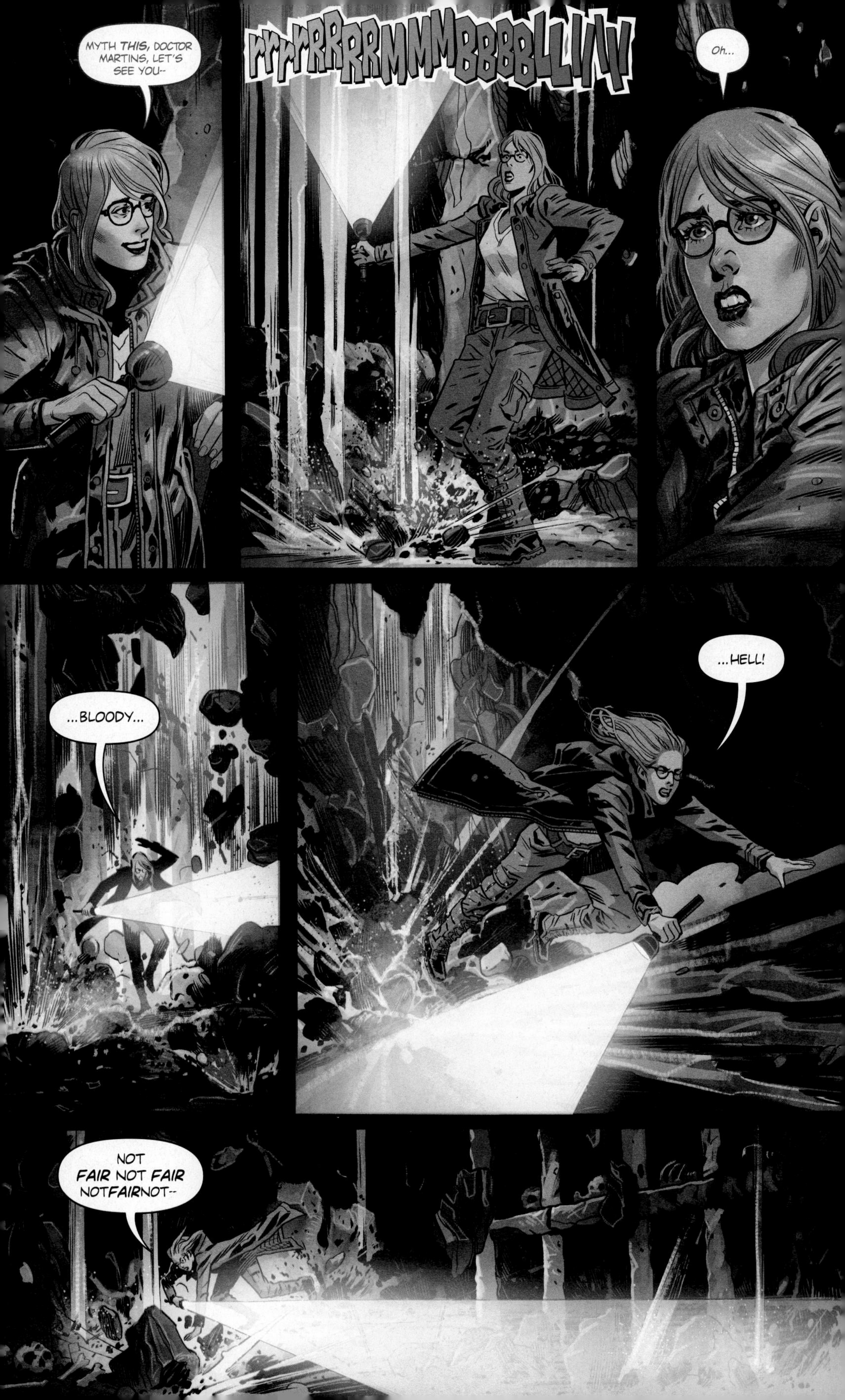
MYTH THIS, DOCTOR MARTINS, LET'S SEE YOU--
rrrrRRRRMMMMBBBBLLLIVV
Oh...
...BLOODY...
...HELL!
NOT FAIR NOT FAIR NOTFAIRNOT--

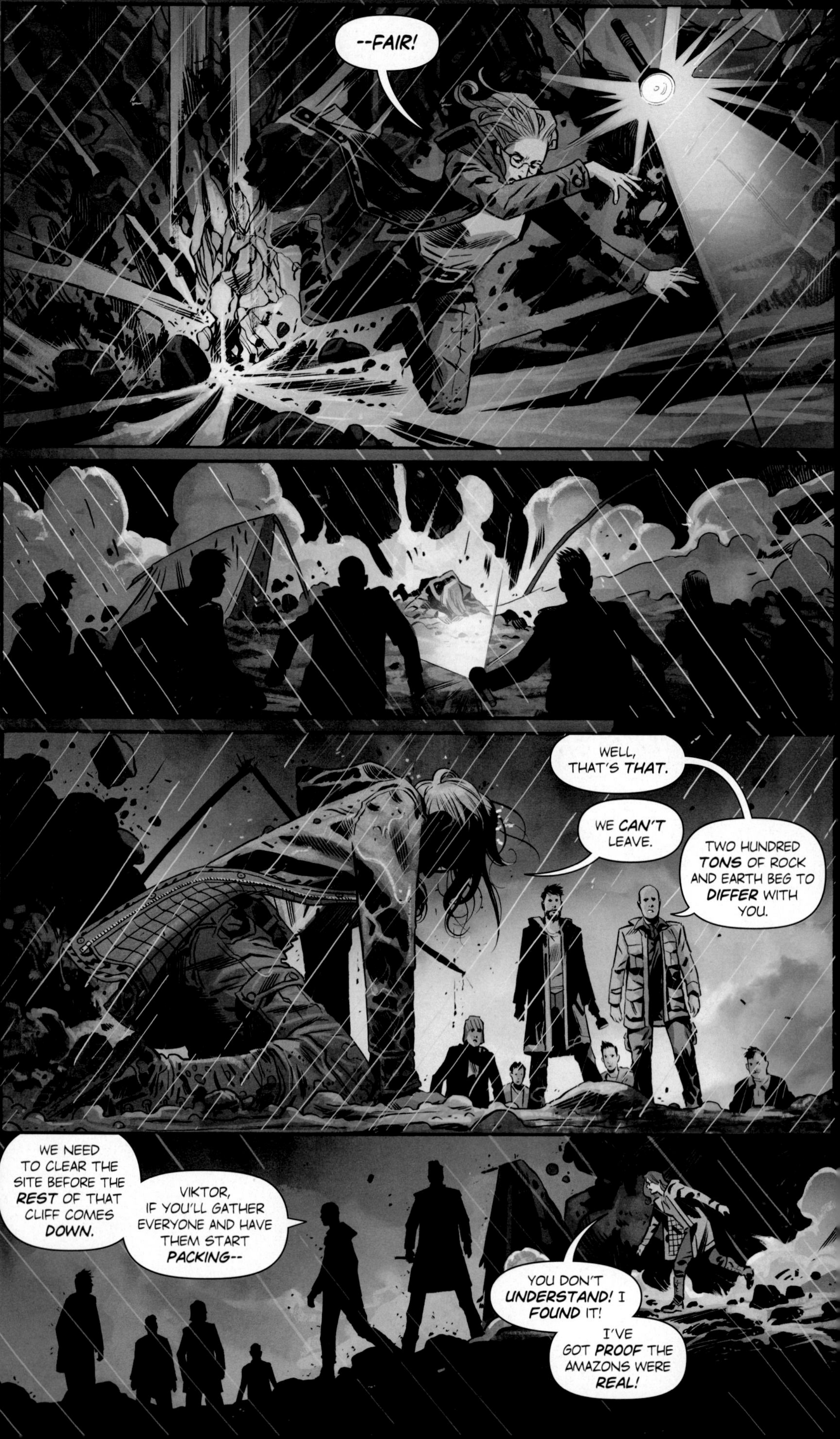
--FAIR!
WELL, THAT'S THAT.
WE CAN'T LEAVE.
TWO HUNDRED TONS OF ROCK AND EARTH BEG TO DIFFER WITH YOU.
WE NEED TO CLEAR THE SITE BEFORE THE REST OF THAT CLIFF COMES DOWN.
VIKTOR, IF YOU'LL GATHER EVERYONE AND HAVE THEM START PACKING--
YOU DON'T UNDERSTAND! I FOUND IT!
I'VE GOT PROOF THE AMAZONS WERE REAL!

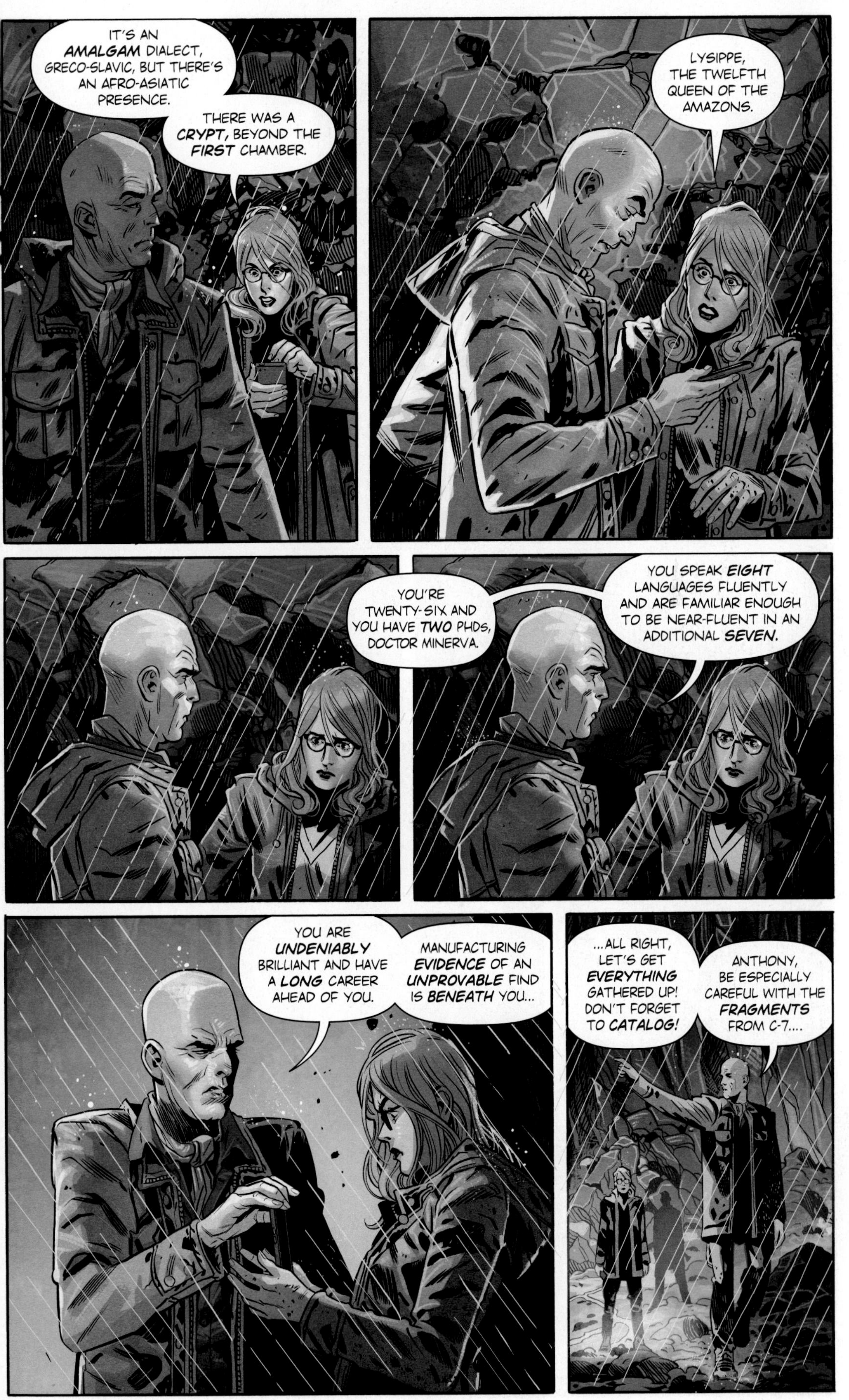
IT'S AN AMALGAM DIALECT, GRECO-SLAVIC, BUT THERE'S AN AFRO-ASIATIC PRESENCE.
THERE WAS A CRYPT, BEYOND THE FIRST CHAMBER.
LYSIPPE, THE TWELFTH QUEEN OF THE AMAZONS.
YOU'RE TWENTY-SIX AND YOU HAVE TWO PHDs, DOCTOR MINERVA.
YOU SPEAK EIGHT LANGUAGES FLUENTLY AND ARE FAMILIAR ENOUGH TO BE NEAR-FLUENT IN AN ADDITIONAL SEVEN.
YOU ARE UNDENIABLY BRILLIANT AND HAVE A LONG CAREER AHEAD OF YOU.
MANUFACTURING EVIDENCE OF AN UNPROVABLE FIND IS BENEATH YOU...
...ALL RIGHT, LET'S GET EVERYTHING GATHERED UP! DON'T FORGET TO CATALOG!
ANTHONY, BE ESPECIALLY CAREFUL WITH THE FRAGMENTS FROM C-7....

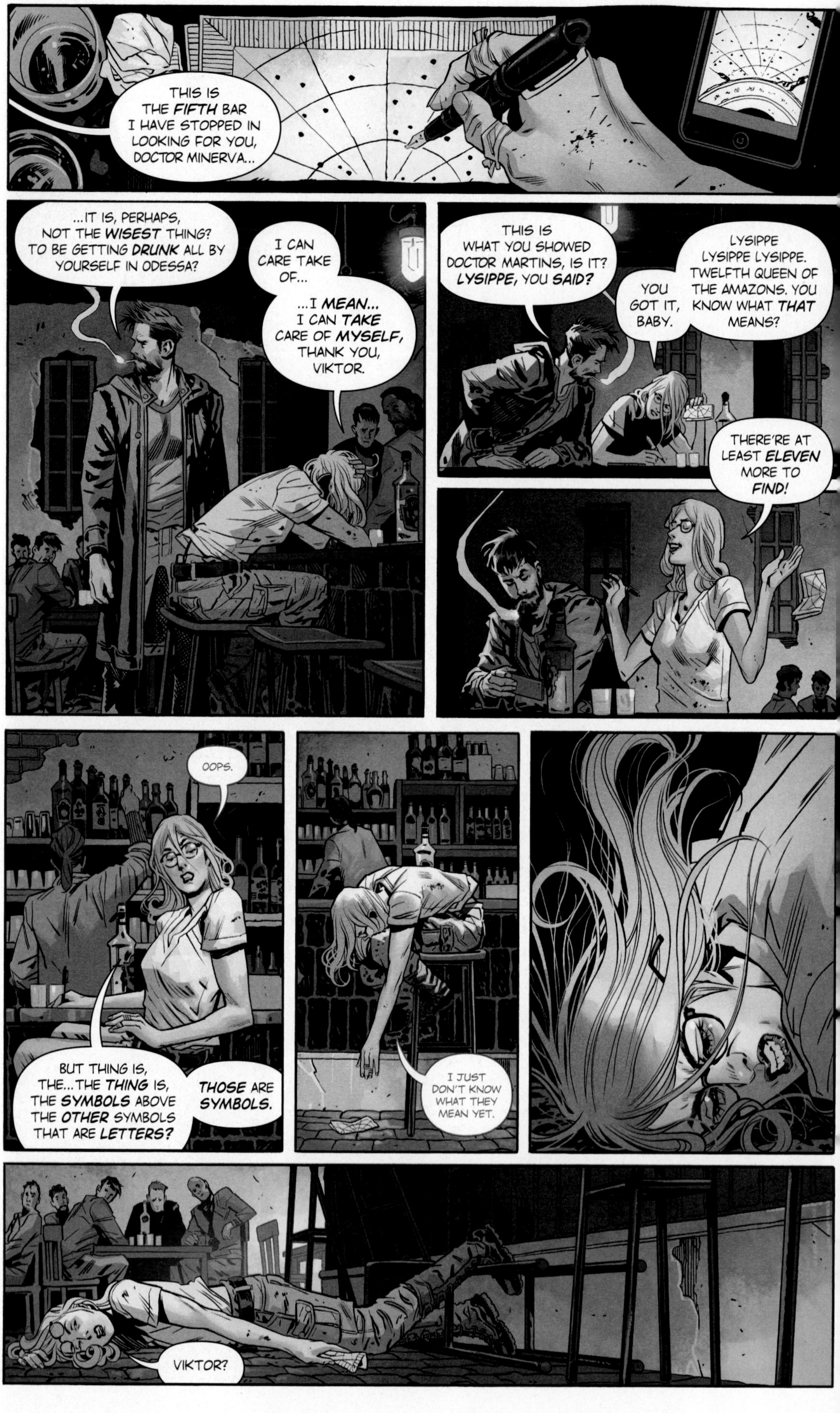

THIS IS THE FIFTH BAR I HAVE STOPPED IN LOOKING FOR YOU, DOCTOR MINERVA...
...IT IS, PERHAPS, NOT THE WISEST THING? TO BE GETTING DRUNK ALL BY YOURSELF IN ODESSA?
I CAN CARE TAKE OF...
...I MEAN... I CAN TAKE CARE OF MYSELF, THANK YOU, VIKTOR.
THIS IS WHAT YOU SHOWED DOCTOR MARTINS, IS IT? LYSIPPE, YOU SAID?
YOU GOT IT, BABY.
LYSIPPE LYSIPPE LYSIPPE. TWELFTH QUEEN OF THE AMAZONS. YOU KNOW WHAT THAT MEANS?
THERE'RE AT LEAST ELEVEN MORE TO FIND!
OOPS.
BUT THING IS, THE...THE THING IS, THE SYMBOLS ABOVE THE OTHER SYMBOLS THAT ARE LETTERS?
THOSE ARE SYMBOLS.
I JUST DON'T KNOW WHAT THEY MEAN YET.
VIKTOR?

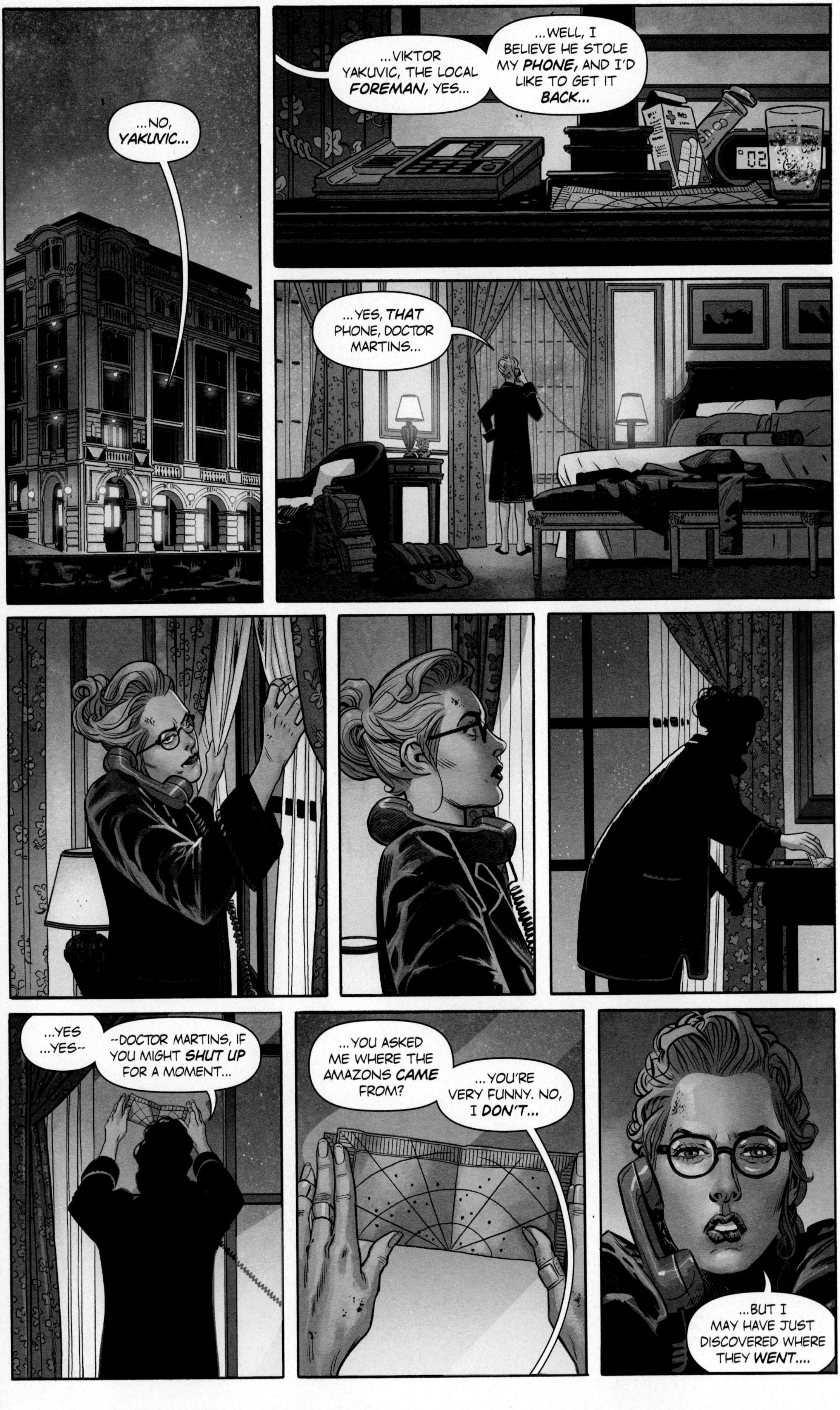
...NO, YAKUVIC...
...VIKTOR YAKUVIC, THE LOCAL FOREMAN, YES...
...WELL, I BELIEVE HE STOLE MY PHONE, AND I'D LIKE TO GET IT BACK...
...YES, THAT PHONE, DOCTOR MARTINS...
...YES ...YES--
--DOCTOR MARTINS, IF YOU MIGHT SHUT UP FOR A MOMENT...
...YOU ASKED ME WHERE THE AMAZONS CAME FROM?
...YOU'RE VERY FUNNY. NO, I DON'T...
...BUT I MAY HAVE JUST DISCOVERED WHERE THEY WENT....

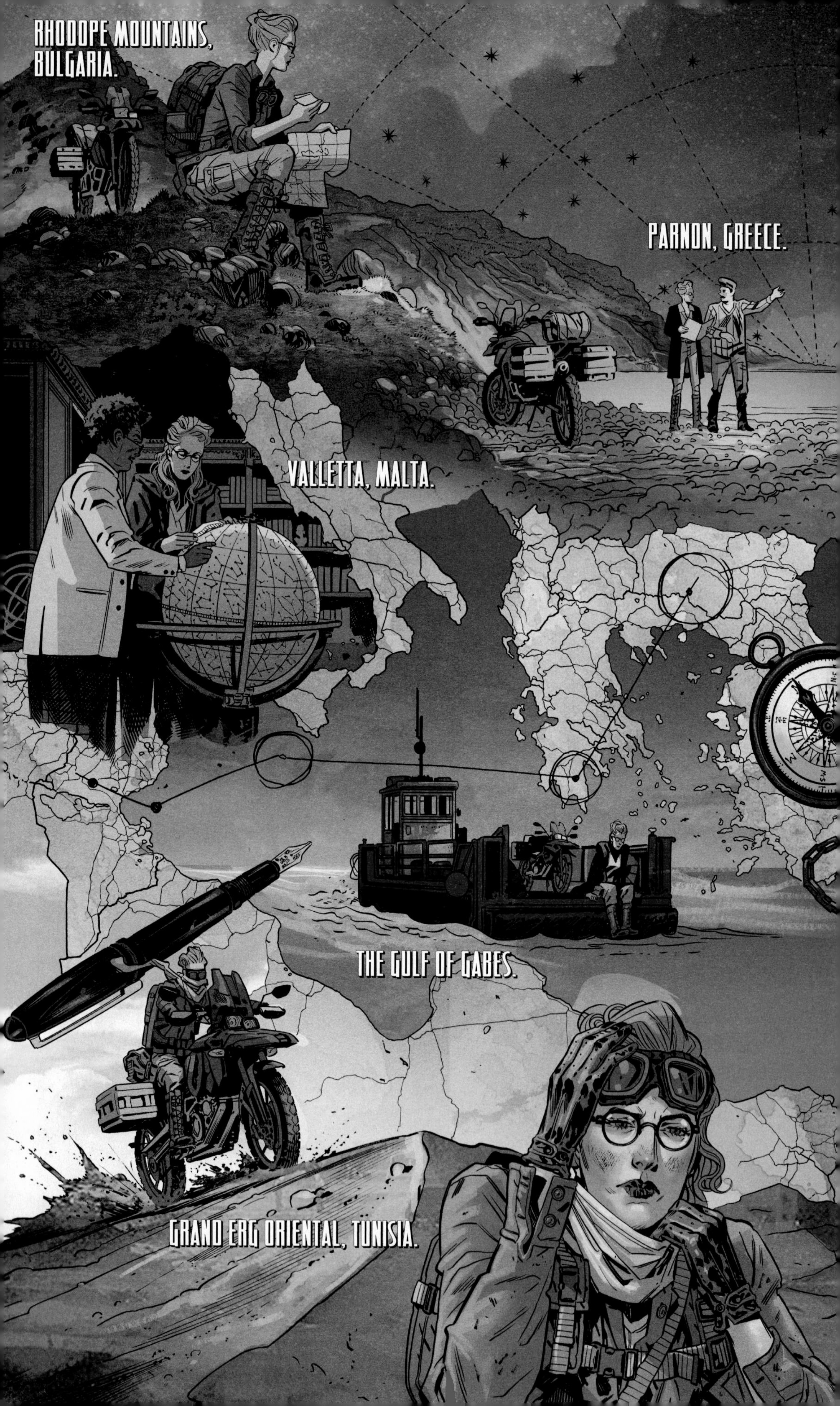
RHODOPE MOUNTAINS,
BULGARIA.
PARNON, GREECE.
VALLETTA, MALTA.
THE GULF OF GABES.
GRAND ERG ORIENTAL, TUNISIA.

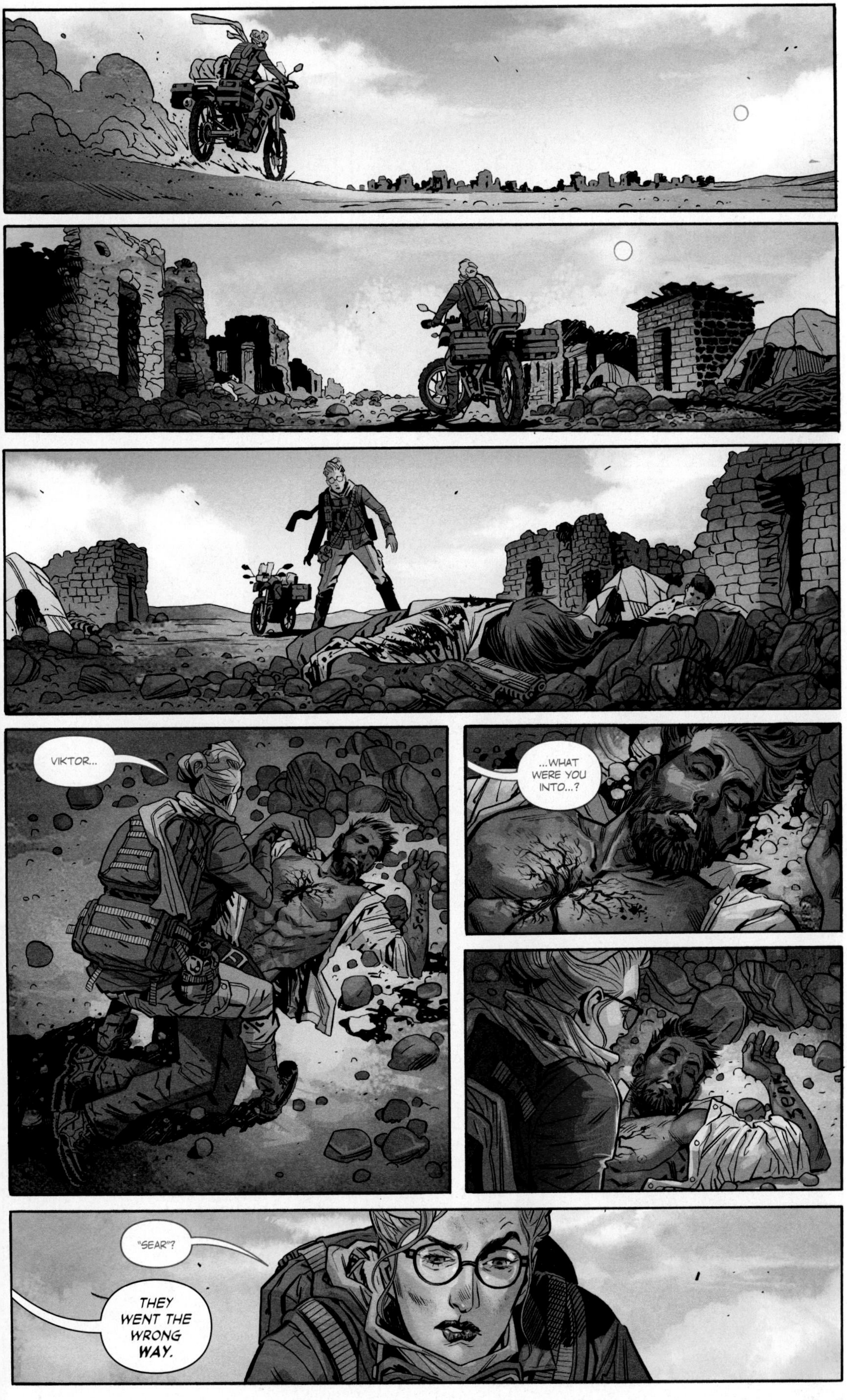
VIKTOR...
...WHAT WERE YOU INTO...?
"SEAR"?
THEY WENT THE WRONG WAY.

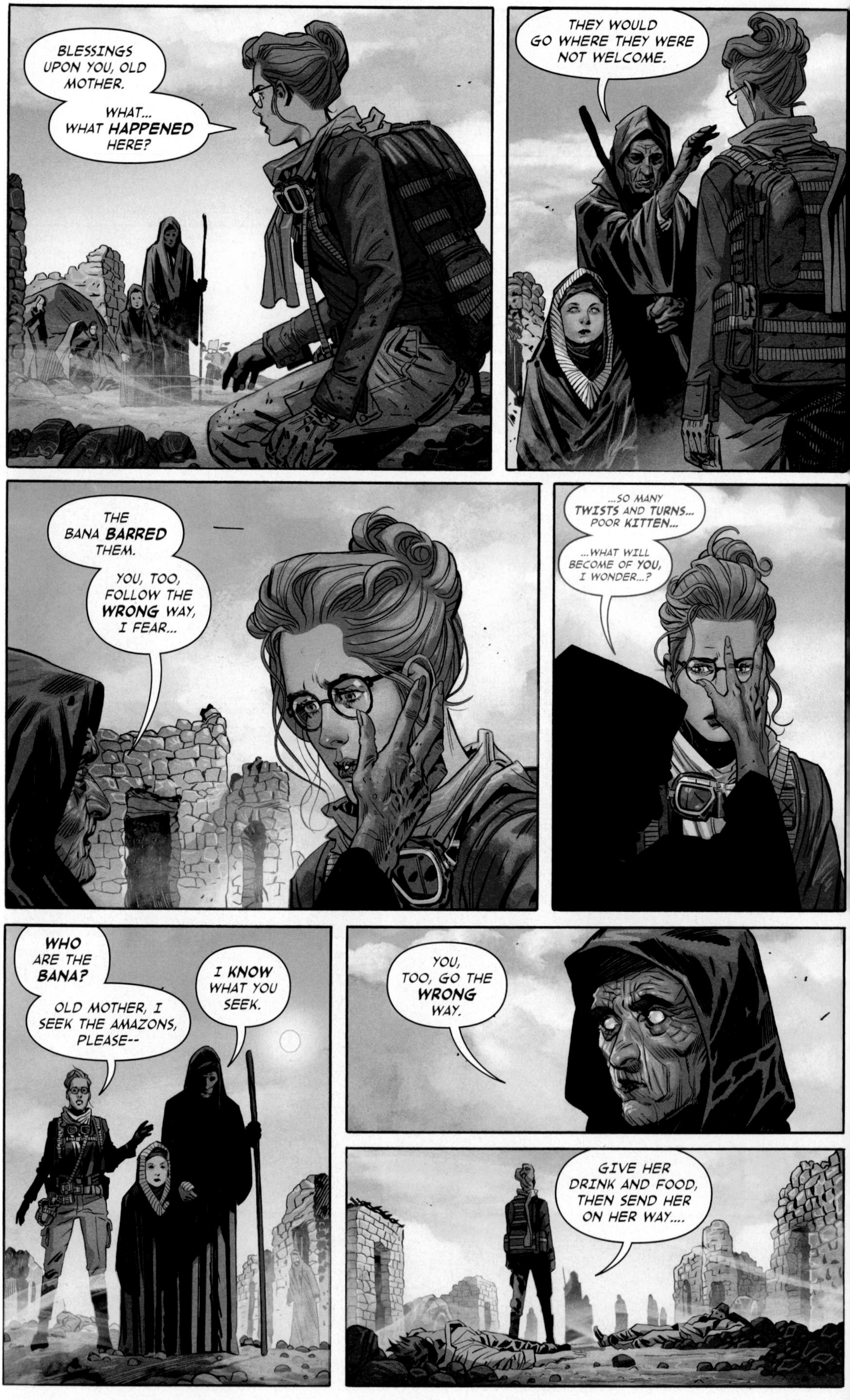
BLESSINGS UPON YOU, OLD MOTHER.
WHAT... WHAT HAPPENED HERE?
THEY WOULD GO WHERE THEY WERE NOT WELCOME.
THE BANA BARRED THEM.
YOU, TOO, FOLLOW THE WRONG WAY, I FEAR...
...SO MANY TWISTS AND TURNS... POOR KITTEN...
...WHAT WILL BECOME OF YOU, I WONDER...?
WHO ARE THE BANA?
OLD MOTHER, I SEEK THE AMAZONS, PLEASE--
I KNOW WHAT YOU SEEK.
YOU, TOO, GO THE WRONG WAY.
GIVE HER DRINK AND FOOD, THEN SEND HER ON HER WAY....

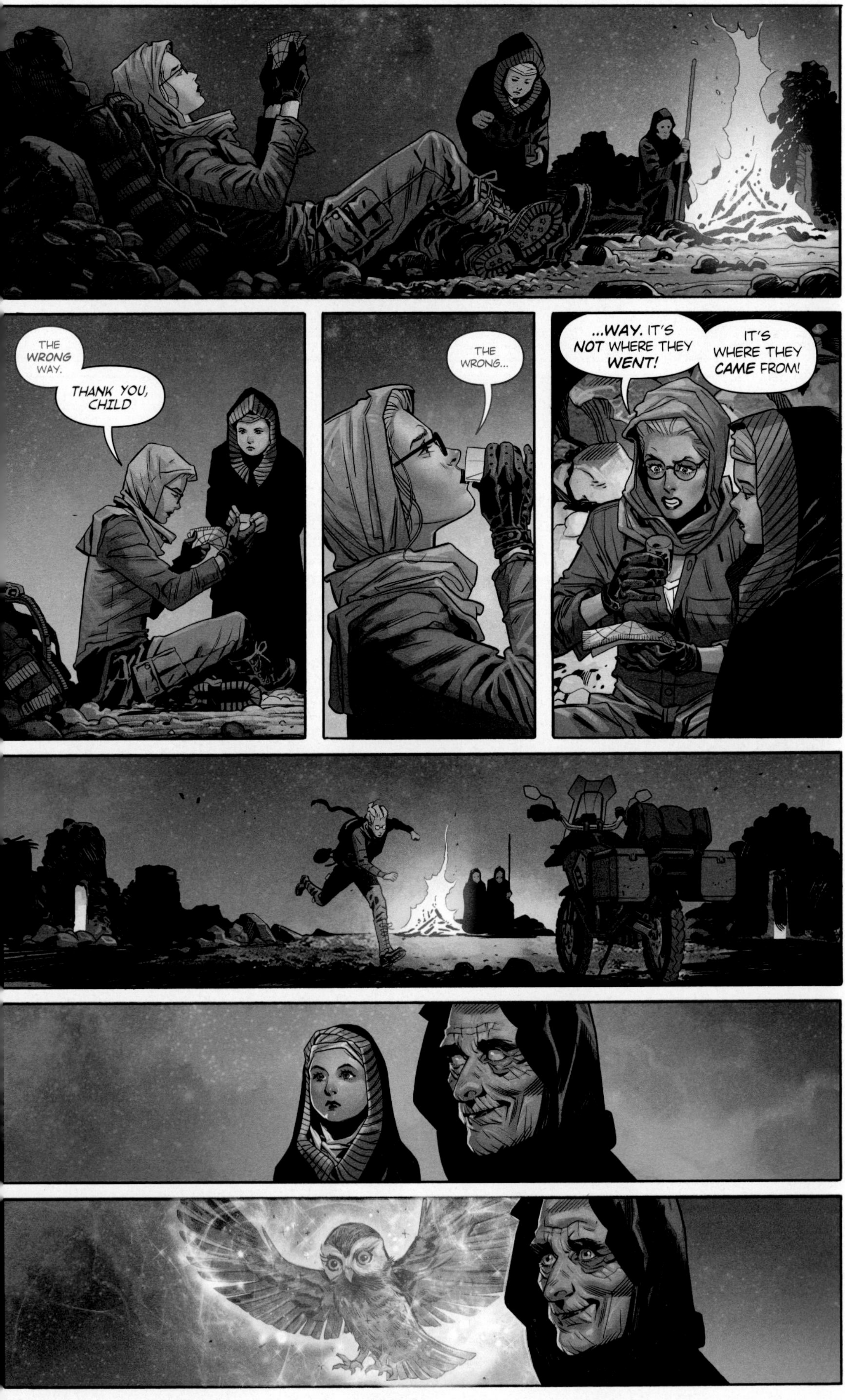
THE WRONG WAY.
THANK YOU, CHILD
THE WRONG...
...WAY. IT'S NOT WHERE THEY WENT!
IT'S WHERE THEY CAME FROM!

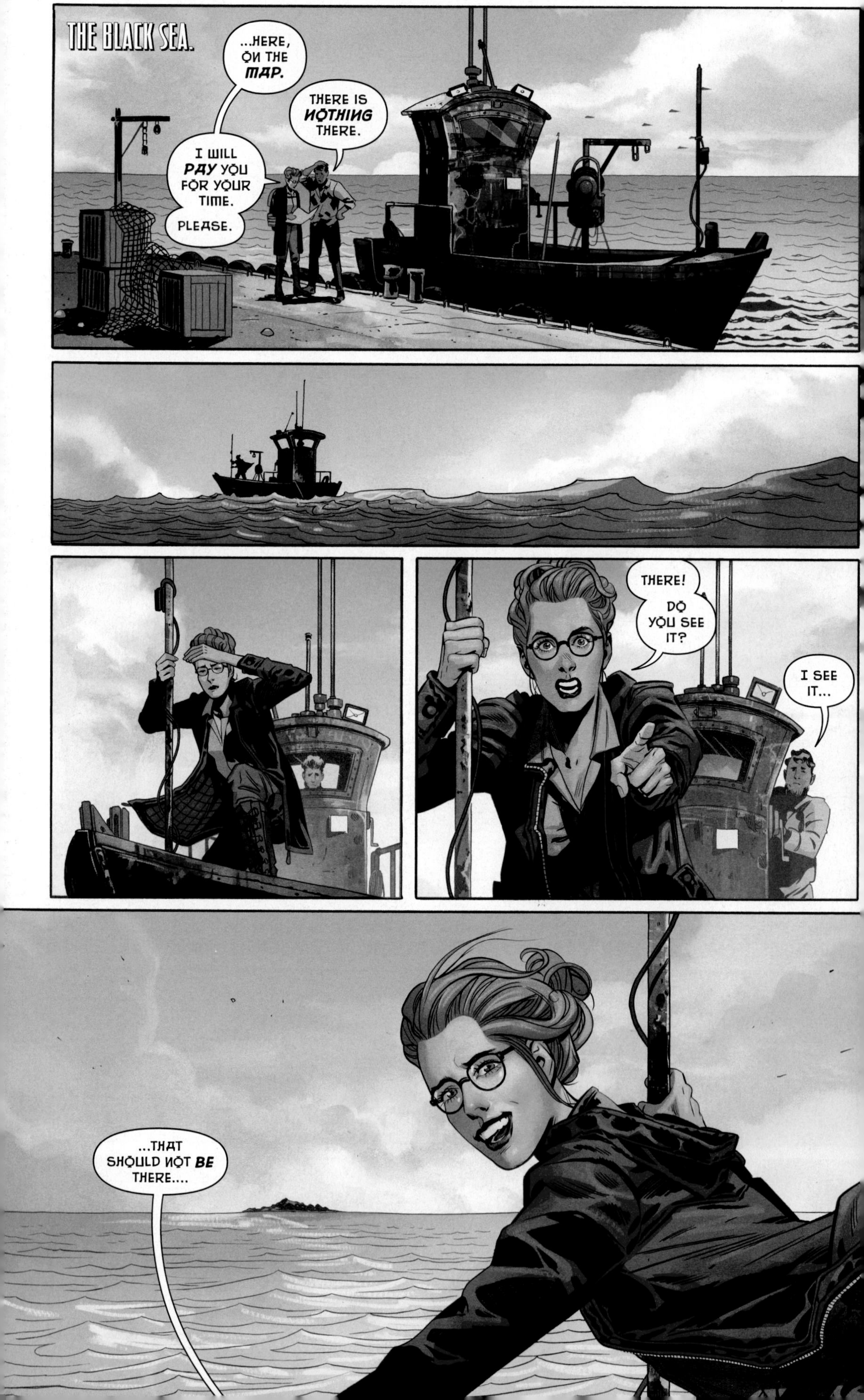
THE BLACK SEA.
...HERE, ON THE MAP.
THERE IS NOTHING THERE.
I WILL PAY YOU FOR YOUR TIME.
PLEASE.
THERE! DO YOU SEE IT?
I SEE IT...
...THAT SHOULD NOT BE THERE....

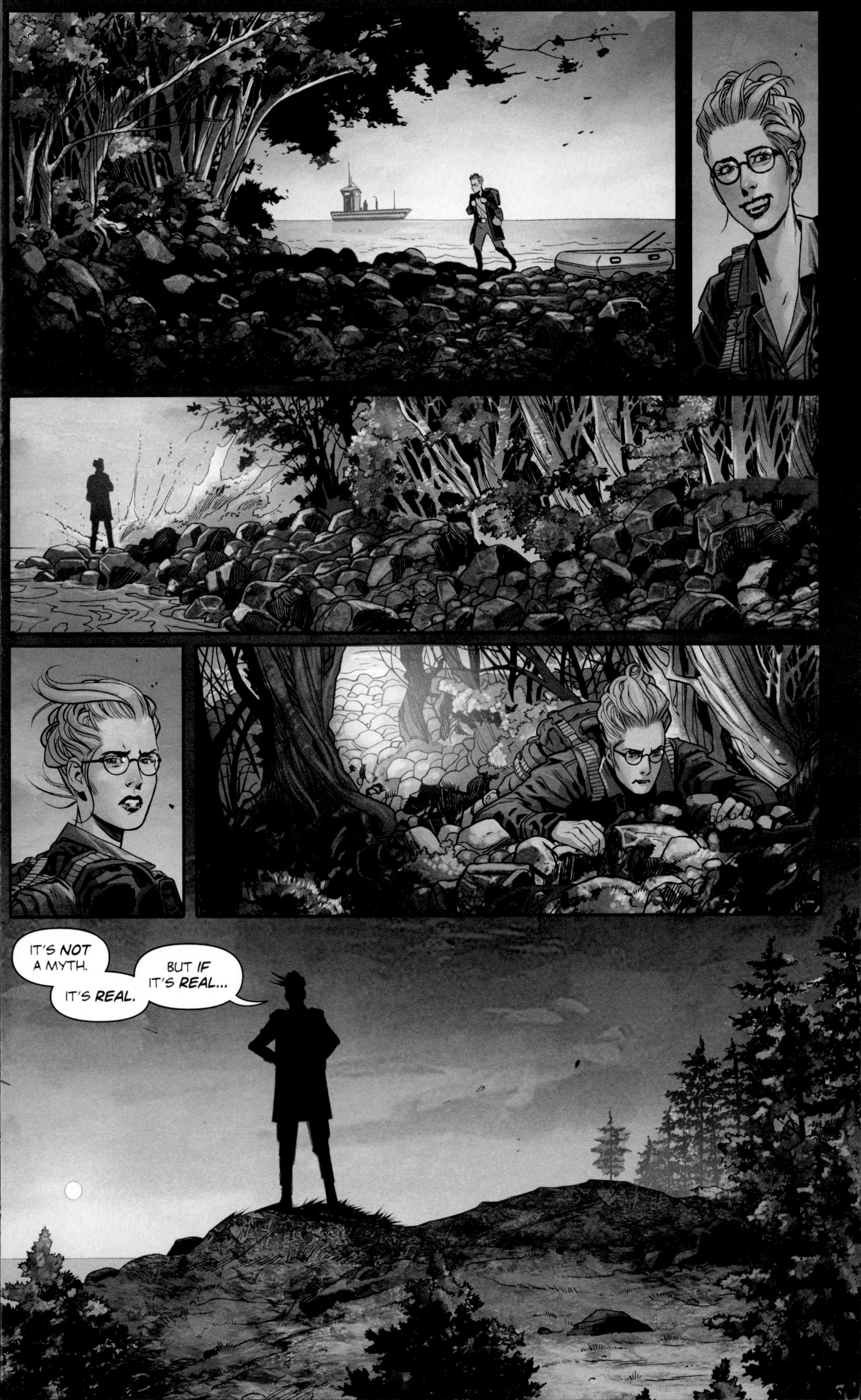
IT'S NOT A MYTH.
IT'S REAL.
BUT IF IT'S REAL...

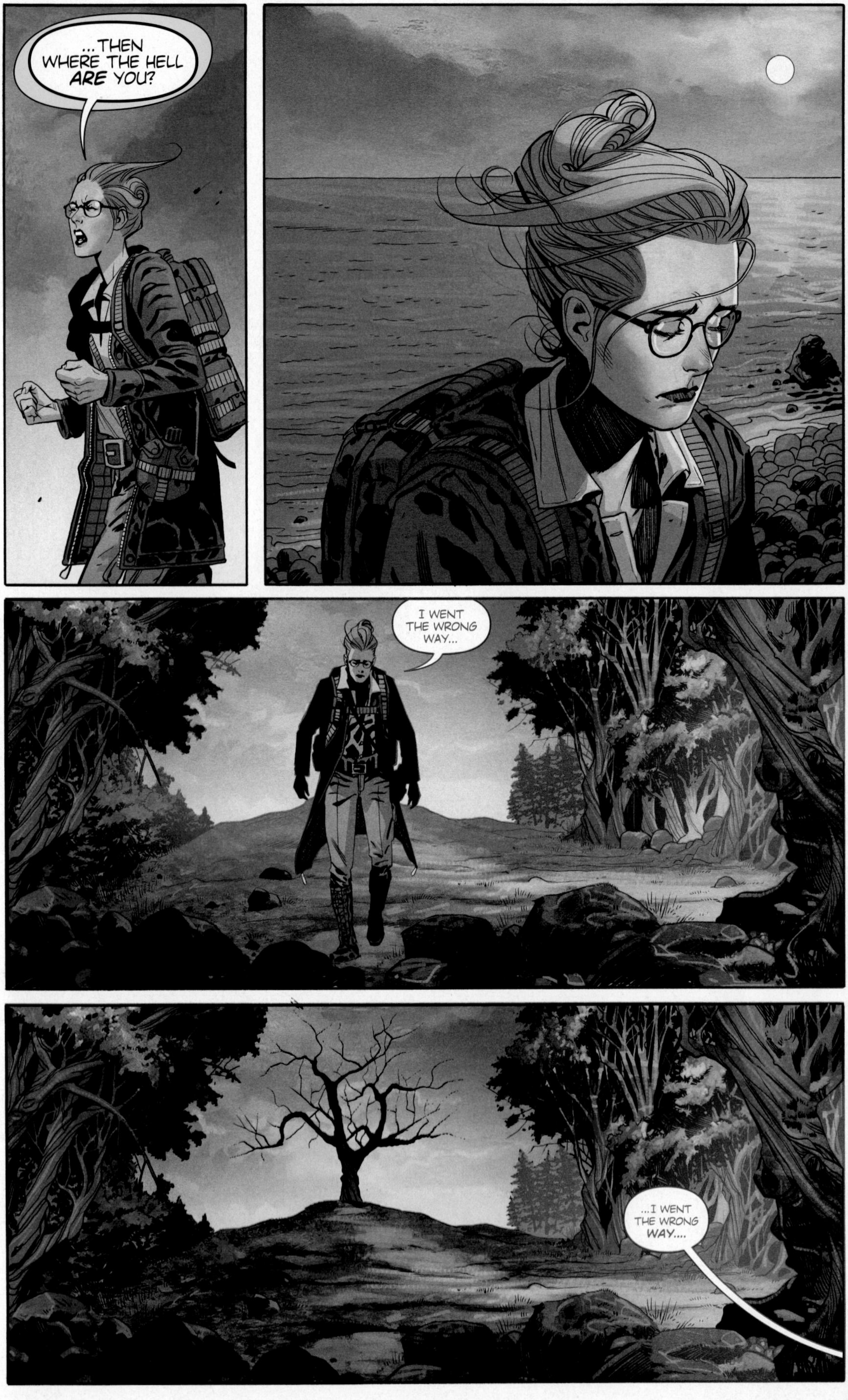
...THEN WHERE THE HELL ARE YOU?
I WENT THE WRONG WAY...
...I WENT THE WRONG WAY....

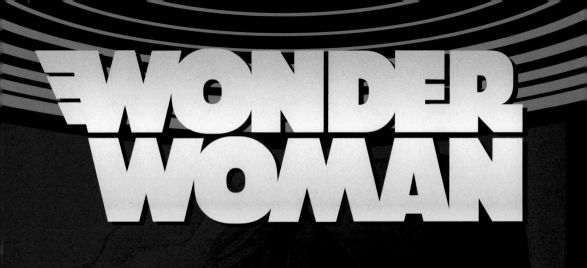

WONDER WOMAN

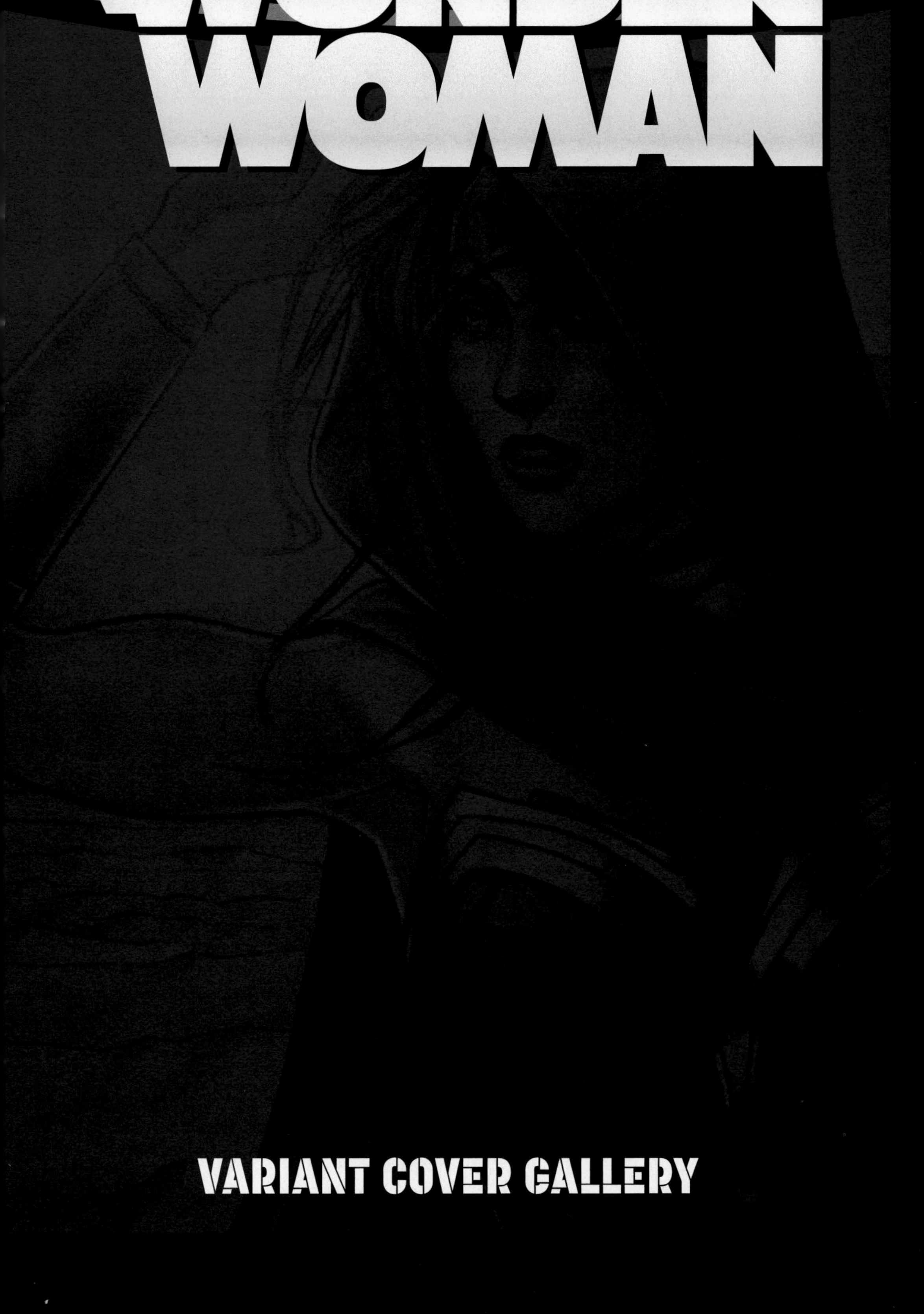

VARIANT COVER GALLERY

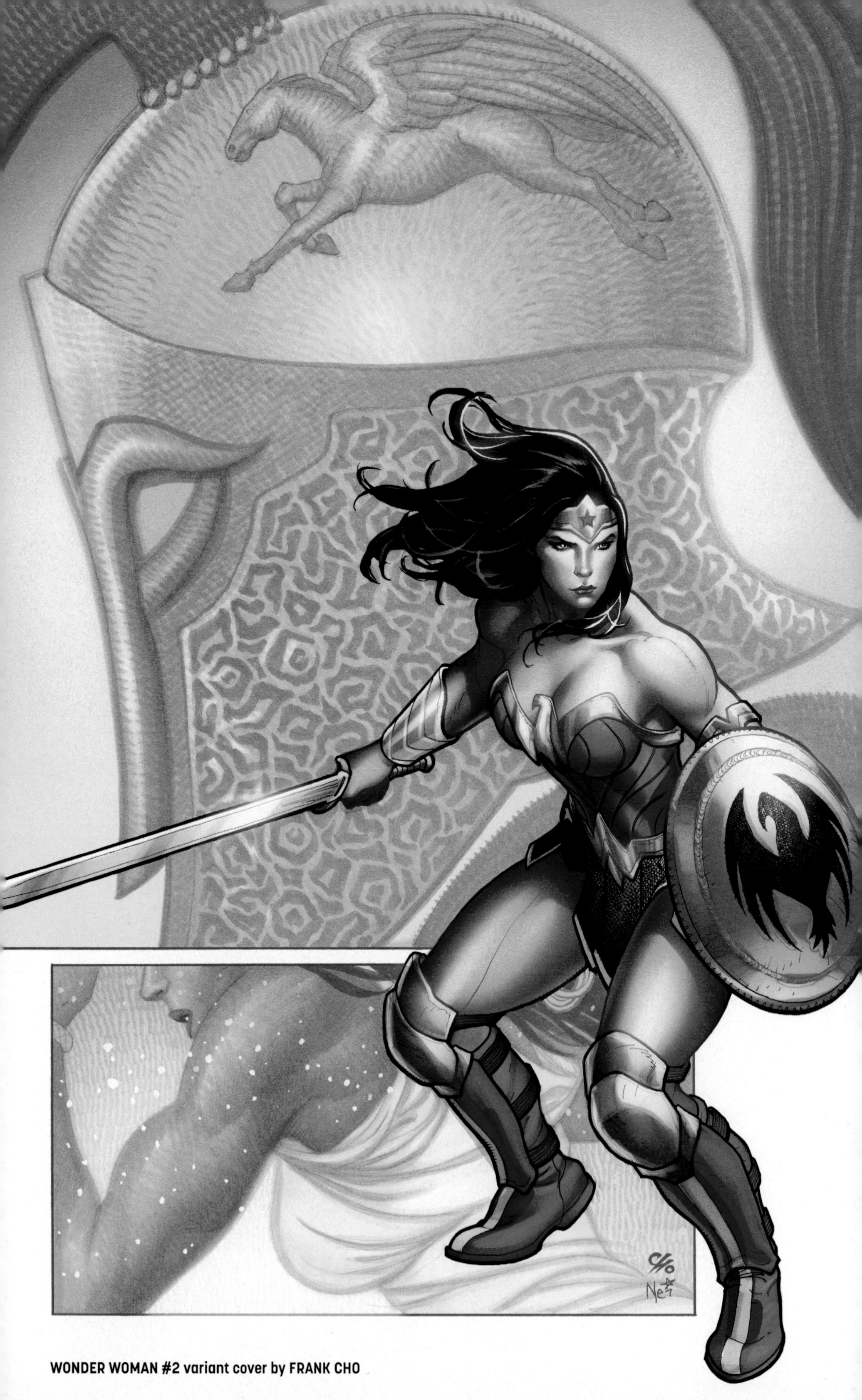
CHO
Ne

WONDER WOMAN #2 variant cover by FRANK CHO

WONDER WOMAN #4 variant cover by FRANK CHO

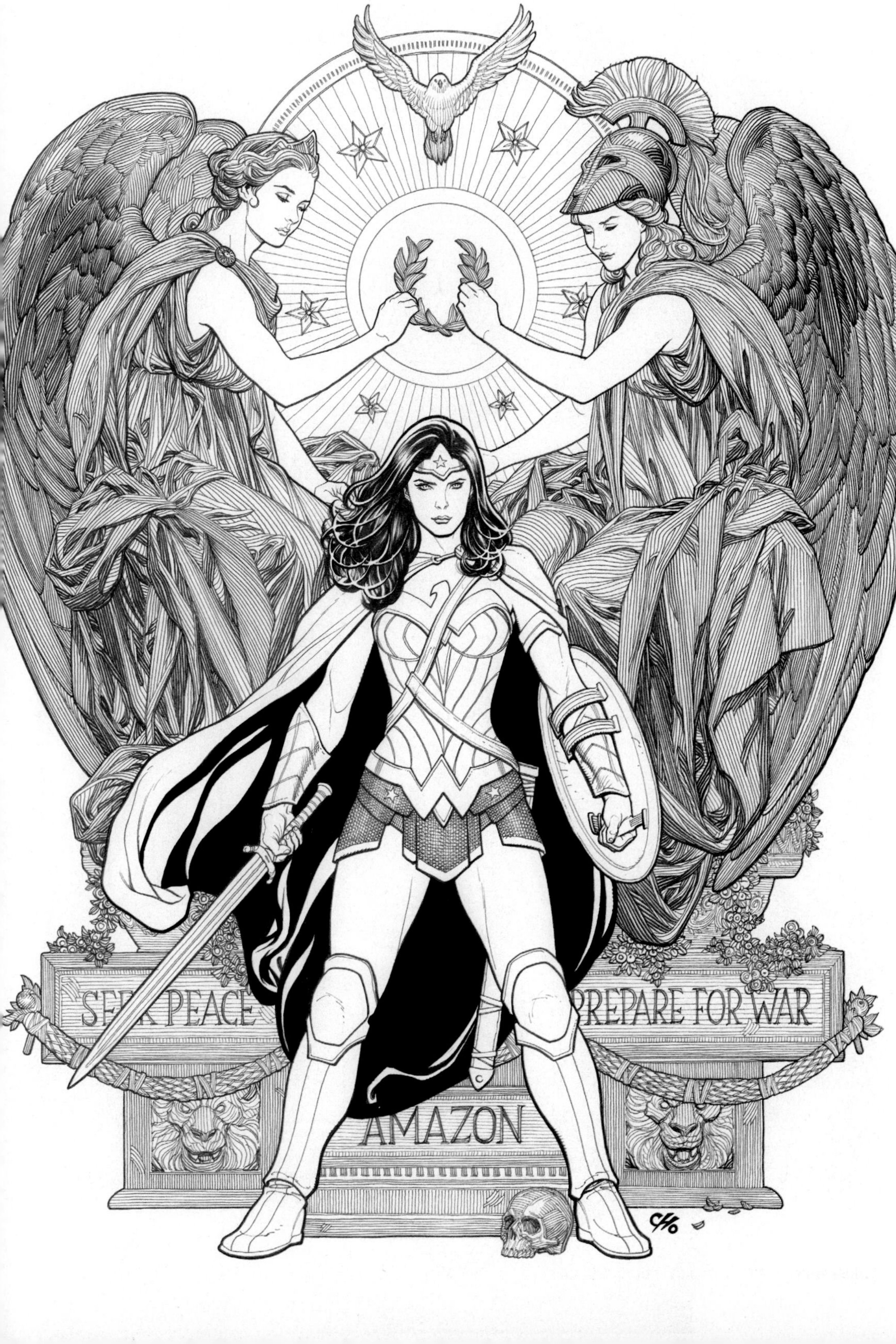
PREPARE FOR WAR
AMAZON
CHO

WONDER WOMAN #6 variant cover by FRANK CHO

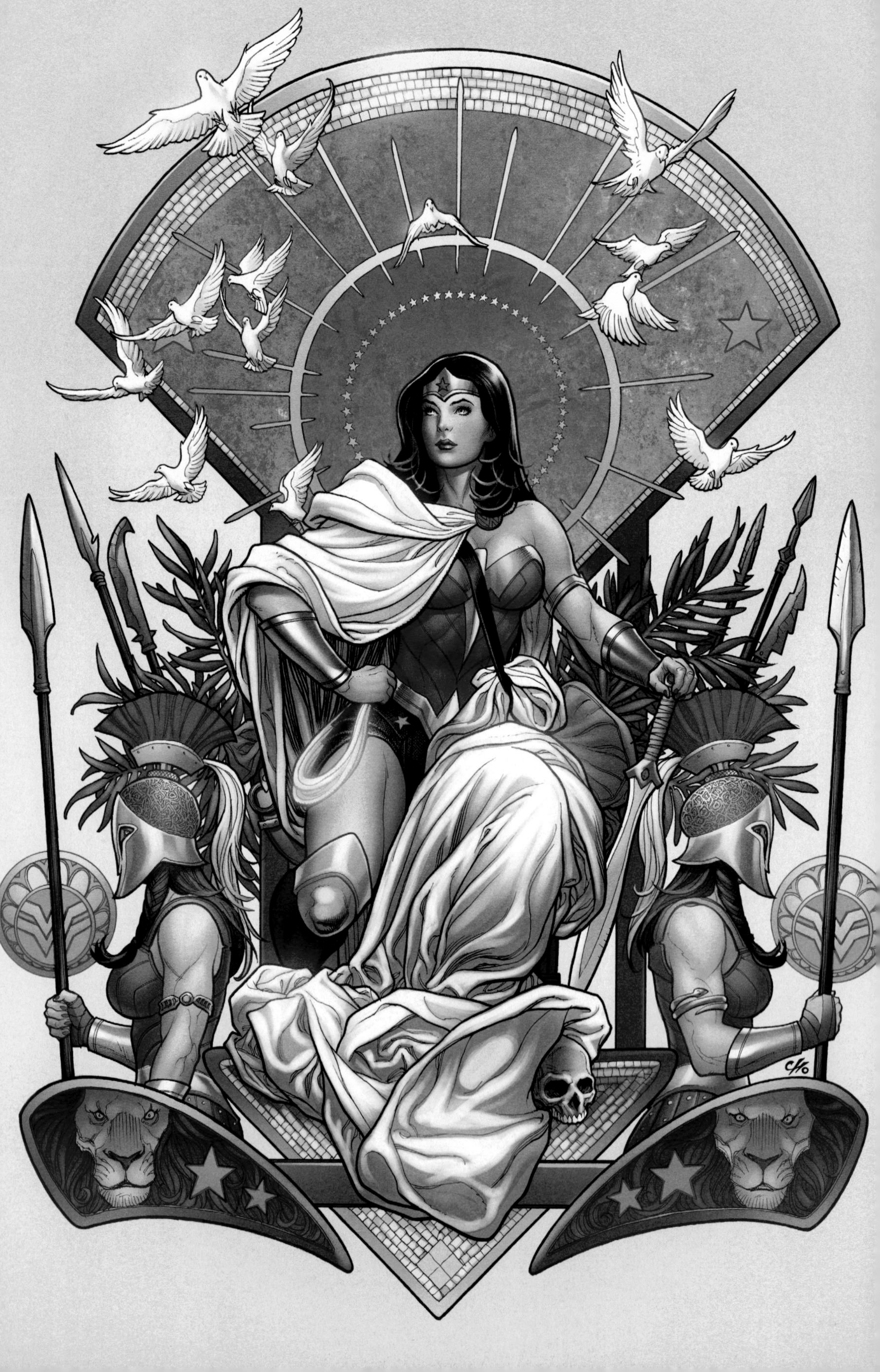

WONDER WOMAN #8 variant cover by JENNY FRISON

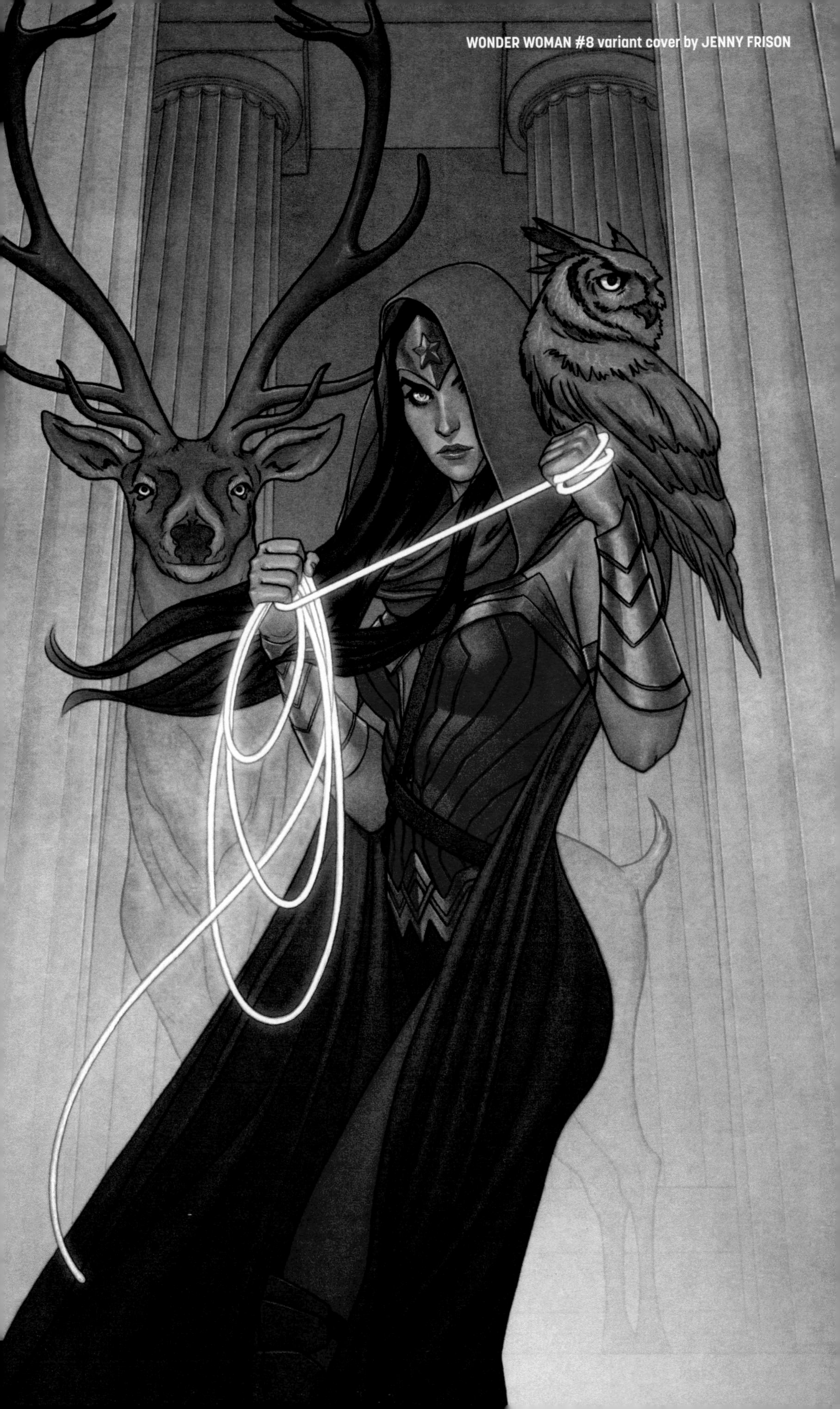

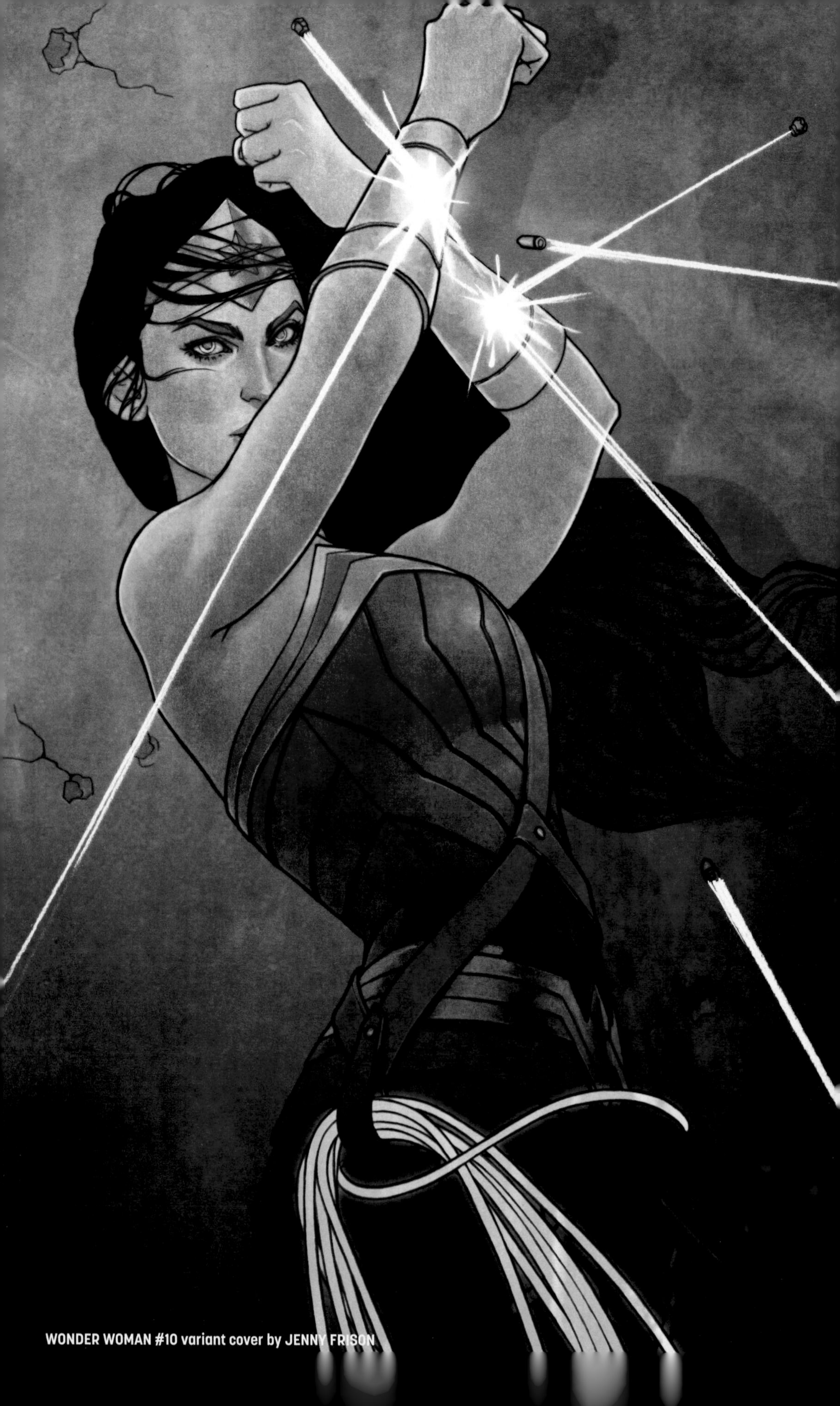

WONDER WOMAN #10 variant cover by JENNY FRISON

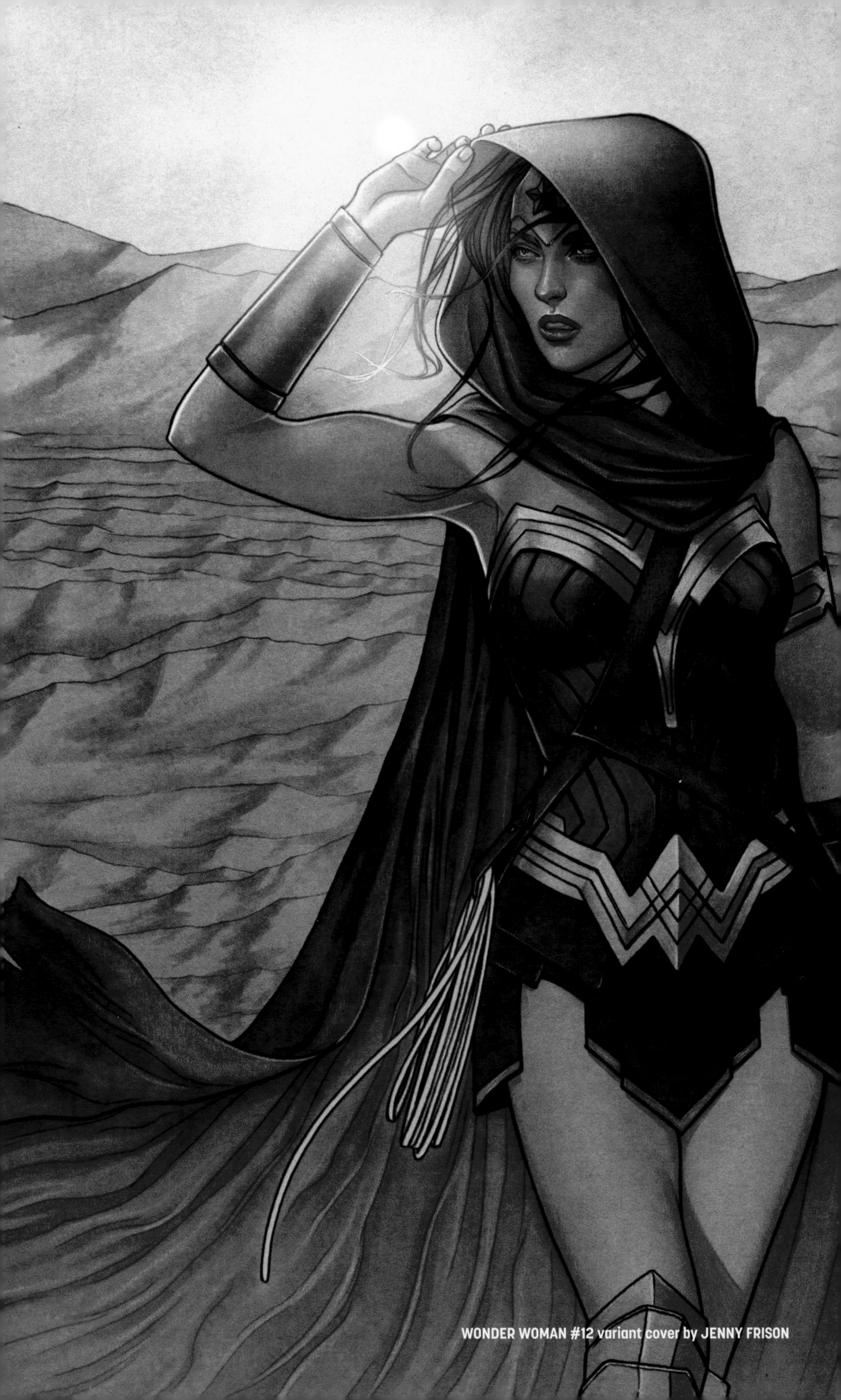

WONDER WOMAN #12 variant cover by JENNY FRISON

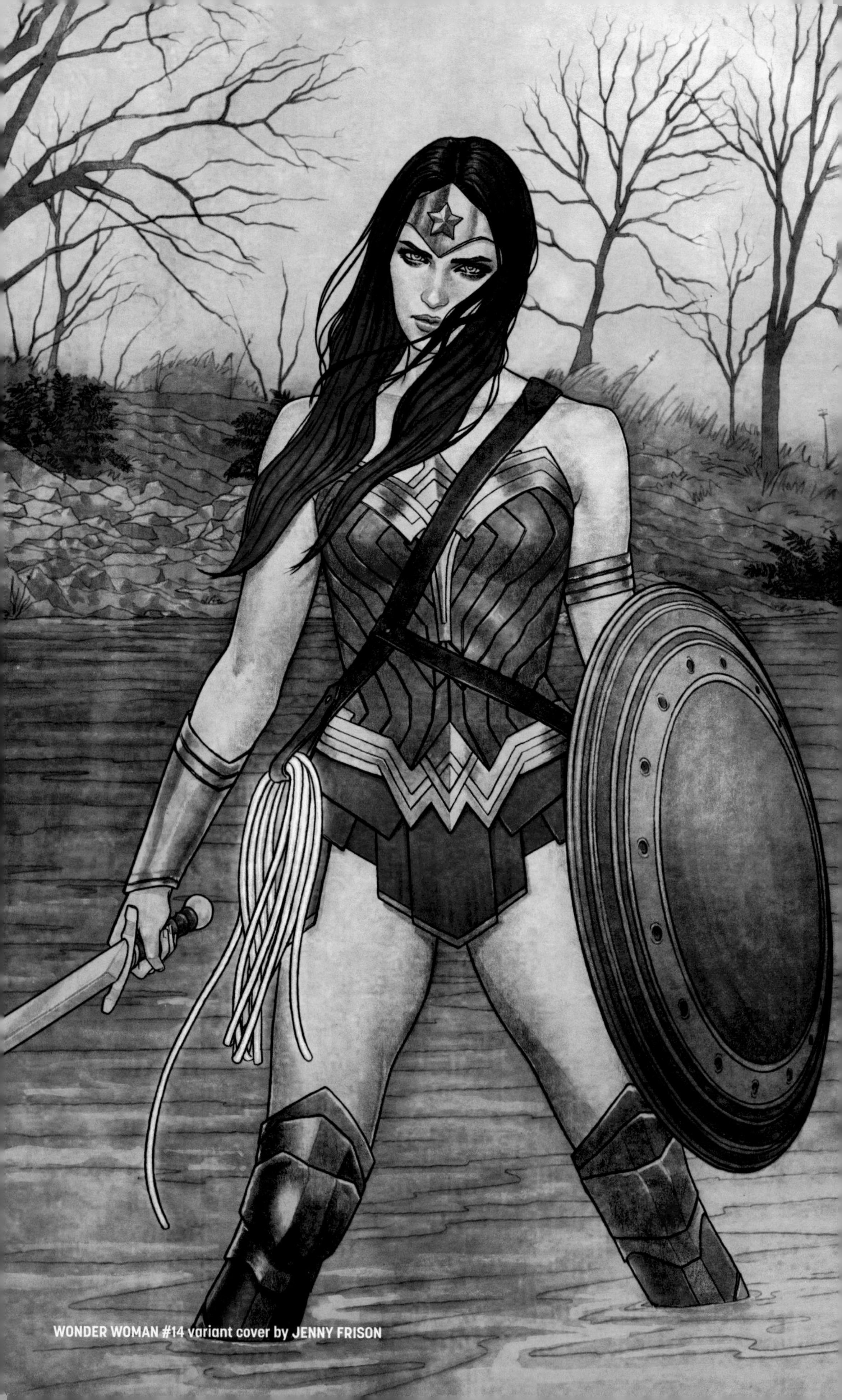

WONDER WOMAN #14 variant cover by JENNY FRISON

DC UNIVERSE REBIRTH

WONDER WOMAN

VOL. 1: THE LIES

GREG RUCKA
with LIAM SHARP

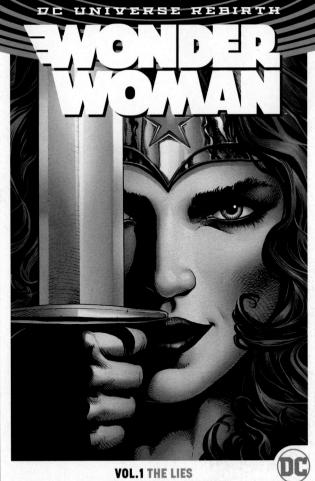

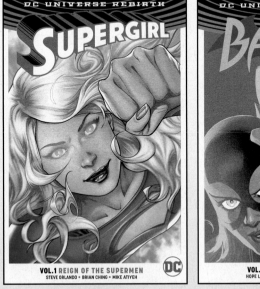

JUSTICE LEAGUE VOL. 1:
THE EXTINCTION MACHINES

SUPERGIRL VOL. 1:
REIGN OF THE SUPERMEN

BATGIRL VOL. 1:
BEYOND BURNSIDE

"Clear storytelling at its best. It's an intriguing concept and easy to grasp."
– THE NEW YORK TIMES

"Azzarello is rebuilding the mythology of Wonder Woman."
– CRAVE ONLINE

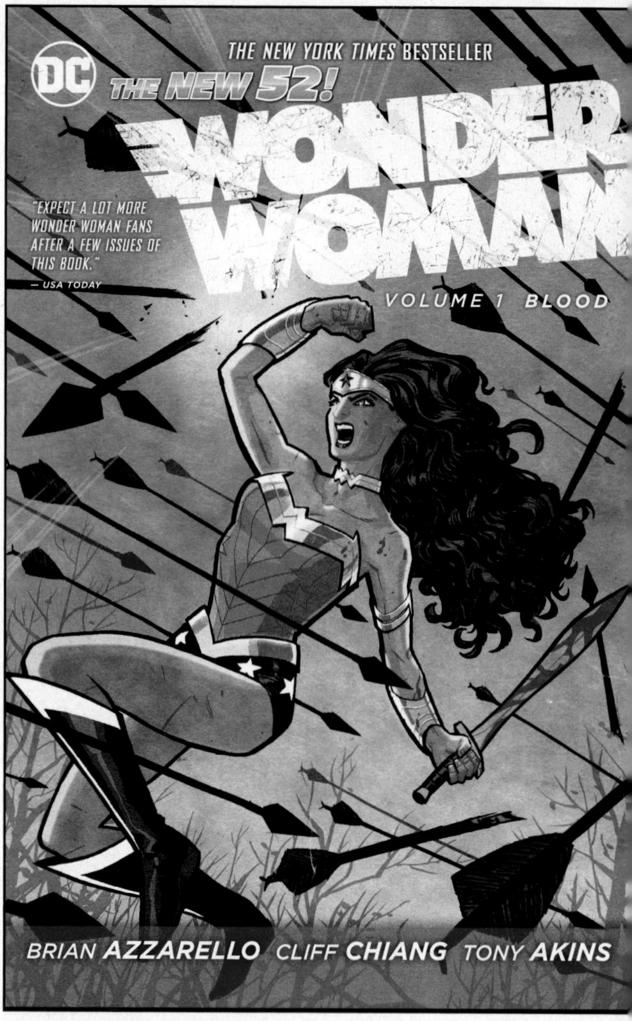
THE NEW YORK TIMES BESTSELLER
THE NEW 52!
WONDER WOMAN
"EXPECT A LOT MORE WONDER WOMAN FANS AFTER A FEW ISSUES OF THIS BOOK."
— USA TODAY
VOLUME 1 BLOOD
BRIAN AZZARELLO CLIFF CHIANG TONY AKINS

WONDER WOMAN

VOL. 1: BLOOD

BRIAN AZZARELLO
with CLIFF CHIANG

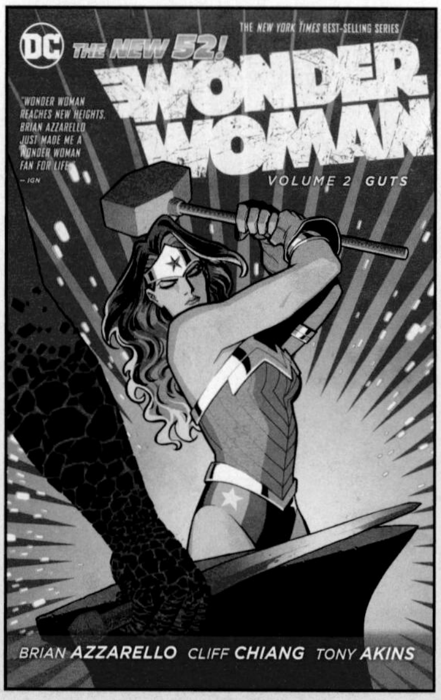
THE NEW YORK TIMES BEST-SELLING SERIES
THE NEW 52!
WONDER WOMAN
"WONDER WOMAN REACHES NEW HEIGHTS. BRIAN AZZARELLO JUST MADE ME A WONDER WOMAN FAN FOR LIFE."
— IGN
VOLUME 2 GUTS
BRIAN AZZARELLO CLIFF CHIANG TONY AKINS

WONDER WOMAN
VOL. 2: GUTS

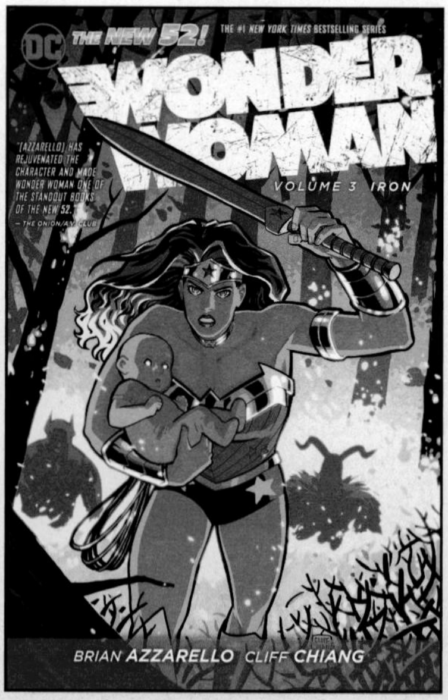
THE #1 NEW YORK TIMES BESTSELLING SERIES
THE NEW 52!
WONDER WOMAN
"[AZZARELLO] HAS REJUVENATED THE CHARACTER AND MADE WONDER WOMAN ONE OF THE STANDOUT BOOKS OF THE NEW 52."
— THE ONION/AV CLUB
VOLUME 3 IRON
BRIAN AZZARELLO CLIFF CHIANG

WONDER WOMAN
VOL. 3: IRON

READ THE ENTIRE EPIC

WONDER WOMAN VOL.
WA

WONDER WOMAN VOL.
FLES

WONDER WOMAN VOL.
BONE

WONDER WOMAN VOL.
WAR-TOR

WONDER WOMAN VOL.
A TWIST OF FA

WONDER WOMAN VOL.
RESURRECTIC

Get more DC graphic novels wherever comics and books are sold!